AT THE FESTIVAL

This book is dedicated to my grandfathers George Morris and Vernon Austen, and to the sight of Birds Nest in action under Andy Turnell, Steve Knight and John Francome

AT THE FESTIVAL

RICHARD AUSTEN

SPORTS
BOOKS

Published in Great Britain by
SportsBooks Limited
9 St Aubyns Place
York
YO24 1EQ

© Richard Austen 2015
First Published November 2015
Reprinted February 2016

Cover designed by Alan Hunns.

Back cover photograph taken by Julie Drewett

A catalogue record for this book is available from the British Library.

ISBN 9781907524509

Printed and bound in England by TJ International.

CONTENTS

ACKNOWLEDGEMENTS

IT WILL NOT take the reader long to recognise that I owe a huge debt of gratitude to my multitude of interviewees, for their generosity and patience and for their willingness to talk about events that weren't necessarily flattering to themselves, about losing as well as winning and tragedy as well as triumph.

To Brod Munro-Wilson, Tony Fowler and Colin Russell I would like to give particular thanks for getting the ball rolling and confirming so rapidly that I would have some superb material to work with. Brod also introduced me to two excellent establishments in London at which to find a good lunch.

I am indebted to my employers at the *Racing Post* for allowing me to pursue this project. Many others have given their assistance in researching frequently obscure pieces of information but I would like to thank in particular Paul Johnson and Frank Carter for the use of their form books, and both Phil Turner of Timeform and Adrian Cook of the *Racing Post* for dipping into the wealth of expertise and reference works at their disposal. Simon Rowlands of Timeform has very generously provided valuable insights for chapters 1 and 2. Richard Scoble of Weatherbys kindly unearthed some pedigree information.

Many thanks to Randall Northam of SportsBooks Ltd for his enthusiasm for this project and the constructive relationship we had in bringing *At The Festival* to publication, and to my father John Austen for enabling that publication to take place.

Thanks also to the photographers (chiefly Bernard Parkin, Mark Cranham and Caroline Norris) and press agencies who contributed their magnificent work and were incredibly helpful in doing so. Peter Savill, the *Gloucestershire Echo*, Brod

Munro-Wilson, Dinah Nicholson and Eimear Mulhern also volunteered some striking images.

In the three years and more that it took me to write this book, I may well have buckled without the support of Richard O'Brien and Emily Weber, who have given their encouragement and great help at all stages from the Introduction through to Chapter 12, and back again. Brookes, Sam, Mum and many others, thank you for your help and for putting up with me. It must have been a test when I was subjecting you to blow-by-blow accounts of the book's progress and my excited reactions to the latest interview or piece of research.

I am also very grateful for the help and encouragement given to me by Lydia Hislop, Graham Cunningham, Peter Savill, Edward Gillespie, Simon Claisse, David Cleary, Julie Drewett, Melanie Bloxham and Chris Pitt.

John Francome has inspired me and countless others with his unsurpassed artistry as a jockey and all the work he has done since for the sport and its participants. To interview him was invaluable for the book's content and a huge thrill, and then for him to participate so generously by contributing the book's foreword is something for which I cannot thank him enough.

John figures prominently among the countless competitors, administrators, staff and enthusiasts over many generations who have made the Cheltenham Festival the highlight of my racing year, something in which friends including Martin Davies, Andrew Lynn and David Moon have also played a huge part. To them all, my profound thanks. Hopefully this book has captured something of the Festival experience which they have created.

FOREWORD

BY JOHN FRANCOME

THE ATMOSPHERE AMONG the jockeys in the weighing room at the Cheltenham Festival is totally different from any other race meeting, even Aintree. There are far more Irish jockeys, for a start, and there is also a lot more tension. Every horse has been mapped out to go there. The people who are usually really chatty are quiet, and the quiet ones can't stop talking.

For a normal race meeting you arrive an hour before your first ride, but if you try to do that at the Festival you don't get in the car park. So you have to be there very early; you've got all this time to kill, the tension builds and it's tense whether you're riding a 33-1 shot or whether you're riding the favourite.

People would chat with you on the way from the car park to the weighing room but it all started a lot earlier in the morning. The postman wants to know what's going to win; everyone's had a bet and people you know would not normally go racing want to be at Cheltenham. For a lot it's a big social event. For the jockeys it's just more pressure.

I'd have started the day riding out as usual at Fred Winter's. I'd probably have mucked out as well, never mind ridden out. We were a team but when you got beaten on something that the lads thought was going to win you would get dog's abuse in the morning. Or they'd cut the result out of *The Sporting Life* and write their own commentary, saying you should have won. Then they'd pin it to the noticeboard.

At the racecourse, I used to sit next to Steve Smith Eccles, Hywel Davies, Graham Thorner, until he packed up, and

Scu – all good lads – and the Irish would be on the other side of the weighing room. The two groups got on well enough but there was always that element of them and us, a competitive rivalry.

Nerves did not affect me much going out to ride and I was lucky, because if a jockey is nervous it will be transmitted to the horse within a second of you getting on it. Once you get legged into the saddle your job begins. You give them a pat on the neck and do everything you can to get them to relax if they are on edge. I like to see horses walk round the paddock with the jockeys' legs dangling down, feet out of the irons. Nothing settles horses better.

You've got to keep them settled all the way down to the start, make sure you look after them, keep them on the best ground. The Festival is no different in that respect, but the buzz, the atmosphere and the mass of people is very different, everybody hoping and wanting to have a winner.

I wouldn't have sounded out the other jockeys about their prospects but when you get down to the start you might be looking at an Irish horse you'd not seen before and you'd think, 'Crikey – that looks a different class to the ones we're riding.'

I'd have done my research before raceday and you needed to have the shape of the race sorted out in your mind well before you got down to the start or even the parade ring. If you don't know pretty much how the race is going to be run, there's something wrong with you. You know the horses that are going to go on and lead; you know the ones who you don't want to be behind.

The thing about a Festival race is that they go so fast. You can go out there with the idea of sitting third or fourth on the inside, which is where I normally liked to be, and by the time you get to the first hurdle or fence you could have been shuffled back to 15th. Then you've got problems.

Many horses which have looked good through the year

can't cope when it comes to going that little bit quicker. Some can.

As a jockey, it's very easy to just get sucked along and stop doing what you normally do. You start riding the race instead of riding the horse, and once that happens you've had it. You've got to get the horse from A to B in the quickest possible time and that isn't by going flat out early or being sucked into going too fast. And you must make sure that every time the horse comes to a hurdle or fence it can see what it's doing.

When you get to the top of the hill on the far side and you look up and see where the winning post is, it's further than you'd ever ride work in your whole life. And yet I see people start going for home from there. That's like riding a bit of work and going flat out from the start – you can't do it. And they've already gone a mile and a bit. It may be the Festival, but you've still got to be completely aware of what the horse underneath you is doing. You've got to get somewhere where you can go at a nice even pace and they've got to be in that rhythm for as long as you can keep them there.

If you're on a horse good enough to get a breather round Cheltenham and able to fill its lungs, you're on a very rare animal indeed. And you're very lucky if you're going well enough in a race to think about saving something for the final hill – most of the time you're just trying to keep them on the bridle for as long as you can.

In the closing stages the noise from the crowd is incredible, but when I was riding I wasn't aware of it at all because I was so focused on what I was doing. If a bomb went off, I don't think I would have heard it. You're just focusing on a fence or a hurdle and making sure that you get the job done.

If you haven't had a ride in the race you'll have watched it on the TV and it's nice when something unexpected happens, when somebody rides a winner who doesn't have many rides at Cheltenham. There are some excellent examples of that in *At The Festival*. They work hard all through the year and there's only a spit between the best and the worst jockeys – a lot of it's just getting on the right horses.

If you rode a winner in the last race of the day, then the celebrations were of a different order. I was a teetotaller, but there's plenty who weren't and some would go on celebrating. There was a bar underneath one of the grandstands and in my earlier years at Cheltenham some of the older jockeys would be down there, hardly coming out until one in the morning. They were from a generation before me and they wouldn't have been riding out in the morning; they'd just get back to the course, get in the sauna, sweat the drink out and off they'd go again. Whether they rode a winner or not, some of them would have a crate of beer under the bench, and they might stop on the way to the races to have a drink. But in my era they were just starting to get a little bit more professional.

You're always pleased if one of your mates has ridden a winner. Invariably it means that you haven't and when Steve Smith Eccles won the Champion Hurdle in 1985 it was because I missed out. I was due to ride See You Then but in the race before I fell on a horse called The Reject and I got 'hung up'. When the horse got to its feet and set off again I was on the ground and my foot was caught in the stirrup iron. Steve got the call-up for See You Then and somebody said to me after the Champion, 'You must be really disappointed to have missed the ride.' But I was just so relieved to be in one piece – I was just delighted to be sitting down under my peg I can assure you.

I rode again on the Wednesday and Thursday but the only time I finished in the first four that year was in the Champion Chase and that was only because I was the last of four finishers. It was my final Festival as a jockey.

My overriding memory of the Festival is that you go there expecting it to be tough and you're never disappointed

– it *is* always tough. But every now and again you'd be on something that's travelled well enough through the race that you could actually time your run and decide when you were going to go for home.

To have been on those horses at championship pace round Cheltenham, just galloping and jumping, was an absolute thrill, and the stories behind two of those races are included in the opening chapters of this terrific book.

INTRODUCTION

AT VARIOUS STAGES of a horserace, in exhortation (usually) or exaltation (sometimes), I often experience a compelling urge to shout something, and in that at the Cheltenham Festival I am not alone. In most races from the turn for home, over the final fence or hurdle and up the hill to the winning line the noise becomes all-enveloping. The crowd's reaction will also be heard at other junctures throughout the race, and that is not so different from race meetings elsewhere, except in its scale. But the Festival is the first event at which I ever heard an irresistible roar go up not just at the finish of a race but at the start. When the field is sent on its way for the Supreme Novices' Hurdle, the first race of the meeting, with the most anticipated action of the racing year all set to unfold over the next four days, the joy contained in that sound feels unmatched.

The cry to which I am most prone is 'Stay On!', although to shout this at the start of the race would be overdoing it. A horse described as 'staying on' is one who still has more to give and is giving it, one who is galloping on with some vigour rather than visibly wilting. It may not actually be moving at a faster speed than at all earlier stages of the race but hopefully, if I have backed it, tipped it or otherwise placed some vested interest in it, that horse will be moving faster than all of his or her opponents.

The shout is above all for the horse. If the individual concerned is of questionable enthusiasm perhaps 'Run On!' would be more appropriate; a token 'Get Fourth!' (for each-way bets) or a muttered 'Quicken up … dramatically' might be heard when hopes have subsided to a fairly pitiful level, but when a serious involvement in the finish looks like materialising then 'Stay On!' usually serves the purpose. Many racegoers shout the jockey on by name, rather than the horse, which for my personal preferences seldom does justice to the importance of their relative exertions. But I concede that in horseracing over jumps the phrase 'Stay On!' possesses an alternative meaning and can sometimes be highly appropriate for the rider as well.

Those two words can act as encouragement for any number of life's challenges, but in racing the cry 'Stay On!' seems especially to the point at Cheltenham. Put the breathtaking aesthetic appeal of Cheltenham Racecourse – also known as Prestbury Park – to one side. For participants, that spectacular topography beneath Cleeve Hill has implications. Both the Old and New Courses at Cheltenham feature a major descent before the final turn, and on the Old Course, where the field turns sharply left as soon as the highest point on the course is reached, that descent is steep. As well as that downhill section, much of what precedes it is on a turn. Many good judges describe the Old Course as a sharp track and they have a point. Coming around the final turn, however, the race is still to be won.

From a detailed survey I have seen, the overall difference between the highest and lowest points on the track is about 18 metres. There are other British racecourses with much greater variations. From the turn for home up to the winning line there is a climb of about ten metres on the New Course, 7.5 metres on the Old. There are other British racecourses with much greater sustained ascents to the finish. But at Cheltenham most of that climb takes place after the final fence. In the extent of that final demand, in conjunction with the pace it has taken to get there at the most keenly contested meeting of the year, Cheltenham is unique.

When confronted by that climb, the horse who is trying

only to hang on will probably be beaten; another who is well off the pace rounding the final turn but staying on could still have a chance, and the ultimate prize at stake for man and horse at this meeting is that their names will henceforth be counted among the sport's immortals. The prospect of witnessing who will join that list has now produced what must be the most dedicated following, from two countries, of any event in the racing calendar, nurtured by more than 100 years of Festival history and the promise renewed in the course of each and every season that this will be the best action of the racing year. Up that final climb the shouting and cheering attains its peak. Every autumn, on my first visit of the season to Cheltenham, I am surprised anew by the volume of it compared to race meetings elsewhere, but in a Festival finish we are at the centre of a world of sound. I have often wondered what watching and listening to a Festival race must be like from the top of Cleeve Hill. I have often wondered but never wanted to find out.

~

There are two categories of anxiety dreams that just keep returning to me. The first is that I am back at school or university and due to take an exam the next day but have done no revision. There is a moment of revelation about exactly how long has passed since this revision last took place and, at the time of writing, it is 28 years. That this anxiety is centred on impending exams is a little baffling, because I was not so concerned at the time. For the second category, however, the derivation is not oblique in the slightest and the dream is far more horrific. It is my night terror. There have been countless variations but the basic plot is always that by some or other outlandish conspiracy of circumstance I am being prevented from reaching Cheltenham Racecourse in time for the start of the Festival.

All manner of fiendish obstacles have been placed in my path and, try as I might, it looks as if there is no way that I can arrive in time for the Supreme Novices'. The Festival has that effect on people. It has that effect on the whole sport, and its primacy in the jumps racing calendar is long and very firmly established.

The Grand National may provide the highest-profile single day in British racing but with the Cheltenham Festival the sport is in the grip of a year-round obsession. When one Festival ends, betting is already underway for the next, and with almost any good horse that emerges in the 12 months in between, the question always seems to be whether it is good enough to run at Cheltenham.

It is possible to have a relationship with a place or an institution, and mine with the Festival has been one of the longest-standing in my life, and fantastically rewarding. My career in racing journalism has been devoted to objective appraisals of horses and races, but when I reflect on more than 30 years at the Festival objectivity is not the chief response. Racing is a sport in which even non-participants can feel a powerful emotional stake and all of the chapters in this book are about races I witnessed, races which made an impact on me. I may not have been in the saddle or had anything to do with the ownership or the training, but these were events that I experienced. They mattered and it felt personal.

There was a time, I admit, in which for nearly 16 years I failed to attend a single Festival, but at the onset of that barren period Arkle was the name on the lips of the racing public, while I was still struggling to say 'Mummy' or 'Daddy'. A few years later, with my attachment to horseracing already fixed, attendance at the Festival could not be reasonably hoped for during schooldays but my failure to be at the racecourse for those three afternoons in March, instead of sitting distractedly in the classroom or slouching about the school sports field, was still the height of exasperation because the most crucial action of the racing year was unfolding on only the other side of town. I lived near Cheltenham, went to school in Cheltenham and the racecourse was just three miles away.

On the face of it, Dean Close School was an unpromising nursery for devotees of the sport, given the man the school was named after. In 30 years as Rector of Cheltenham during the 19th century, the Reverend Francis Close (later Dean of Carlisle Cathedral) railed against many things in his evangelical preaching, and racing was certainly one. During one Sunday sermon in 1827, for instance, he revealed that: 'Every species of profligacy – adultery, fornication, uncleanness, lasciviousness, hatred, variance, emulations, wrath, strife, envying, drunkenness, revellings and such like are promoted by a race week. If you wish your child to plunge into the world's vain pleasures, to acquire a taste for dissipation, send him to Cheltenham races.'

Three years later his followers burned down the grandstand. As a direct result, the race meetings moved from Cleeve Hill to Prestbury Park, so the longer-term consequences were probably not what those arsonists were aiming for. Apparently, Dean Close School did send some of its earliest pupils to the new venue on racedays but this was so that they could be marched up and down outside brandishing anti-racing banners.

The school did not lay on transport to the track in my day but at least we were not instructed from the pulpit that to enter the gates was tantamount to a mortal sin, and of horseracing I simply could not get enough. Those teachers who knew about it regarded my hobby with a mostly tolerant and sometimes benevolent eye. During repeated seasons of underachievement in the 2nd XV, Saturday home matches were played on the other side of the road from the school and while my team-mates would jog down to the road and on to the pitch in a purposeful group, with the imposing sound of studded boots on tarmac reverberating around them, I would often watch as much of the racing as I could on a television in the school buildings before making my way on to the field of play on my own, and not so imposingly, from another gate some 50 yards distant.

On another Saturday when there were lessons as usual but no school sport was required and getting to Prestbury Park was the day's primary purpose, I once soft-footed it out of the back of a Physics class while the teacher was writing on the blackboard. His lesson threatened to overlap with the first race. Outside the school, parked with the engine running, were one set of grandparents who whisked me to the racecourse where my other grandfather was already present.

My grandfathers, accomplices and inspirations, Vernon Austen and George Morris, were old friends who in former years used to go racing a great deal together. They were enthusiasts for the sport in a major way and happy to share that enthusiasm with me. It was my life-directing good fortune. There can have been very few meetings at Cheltenham or Newbury that Grandpa Morris did not attend, and if they took place during the school holidays I would probably be with him. He was a quiet, even reticent, man in whom a love of racing was deeply ingrained – a love of racing and of horses. As a tenant farmer, he grew up with horses. He lived about eight miles from Cheltenham, at Deerhurst, on the banks of the River Severn, where his home and farm buildings stand in the shadow of one of the oldest churches in England. It is a place that was better known in Saxon times. Saint Alphege embarked here on the monastical life that led him to the Archbishopric of Canterbury, and to martyrdom in 1012 at the hands of the drunken Danish raiders who held him hostage and then pelted him with animal bones.

In 21st-century Britain, horses are essentially a luxury to those not involved in the racing industry but for a large part of my grandfather's life, for the farming community,

Introduction

horses and horsepower were a necessity and a big part of their way of life. My mother and uncle recollect that when they were children there would be perhaps four carthorses at a time on the farm, and as a young man their father also rode in point-to-points. He told me that enforced changes in farming practice after the Second World War were what turned his attention to keeping broodmares (he never had more than two) but I strongly suspect that he felt such a bond to horses and racing that he would have done it anyway. Certainly, when the economic advantage had long since disappeared, he kept a mare for as long as he could.

Kantabiri, a 1951 bay by Birikan out of his mare Easton Square, was the best horse my grandfather owned and raced, and he was sent racing only after two seasons being proudly taken on a tour of agricultural shows in the south west. As a foal, 'Biri' went to Cheltenham and to Gloucester and was awarded first prize. As a yearling colt, he won first at the Three Counties (for a prize of £15), Evesham (Champion), Berkeley (£5), Cotswold Hunt and Withington, Thame (for the Chesham Perpetual Challenge Cup), Monmouth and Bradford on Avon; he was runner-up at Yeovil (£5) and Pilning.

Biri had originally been owned in partnership but Sid Freeman relinquished his share when my grandfather started thinking that this could be his first horse in training. In a letter, Freeman warned: 'I would George strongly advise you to think hard and long before deciding to what trainer you send him, knowing a good deal about them!!! It may not be a bad idea to have another word with the Paynes. I do know they are honest.'

Bill Payne at Seven Barrows (now Nicky Henderson's yard) in Lambourn did indeed take charge of Biri, who in February as a three-year-old became registered as Kantabiri with racing's secretariat Weatherby & Sons as were the new owner's colours of chocolate, silver grey and chocolate quartered cap.

June 7 that year was to be the day of days in Kantabiri's Flat career. Lester Piggott was booked to ride. A large contingent from Deerhurst made the very scenic journey down the Wye valley to Chepstow and Kantabiri was backed down to 5-4 favourite in a maiden race over one mile (1m). According to my uncle, William Morris, his father gave strict instructions that the bets were not to be placed until shortly before the off, in order to protect the price. Straining at the leash, the eager backers were to wait for my grandfather to give a signal as he stood in the grandstand.

'When he raised his hat, that was the time for us to go and put our money on,' relates my uncle, 'and then we all got on the stand and watched the race and it was just a formality really, of him coming through and winning. Then I think one of the reins broke. Kantabiri veered off to the right towards the stands and the other horses just ran on through. We just stood there and poor old Dad was so upset, because a lot of people had put a lot of money on. He thought he was doing them a favour by making a good investment. I can remember now, us all standing there after the race in pretty grim silence. We just couldn't believe it really.'

After that three-year-old career on the Flat of six races and one placing, Kantabiri was described in the Timeform *Racehorses* Flat annual, then in its infancy, as 'of little account' but Lester advised that he should have a go over hurdles and at Stratford in October Kantabiri made his hurdling debut and won at 6-1. My uncle was present. Hopefully the Chepstow losses had been only lent. Kantabiri also won one race at Stratford over fences.

My grandparents were frequent visitors to the Paynes, sometimes taking my mother and uncle, and as a result of one such visit they ended up taking something else back with them. A two-year-old filly in 1956, Fair Sabrina sustained an injury that was too bad for her ever to race but she had a notable half-brother in Halloween; he won the King George VI Chase in 1952 and 1954, and from 1953 to 1956 he was runner-up in two Cheltenham Gold Cups and third in two more. Fair Sabrina's injury was serious enough that her being put down was a strong possibility, but instead of that my grandfather bought her, took her home and nursed her back to health.

Nine foals followed for Fair Sabrina, three winning as point-to-pointers, while Fair Pinch and Horatio Sparkins were fair jumps winners under rules in the early 1970s. In the winter of 1968/1969 my grandfather considered whom he should have Fair Sabrina covered by next. Among his paperwork, I have since come across a 21cm by 16cm advertising card, on which is glued a small photograph of a bay stallion:

ENTANGLEMENT
Now standing at Burley Lodge Stud, Epsom
Under the direct supervision of Mr and Mrs GEORGE
FORBES

Under the photograph, it states that Entanglement is 16.2 hands high, has 8½-inch bone and is 'Proven sire of winners throughout the world'. Foremost among those winners, it expounds inside, were the French winners Castagniccia and Stengah, also Bunkered who had 9st 6lb in the 1968 Irish Free Handicap, and Maspalomas whose successes in Spain apparently included their Gran Criterium and three Classics, earning the description 'best racehorse in Spain for over 20 years'.

I doubt very much whether my grandfather would previously have heard of any of those flagbearers.

The advertisement went on: 'Entanglement's yearlings were fetching up to 1,900 gns in 1968. Fertility for 1968 over 80%.' Entanglement himself, it reported, had won handicaps at Newbury (1m2f) and Sandown (1m and 1m2f) as a three-year-old in 1961, and been fourth in the Champion Stakes at Newmarket. In 1962 he finished a close third in the 1m4f Jockey Club Cup. He was the 'Highest stakes winning 3-y-o sired in England by King Of The Tudors'. Among further details in Entanglement's 'impeccable pedigree', his once-raced dam had also produced Coral Cluster, who had registered '13 wins under N. H. Rules, including George Duller Hurdle, Cheltenham'. Infra red lamps were present in all boxes at the stud 'to induce early conception' and there would be 'free routine veterinary charges'.

On February 10, 1969, the secretary to Mr Forbes wrote to a wavering Mr Morris outlining again the price of a nomination to Entanglement and extolling the merits of the live foal concession: 'Perhaps you would telephone on receipt of this letter and confirm whether you wish to take a nomination to this stallion for 1969, as there are only two nominations available and Mr Forbes has requested me to reserve one for you, pending your decision. Yours truly.'

Fair Sabrina arrived at Burley Lodge Stud on February 17. The nomination had been purchased for 198 sovereigns, 'returnable if mare not in foal or aborts, or foal fails to live within 48 hours of birth,' and Fair Sabrina visited Entanglement on March 6 and 9. On April 23 Mr Forbes's secretary wrote to my grandfather informing him that 'I enclose our card, from which you will note the good news that Fair Sabrina has been tested for pregnancy diagnosis and found to be in foal to Entanglement to her service of the March 9 1969.'

According to a note in my grandfather's hand, written on that stallion advertising card, the foal was born on February 21, 1970. Grandpa told me that he arrived at four o'clock in the morning. I have some photos of my brother and me, two very small boys, and other members of our family looking on in wonder, being introduced to the newcomer. He was a chestnut with a smudge of white on his forehead and a small white band just above the near-hind hoof. At Deerhurst, he became known as 'Muddles', and not because of his sire's name.

He was Fair Sabrina's last foal because she died of cancer in the same year. My grandfather kept Muddles until he was a three-year-old, not wanting to send him to the sales but also, after an earlier half-brother to Kantabiri had broken his back on the gallops, not wanting to put him into training himself. In the spring of 1973, his friend Ian Scott, a Shropshire farmer, was telephoned and asked whether he knew of anyone who might be interested. Having combined his visit to a Cheltenham osteopath with one to Deerhurst, Scott then persuaded the trainer Bob Turnell to call in as well the following day. Scott and Turnell took half shares.

Scott later told me that when he pondered what to call his new horse, the answer came to him in an Archimedes-like 'Eureka' moment while he was having a bath. Referring back to the sire's name Entanglement, he settled on a fishing reference. According to one website, it means 'a monumental tangle of line on your reel resulting from a spectacular overrun. A fishing term that's often preceded by an expletive.' The intended spelling is not entirely clear, as Turnell's secretary apparently made a mistake when typing out the registration form, and it would later appear with and without an apostrophe depending on the publication, but when the chestnut three-year-old was entered for his first race that October he was now called Birds Nest.

CHAPTER ONE

1981 WATERFORD CRYSTAL CHAMPION HURDLE

The Golden Age of Hurdling

ON MARCH 7, 1970, two weeks after the birth of Birds Nest, and also at four in the morning, a son of Sea-Bird was foaled at the Greentree Stud in Kentucky. He would soon be named Sea Pigeon. On May 26, 1971, at the Cloghran Stud near Dublin, a colt by Falcon arrived who would later be called Night Nurse and on June 7, 1972, the Lismacue Stud in County Tipperary was the birthplace of the Gala Performance colt who would be Monksfield. A group of the most celebrated hurdlers of all time were on their way to Cheltenham.

For me, looking at the arrival and positioning of these horses in the top rank of hurdlers feels almost akin to describing the creation of the planets. The four of them were the heroes of my youth and there has never quite been a horse, let alone a group of horses, to supplant them. At that age my wonder years were a contributory factor, for sure, but I am not the only one who was so enraptured and felt that this collection was different from 99.999 per cent of other horses, and I cannot believe that any rivalry on the racecourse has yielded so much to the sport as that between Birds Nest, Sea Pigeon, Night Nurse and

Monksfield. They are listed here in age order, and the battles to see how they should be listed on a race-by-race basis and in terms of absolute merit would soon result in this being called the Golden Age Of Hurdling, a label that continues to stand the test of time. At stake were not only the top prizes in 2m hurdle racing over a six-year period, but also the highest figures ever in the history of ratings for horseracing over hurdles. Persian War, Bula, Comedy Of Errors and Lanzarote were impressive as they monopolised the Champion Hurdle from 1968 to 1975, but the stars of this next generation would push each other to even greater heights.

Timeform's *Chasers & Hurdlers* commenced in 1975/76 but they were rating jumps horses long before that, and this group of hurdlers is their most garlanded. Simon Rowlands of Timeform states: 'What is remarkable about any list of the most highly rated jumps horses since the mid-1970s is just how many of the best hurdlers came from a brief period around that time and a little later. There have been some great hurdlers since, not least Istabraq and Big Buck's, but there has never, even remotely, been such a clustering of great hurdlers at one time. It was quite remarkable. And it seems very likely that there was not an era quite like it previously, either. Timeform scrutinised and validated its ratings for hurdlers in the 1960s and early 1970s as part of its contribution to Cheltenham's Hall of Fame in the early 1990s. Again, there were some great hurdlers around – notably Persian War and Magic Court – but there were not *many* great hurdlers almost all at once as was to occur some years later.'

In 2015, Birds Nest, Sea Pigeon, Night Nurse and Monksfield still provided two of the top three hurdlers ever on Timeform ratings, three of the top 11, and the other is 1lb further back in equal twelfth. To state their standing on the ratings history, however, conveys so little, because this group contained some of the most striking individuals of jumps racing that I can remember. Their distinction resided in far more than calculations of pounds per length.

Racehorses tend to be viewed with a good deal of anthropomorphism, including a fondness and hastiness for identifying in them some of the most vaunted virtues possessed by human competitors, particularly concepts of courage and the will to win. With Night Nurse and Monksfield, it has to be conceded, there was every opportunity. On the other hand, for those more intrigued by ideas of the wayward genius or by the unfathomable mysteries of nature, Sea Pigeon and in particular Birds Nest would show that the process of getting from A to B before the other horses need not always be so straightforward.

~

Birds Nest was the first of them to race over hurdles. 'He wasn't a particularly tall horse but he was very thickset, strong. He was a very good-looking horse,' remembers Andy Turnell, his regular jockey and the son of trainer Bob Turnell. On Birds Nest, he would experience some of the best moments in his career: 'Whenever I'm asked what was the best horse I rode, he is the first one you think of. I was lucky enough to ride three or four very, very good horses but on his day he was probably the best horse I ever rode.'

Success was not instant though and it was never to be relied upon. Sport provides life lessons and if one of those is not to take anything for granted then Birds Nest was the perfect instructor. Following Birds Nest, the horse my grandfather bred, was as thrilling as one could hope for but it was certainly a life lesson and one that commenced almost as soon as he set foot on a racecourse. After promise on his first start and a lot of promise on his second, he was second favourite for the Finale Junior Hurdle at Chepstow and within the Turnell yard he was thought to be a certainty. Andy Turnell was unavailable for the ride, which went to the stable's young claiming jockey Steve Knight. Some of the lads did not want him on board, thinking that he was too inexperienced, but Bob Turnell was a great one for giving his young riders opportunities.

'He fell with me at the second last,' Knight reflects. 'And he would have won. There was no question about it, he would have won. I remember going into work the next morning and hardly anybody spoke to me. I think they'd all lost their holiday money.'

In his next race, Birds Nest justified favouritism at Wolverhampton. When he ran at Newbury second time out the following season, it was at Christmas so I was able to go and watch him, as did a sizeable proportion of my family. Starting favourite, and with Turnell in the saddle, Birds Nest fell at the fifth hurdle and, as I remember it, with the life lessons clearly not yet taken on board, I spent a good deal of the rest of the afternoon crying in the car park. Thankfully, I was not back at Newbury six weeks later for the Schweppes. I can, however, remember vividly watching the race at my other grandparents' house. A long time earlier, Bob Turnell had predicted that Birds Nest would win this biggest handicap hurdle of the season off 10st 6lb. In fact, Birds Nest carried 10st 7lb and he didn't win. Trainer and jockey took the preceding race on 25-1 shot Shock Result, who stole a lead to beat Pendil and Bula no less, but the real shock result for the stable and others rooting for the gambled-on co-second favourite Birds Nest came when Mr Straight fell at the second and brought Birds Nest down with him. Grouping together that tumble at Chepstow and the two at Newbury, Steve Knight reports soberly, 'that was the three times they backed him'.

Up until that point, Birds Nest had won only one race. After it, he won three on the trot and on the second occasion, at Doncaster, he inflicted the only defeat that season on Sea Pigeon. The pair would go on to race against each other another 13 times.

Born amid the sprawling acres of Greentree Stud, Kentucky, Sea Pigeon was a son of the 1965 Derby and Prix de l'Arc de Triomphe winner Sea-Bird, one of the very best Flat horses of all time – he was easily Timeform's highest rated before Frankel came along in the next century. Sea Pigeon's dam Around The Roses had not done badly herself, finishing second in one leg of the United States fillies' triple crown, and his breeder was the multi-multi-millionaire John Hay 'Jock' Whitney, former US Ambassador to Britain. Whitney's mother had been known as 'First Lady of the American Turf' and he and his sister Joan Whitney Payson made a decent stab at keeping it in the family.

Of the four main players in this chapter, Sea Pigeon was the first to race, doing so on the Flat and winning easily at Ascot in October as a two-year-old, but although the list of races he contested at three was of the highest order, his performances in them were not. He was fourth in the Dante and seventh in the Derby but, highly strung, he was gelded at the end of the season and a private bid of £10,000 (about £108,000 in 2015 after inflation) took him into the ownership of wine merchant Pat Muldoon, and from being trained by Jeremy Tree at Beckhampton in Wiltshire he was sent north to Gordon Richards at Greystoke Castle, near Ullswater, not far south of the Scottish border. Given two runs on the Flat in 1974, he was not an immediate success. The *Timeform Black Book* commented that Sea Pigeon 'had apparently very simple task at weights in amateur riders' event at Beverley ... but went under by 1½ lengths...and looked ungenuine in the process'. Sea Pigeon was not given their notorious black mark the Timeform squiggle (§), but that sort of terminology is used sparingly and he must have come very close.

If at this stage there was an element both of disappointment in Sea Pigeon's racing career and depreciation in his value, the merit he showed and the sums involved nevertheless make those of Night Nurse on the Flat look minuscule.

Night Nurse was bred by Mrs Eleanor Samuelson's huge and historic Cloghran Stud. Close to Dublin Airport, the site is now owned by the Dublin Airport Authority. Its buildings have been left to decay steadily but they were once home to Blandford, the sire of four Derby winners. Unlike Sea Pigeon, Night Nurse was not bred to be a Derby horse. Neither though was he bred for the Champion Hurdle. As his trainer Peter Easterby puts it, 'his father was a short-runner over five furlongs – you work that one out.'

Night Nurse's dam Florence Nightingale ran only as a two-year-old and she was by a 1m St James's Palace Stakes winner. There were good Flat winners a bit further back in the pedigree but when Night Nurse was sent to the Houghton Sales at Newmarket in 1972, seven yearlings from Cloghran were sold that day and he fetched the least, at 1,300 guineas. Easterby remembers well what he looked like: 'A great big, plain horse he was, nobody would want him for a Flat horse. One reason why I bought him was I had his half-sister – she was pretty useful. She won, then she ran again and she had a bad fall. They took the knacker cart down and when they got down she got up but she wasn't any good after that. I liked him anyway and he wasn't much money either.'

The muted response to the youngster from others beside the sales ring was replicated when Easterby got him home: 'I tried to sell him. My job is to sell them, not keep them. You'll go skint if you keep them all and the ninth man that saw him he bought him; a fella called Mr Rudkin from Leicester and he had glasses that thick – he couldn't see, could he?'

The aforementioned half-sister was Leca, who won a 1m2f Flat maiden and was gambled on for a juvenile event on her hurdling debut at Catterick, only to fall at the first. Night Nurse's Flat career was similar, comprising no success as a two-year-old, when five of his six runs were over five or six furlongs, and a solitary maiden win at three, in his case over 1m1f at Ripon in June with a Timeform rating of 74 (Sea Pigeon's as a three-year-old had been 109). Easterby says Night Nurse pinched that race from the front and he does not speak highly of the horse's Flat career.

The trainer did, however, see a future for the three-year-old Night Nurse over hurdles but in this he did not see eye to eye with the owner, or more precisely with the owner's girlfriend. The trainer recalls, 'I rang Mr Rudkin up and said, "I've schooled this horse over hurdles, and he didn't shape so bad you know."'

The owner thanked him very much. It was not long, however, before Easterby's call was returned: 'He was 85 and had a girlfriend – she was 65 – and the next thing the telephone goes and it's his girlfriend: "You run that horse over hurdles over my dead body." How do I get out of this one?'

Reports and memories vary but at some point, and this may well have been it, Night Nurse was entered for the Doncaster Sales. August 14 at the Great Annual York Race Sales looks the most likely candidate. Whatever the date, it is not one which Night Nurse's potential buyers will remember with any affection. As Easterby recalls, 'Nobody bid, thank God. He was supposed to have a heart murmur.' In a 1983 television interview, he elaborated. 'He went to Doncaster Sales with a £2,000 reserve on him and we couldn't produce a vet's certificate. Therefore there wasn't a bid for him. And he came back and that was it.'

The person I spoke to at Doncaster Sales confirms that the veterinary world now understands some of the nuances of equine cardiology a great deal better. Whether Mr Rudkin's girlfriend was the one to suffer heart failure is not recorded but three days after that probable 'sale' date, Night Nurse ran in the Grimsby Maiden Juvenile Hurdle at Market Rasen and he won it, according to *The Sporting*

Life and *Sporting Chronicle* while still in the ownership of Mr Rudkin. Of the manner of this win, comfortably and at 10-11, the trainer asserts: 'We didn't know he was any good. We knew he jumped well – he jumped very well.'

Another week on and Night Nurse was back at Market Rasen and this time he was 1-2 and carrying new colours, as Easterby explains: 'So I gave him [Rudkin] 1,000 quid for him back, and I turned around and sold him to my schoolfriend Reg Spencer for 1,500. How's that?'

At Cheltenham in September – on the day that Sea Pigeon flirted with the Timeform squiggle on the Flat at Beverley – Night Nurse won by six lengths and after further wins in October and February, with a second at Chepstow in between, *The Sporting Life* was reporting on 'undoubtedly the best juvenile hurdler in the North. Night Nurse is a breathtaking jumper for a beginner'. His odds for the Triumph Hurdle (a race Birds Nest had missed the year before because of injury) were down to 6-1.

Eventually sent off 10-1 when the ground turned heavy, Night Nurse was well beaten. However, like the 'heart murmur', that particular cloud was another that turned out to have silver linings for his trainer. Interest in Night Nurse had become much more animated since the putative sale at Doncaster and there was one particularly persistent source of enquiry, as Easterby relates: 'Another fella wanted to buy him. He always had a bag in his hand, a little bag, and every time Night Nurse won he used to dive in, not announced, and say, "He's a good horse, isn't he? Would you sell him?"'

Holding up the bag, the man would proclaim, 'I'll give you 25 grand for him. I've got the readies here.' Easterby continues: 'Night Nurse ran in the Triumph Hurdle and he finished last and he coughed all the way home, from Cheltenham to here. Coughing his guts out. And he was that ill he never got his summer coat 'til July, that's how bad it was. So that was another stroke of luck. I couldn't sell him then could I? I think he [the owner] would have taken 25 grand.'

~

1976 CHAMPION HURDLE

In the run-up to the 1976 Champion Hurdle, Night Nurse had five starts unbeaten. These included the Fighting Fifth at Newcastle and the Sweeps Hurdle (in its last year as a conditions race) at Leopardstown. The one his trainer seems to remember with particular fondness, however, was the Free Handicap at Chepstow, which kicked off that campaign, in which Night Nurse was so well handicapped (nevertheless carrying 11st 5lb) that in Easterby's words he was 'running loose.' Did they have a few bets on Night Nurse over the years? Easterby confirms in no uncertain terms that they did.

Meanwhile, Sea Pigeon won three of six starts before the Festival and even in defeat, including at the hands of Night Nurse in the Fighting Fifth, he too looked a contender for the Champion. Ten days before the Festival, Gordon Richards took him to Wetherby for a racecourse workout under Jonjo O'Neill in which Sea Pigeon breezed home after giving his galloping companions a 20-length head start. The following day he was found to have a warble on his withers and therefore could not run at Cheltenham.

Birds Nest, however, would be there, although his build-up had been limited to two starts in a dry winter. The 1975 Champion on heavy going had been won by Comedy Of Errors by eight lengths. Going into the 1976 renewal, Night Nurse and Sea Pigeon had both defeated Comedy Of Errors when receiving weight from him and in the Wolverhampton Trial Birds Nest became another to do so. Not greatly remarked on at the time, after coming through smoothly to lead, Birds Nest swerved badly to his left halfway up the run-in.

In terms of weight carried and distance beaten, Comedy Of Errors was still the best horse on form going into the 1976 Champion. The eight-year-old Lanzarote too had demonstrated that he was still a major force. Such, however, was the visual impact made by Night Nurse and Birds Nest that many felt there was about to be a change at the top. Among those with such an inkling were Peter Easterby and Bob Turnell, and Michael Phillips related in his preview in *The Times* on the morning of the race: 'My colleague, Michael Seely, has reminded us often recently that there is an air of confidence at Malton, where Night Nurse is trained by Peter Easterby. Easterby considers that Night Nurse is better than Saucy Kit, his winner of the Champion Hurdle in 1967. Talking of confidence, I have never known Bob Turnell more hopeful of winning a race of this nature. He has trained Birds Nest all winter with today in mind and, having won the Champion Hurdle once with Salmon Spray, he knows precisely what is required.'

From what I remember of him, Bob Turnell did not seem the type of man who was easily prone to such confidence, or to expressing it, but he certainly did know what was required. He habitually brought his best horses to a peak at the Festival. Of the 18 races then at the meeting, he had won 12 at least once; four of the others had been instituted only recently; of the long-established races, the Kim Muir and Triumph were the only ones that had eluded him.

On officially firm going, Night Nurse was 2-1, Birds Nest 100-30, the nine-year-old Comedy Of Errors 4-1 and Lanzarote 9-2. The script to two out was already known, because Night Nurse's style of running under Paddy Broderick was well set. 'He was a front-runner of course – only because the jockey was,' says Easterby. 'It was no good giving Brod orders; it was a waste of time, that's why. He used to make the running on them all, mostly.' From two out in the Champion it would simply be a case of who could challenge them.

Broderick had ridden his first winner in 1953 and, as Brough Scott described it the day after the Champion, his 'riding style is the upright long legged method more usually associated with old sporting prints.' He had suffered some heavy falls – in 1967 being rendered unconscious for a fortnight – and some bad after-effects, struggling for rides at one stage before he teamed up with Easterby.

In riding style, Andy Turnell was a polar opposite. I doubt that anyone has ridden with shorter stirrup leathers over jumps and it comes as no surprise to learn that in his youth he was a huge fan of Lester Piggott. Turnell's preferred approach was that 'the longer you can hold a horse together the better' and Birds Nest was in many ways the perfect Turnell mount. 'He used to travel so well,' recalls his rider, a hint of awe still in his voice. Birds Nest could do it for a long way too, before producing a comparatively short but potent burst of finishing speed.

Turnell's style sometimes fooled those in the grandstand into thinking that his mounts had more left to give than they really did. Two out in the 1976 Champion, just how much horse he had under him was the issue of the moment. Birds Nest had moved up about a length behind Night Nurse and while Lanzarote and Comedy Of Errors were third and fourth they were flagging. I doubt there can be many readers who do not know the result of this race. Attempting to transmit any cliff-hanging element as it came to a climax may therefore be a vain enterprise but, with Night Nurse having accelerated into a three-length lead entering the straight, I will leave it to Peter O'Sullevan's BBC commentary. The memory of it is clear from when I watched it on a television at school:

'Over the final flight, Night Nurse from Birds Nest then Lanzarote and racing into the final 150 yards and Birds Nest putting in a tremendous run. It's Night Nurse from Birds Nest, racing up towards the line and Birds Nest beginning to get up on the far side ...'

What O'Sullevan did not mention when describing Birds Nest challenging on the far side is that he started off on the near side. Birds Nest produced a terrific surge, starting as he went into the last hurdle, which he stood off by a huge distance. But it is hard to judge just how close he got to Night Nurse on the run-in because he was drifting so far to his left, ending up on the far rail. A dozen strides from the line, Birds Nest clearly had no more to give. Staying on with gun-barrel directness and efficiency, Night Nurse was the new champion by two and a half lengths. It was another eight lengths back to Flash Imp, who stayed on past the two thoroughly vanquished former Champion Hurdle winners for third.

~

Also present at the 1976 Festival, in the Triumph Hurdle, was the four-year-old colt Monksfield. Two years earlier, trainer Des McDonogh had been watching the meeting from an Irish hospital bed, his operation the extremely drawn-out consequence of a broken shin suffered in a fall. With his wife Helen, he started training in November 1972 and they had their first winner in February 1973.

Remembering the impressions Cheltenham made on him in his youth, McDonogh says: 'Well, like every young fella looking into it, you couldn't wait to see it every year. Unfortunately we missed an awful lot of it, we hadn't television down in the south and you'd have to wait for Pathé news or something in the films to see the big races, but you'd read about them in the paper. I knew it was the place.'

Two months after watching Lanzarote win the 1974 Champion Hurdle and Captain Christy win the Gold Cup, and not long after his 28th birthday, the now discharged

McDonogh (with his leg in plaster) and his wife went to the Ballsbridge Sales, caught their first sight of the two-year-old by Gala Performance out of Regina and bought him for 740 guineas. In Jonathan Powell's superb book *Monksfield*, McDonogh recalled what happened when they first asked to see him in his box at the sale-ground. 'I opened the door and *that* was it, the way he looked at me from the corner of his box. He perked up as if to say, "What the hell do you want?" I loved that head, that *fabulous* head, the instant I saw it.'

At that stage, McDonogh had trained the winners of three races and one of those was in a walkover. His new purchase had already made one previous visit to the sales ring, as a yearling, and been led out unsold at 1,200 guineas. His dam Regina was no stranger to the sales ring either. She came from one of those Aga Khan families from which every breeder wants to have a member – but in her case they didn't. When she was a filly in training with Alec Head she was small in stature and, as Timeform put it, perhaps kindly, she 'ran a few times on the Flat in France without distinction'. Sales followed for 4,000 guineas in 1960, 120 guineas in 1965 and 1,500 guineas in 1968. Her buyer on the third occasion was Peter Ryan, a young science writer soon to be author of *The Invasion Of The Moon 1969: The Story Of Apollo 11*, who was at the sale only to meet his cousin Arthur Ryan. What neither Ryan had been aware of was that although Regina was in foal when they bought her, she had managed only one foal in the previous six years. While Peter Ryan lived in Chelsea, Arthur Ryan looked after Regina and her offspring on his farm at Inch, County Tipperary. It was their joint decision in 1971 to have Regina covered, at a fee of £300, by Coolmore's US-raced stallion Gala Performance, a union from which Monksfield was the result. He was sold to Dr Michael Mangan that June for £1,125 and named after the guesthouse his mother used to run in Galway.

Like Night Nurse, Monksfield was foaled very late in the year compared to the general thoroughbred population, and whereas Night Nurse had been too large for commercial tastes as a yearling, Monksfield was too small. Like Sea Pigeon, however, he won in October on his only race as a two-year-old, but whereas Sea Pigeon had been second favourite, Monksfield, in his maiden over the extended seven furlongs at Punchestown, was 25-1. On the Tote he was 647-1. He did not win at three on the Flat but was third (at 33-1) in the Irish Cesarewitch that October and the following month a maiden at Navan was the first of an eventual 14 wins over hurdles. By the time Monksfield went to Cheltenham for the 1976 Triumph, he had already raced eight times as a juvenile hurdler, in addition to an extensive Flat campaign, and he would also run twice that season after Cheltenham. At 28-1, he finished second in the Triumph to Peterhof, trained by Peter Easterby's brother Mick. In Monksfield's essay that season, *Chasers & Hurdlers* concluded that 'Lightly built, he probably lacks the physical scope to make a really good horse but nevertheless he should be a smart handicapper.' Twelve months later they were writing about him again, more expansively, and their opening sentence this time, following his first Champion Hurdle bid, was 'We owe Monksfield an apology.'

As already recorded, Timeform's views on Sea Pigeon had also required some revision and he too was there to bid for the 1977 hurdling crown, but Gordon Richards was no longer his trainer. Richards was not averse to running more than one horse in the same race and sometimes the longer-priced runner won. When this happened in October 1976 and, not for the first time, the shorter-priced runner was owned by Pat Muldoon, the owner decided to take his horses elsewhere and Peter Easterby's stables were the recipient.

After the final start of his three-year-old Flat career, Sea Pigeon had been described by his jockey Tony Murray as 'like a person on the edge of a nervous breakdown', so when the horse arrived at Greystoke the imperative had been to calm him down and relax him. In *The Boss*, the colourful biography of Richards by John Budden, the trainer's son Nicky described how 'Father was fascinated with Sea Pigeon. He was convinced that the way to release his latent potential was to get him interested and happy in himself.' Consequently, Sea Pigeon seems to have lived in a bucolic idyll, Budden detailing how 'as far as possible, he would be divorced from the regimental routine of everday training' and that he 'revelled in the quiet life, the jogging up hills, the roaming through the woods and the occasional jumping over fallen trees or narrow water splashes'.

Peter Easterby had a high regard for Richards as a trainer but with Sea Pigeon he decided the job was not yet completed and he seems to have gone about it very differently. 'When I got him he hadn't any brakes,' declares Easterby. 'All he knew was "*phew*" [he indicates something shooting forward]. They don't win like that. We brainwashed him and got him settled down.'

Asked whether this involved exploring different tactics and different positions on the gallops, Easterby states, 'No, that's the last thing you do. You do the same thing every day, day in day out, no variation at all, then they get the message. No good taking him a different route and all that, that's the worst thing you can do. But they're all different. There's no set rules with what you do with a racehorse.'

It was three months before Sea Pigeon ran for his new trainer. A number of engagements were made and some journeys wasted in a bid to avoid soft ground, but the trainer's view swiftly became one that 'It wasn't the ground that was stopping him, it was his brain. He wasn't relaxed. If you don't relax them you won't win anything. That was what was up with him. He got the message eventually.'

With the combustible talent that was Sea Pigeon, ensuring that he was settled in his races and deciding exactly when to deploy his almost unique finishing speed would be perpetual issues.

~

1977 CHAMPION HURDLE

In March 1977, the big guns of Champion Hurdle history were now assembled. Anybody who has ever seen or heard about racing will know that the post-race perspective is often radically different from that as the tapes rise, and in that Champion at the off Birds Nest was favourite at 6-4, Master Monday was 11-2, Dramatist 6-1, Night Nurse 15-2, Sea Pigeon 10-1, Beacon Light 11-1 and Monksfield 15-1 in front of three longshots.

Master Monday had won at Leopardstown in the Sweeps Hurdle and Erin Foods Champion Hurdle; Dramatist had won the Christmas Hurdle at Kempton and the Kingwell Pattern at Wincanton. Birds Nest was three from four for the season, easily the most striking of which was the Fighting Fifth in which he was making his reappearance – Andy Turnell thought he might be short of peak fitness and rode at Ascot instead – against Night Nurse who had been unbeaten in eight starts the previous season and had just increased that sequence to ten. In that Fighting Fifth, Birds Nest beat Night Nurse by 15 lengths. It transpired that Night Nurse had a back problem but Steve Knight makes clear it was also some performance from the winner: 'It was unbelievable because he jumped so well, everything. He never came off the bridle really that day. That was him at his best.'

Knight had ridden four winners the previous season and would end 1976/77 with nine, but in the 1977 Champion Hurdle he was on Birds Nest once again. Not many trainers nowadays, and perhaps not many even then, would countenance putting someone with those totals on board the 6-4 favourite in the Champion but with Bob Turnell that brand of loyalty was not a surprise. Andy Turnell had suffered a freak injury the day before which denied him the ride on Birds Nest and also on Summerville, for whom he had huge hopes in the Gold Cup. In the event, Summerville suffered a career-ending injury when he broke down in the lead after the second last and finished third. Birds Nest would be back for another day, many of them, but in his race at the 1977 Festival he did not show up anything like as creditably as Summerville. Knight says, 'He wasn't the same; he just didn't feel the same.'

Night Nurse, on the other hand, was every bit as good as in 1976, if not better. Beacon Light and Birds Nest were upsides at the third last, then Dramatist and Monksfield had taken their place turning for home; Sea Pigeon, racing very wide, was in extremely serious contention as well. Night Nurse saw them all off, a superior leap at the final flight playing its part. Monksfield challenged strongly halfway up the run-in but Night Nurse went away again in the final twenty strides.

The winner's generous price was influenced by the heavy ground, two defeats and an absence since Christmas, even though two weeks before the race Easterby had challenged: 'If there is any blighter who thinks that anything is wrong with Night Nurse, let him come to Cheltenham and see for himself.'

There was, however, a point at which the negative vibes about Night Nurse threatened to get to even his trainer, as Easterby reveals: 'We had a fright. He had always won on firm ground you see, and it was soft ground. We backed him at 7-2 or something – he drifted out to 5 or 6-1. We backed him again, and bugger me he went out to 7-1. So I said to the lad, Keith Stone, "Have you ever left this horse?", thinking he must have been doped to go out like this. "No, never left him." So I said, "Oh, alright then, we'll have a bit more on." I had too much on. Before I left I had some potatoes. There was five ton left and I said to me brother-in-law, don't sell them potatoes before I go to Cheltenham – I might need them when I come back. Anyway the potatoes were £100 a ton when we left here and when we got back home after he'd won the Champion Hurdle they were 150. How's that for a double! That was better than an insurance policy that, keeping those potatoes back.'

Unlike the potato market, there was no volatility to Night Nurse, not on the racecourse anyway, although his trainer says that 'He was a miserable old bugger in his box – he'd kick you, bite you, he'd do anything. Oh aye, he was miserable in his box.'

As a racehorse, there was nothing to criticise in Night Nurse's behaviour and there was no mystery to him. Sailing forward at the head of his field, he was the steadfast captain who would not be blown off course. Forty years on, the most strikingly individual thing about him is that for two seasons he was clearly the leader among the best group of hurdlers there has ever been. At the time though, it was deemed remarkable that he had made all the running in one Champion Hurdle and nearly all to win another. The last to have made all was, apparently, Victor Norman in 1936 and before him there was only Blaris in a four-runner race for the inaugural Champion in 1927. Since Night Nurse there has been Make A Stand in 1997, Hardy Eustace in 2004 (virtually all) and 2005, and Faugheen in 2015.

Blanket descriptions of front-running as 'doing it the hard way' are grossly simplistic. Assertions of an 'easy lead' can be just as hasty. It all depends on the horse and the race, and in making the running Night Nurse was found a way that suited him incredibly well. While the initiative may have come from Paddy Broderick's default riding preferences, in Peter Easterby's words, 'They clicked, didn't they? He was a natural front-runner and Paddy was a front-runner – that was the answer. He was very good at pacing the race though, Brod. He didn't know he was doing it but he was.'

For those who set off in pursuit of Night Nurse, a very small number of hurdlers might hope to outpace him late on but none could hope that he would weaken. Subsequent events would demonstrate even more clearly that this son of a sprinter had no shortage of stamina. That helped. Something else, though, was as fundamental in his success as a hurdler. 'A competitor who will fight to the last ounce' is how *Chasers & Hurdlers* once described him and that is the horse I remember. Watch his two most famous defeats at Cheltenham and, even then, when he is clearly beaten, Night Nurse is coming back for more. 'He was a brave, brave horse,' is Easterby's summary. If there is a mystery with Night Nurse, it is that he wore blinkers on his last four starts on the Flat as a three-year-old. Nearly 40 years later, his trainer's reaction must be similar to the rest of us when he says, 'Did he? I didn't know that. I couldn't tell you why.'

Going head to head with a sometimes errant Birds Nest helped to point up Night Nurse's irreproachable demeanour – 'I was worried 'til Birds Nest veered off,' says Easterby of the 1976 Champion – but with Monksfield he was up against a competitor cut from his own cloth. For some, Night Nurse's most famous success is not one of his many outright wins but the dead-heat when he gave 6lb to Monksfield over 2m5.5f at Aintree 17 days after the 1977 Champion. To put it simply, neither horse would give in, and the mechanical repetition of whip strokes, in particular from Dessie Hughes on Monksfield, would have fallen very foul of the modern-day rule book. Ten days later Night Nurse ran and won again.

~

1978 AND 1979 CHAMPION HURDLES

'A legend – before I even took him on he was a legend, wasn't he?' is how Des McDonogh assessed Night Nurse. 'He was the best anyone had seen,' adds the trainer, but, in Monksfield, Night Nurse would have a very serious rival for that title.

When I spoke to McDonogh in 2013 and broached the subject of writing about Monksfield, his first response was to ask: 'Oh Lord, will there be anyone around that'll remember him?'

Well, in my memory, Monksfield is the single most distinctive jumps horse bar Desert Orchid. For catching the eye, the latter had the significant advantage of being not just grey but for much of his career almost white. The first thing which people tended to latch on to with Monksfield was his size. In the course of his five seasons hurdling, Monksfield's physical description with Timeform progressed from 'lightly built' to 'small'. Peter O'Sullevan called him 'little Monksfield' in his Cheltenham commentary, but McDonogh remembers him slightly differently: 'Everyone said he was a little horse. He wasn't, he was a strong 16 hands. He was just running against Night Nurse and Sea Pigeon who were great big horses alongside him.'

Then there was Monksfield's action. Describing him in his slower paces, McDonogh says, 'When he walked, his knee, fetlock, ankle, hoof and the lot were all in a straight line.' So far so textbook. From the trot upwards, though, that line and Monksfield experienced a parting of the ways. In *Monksfield*, Arthur Ryan, one of the first to see Monksfield in his faster paces, says: 'we call it winding, as his two front legs go out and round in a great big circle' and the adjective used most often in that book to describe his action at the gallop seems to be 'appalling'.

None of which mattered, of course. Dessie Hughes's description of Monksfield's forelegs is that 'He swung them around a bit. He wasn't a very straight mover and he turned them out a bit, but he got them down quick enough,' while McDonogh says, 'To ride him was just amazing because he didn't feel like he looked.'

The idiosyncratic nature of Monksfield's action was slight compared to other aspects he displayed in a race. When horses race against each other and are reported to have 'stuck their necks out' or 'put their heads down', these words are often employed metaphorically. Monksfield, however, took it very literally. Surely none can have done so more and, for anyone who saw him do it, those traits will forever be fused to concepts of tenacity, courage and a horse's willingness to answer his rider's every call. 'He had a great will to win alright,' says McDonogh. As the competition began to hot up, Monksfield would lower his head and stick his neck out, straining and stretching to do his best, and McDonogh reports that his horse would feel similarly inclined on the gallops: 'If you were riding him at home you wanted to be fairly fit and strong now to be able to hold him, because when he decided he'd go and do his piece of work he got lower and lower and farther away from you.'

No horse has embodied competitiveness more vividly in its actions, and the stiff finish at Cheltenham, when others might be flagging, brought it into sharp relief. He would not peak in his campaign before the Festival but after it the Aintree Hurdle over its longer distance of 2m5.5f was also made for him and he won that race three times.

In the 1977/78 campaign Night Nurse was well below his best. In the Christmas Hurdle at Kempton he fell badly and effectively ended Paddy Broderick's riding career. But when the field set off for the 1978 Champion it was still Night Nurse who started 3-1 favourite, followed by Birds Nest (blinkered for the first and only time) and Sea Pigeon at 5-1, Monksfield at 11-2. Easterby's stable jockey Jonjo O'Neill stuck with Sea Pigeon rather than switching to the favourite but whatever soul-searching there had been behind that decision proved a waste, because O'Neill was injured on the first day of the meeting. So was Night Nurse's intended partner Colin Tinkler but he recovered in time. The ride on Sea Pigeon, though, was taken by Frank Berry.

Night Nurse's reign was over when three challengers quickly went past him after the second last. At the final flight Sea Pigeon was the only threat to Monksfield but it was not for long and the Champion Hurdle went to the Irish challenger by two lengths; Night Nurse rallied into third, a further six lengths back, while Birds Nest was a never-dangerous seventh. It was Night Nurse's final Champion Hurdle before being sent chasing the following season. At 44, Tommy Kinane was the oldest jockey to win the race. It was also trainer Des McDonogh's first win for ten months.

Twelve months on, in the 1979 Champion, Monksfield was bidding to be McDonogh's first winner for an hour and 20 minutes, the day having started with his Stranfield winning the Supreme Novices'. Kinane was on Stranfield but he was not on Monksfield. A week earlier the trainer had told him that he would be replaced, so when Monksfield set forth it was under Dessie Hughes, having his first ride in the race and his first ride on Monksfield at Cheltenham. Hughes felt some pressure. 'I had 12 stone 7 on myself going out alright,' he told me in 2013. In the days immediately before the race there were adverse rumours, which found their way into front-page stories in *The Sporting Life*, about the fitness and participation of both Monksfield and Sea Pigeon. The public still made Monksfield favourite but Sea Pigeon drifted to 6-1, the third choice. Had there been any truth in the rumours, one of the greatest head-to-heads for the hurdling crown would never have taken place.

In very heavy ground the field split in two, with Hughes on Monksfield setting the pace in his group and looking for, in the jockey's words, 'a bit of half-reasonable ground' in a most unorthodox path around the wide outside. Birds Nest led those who took the shorter, inside route, but the eventual first four were in the Monksfield group and it would have been the first five had second-favourite Kybo not fallen at the second last when disputing the lead; trying to stay with Monksfield over that flight proved too much. Sea Pigeon, however, looked as if he would more than match the leader. In his autobiography, *Jonjo*, Sea Pigeon's jockey wrote: 'We joined Monksfield on the inside at the elbow and I knew Pigeon would win. The tank was full and I only needed to press the button and Sea Pigeon's instant answer would carry us home.'

Sea Pigeon had a slight lead turning for home until the last, which both horses flew, but a dozen yards up the run-in Sea Pigeon's bid began to ebb and Monksfield was all the time scrapping away to claw back his crown. He succeeded, winning by three-quarters of a length. 'I'd say the best thrill of my life was the day I rode him to win the Champion Hurdle,' said Hughes to me. 'You know, you have a plan in your head in those races and everything went exactly like it was written, and it had to [he stressed] for him to win.'

This is how Hughes remembered Monksfield in a battle: 'He'd get down to it proper; he'd get down to a proper fight. His head would be down and he would try very, very hard for you.' The low head carriage and the extended neck were totally accurate indicators: 'He just wanted to win and he enjoyed racing,' asserted Hughes.

～

Watching Monksfield and Sea Pigeon at the final flight of that 1979 Champion, I am struck by a fact so obvious perhaps that it might be overlooked. As Dessie Hughes put it, 'The Champion Hurdle horses are champion hurdlers.' The four chief players in this chapter were all fabulous jumpers of a hurdle. Hughes's description was that 'they take very little out of themselves, measure them and jump them very quickly and get away at the other side. A totally different method of jumping to a horse jumping a fence.'

His mount Monksfield is the one who made the greatest impression on me in this respect; his approach to hurdling being one of incredible attack. 'Oh absolutely, but he was like that from day one,' confirms his trainer. 'The late Bobby Coonan rode him first time out at Navan and he said you'd get up out of bed at midnight to ride him over a jump; that was the feeling he gave him. When he was five strides off a hurdle you could know that he was going to let fly.'

McDonogh can remember Monksfield making only one jumping mistake during a race and is adamant that it was not his fault. It happened at the final flight in the 1977 Champion Hurdle when, contrary to the best-laid plans, Monksfield ran through a bad patch of ground on the approach. Watching a recording of the race, he clearly loses his action.

Even at the end of his career, Monksfield still made a deep impression with his jumping, as the trainer remembers: 'Helen [Mrs McDonogh] rode him in his last ever win, at Down Royal in an amateur conditions race, and she had previously ridden about 126 winners in point-to-points. She said she'd swap the whole 126 for that one race. She didn't remember leaving the ground on him, he just went from hurdle to hurdle as if it was a flat race.'

When Night Nurse had his first schooling session, the reaction of Peter Easterby was that the horse was 'A natural. Make your hair stand up. "Christ," I said, "What's this then?"'

Easterby continues, 'A top hurdler, he touches the ground, then he's gone again. They've either got it or they haven't.'

Of Sea Pigeon, the words he uses are: 'Brilliant – he were like a gazelle. With a top hurdler you don't see them take off or land you know.' John Francome states of Sea

Pigeon that 'Jumping-wise he was as fast as anything I ever sat on.'

As ever, with Birds Nest things were not quite so straightforward, because as Steve Knight describes it: 'He would never shorten, everything was long with him. Probably that's why you had them two crashing falls because he used to stand off it all the time.' In his best years though, Birds Nest got it right the vast majority of the time. The result, for Andy Turnell, was that 'I've never sat on a horse cross a hurdle any quicker. He was just electric.'

~

When Monksfield won his second Champion Hurdle, Birds Nest had been sent off at 13-1. Confidence in him for the championship had started to wane. Assessing his own path-finding that day, sticking to the inside, Andy Turnell says with dry humour that 'I was almost certainly proved wrong,' but it was not just punters whose patience with the horse now started to wear thin. When Birds Nest ran next in a good handicap at Aintree, Turnell opted to ride Beacon Light. As Beacon Light had been 13 lengths ahead of his stablemate in the Champion, finishing third – yet Birds Nest now had to give him 2lb (plus 18lb to the Supreme Novices' winner Stranfield) – the jockey certainly had a point. Writing off Birds Nest, however, tended to be a perilous business, as this race illustrated graphically. Under John Francome (who had ridden Beacon Light at Cheltenham) Birds Nest won comfortably by three lengths. Settling much better than in his youth, and with Francome therefore able to dictate a steady pace, Birds Nest had a great deal going for him in the way the race was run. But Francome also remembers being given some advice while going onto the track: 'The lad who looked after him, he said if you hit this horse down the left side he'll take off with you, he said he's never been hit down the left side. And he was absolutely right, he just took off.'

Everybody had their theories of how best to ride Birds Nest – when to challenge, where to challenge and what to do once getting there – and I dare say he confounded every single one of them at one stage or another. Turnell and Francome drove up together for that Aintree race and when they returned to the car after racing someone had written 'Cheating bastards', or words to that effect, in the mud on their car. 'It certainly wasn't the case,' Turnell assures me, and I do not think that whoever was responsible for that graffiti could have had much prior knowledge of Birds Nest. In his six seasons in the top flight, challenging on the bridle and then sometimes – but not always – hanging left was initially the glaring issue with him. There was no sign of him hanging at home but on the racecourse it would become his trademark. Some inconsistency crept in with it. Swishing his tail also became a feature, albeit often while he was running on strongly, but from the end of the 1977/78 season the causes to question his enthusiasm were not confined to the closing stages. 'In his younger days he just gave everything. Later in his career I thought he probably got a little bit knowing,' says Turnell.

More surprisingly, Birds Nest's usual rider says, 'He was comparatively straightforward to ride. I know it sounds silly because of his hanging, but most races you had to get him settled and just ride a race on him, produce him.'

For those incapable of a phlegmatic response, it must have seemed that Birds Nest's career veered between triumph and travesty. There were races he should have won but didn't and there were others he looked like winning but didn't, but in those 62 races overall he also won 19. Ten of the losses came in the last of his nine seasons. *Chasers & Hurdlers 1977/78* gave him the 'squiggle' notation next to his rating, indicating 'a horse who is somewhat ungenerous, faint-hearted or a bit of a coward; one who may give his running on occasions, but cannot be relied upon to do so'.

It was hard to argue with, but in 1978/79 the squiggle was removed. In 1979/80 it came back.

In seven of his wins the horses he beat included Night Nurse or Sea Pigeon. Against Monksfield in the 1979 Welsh Champion, you would be very hasty to conclude that Birds Nest would have won had he not blundered at the last, but he was challenging strongly at the time. 'I always went out on this fella thinking that I could beat them and obviously sometimes I did, sometimes I didn't,' states Turnell.

What often comes across as an ungenuine nature to the grandstand and unreliablility in the form book can be caused by physical problems and Birds Nest seems to have had his share of possible explanations on that front. As recorded in Michael Tanner's *The Champion Hurdle*, Bob Turnell was once quoted as saying, 'He's genuine enough but he's no fool. If things don't suit him, he doesn't run well. He has a fairly serious heart murmur. The only time he swerves is when the old heart pinches him.'

As a four-year-old, Birds Nest had his joints pin-fired and they would be an ongoing concern, particularly as the season wore on. Andy Turnell expounds: 'I'm just of the opinion that he was a better horse in the autumn, and not through anything other than the wear and tear on his joints. He looked a picture and everything but I'm pretty convinced that that's why the hanging started, because he was doing things that hurt him.'

Whatever its cause, Birds Nest's hanging under pressure presented his jockey with a dilemma, as Turnell relates: 'I felt that it was better, when he quickened up and was running like that, to let him hang rather than try and straighten him, because you slow horses up straightening them. I thought he'd got into a rhythm and was running on, so if he went a bit left it wasn't the end of the world.'

Birds Nest's jockey concedes, 'I think probably there were occasions when I should've pulled it [the whip] through and tried to straighten him.' But he was above all trying not to cancel out the turn of finishing speed, which he describes as breathtaking.

The quietly spoken Turnell is very modest about his achievements. At the time he was widely praised, including by Timeform, for his sympathetic riding of the horse and it is not hard to believe that this handling played a part in Birds Nest's extraordinary longevity in the top flight, though the man himself attributes it far more to the way he was trained by his father. Confronted by Birds Nest, many other jockeys would have resorted to using the whip and some would have done so in liberal quantities, but Turnell states: 'There were horses that wanted a hiding and he wasn't one of them. When you've got a horse quickening under you like he did, there was no point hitting them because you knew very well they were going as fast as they could go. I think nowadays a few of the jockeys would be a bit better keeping still and keeping balanced. It's all for the camera now isn't it? If you don't hit them you're not trying hard enough.'

~

1980 CHAMPION HURDLE

In his autobiography, Jonjo O'Neill recalled sorrowfully the closing stages of the 1979 Champion when it had become clear that his mount would not, after all, be quickening clear from Monksfield: 'I was helpless but still did the unforgiveable and cracked Sea Pigeon three times with the whip, knowing full well it would make not the slightest difference. Pigeon never went for the whip and to this day I wince with shame when I think how I resorted to hitting him.'

With his almost matchless ability to quicken, but some quirks to go with it, the riding tactics and use of the whip on Sea Pigeon needed to be every bit as cute as those on

Birds Nest. As described earlier, getting him to settle was the first step. In the 1977 Champion in which he finished fourth, Sea Pigeon had been described in his Raceform note commentary as 'not resolute'.

Even once he was able to race with a more relaxed demeanour, the timing of his run had to be perfected because, in Easterby's words 'he only had one run but it was fast. It didn't last long though'. John Francome had the leg up later in Sea Pigeon's career when Jonjo was injured, and his description is that 'he'd get to the front and then think he'd done enough. It was never that he'd got tired or anything, he'd just say "Well, that's it, I can beat everything else."'

There are different ways of finishing off rivals in a race, as I hope this chapter shows, and while Night Nurse and Monksfield could seem like rather blunt instruments in this regard, Sea Pigeon could administer the swiftest of coups de grâce. Birds Nest was similar, except with him the kill could get rather messy. Comparing the contrasting running styles of his two stars, Peter Easterby says 'I think the horse coming from behind is more exciting for the public like Sea Pigeon – Will he get there? Will he get there? – while old Night Nurse is battling away.' It is certainly hard to think that there have been many more exciting racehorses than Sea Pigeon.

As with Night Nurse, there was a point when the horse might have left Peter Easterby's yard at Great Habton near Malton in Yorkshire. In *The Sea Pigeon Story* by Bill Curling it is reported that a would-be purchaser, the American trainer W Burley Cocks, travelled over to see him but turned him down. Sea Pigeon did travel to the United States but it was in Easterby's care, to Camden in South Carolina in November 1977 for the Colonial Cup, a chase over 2m6f in which, three out, as his trainer, puts it now, 'he made the biggest bloody hole that has ever been made in a fence.'

Incidentally, Birds Nest was schooled over fences at one point and that experiment did not go well either. Steve Knight was in the saddle and he says, 'It was a bit slippery that morning and he didn't actually fall as such, he jumped the fence super, but he just slid on landing and laid down and that was the only time he ever saw a fence. He only ever jumped one fence.'

Without fences, or even hurdles, in his path, 1977 was the year in which Sea Pigeon began to set out with purpose towards racing immortality. In between the 1977 Champion and the Colonial Cup, he raced six times on the Flat. First of all, Easterby ran both him and Night Nurse in the Chester Cup. In addition to his maiden at three, Night Nurse had won two Flat handicaps as a four-year-old but at Chester he was a well-beaten fifth and Easterby explains, 'He didn't get round the corners. That were it.'

However, Sea Pigeon, giving his stablemate 14lb, won that Chester Cup, the first of three wins that season, and he was also second in the Northumberland Plate. In 1978, Sea Pigeon won five of ten Flat races, including retaining the Chester Cup, and in 1979 it was a case of third in the Chester Cup but victory in another four races, including the famous – but nearly infamous – Ebor Handicap at York in which O'Neill switched codes to take the ride and Sea Pigeon set a new weight-carrying record, but did so only after a long wait for the result of a photo-finish, the jockey having dropped his hands on him before the winning line.

At this point, Sea Pigeon was being described by Timeform as one of the most popular racehorses of the decade, and this was without him yet having risen to the top at his day job – he had not won a Champion Hurdle. His trainer is in no doubt that he should have done so in the epic 1979 race, roundly blaming the owner Pat Muldoon for telling O'Neill, as he got into the saddle, not to leave it too late. 'When Jonjo came in I just looked at him and he looked at me and we never spoke,' says Easterby. 'We knew what had happened – he just went too soon.'

'It's amazing that, you know,' the trainer adds. 'At that age, to be second twice, you'd never think you were going to win, would you?'

At the start of the new decade, Sea Pigeon and Birds Nest were now ten-year-olds. Since Hatton's Grace won the Champion aged nine, ten and eleven in 1949–51, no horse aged even nine had taken the race. Only four eight-year-olds had prevailed in that period. Going into the 1980 renewal, Monksfield looked to be on his way back to form but Sea Pigeon, troubled by a foot infection, had been absent since November when Birds Nest beat him in the Fighting Fifth, the first of three Birds Nest wins that season before the Champion. The younger generations were represented by Connaught Ranger and Pollardstown, winners of the two previous Triumph Hurdles.

As well as younger faces to take them on, the old guard were confronted by an altered course. Having in previous years been run on the Wednesday, the Champion was moved to the first day of the meeting to avoid a repeat of the previous renewal when the course was so cut up that all the runners had done their best to avoid running on it. Hitherto run over two miles and 200 yards, the Champion was still on the Old Course but had the 200 yards lopped off it, as the runners no longer had to take a longer loop (around what is now the Best Mate Enclosure) that involved going past the winning post on the first circuit. The going was soft and Monksfield was sent off 6-5, with Pollardstown 7-2, Sea Pigeon 13-2 and Birds Nest 11-1.

Facing up to the hill for the final time, Monksfield was just over a length in front of Sea Pigeon and Birds Nest and they were the only ones in serious contention. Birds Nest was given two cracks down his left side by Andy Turnell and finished probably the closest he ever managed at Cheltenham to the stands rail, but it was good enough only for third, one and a half lengths behind the runner-up. As he had 12 months earlier, Sea Pigeon approached the last apparently travelling much the best. Jumping it, this time he was three-quarters of a length down and when O'Neill asked his mount to go on shortly afterwards Peter O'Sullevan was soon able to call: 'He's won it at last. Sea Pigeon wins the Champion Hurdle.'

At the line there were seven lengths between Sea Pigeon and Monksfield. Racing up with the front-running Paiute, winner of France's most important hurdle race, may have adversely affected Monksfield's chance. There was also the fine-tuning of tactics on Sea Pigeon and the less testing ground. When the season-long evidence was available it seemed that Monksfield had simply not been at his best in that campaign, which is probably the key point, but the changed course layout was also very much to Sea Pigeon's advantage.

'I'd say it was very important. It was in our favour definitely,' states the winner's trainer. 'Of course we did know how to ride him. Monksfield was a very tough staying horse, and we felt you could beat him for speed if you waited long enough – which we did do once.'

Giving his assessment of Monksfield's performance, Des McDonogh says, 'Well, my jockey on the day, Dessie Hughes, said he wasn't as good as he was and I have to accept what he says, although three months before Cheltenham I rang Michael Mangan, his owner, and told him that I didn't think he'd be able to win it a third time in a row because they had changed the track layout. Sea Pigeon didn't like to go up the hill twice; that's what I was thinking anyway.'

It was Monksfield's final appearance at Cheltenham. The decision had been taken well beforehand that this would be his last season before retirement to stud. In five visits to the Festival, he finished second three times and won twice. 'That night, I remember a lot of people saying I wasn't a great loser or whatever,' recalls McDonogh. 'I was a bit down and a bit upset, the reason being I never mind being beaten, it was the fact that I knew I'd never have one again like him.'

~

1981 CHAMPION HURDLE

My introduction to the Festival proper was on Champion Hurdle day 1981, Tuesday 17 March, roughly half an hour after Physics or some other lesson that was not that day the prime focus of my attention. In 1978 the Triumph Hurdle and Gold Cup had been postponed by snow until the April meeting, during the school holidays, and watching Connaught Ranger and Midnight Court prevail that afternoon seemed excellent at the time, but that experience as a racegoer was about to pale severely.

Having been brought up on the Golden Age of Hurdling, the question was whether it could last long enough for me to witness its final major action. I was desperate for Birds Nest to win a Champion. As Andy Turnell says of his challenges for the race, 'I don't remember going to Cheltenham and riding him and not being hopeful – he was that sort of horse. He was a very, very good horse at his best and it just depended which Birds Nest turned up.' But we were both probably realistic enough by 1981 to accept that it was now unlikely to happen. However, Sea Pigeon, too, was a hero, as he was to almost everyone by then. The horse who was too highly strung as a three-year-old and whose honesty had been doubted by the foremost form organisations in the land was now famous for his enduring zest for racing. With this harnessed and channelled, he was top class over hurdles and not far off it on the Flat. To be so good in both spheres was extraordinary and to do it at his age was almost incredible. Over the past four years

Sea Pigeon had been not just an adornment to the sport but an integral part of it, and he had done it in spring and summer, autumn and winter.

Having had Timeform Flat ratings (which are on a different scale to those over jumps) of 113 in 1977, 120 in 1978 and 121 in 1979, he increased it to 123 as a ten-year-old during his ten-race programme in 1980. He was doing it under big weights in major handicaps but these are the ratings of a good Group-race horse. Timeform, the company renowned for its detached and cool-headed assessments, was moved to write of Sea Pigeon in *Racehorses of 1980* that 'His story is one of the most extraordinary sports stories ever told. He has been a magnificent ambassador for the sport; his achievements have transcended the confines of racing in a similar way to those of Brown Jack, Golden Miller, Arkle and Red Rum, probably the most famous geldings to race in Britain in living memory.'

When Sea Pigeon returned to hurdling for the 1980/81 season, it was, however, without Jonjo O'Neill, who had suffered a horrific leg injury in October 1980 and would not be able to return to raceriding until December 1981. John Francome guided the horse to his reappearance win at Sandown in November and Alan Brown was on board in the Fighting Fifth at Newcastle, where, of course, Sea Pigeon was once again up against Birds Nest. Both mustered terrific late efforts in pursuit of the front-running Pollardstown, getting to him so late that commentator Raleigh Gilbert called Pollardstown the winner when in fact he had finished third, and by half a length. It was Birds Nest who, for a fourth time in the race, passed the post first. Sea Pigeon, though, had been checked on the run-in. Steve Knight, who rode Birds Nest that day, is adamant that 'the horse raced dead straight' and that it was the rails which deviated, not his mount, but for the only time in Birds Nest's wayward history the stewards demoted him.

At an age when most horses would have long since

reached for their metaphorical pipe and slippers, Sea Pigeon and Birds Nest were still among the foremost hurdlers. Naturally Birds Nest did not show it on every occasion, but next time out, going for a third win in the Bula at Cheltenham, came the most extraordinary display of his extraordinary career. As outlined earlier, he may well have had physical issues, but in this Bula it was difficult to ignore the mental. As Andy Turnell relates, 'They went absolutely no pace and when we got over the second I thought, "Well, this is ridiculous" and stole about 20 lengths. I thought I was being clever but then as soon as we turned down towards the water he pulled himself up.' Birds Nest's turn to be clever resulted in the complete loss of his lead but he did at least continue with the others. Those rivals included Celtic Ryde, Heighlin, Connaught Ranger and Gay George, all serious talents, and in the run to the line Birds Nest got back up to win by a neck.

In the Champion, Heighlin and Celtic Ryde started second and third favourites to Sea Pigeon with Daring Run (a rising force in Ireland) and Pollardstown next. Birds Nest, with three defeats since the Bula, was 16-1. Sea Pigeon, contrastingly, had not been seen since the Fighting Fifth. His absence may have emboldened both the connections of the younger generations, who ensured a 14-strong field, and the bookmakers, who opened up on course with Sea Pigeon at 11-4, but Sea Pigeon was sent off 7-4 favourite. The Supreme Novices' and Arkle had just been won by the market leaders but this was not just a crowd playing up its winnings. Its emotional stake in Sea Pigeon was worth vastly more.

Whereas getting to the 1980 renewal had been hard work and rushed – O'Neill says the horse was not fully fit and at halfway he 'started to let out the most disturbing gasps and pants' – there were no such problems in 1981. 'No, no, we weren't worried about that. He was a very clean-winded horse,' says Easterby. John Francome was back on board and the jockey says that the final instructions he received from the trainer amounted to little more than a statement that 'He's better than he was last year.'

What followed was one of the most famous races, and rides, in Festival history. The shape of it was determined chiefly by the needs of Pollardstown, a thorough stayer at the trip, whose connections did everything they could to secure a strong pace by buying Meladon (the 1977 Triumph Hurdle winner) and using him as a pacemaker. He set about his task in earnest. Pollardstown kept close to him and as the field turned away from the grandstands after two flights the first six runners were stretched out over 15 lengths, preceding the pack. Birds Nest raced in a clear fourth in those early stages but hopes for a Champion Hurdle win at the sixth attempt ended between the fourth and fifth flights when he took himself back to last. Sea Pigeon, meanwhile, crept closer towards the outside and, with Francome crouching low and still, could be spotted at various points thereafter asking for his head, but not being allowed it. As Pollardstown turned for home in the lead with Daring Run second, Daring Run's jockey Ted Walsh glanced to his right. He looked again, presumably not quite believing what he saw the first time. To rising excitement in the crowd, Sea Pigeon was close on Daring Run's outer and still under highly conspicuous restraint.

John Francome describes the race up to that point and shortly after it: 'It's just how your luck goes. Going to the first hurdle there was a horse in front of me and I thought, "Will I go to the left of it or right of it?" and it fell. If I'd gone the other side he'd more than likely have been brought down. It's just how things go. At the top of the hill it was like he'd just started. With most horses they're just trying to get some air into themselves but he was nearly running away at the top of the hill. He always travelled well in the race and people say it was a really good ride but it was like riding a piece of work.

In most jump races you can't be messing around trying to come really late because if you don't jump the last flight of hurdles well you check your momentum and your chance has gone, but with him he came up out of my hands, he came up almost a stride earlier than I'd expected. Even if he'd got in close, you knew that he was never going to land flat-footed over anything.'

Even if Francome's ride was not conceived as an act of showmanship – Sea Pigeon still had a superb turn of foot, the going was soft, officially heavy – it certainly had that effect, electrifyingly so. After jumping the last, Pollardstown and Daring Run were two lengths ahead and they were not stopping. Francome opted to wait a little longer. Was Peter Easterby expecting him to be delivered so late? 'Oh yes,' he says. 'We'd learned by then. It took a long time to learn, didn't it?' Was he confident that Sea Pigeon could bridge the gap? 'Yes. Well, sort of. You could see he was travelling but it's a long hill that one at Cheltenham, isn't it?'

About ten strides after the last, Francome started to nudge and by the time that nudge became a push another dozen strides later, about halfway up the run-in, Sea Pigeon had already launched his winning surge. Pollardstown, keeping on remarkably well given his earlier effort up front, wrested back second from Daring Run (Birds Nest stayed on again to be seventh). On the television commentary Peter O'Sullevan exclaimed, 'It's the old man Sea Pigeon coming to take it up and he's going to win it ... you've never heard such cheers from the crowd.' The first taste of something is often particularly special, simply by being the first, but I do not think it is any rose-tinted delusion by the Festival new boy that places this race among the very best I have ever seen.

Francome downplays the famous ride which brought Sea Pigeon home in front by one and a half lengths. He says, 'It was famous for everybody else, it wasn't famous for me. If you're a jockey you'd give your right arm to get on a horse like him and I only got on him because Jonjo O'Neill had broken his leg.' Peter Easterby sums up Francome's contribution simply as 'He rode him to perfection.'

I did not think that there was any way in which the man on board Sea Pigeon could have made this race a more fantastic spectacle. When I interviewed Easterby, however, the trainer revealed that I may have been wrong: 'I tell you who was going to ride him if we couldn't get Francome – Lester. He was going to ride him. He was one hell of a jockey over hurdles, Lester. I was sat next to him at the Derby Awards and I said, "Hey, I might want a jockey for Pigeon, at Cheltenham, can you ride him?" "Yeah, I'll ride him," he said. It was on the cards for Lester to ride him, I'll tell you now. He agreed to ride him.'

Perhaps I showed some surprise at this point, but Easterby continued: 'He was on call, don't you worry about that. Oh yes. Aye, some memory that Lester. He rode a winner for me at Pontefract. I rung him up and said, "Ride this Lester, it'll win. You're going for the championship. You don't get any pay you know, you won't get any bonus and all that balls, you get nothing." "Oh, I'll ride it," he said. "It belongs to a little old farmer, he can't afford it," I said – he farmed over 2,000 acres this fella. Anyway, that was it, he won alright. He gets off and Lester says, "Send us a bag of spuds." And I was playing golf with him in Dubai, it's got to be 20 year after. Now I wasn't very good at golf and he was worse, and we'd just been going on a bit when he said, "I never got them spuds, you know." Twenty year after. How's that then? Christ, he was some jockey, that Lester. It would have been interesting at Cheltenham, wouldn't it? He rode a few winners at Cheltenham you know, Lester did, and all his family were jumping jockeys.'

It would have been unreasonable to have asked for any more of the Golden Age of Hurdling but Lester Piggott riding Sea Pigeon might just have provided it.

～

I wonder how many people could possibly have attended that day's racing and not gone back. I have been there for every Champion Hurdle since and for the vast majority of other Festival days. Of the four leading protagonists in the Golden Age of Hurdling, though, Night Nurse would return for the Gold Cup (see Chapter 7) but none would be seen again in the race they had made their own.

By 1981 Monksfield was retired. He had raced 49 times over hurdles, winning 14, and had 76 races overall, five further wins coming on the Flat. Monksfield had been the exemplar of toughness, both during his races and in that he was able to take so many of them. Des McDonogh was often described as Monksfield's lad as well as his trainer, looking after him at home as well as riding him. 'I did indeed,' he says. 'Nobody else did. I wouldn't let them anyway. I enjoyed doing him over, mucking him out and all that. I built his stable myself as well.'

With Monksfield gone, the trainer went back to Cheltenham with Herbert United, who was fifth in the 1984 Supreme Novices', third in the 1985 County Hurdle, ninth in the 1986 Champion, seventh in the 1987 Champion and well beaten in the County two days later. He has not had a runner there since nor been back to the meeting. The McDonoghs' son Declan is a leading jockey on the Flat.

Monksfield's progeny won 133 jump races in Britain and Ireland for £676,977, along with 22 Flat races for £41,210. I asked McDonogh what sort of physical resemblance the offspring had to their sire and he replied, 'I never saw one that looked like him.'

And what about in their action or sticking their necks out? 'No, no,' he laughs, 'you wouldn't get any one that moved like him.' Dessie Hughes also replied in the negative. Monksfield, it seems, was a one-off, although at the time of writing McDonogh also has two unnamed fillies (a four-year-old and three-year-old in 2015) who are distant relations to him and whose faces are marked exactly the same as his was.

'He had a fantastic broodmare line,' says the trainer, 'and the mares that were by him were very tough breeders and bred very good horses.' He has every reason to say it given that two of those mares, the sisters Friars Pass and Las-Cancellas, whom McDonogh trained himself, went on to produce the Grand National winner Monty's Pass and dual Gold Cup third Harbour Pilot. The most successful of Monksfield's offspring on the racecourse was the smart Toranfield, later runner-up in the 1992 Cathcart, who first came to prominence with a hurdles win one day after the death of his sire, put down after breaking a hind leg when having his morning roll two weeks before the 1989 Festival.

The good behaviour that characterised his time in training did not, apparently, carry over into his stallion days. 'No, he wasn't easy to handle I believe,' says McDonogh. 'I went down with four mares one day and they were trying to do an insurance thing, a heart monitor or something, and I went into the stable and there were about three of them holding him, and there were vets and the whole lot, and he was going mad. I said, "Oh, what's going on here?" Didn't he hear me, and he just downed tools and came over, licked my hand and they were able to do whatever they liked with him. Amazing, and I hadn't been there from the previous stud season. He was an amazing horse. That would have been the last time I saw him. He's buried here. I brought him home and he's buried here at the front gate.'

Night Nurse and Sea Pigeon are together not many yards from Peter Easterby's front door, beneath a beech tree and an inscription 'Legends In Their Lifetimes'. 'And my wife's ashes are there as well now,' he says. 'She wanted her ashes to be put there so we did.' Sea Pigeon had been ante-post favourite for the 1982 Champion but suffered a serious virus in the spring of 1981 and did not recapture his form, his retirement being announced just before the

1982 Festival. He lived until October 2000 and spent most of his retirement at the Etchingham Stud not far from the Easterby stables. The trainer remembers Sea Pigeon as being very intelligent, citing the following story as an example of it and also of his attachment to a routine: 'He used to go out in the field every day and he wouldn't come in 'til half past 12. One day I thought I'll just go and bring the old horse in before Sunday dinner and the old bugger was on the other side – you'd never catch him. I went out after I'd had my dinner, at 1.30, and there he was, waiting. The clocks had altered, hadn't they?'

In all, Sea Pigeon won 16 of 45 races on the Flat and 21 of 40 over hurdles. Night Nurse won half of his 64 races over jumps and three of 18 starts on the Flat, and after his retirement on New Year's Day 1983, Timeform stated that 'For almost a decade the name Night Nurse has been synonymous with what is best in National Hunt racing.' He died in November 1998 after a retirement at Habton Grange. At one stage the two stable stars kept each other company in the same field.

'They both ran together,' says Easterby of their retirement. 'They took to it all right. They were ready for it.' Asked what those two horses meant to his life, he replies: 'Everything, but it meant more after they'd done it. Because you're doing your job and you're flat out busy and then all of a sudden, when they've gone, you haven't got one like 'em.'

Hardly anyone has. Night Nurse on 182 is still the highest-rated hurdler in the history of Timeform ratings. When I asked Peter Easterby whether at the time he thought it was a golden age of hurdling, his response was 'No, did I hell? It's for other people to assess that, not me. I'd be biased, wouldn't I? It's no good me assessing it.'

Would he agree that Night Nurse was the best hurdler? 'Well, I wouldn't disagree with them, would I? Put it like that. I don't know how they arrive at it.'

As assessed by Timeform, Monksfield is joint second

highest (with Istabraq) on 180, while Birds Nest is joint ninth on 176 and Sea Pigeon joint twelfth on 175. On the same mark as Birds Nest is another horse from the same period. The Irish six-year-old Golden Cygnet won the 1978 Supreme Novices' by 15 lengths and it looked as if he was about to win the following month's Scottish Champion as well when he fell at the final flight. He was challenging the leader Night Nurse at the time and the novice was giving the former champion 5lb. The eventual winner Sea Pigeon was conceding Golden Cygnet just 1lb, but there never would be a Champion Hurdle for Golden Cygnet, whose fall at Ayr caused him fatal injuries.

~

In the midst of these six years of peerless excellence among hurdlers, most observers probably recognised them as great horses, but with the benefit of more than thirty years since and the arrival and departure of countless other hurdlers, they seem more special not less so. Among hurdlers to have contested the Champion, Birds Nest is generally recognised as the best hurdler never to have won it. The first of the four main protagonists in this chapter to have raced over hurdles, he was also the last to do so, before his retirement aged 12 at the end of the 1981/82 campaign.

Birds Nest was basically Steve Knight's ride at home but in later years, when the careers of both the horse and his owner-trainer were drawing to a close, Bob Turnell would also sometimes take him out. 'He would very often go up on his own on Birds Nest and hack about,' recalls Andy Turnell. 'You used to see him in the distance, hacking up a hill somewhere. We rode him when he worked, but at Ogbourne there were some pretty good gallops and some were a fair way apart, and you used to see him hacking on Birds Nest from one to the other to see horses work. He obviously had a soft spot for him.'

At The Festival

Birds Nest had been retired for a matter of months when Bob Turnell died aged 67 following a stroke in September 1982. He was a man who had known how hard a life in racing could be before he eventually became a master of his profession as a trainer. Andy Turnell, forced to take up training earlier than he had expected, went on to win the Grand National with Maori Venture and the Champion Chase with Katabatic. When his mother Kathleen, known to all as Betty, moved to Marlborough following her husband's death, she called her new house Birds Nest.

The horse himself lived until 1994, impeccably behaved as a hunter before taking up a more sedate life when he got arthritic. Much of his time was spent with his other owner, Ian Scott, who described him in a 1988 interview with Emily Weber as 'The kindest, nicest chap. He has a marvellous, charming temperament, and would do anything. We don't even put a head collar on him when we need to do anything to him.'

Fewer than four weeks after the 1981 Champion, Sea Pigeon and Birds Nest gave battle against each other in the Scottish Champion at Ayr. Giving weight to the young guns Gay George and Ekbalco was recognised as a tricky task and, for all their Cheltenham heroics, Sea Pigeon and John Francome did not start favourite. That honour went to Gay George and, with Sea Pigeon feeling the first effects of his virus, it was Gay George who led by a length and a half at the final flight. He made a mistake. Closing, Birds Nest put in a superb leap, quickened up and won by three-quarters of a length. I may be biased but no group of horses could have inspired a biased outlook more effectively and it is this race, Birds Nest's final win, that I always think of as having brought the Golden Age of Hurdling to a close.

CHAPTER TWO

1981 WATERFORD CRYSTAL STAYERS' HURDLE

Derring Rose – the horse who preferred to go backwards

SEA PIGEON'S CHAMPION Hurdle on its own would have been more than enough. With the benefit of more than 30 years of hindsight, however, it is clear that his was far from being the only remarkable race that day in 1981. The Supreme Novices' felt remarkable because it always does, regardless of the horses involved or what happens. As the first race of the meeting, there can be hardly any other in the entire calendar that is more longed for. On this occasion the usual acclaim at the start was greatly boosted at the finish by the late arrival in front of Hartstown, a heavily backed Irish-trained favourite. Thirty-five minutes later, the Arkle went to another favourite, but Clayside had to overcome surely one of the worst mistakes ever by a Festival winner, almost coming to a juddering halt when he hit the ditch at the top of the hill four from home: jockey Alan Brown needed the sturdiest reins and the keenest sense of self-preservation to prevent himself from bidding adieu to his mount via the back door and various other exits.

The superlative achievement among that supporting card, however, and it would not have been categorised as a supporting role on almost any other day, was in the Stayers' Hurdle from its incredible winner Derring Rose. Superlative; incredible – such words can easily be bandied about but this performance is virtually on its own in my experience at the Festival for its overwhelming authority. It was not until 2008 when Master Minded won the Champion Chase that I felt a comparable thrill at dominance revealed again on such a scale.

John Francome rode three winners on the Tuesday in 1981 and, as he describes it, 'they all bolted up' – the third was by 15 lengths on Friendly Alliance, when wearing the white question mark of John Mulhern in the Grand Annual – but I severely doubt whether the seven-time champion jockey's 1,138 wins contained any that were easier than Derring Rose's that afternoon, and this despite it being a championship race.

Over the first two flights the pace was slow, with 3-1 second favourite Derring Rose mostly setting it, having found himself in front, more by accident than design, when the tapes rose. From there on, he was always close up and raced on the inside for the first circuit, after which the favourite Richdee took up the running while Francome bided his time.

Making the final turn downhill, there was a line of five up front with Derring Rose and Celtic Isle on their heels. Derring Rose narrowly avoided a faller three out and when a new line of five jumped the second last almost together he was one of them, second from the left as the crowd looked at it. At this point Derring Rose was travelling so strongly in comparison to the others that a win for him was a long odds-on certainty. But what followed was a jaw-dropping experience nevertheless for all who witnessed it. In a narrow lead turning for home, Francome moved on him a dozen strides before the last and gave him a slap down the shoulder five strides before it. That was the only time he raised his whip and, having gathered momentum to jump in a lead of three lengths, Derring Rose then passed the post in front by 30. Runner-up Celtic Isle was floundering but, make no mistake, Derring Rose was in overdrive. He rocketed clear.

Peter O'Sullevan's television commentary went: 'It's Derring Rose producing a sprint as he races towards the line. You'll think this was top-of-the-ground conditions. He's sprinting away to win the Waterford Crystal Stayers' Hurdle.' In fact, the official going was heavy. 'He never came off the bridle,' reflects Francome. 'There was one stage in the race when I thought maybe I had to go round again.'

On those BBC pictures, once Derring Rose has exited stage right to receive his plaudits, there is a hiatus of a couple of seconds before any other horse enters the camera shot. In the end, Celtic Isle gets to the line 6.82 seconds behind the winner.

Derring Rose was small in size, much more of a Flat sort in appearance, but over 3m1f in the mud the chasing types had proved hugely his inferior. 'Jump racing, it's just stamina at the end of the day,' says Francome. 'They are all staying races and he had limitless amounts of stamina. His strength-to-weight ratio was phenomenal.'

Limitless stamina was by no means the only attribute Derring Rose displayed in that race, though, and I do not think that the winning distance is the most remarkable statistic about his victory. Sea Pigeon's burst of speed to close out that year's Champion Hurdle is one of the most famous finishes in the sport, yet Derring Rose did it in only a fraction of a second longer, despite having raced over an extra mile and one furlong.

Judged solely on his 1981 Stayers' Hurdle win, he could have been a world-beater: he was perfectly amenable to restraint, jumped rapidly and efficiently, and he demonstrated stamina, a high cruising speed and startling acceleration at the finish. In short, he looked a paragon

among racehorses. The true situation, however, was nothing like that simple or that positive.

~

Sea Pigeon and Derring Rose were the leading players in what was probably the most influential day in my racing life. After that, attending the Festival and doing so for as many days as possible was a compulsion, an absolute necessity. The following year, one afternoon in late February or early March, a bone in my hand was fractured during a hockey match. Realising instantly that it was broken, I was ecstatic; in mid-March that year, school sports would have to do without me and I would again be at the racecourse instead.

One individual not so thrilled about a return to Prestbury Park was Derring Rose. As outlined already, he was in possession of many virtues. What he lacked, however, was the inclination to put them regularly on display. Even at the time of his Stayers' triumph, those who knew him well knew that there were substantial (and growing) entries in the debit as well as credit column.

Anyone with even mild mood swings tends to be described as a Jekyll and Hyde character, it has become such a cliché. Except in his name – by Derring-Do out of Bandi Rosa – Derring Rose was absolutely no cliché but you can see why those two creations of Robert Louis Stevenson have often been mentioned in his connection. I cannot think of another horse like him, of any horse with such positive and negative sides displayed so glaringly. Stevenson's work was titled *The Strange Case of Dr Jekyll and Mr Hyde* and the story of Derring Rose that arises from the racecourse evidence and witness statements is strange indeed in the world of top-level racing. He never killed anyone, to the best of my knowledge, but those who kept backing him to the bitter end may well have gazed upwards at the top of the grandstand and considered various points from which to disembark. He was the hero of the 1981 Stayers' but Derring Rose also indulged in a series of slapstick comedy routines with his unwitting riders, became notorious throughout Lambourn and on the racecourse, and he was the scourge as well as the delight of his owners and a legendary trainer.

Derring Rose's first trainer in Britain was Alan Jarvis, who early in 1980 was asked by Peter Savill to go to France to look at a certain horse and if he liked him to buy him. Savill had been pointed in that direction by David Margulies (who would be the co-owner) and his agent Frederic Sauque. On arrival in Paris, Jarvis caught the overnight train to the south and early the next morning he was in Pau, in the shadow of the Pyrenees. 'It was right by the mountains. It was beautiful and the air was fantastic,' remembers the visitor. In these idyllic surroundings, however, there was a malcontent.

'I always used to give the head lad or the lad looking after the horse a couple of hundred francs to get an honest opinion,' relates the trainer, 'and I said, "What do you think of him? Is he worth buying?"'

The reply Jarvis received was 'He's a very good hoss, very good hoss.' So far so good. 'But they put blinkers on and he not like. He very funny horse, he savage you in the box, but if you treat him right, he treat you right.'

Doing business the French way, Jarvis waited all day to meet the man who was selling and they clinched the deal over a good dinner. He caught the train back to Paris, with Derring Rose to follow. 'We only paid five grand for the horse,' says the buyer. However, on arrival at his Withybrook stables, near Coventry, Derring Rose was not greeted with unalloyed pleasure by the trainer's staff.

'The first day they were all frightened to go in his box because he used to lay his ears back and run at you,' he relates. 'With his teeth he looked a bit fierce. My son went in the box and Derring Rose pinned him in the corner, but Stephen came out, got some Polos and some carrots and grass and spent all afternoon feeding him over the door, making a fuss of him, and they bonded straight away. He used to ride him all the time and do him and he got on great with him and really never had any more problems.'

There was, however, an issue of a different sort: 'The one problem which we established very quickly was that he was wrong in the back. He was stiff behind and obviously wasn't right but I had a brilliant man who was a surgeon, at I think Leicester Hospital, and his hobby was treating racehorses. He used to go to Ireland and treat jumpers, manipulating them. He said, "Can I have a go at him? I'll put him right", and I said, "Yes, sure."'

With Derring Rose under anaesthetic and laid out in the indoor school, the hospital surgeon went to work, with some assistance. Watching on, there were nervous moments for the trainer: 'He had about four great labourers, huge guys who looked like rugby players, and they laid him down on the floor, they tied ropes round his joints and pulled him over. Two of them sat on his back end and they pulled the front end over and it cracked like a gun going off. They pulled and manipulated him and I thought they were going to kill him, but he said "Just walk him for two days in a straight line and trot him for the rest of the week, then kick on with him and he'll be fine."'

Corroboration for this prognosis was rapidly forth-coming. Under Andy Turnell in the Rendlesham Hurdle at Kempton on February 23, the newcomer to our shores was sent off at 50-1. In *The Sporting Life* and *Sporting Chronicle*, he was correctly listed as an entire five-year-old but there was no form for Derring Rose, not even form figures next to his name. There was no indication that he had ever run before. Did connections back him? Jarvis remembers doing so; Savill, who listened to the race in America, says 'definitely not'. Turnell recollects the trainer briefing him with the words 'Don't be surprised if this runs pretty well.'

If they did not realise quite what a quality horse they had going into the race, they were in little doubt after it. The 5-6 favourite John Cherry fell at the second last but the issue affected was surely only that of who came second. Derring Rose put eight lengths between himself and Major Swallow on the run-in; in *Chaseform*, the distance back to the third horse is recorded as 'bad'. In *The Sporting Life*, George Ennor wrote that this win 'reduced the crowd to silence. To the best of public knowledge Derring Rose had no public form but he has won and been placed in good company at Pau, in South West France, and has also won on the Flat at Evry.'

High on the list of those on whom this performance made a sizeable impression were John Francome and workers at Fred Winter's yard, who had fully expected their Major Swallow to win that race. They still thought he would when the field turned for home but when Derring Rose was unleashed he flew past. The bare result was striking and Derring Rose displayed a highly idiosyncratic style of running with it, making giant strides from out the back.

Coming from well off the pace was largely typical of his first British campaign and at that stage it was not too concerning to connections that his being there had nothing to do with the preferences of his jockey. Turnell swiftly abandoned attempts to modify the horse's French style of jumping – 'he ran into the bottom of every hurdle and just bent his legs; he didn't touch a hurdle' – and then found he had to adopt a similar approach to their position in the race. 'You couldn't keep him in a race sometimes,' admits Derring Rose's helpless partner, 'and then he'd gradually warm to it and then run on. It's a typical example of it's the horse not the jockey [that matters] because you couldn't make him do anything.'

After just that one run in Britain, however, Derring Rose was undoubtedly a serious contender for the Stayers' Hurdle less than three weeks later and sent off 10-1 in a field of 19. He finished third, but there would not have been nine lengths between him and the winner Mountrivers had the saddle not slipped. Two starts later, following a successful step down to 2m5f in a handicap at Aintree, there was hard-to-ignore evidence that Derring Rose was in fact markedly the better horse than his Cheltenham conqueror when he beat Mountrivers by 11 lengths into third at level weights in the Long Distance Hurdle at Ascot.

As described in *Chasers & Hurdlers*, Derring Rose kidded the Timeform racereaders in the course of both wins into thinking he had little chance approaching the second last, so far off the pace was he, and the organisation was on safe ground when concluding that 'he can produce a turn of speed that none of the present batch of three-milers can match and will be very difficult to beat when ground conditions are in his favour'.

Firm going was not in his favour back at Ascot later in April but the campaign ended on a lower note when he was sent to France in June for the Grande Course de Haies d'Auteuil, commonly known as the French Champion Hurdle. Derring Rose was unplaced and Peter Savill describes why: 'As soon as he got back to France – he probably heard all the French people talking – the horse was just a nervous wreck and clearly there were some memories there which he didn't enjoy. He fretted all day from the time he arrived and he was just not himself at all. He was normally quite relaxed when he got to the races, laid back, but there he was in a muck sweat and never ran his race in any shape or form.'

Jarvis elaborates: 'He went to bite one of the French handlers. It was unbelievable. The minute he landed and got in the horsebox and heard the French voice he changed completely. He lunged and was lucky not to bite this guy's face.'

As an indirect result that race turned out to be Derring Rose's last for Jarvis. The horse's passport had not been correctly updated on his return to Britain and the trainer was informed of this at Lingfield when Derring Rose was due to race on the Flat and Margulies had travelled over from the United States to see him run. Unimpressed, Margulies decided on a change of trainer. Fruitless journeys would become an occupational hazard with Derring Rose but, for now, it was Jarvis who felt it most keenly: 'I schooled him over fences and he jumped like a stag. He went over three fences, my daughter Elaine rode him, and I'd never seen a horse jump so well. I thought I'll win three Gold Cups with this horse and I was very, very disappointed to lose him. You're always going to lose good horses, horses you have done well with, but that's life. It happens to everybody.'

~

Derring Rose was sent to Uplands Stables in Lambourn to be trained by Fred Winter. A revered figure and a giant of the sport, Winter was the hero of Mandarin's 1962 Grand Steeple-Chase de Paris (won despite the bit snapping after four fences) and countless other races as a jumps jockey. He was widely considered one of the greatest of the 20th century. Taking out a training licence in 1964, he had established a not dissimilar standing and was already champion trainer seven times, a distinction he would achieve again in 1984/85.

If a phobia of French speakers was all that bothered his new charge, that could probably be managed, but it turned out that this was only a very small element in Derring Rose's eccentricities. The first impression those at Uplands had of their new charge was how small he was, but it was not long before the horse's physical characteristics were rather eclipsed by the mental. Brian Delaney was head lad at Fred Winter's and his pithy summary now of Derring Rose is that 'he was a quite a character, to say the least.'

At first there was a honeymoon period. Derring Rose became acquainted with his strange surroundings and what was required of him. When he was used to it, however, it rapidly became clear that he would rather be doing something else or at least doing it in a manner that was very different from the norm. In his stable there was no particularly untoward behaviour – Francome says he was 'as good as gold'. Reports vary on how he worked on the gallops, and Derring Rose may well have felt differently about the task from one day to the next, but there is unanimity that getting him there at all was often a stern challenge and that his work when with the string was less of an issue than getting him with the string in the first place.

'Once he got used to where he was heading and what he was going to do, that was when he used to just plant himself,' remembers Delaney. And how long did it take before he got to the gallops? 'As long as he wanted,' states Francome. 'That was the bottom line. He'd go when he wanted and not before.'

Even when he did make his way to the gallops, Derring Rose declined to do so in a straightforward manner. Instead, he developed a preference for doing it backwards. 'He was more adept at walking backwards than forwards,' declares Francome. 'You'd walk up the road, get within 300 yards of the gallops, he'd whip round and then he'd walk backwards all the way. He used to do it with his ears pricked. It wasn't that he wasn't enjoying himself, he was just a piss-taker. That was him. He wasn't nasty. He wasn't a complete dog. I think he just thought it was a bit of a craic, and it wasn't as if he'd be walking backwards slowly – he'd be walking back with the others that were walking the right way, at the same pace. He wasn't dragging his heels.'

Derring Rose – the horse who preferred to go backwards

Richard Cullen was the lad entrusted with Derring Rose and it was a considerable responsibility. On the plus side, morning exercise could be even more of a social affair than usual, walking backwards and having a conversation with the lad next to him face to face. However, when the horse decided not to move forwards or backwards, and with all the variations to try and persuade him becoming rapidly exhausted, the Winter team used to leave them behind. In the words of Brian Delaney, 'Richard would just do what he could with him. Some days he probably didn't do anything.

'Richard would have thought the world of him, he was that sort of lad. I used to use him like that all the time because anything that wanted a lot of riding, Richard was probably the first name I'd put beside it. He had very good hands and a very good temperament. I suspect old Derring Rose tried his temperament a fair bit but I don't think he even carried a stick on him, because it was a waste of time, and Mr Winter wouldn't have him knocked about either. Richard used to coax him. He'd take his feet out of the irons and pull him one way and pull him another. We'd leave him and go on up the downs and all of a sudden you'd see him coming. We'd see him coming round with Richard on him, doing his work, and then he'd probably come back into the yard half an hour after everybody else.'

For all its novelty, and in the case of Derring Rose his great proficiency at it, an aptitude for going backwards rather than forwards is not greatly admired or encouraged in a racehorse. In his first season with Fred Winter, Derring Rose's behaviour was not so bad that he could not be trained, but now that his phobia of French speakers had been joined by a reluctance to go to the gallops and a preference for walking in reverse, there had to be some nervous questions about whether this nonconformist outlook would also manifest itself when it came for him to race again. He gave his answer at Ascot in November. With Andy Turnell retaining the ride, Derring Rose was behind until, on turning out into the country, he tried to refuse at the fifth and then pulled himself up.

One month later Derring Rose returned to Ascot with both John Francome and blinkers enlisted in the 3m2f Long Walk Hurdle and he not only completed the course but did so comfortably in front of his eight rivals, by five lengths from John Cherry. Derring Rose also won another Rendlesham on his final start before the Stayers' and did so with ease, having led at the sixth, but in between those victories in the Long Walk and Rendlesham there was a sequence of three seconds. A run of seconds tends to sound a warning note and the increasingly unsympathetic reaction to Derring Rose's sequence was well summed up in *Chasers & Hurdlers*, which reported that he 'performed very creditably' in a very slowly run Corinium Hurdle at Cheltenham on New Year's Eve, 'getting the worse of a good, long battle by only a short head'; losing out narrowly again the next time, however, he 'just wouldn't consent to do his best', and of the third race they observed that 'Richdee won by three lengths, his enthusiasm from two out contrasting with Derring Rose's lack of it, though it must be said that the second had had a lot of ground to make up from Swinley Bottom.' In addition to a phobia of French speakers, a reluctance to go to the gallops, a preference for walking backwards and sometimes coming to a halt in his races, Derring Rose had now added a tendency to hang fire in the finish.

After the Long Walk win, Fred Winter was called before the stewards to explain the discrepancy with the horse's previous, lamentable performance. This was not an experience to which the trainer was accustomed. 'In 15 years of being with Fred Winter we never had a horse that did less than its best,' states Francome. 'The only thing he wanted every time you went out to ride was that at some stage during the race, the horse had to have some chance of winning.' Winter informed the Ascot stewards that Derring

Rose had been fitted with blinkers and that his instructions to the jockey were to keep the horse more in the race than on his reappearance. The blinkers were retained for his next four starts, the last of which was his seven-length win in the Rendlesham, but at Cheltenham for the Stayers' they were absent. It was not by design. Winter's assistant was Oliver Sherwood and one of his duties was declaring the headgear.

'I forgot to declare a pair of blinkers on him,' he confesses, 'and when I realised it was past declaration time I promise you my heart missed about twenty beats. I had to go down and tell Fred Winter that I'd forgotten to declare the blinkers which he wanted and I won't say to you what Mr Winter said back. Prior to going to see him I rang John Francome up and he said, "It won't make any bloody difference mate" and the rest is history. He won by 30 lengths. Mr Winter was a man of few words but his face said it all afterwards and I was a very relieved man.'

Watching the BBC coverage of the 1981 Stayers' and knowing now what Derring Rose's habits were at home, it seems probable to me that all those in his camp, and Sherwood in particular, were given cause for serious jitters even at the start, because when the field are pictured side-on, all lined up almost ready for the race to commence, Derring Rose reverses out of camera shot. The field were under starter's orders for about a minute before the starter let them go, with Derring Rose now to the fore.

Tactics, according to Francome, did not really come into it with Derring Rose. 'You had to ride him how you found him. If he was going forward, it didn't matter where he was, you used to just be happy that he was going forward. It was never a question of him not being good enough or of riding a race. He was always much better than anything else. Getting the best out of him was the key but easier said than done.'

~

When it was just as easily done as said in that 1981 Stayers', Derring Rose was a champion. The staying hurdlers were nothing like so strong a division as in later years, but Derring Rose was top of the pile by a massive margin. He had recorded two impressive wins in a row. There was a fall (three out, when holding every chance) at Ascot in April, but he was then given a Flat campaign and although not as good in that discipline, he ended the season with a Timeform Flat rating of 97 to go with his 164 (on a different scale) as a hurdler, having won the 13.3f Aston Park Stakes at Newbury and finished well when fifth in the Cesarewitch, not getting the best of runs. In public at least, he performed without demur.

In *Dr Jekyll And Mr Hyde*, this period would perhaps be the equivalent of when Jekyll repents following Hyde's murder of Sir Danvers Carew: 'He came out of his seclusion, renewed relations with his friends, became once more their familiar guest and entertainer; and whilst he had always been known for charities, he was now no less distinguished for religion. He was busy, he was much in the open air, he did good; his face seemed to open and brighten, as if with an inward consciousness of service; and for more than two months the doctor was at peace.'

Giving thanks for his charitable works may well be how Oliver Sherwood treated Derring Rose after that win without the blinkers, while owner and trainer were encouraged to be ambitious in formulating plans for the horse in the forthcoming jumps season. 'We decided we'd won the Stayers' Hurdle and beaten the stayers so comprehensively, we might as well have a go at the Champion Hurdle,' says Savill. 'We knew he had plenty of speed and those were the days when you got bottomless ground at Cheltenham, so the whole aim was towards that. We didn't feel there was anything to be gained by running him in another Stayers' Hurdle.'

Derring Rose – the horse who preferred to go backwards

The first step in his reinvention as a Champion Hurdle horse was the Fighting Fifth over 2m at Newcastle in November. With John Francome appearing instead on the Mackeson card at Cheltenham, the pleasure of riding Derring Rose went to Sherwood. Savill flew in from the United States on the morning of the race and was picked up from Heathrow by the leading amateur before they caught a small plane up to Newcastle. Derring Rose jumped three hurdles then refused to go any further. Sherwood and Savill flew down south again and Savill flew out of Heathrow on the Sunday morning.

Like that of Dr Jekyll, Derring Rose's period of redemption had lasted for only a matter of months. Jekyll confessed that 'I was still cursed with my duality of purpose; and as the first edge of my penitence wore off, the lower side of me, so long indulged, so recently chained down, began to growl for licence.' For Derring Rose too, the balance was beginning to tip.

'It was always at the back of my mind that he might do it one day,' reflects Sherwood on that refusal in the Fighting Fifth, 'but it was a bloody long way to go up to Newcastle for him to do it. I wouldn't have been nearly as strong a rider as J Francome and probably if J Francome had been on him he might have got him going again.'

Savill, of course, had had a rather longer journey for the 'race', so when Derring Rose appeared in a 2m4f event at Ascot six days later and the owner considered whether to travel over again, he did not have to think that long or hard before on this occasion deciding against it. Sherwood's soul-searching about whether Francome could have done better was immediately put to the test, with blinkers reinstalled as well, and Derring Rose did get further than at Newcastle. But it was only as far as the fifth, after which he once more concluded that he had had enough and the efforts of the champion jockey proved no more persuasive than those of the stable's amateur.

Later in the decade, punters endured similar anxiety from another otherwise high-class horse, the chaser Vodkatini, but at least the moment of truth with him was at the start, so would-be supporters could skulk about by the bookmakers waiting for the tapes to go up, after which there would either be a rush to place the bets or the crowd would disperse, depending on what Vodkatini had opted for. They did not have even that refuge with Derring Rose and there now followed a race, which, in the parlance resulting from modern punting opportunities, would be described as causing 'in-running betting carnage'. For virtually all my Derring Rose interviewees, this race made as big an impression as his astonishing win in the Stayers' Hurdle.

It was the Colt Car Corinium Hurdle over 2m4f at Chelt-enham on the last day of 1981, in which he had to give 8lb to the David Elsworth-trained Heighlin and Heighlin was ante-post favourite for the Champion Hurdle. The latter started 6-4 on, with punters showing a by-now understandable wariness about Derring Rose, who was 11-1. But Derring Rose beat Heighlin by three lengths. That was striking enough but it tells a fraction of the story.

'Getting to the start, starting, throughout the race and even getting him back in – he could down tools at any time,' says Francome, and in the Corinium Derring Rose went through almost his full repertoire. First, he took root and his jockey had to dismount and drag him all the way to the 2m4f start. He then showed reluctance to jump off before leading over the first four flights. In sight of the fifth, as they completed the turn away from the grandstand, he still had a two-and-a-half-length lead. On that approach to the fifth, however, he dropped back to last. About ten lengths were thrown away as connections and supporters steeled themselves for the inevitable premature conclusion of his race but, for the first time, Derring Rose not only put on the brakes, he then took them off again. He never actually stopped and, jumping the fifth well, he soon started to move forward again.

What was Francome doing on board? 'Just squeezing him,' he relates. 'I didn't ride very short, so just kicking and shoving and pushing. It's like the things you used to do when you were a seven-year-old kid and your pony wouldn't want to go into the main ring. Or what you're doing at gymkhanas. Anything just to try and keep him going. Flapping and shouting at him.'

At various points afterwards, there were strong signs from the jockey that Derring Rose was by no means fully persuaded on his new course of action and at the second last, coming down the hill, he was in fourth place about 15 lengths off the leader and ten off Heighlin who was disputing second. Rounding the turn, Heighlin had moved through smoothly to take up the lead and Derring Rose was maybe 12 lengths adrift. Then something changed.

The leaders were tying up, for sure, but Derring Rose was running on. He was at Heighlin's quarters jumping the last, took it much the quicker and was rapidly in a four-length lead. In the closing stages a jockey is often described as keeping his mount up to his work. In this race, however, it was surely Derring Rose who kept Francome up to his work because after a dozen strides he once again started to show an aversion to forward motion and he had the jockey working more frantically than ever. *Chasers & Hurdlers* described it as: 'Derring Rose began to behave like a mule again; he had to be coaxed, nagged, pushed, up the hill to the line.' Close to the line, Francome used the whip twice. Derring Rose flashed his tail. Oliver Sherwood remembers Francome being physically sick afterwards, so great were the jockey's efforts.

This has frequently been described as John Francome's greatest ride, but 30 years on he disagrees: 'Oh God no. Good rides are when horses don't have the ability. He had all the ability in the world.' Francome's efforts were extensive and successful, but it was his mount who was fully in charge of the decision-making.

Although he was the winner, Derring Rose had not covered himself in glory. The phobia of French speakers might or might not have still been there but the reluctance to go to the gallops, a preference for walking backwards, coming to a halt in his races and hanging fire in the finish, they had all become far worse. His deteriorating behaviour on the racecourse merely mirrored what was happening at home. After his 1981 Stayers' win, *The Sporting Life* recorded that 'it can sometimes take as much as ten minutes to get him to take part in a gallop. Once he is convinced of what is required Derring Rose does precisely what's wanted.' If it was true then, it most certainly was not now, and his trainer must have pined for a return to such saintly behaviour.

With Derring Rose, the usual pre-race discussion in the parade ring between connections about their horse's chance had been rendered largely superfluous. 'You used to go in,' remembers Francome, 'the owner would say, "Well, I wonder what he's going to do today.. Fred Winter would just smile and say, "Who knows?" and that was it.'

In the salad days, Winter had once told Savill that Derring Rose showed him ability that was as good as any horse he had ever trained. Before the 1981 Stayers' the trainer and jockey were apparently quite bullish about his chances and reported that he was in really good form and had been working very well. In that second season at Uplands, however, Winter's reports to the owner on Derring Rose became less cheerful. Savill says: 'I remember him telling me that Derring Rose had destroyed the rose bushes in his garden. I don't know how he got in there but they were Fred's pride and joy and one day he trampled the whole lot.' Brian Delaney describes this incident as: 'He jumped and kicked and galloped through whatever he could.' Delaney confirms that this garden, with its roses and carefully tended lawn, was indeed Fred Winter's pride and joy.

Derring Rose – the horse who preferred to go backwards

In his highly entertaining 1985 autobiography *Born Lucky*, John Francome wrote that 'Every now and again the Governor falls in love with one particular horse that has usually got lots of ability but which is mulish and he doesn't take kindly to anybody even suggesting that the animal might be ungenuine.' In 2012, Francome elaborates: 'That's right. It was never the horse's problem. He'd say it was just a bit of a character. He was very protective of all his horses. The year that Crisp got beaten in the Grand National, there was a picture of Crisp on the Injured Jockeys Fund Christmas card and when I sent him a Christmas card I put a pair of blinkers on. It was so far from the truth – a horse who had done everything bar kill itself trying to win – but he didn't think that was very funny.'

One can only speculate whether Derring Rose was one of those 'mulish' horses to whom the trainer developed an attachment and to what degree Winter was amused at the various and multiplying indignities with which Derring Rose was now assailing him. 'Best bloke in the world' is how Francome describes his boss. 'I've only worked for one trainer but I rode for hundreds and he was the best loser that I've ever known. Great integrity.' At some point during that winter of 1981/82, however, the trainer's patience with Derring Rose was wearing thin and he decided that plans for him needed to be revised. The Champion Hurdle would remain the target but it hardly mattered which race he ran in if he continued in his current mood. Winter suggested a change of scenery for the horse to try and sweeten his mind and restore his enthusiasm for racing, and the medium for this rehab would be a spell out hunting. Derring Rose was dispatched to Francome's brother-in-law Derek Ricketts, master of the Bicester Hunt and the former world champion showjumper.

Overall, the horse apparently enjoyed his new routine and appeared to have been freshened up, but his time with the hunt was not without incident. One day, walking alongside a canal, Derring Rose spooked at something and would not walk on. He started going backwards. Towards the canal. On board was a young lad who worked for Ricketts and he began to feel some alarm. His boss reassured him that there was no way the horse would reverse all the way into the canal. This, perhaps, was where Ricketts had not been fully briefed. The lad was fished out and Derring Rose had to swim about 100 yards before a suitable place was found for him to return to dry land.

In his widespread experience with horses, has Ricketts ever seen another behave that way? 'No, never,' he says. 'I couldn't believe it when he did it. I couldn't believe it when he did it the first time but I was even more astonished when he did it twice.'

On returning to the same spot on the canal path, Derring Rose did exactly the same again, although presumably on this occasion without taking his rider with him. Second time round he had a longer swim and ended up in a lock. For anyone patiently waiting their turn on the other side, enjoying their John Constable-like scene of tranquillity in the British countryside, it must have been a surprise when the lock gates were opened and out swam Derring Rose, attended by a group of anxious hunt followers.

Thirty years on, the exact chronology of his time with the hunt and his races is not clear, but when Derring Rose appeared at Kempton in February 1982 bidding for his third win in the Rendlesham, his performance was nothing like those previous two renewals and as 2-1 favourite he finished a well-beaten fourth behind the Jarvis-trained and Turnell-ridden Hill Of Slane. The Champion Hurdle was next. Five days before the race Winter informed the press that 'He worked for a mile this morning, then pulled himself up, which he is always likely to do.' It was decided to remove the headgear again, this time on purpose, but with little or no confidence that this relatively orthodox ploy would prove the cue for a

Derring Rose – the horse who preferred to go backwards

Derring Rose revival. Summing up the horse's attitude to blinkers, Francome now says, 'I think he thought they were just for keeping the rain off.' But connections racked their brains to come up with something else that might just inspire him, as Peter Savill relates: 'Johnny Francome and I and Fred Winter got together and we decided that because he loved hunting, we needed him to have the feeling that he was hunting again. So what we would do was we'd get a huntsman and send him over to the woods over by the hurdle where he'd virtually pulled himself up, and as they came round the bend he'd blow his hunting horn and give him the feeling he was still out hunting. So I remember meeting this fella in the weighing room, and whether this was legal or not I've no idea but he was dressed as a regular bloke with a long coat on and a hunting horn buried inside it. Johnny Francome and I gave him his instructions, pointed out where we wanted him to sneak round and hide behind the trees, so when he saw them coming round in the Champion Hurdle he would start blowing his horn.'

Readers will probably know that Derring Rose does not figure on the list of Champion Hurdle winners. He opened on course at 20-1 and started at 16-1, but start is almost all he did. The very early stages were not that dissimilar to the 1981 Stayers', with Derring Rose disputing the lead over the first, and he rounded the turn away from the stands on the inside in fourth, but almost immediately afterwards the visual effect was that he was reprising his favourite party trick from Uplands and going backwards. In a field of 14 he went to a detached 14th before they reached the next hurdle, the third, and he refused to go over it. Riding Derring Rose in that Champion must be the only resemblance John Francome has to my own minuscule experience on horseback. Sitting on a recalcitrant beast who refuses to move forward is something you expect to see in a riding school but not in the Champion Hurdle.

'It was heavy ground as well, so we had everything perfect and it was just a matter of getting him over that hurdle,' laments Savill. 'We weren't really entirely surprised but we were disappointed and when Johnny Francome finally came back after the race and managed to get the horse back into the paddock, I said to him, "Oh Johnny, what a shame. Did that huntsman blow his horn?" and he replied "Aye, he blew his horn but for all the good it's done he might as well have blown it up his arse." I'll never forget that. It delivered a bit of humour at a glum time.'

The stewards called for Winter and inquired into the running of Derring Rose, to which the trainer replied that the horse would not run again. As the officialese puts it, 'no further action was taken'. Derring Rose's racing career was over.

~

For all the disappointment of that Champion Hurdle, there may well have been a collective sigh of relief in Lambourn at Derring Rose's exit from training. There he had become a notorious figure, as a story from Brian Delaney well illustrates. Richard Cullen had brought Derring Rose back into the yard some time after the others and, having ridden him down the back lanes to and from the gallops, he was preparing to wash the mud off him when Derring Rose gave him the slip. Outside Uplands a dozen horses from another yard were quietly picking grass on the side of the road when Derring Rose emerged and came careering down the road towards them. At the cry 'Loose one! Loose one!' assistance would normally be given to try and catch it. In this instance, however, the shout also went up 'Look out! It's Derring Rose!' and everybody scattered. 'They didn't want to be about if he was going to be about loose,' says Delaney, 'because you wouldn't know what he would do.'

Derring Rose – the horse who preferred to go backwards

Predicting what Derring Rose would do had never been that easy in his last two seasons and there is no definitive or single answer as to why he would or would not do it. Behavioural problems can often be rooted in the physical and Alan Jarvis suspects that the key lies in his old back issue. Oliver Sherwood confirms that chiropractors for horses were very much frowned upon in those days, not so much by the trainers as by their vets. Fred Winter did have various 'back men' to treat his horses in the latter stages of his career, but it is possible that Derring Rose preceded them. Either way, there is no recollection of back problems among those I have interviewed about Derring Rose's time at Uplands. Sherwood remembers him as 'a very clean-limbed horse and very healthy horse'.

He was also an entire horse. It is easier to get a gelding fit than a bulkier entire horse, even when that entire horse is one who consents to go on the gallops, but the gelding operation also minimises the distractions of a wandering eye. Sherwood states: 'If we buy a horse off the Flat and it's a colt the first thing you do is get him cut. The older they get the harder it gets for them to concentrate on the job they're supposed to be doing.'

The prime reason not to geld a jumps horse would be in the hope of turning it into a stallion, but jumps stallions who have themselves raced over jumps are now a rarity in Britain and Ireland (but not in France) and the popularity of stallions who cover hundreds of mares a season leaves less room for others of any ilk. The top-class chaser Nickname is one of the most notable recent examples but jumps horses who became stallions used to be commonplace. Monksfield was the most celebrated of these in my time, at least for his standard as a racehorse. Over The River and, in particular, Roselier were major jumps winners in France. Derring Rose's near-contemporaries Broadsword, Royal Vulcan and Sula Bula were all high-class 2m hurdlers, and the 1990s kicked off with Nomadic Way finishing second in two

Champion Hurdles (1990 and 1991) and on both occasions he was followed home by another entire, first in Past Glories and then Ruling.

Baron Blakeney beat Broadsword in the 1981 Triumph (Saxon Farm and Ikdam were entire Triumph winners later in the decade) and had a resurgence when sent novice chasing. On board for his two most impressive chase wins, Sherwood remembers that Baron Blakeney 'jumped like a proverbial buck' and, with inescapable logic, points out two reasons why an entire horse should be so motivated not to touch a twig. Cruise Missile perhaps owed his entirety more to the exploits of his older half-brother, the top-class hunter chaser Spartan Missile, but he too did much better again when switched to chasing.

The 2m chaser Toirdealbhach was useful and a lot more colourful than the vast majority of racehorses, one much more in the Derring Rose mould, as he used to get himself way behind before often finishing strongly. Some of his best efforts were up the stiff finish at Cheltenham and Timeform were moved to describe him as 'finishing like a train' when he was third as a nine-year-old in the 1983 Grand Annual. Toirdealbhach raced on until he was 13 and won a race at that age and he did sire at least one winner.

No one I have talked to seems at all persuaded that having Derring Rose gelded would have transformed him into a figure of probity. Besides which, his connections had known for some time that he had an assured place at stud, thanks not only to his good days on the racecourse but also because he came from what Timeform described as 'one of the best families in the French Stud Book'. His third dam was the 1,000 Guineas, Oaks and Champion Stakes winner Bella Paola.

So Derring Rose went to the Knockhouse Stud, County Waterford, where he stood initially at a price of £350 no foal no fee (if only punters had been able to enjoy a similar concession in his racing days). He was there for the majority of his stud career before being transferred to England. He died in 1997.

If anything is a test for a bad back it is life as a National Hunt stallion but Sean Kinsella of the stud remembers him thus: 'He was a grand horse to work with. He was no different to any stallion to work with. He wasn't a wicked horse. He was a great horse to cover mares and do all that, there was no problem with him. He wasn't savage or wicked. He was no threat to anybody that way. He was just a normal stallion.' Somewhat surprisingly perhaps, Kinsella reports that his charge had no eccentricities. 'None whatsoever,' he says, 'but his stock weren't that way.

'He got a good few very smart winners, a good few nice bumper horses, but then when they got a taste for the racecourse they turned out a lot of them to be very roguish. They were very smart bumper horses but they didn't like the jumping.' Of the fillies, Kinsella is even more damning, generalising that they 'were no good and they didn't make even middling broodmares. That chink came into them.'

In Britain and Ireland, Derring Rose's progeny won 128 jump races for £668,161 and 14 Flat races for £28,097. The best was The Committee, who was placed at three Cheltenham Festivals – runner-up in the 1990 Sun Alliance Chase, third and second in the 1993 and 1994 Kim Muir – and fourth in the void Grand National of 1993. Among his better offspring, perhaps Derring Bridge came to look most like a chip off the old block, showing a reluctance to race towards the end of his career, but it was a long career of 94 races during which he won under rules 15 times.

Although Derring Rose's stallion career was disappointing overall, he did have a legacy of another sort. Peter Savill become an owner in 1977 and had his first win in 1978 but Derring Rose was his first high-class horse. 'That was something when you're fairly early in your owning career,' he reflects. 'He gave me my one and only win at the Cheltenham Festival and my first really big win and really big thrill. I was over the moon that day.' Savill and some friends used to stay nearby for the week and unsurprisingly had a particularly good evening after the 1981 Stayers' Hurdle, staying up all night drinking. Twelve months later there was contrasting motivation for a stiff drink but that chastening experience did not put Savill off as an owner. Business on the other side of the Atlantic during our winter limited his involvement over jumps but he went on to an extensive and successful involvement on the Flat. He became President of the Racehorse Owners' Association then Chairman of the British Horseracing Board and Derring Rose played an important role in nurturing his participation in the sport.

While the balance of nature versus nurture is unclear in Derring Rose's own rather less enthusiastic and more precarious mindset, the result was undoubtedly one of the game's most extraordinary characters. He was the horse with a phobia of French speakers, a reluctance to go to the gallops, a preference for walking backwards, refusals to race, hanging fire when he did race, innovative ideas on equine swimming and a distaste for horticulture, but he still produced one of the most dominant championship wins in Cheltenham Festival history. Oliver Sherwood sums up his memories of him by saying 'He was an amazing little horse. He was almost human – you could see his brain thinking; he could almost talk to you.' It was a shame that his utterances became largely unprintable, with most of his words surely of the four-letter variety, but in behaving as he did Derring Rose probably added to his legendary status and he certainly did not extinguish it.

~

Footnote:

As mentioned at the start of this chapter, when Derring Rose won the 1981 Stayers' his sprint to the finishing line took only a fraction of a second longer than that of Sea Pigeon in the Champion Hurdle, despite having raced over an extra mile and one furlong.

There are other factors to consider, of course, including that Sea Pigeon carried 12st whereas Derring Rose had 11st 12lb. Another help was that the early pace in the Stayers' was steady, and much steadier for most of the race than that in the Champion, which was pretty much break-neck throughout, but the instinctive reaction that this was an extraordinary performance is not misleading.

Timeform's Simon Rowlands, an expert on sectional timing, has this to say about Derring Rose's finishing effort: 'The visual impressions created by Derring Rose and Sea Pigeon are one thing, but is it possible to quantify more precisely what their finishing efforts were like?

'Some things have clearly changed in the 30-plus years since the 1981 Cheltenham Festival, including almost certainly the exact positioning of hurdles at the course. But one thing that has not changed, in any significant way, is the effect of the famous Cheltenham hill.

'Sectional times taken more recently show that horses tend to finish at a speed slightly slower than their average race speed at Cheltenham. They occasionally finish slightly quicker than that average in races which have been slowly run, and they finish slower still than that average rather more often, especially when races have been run at a generous pace.

'It is possible to use this information to estimate sectional distances and finishing speeds from distant Festivals and to add substance to the impressions of the naked eye. Video analysis shows that Sea Pigeon ran about 19.1 seconds from the last flight to the line and about 40.4 seconds from the second-last to the line, in a sixteen-furlong race run in 251.9 seconds overall. Derring Rose's figures are 19.4 seconds, 42.0 seconds and 436.0 seconds for a 25-furlong race.

'It can be estimated that the distance from the last flight to the line in 1981 was about 260 yards (1.18 furlongs) and that the distance from the second-last flight to the line was about 550 yards (2.5 furlongs). These estimated distances give rise to a finishing speed for Sea Pigeon of 97.3% from the last and 97.4% from the second-last, similar to finishing speeds achieved by Champion Hurdlers in more recent times.

'The same estimated distances give rise to very different finishing speeds in the Stayers' Hurdle, which was, it should be remembered, run over more than a mile further and at a much slower average pace (17.44 seconds per furlong, compared to the Champion Hurdle's 15.74 seconds per furlong). Derring Rose's estimated speed from two out, expressed as a percentage of his average race speed, was an impressive 103.8%.

'By way of comparison, Big Buck's only just exceeded 100% from two out for his World Hurdle wins in 2011 and 2012. But Derring Rose's estimated speed from the run-in alone is a mighty 107.9% of his average race speed, a quite remarkable figure in the context of a staying hurdle with a stiff finish, even when the runners have gone slowly for much of the way. In actual terms, Derring Rose was about 0.3 seconds slower than Sea Pigeon in the closing stages, but in relative terms he was quickening in remarkable style given the nature of the race he was contesting.

'And it is not as if others in the 1981 Stayers' Hurdle field were doing the same. The runner-up, Celtic Isle, can be estimated to have lost about 6.1 seconds on Derring Rose on the run-in, having jumped the last only about three lengths down. That puts his finishing speed at a pedestrian 83.7% of his average race speed. Not only was Derring Rose quickening smartly, his rivals can be seen to have been slowing.

'A sudden injection of pace mid-race when the early gallop has been slow can have strange effects on horse performances, and it is not unusual to find horses slowing again before the

Derring Rose – the horse who preferred to go backwards

end in such circumstances. What is surprising about the 1981 Stayers' Hurdle is that the evidence strongly suggests the beaten horses slowed markedly up the hill while Derring Rose did the complete opposite!'

With Derring Rose, doing the complete opposite of what was expected would become a recurring theme.

CHAPTER THREE

1981 KIM MUIR MEMORIAL HANDICAP CHASE

Prince Charles rides at Cheltenham

On Wednesday March 18, 1981, the Cheltenham Festival was front-page news in all the national daily newspapers – except for the *Morning Star* – and nearly all the coverage was accompanied by one or more photographs. But the race on which they were focused was not Sea Pigeon's Champion Hurdle or Derring Rose's Stayers' Hurdle and the jockey on whom the papers were fixated was not John Francome. The headline race (to the wider world at least) was the usually unheralded Kim Muir.

Named after a local amateur rider and officer in the Tenth Hussars who was killed in action aged 23 during the Second World War, the Kim Muir Memorial Challenge Cup Handicap Chase (now the Fulke Walwyn Kim Muir) was inaugurated in 1946 and is reserved for amateur jockeys. There is something slightly anachronistic but deeply ingrained about the amateur at the Cheltenham Festival. Ted Walsh (father of Ruby and Katie) was there on my first visit, giving his typically forthright encouragement to Daring Run in the Champion Hurdle; that was two days before Jim Wilson won the Gold Cup on Little Owl and the following year Colin Magnier won the Champion on 40-1 shot For Auction. Misters all.

Prince Charles rides at Cheltenham

Wind on 30 years and Sam Waley-Cohen could not have achieved a much higher profile, while the likes of Nina Carberry, Katie Walsh (daughter of Ted), JT McNamara and Patrick Mullins have been as well known as many of the professionals. Three races at the meeting remain for amateurs only and, while watching these events it sometimes seems as if the racing has been plunged into a state of chaos, in most Festivals they nevertheless feature some highly promising young talent on its way to prominence in the paid ranks. Among winners of the Kim Muir in my lifetime, they include Ridley Lamb, Dermot Browne, Simon Sherwood, Gee Armytage, Robert Thornton, Seamus Durack and, perhaps most famously of all, Adrian Maguire who was 19 and claiming 7lb when his services were snapped up by Martin Pipe and he surged to distinction on board Omerta (making his debut for the stable and for the season) in 1991. Kim Muir-winning jockeys bound for notable training careers included Nick Gaselee, Roger Charlton, Michael Dickinson and Ted Walsh.

There are other types of amateur, though, and one hour and ten minutes after the 1981 Champion Hurdle, the rider on board Good Prospect in the Kim Muir was one HRH Prince of Wales claiming 7lb, or as he was described on the racecard in the *Morning Star*, 'Charles (7)'.

His fellow jockeys in the race included Ted Walsh, Jim Wilson, Frank Codd, Paul Webber, Oliver Sherwood, Tim Easterby, Chris Cundall, Tim Thomson Jones, Geordie Dun, Colin Magnier and Brendan Powell, so he was in distinguished equestrian company. The Prince, as was normally the case, put up a little overweight. Among others in the field was a barman, Malcolm Batters, whose own spot of bother doing the weight on Martinstown in a handicap chase that New Year's Day in 1981 had entered racing folklore. For, having celebrated 'in time-honoured manner' the night before, after driving the horsebox to

Cheltenham, he had then been roused from his slumbers on discovery that he had in error been declared as the horse's jockey. Batters had to complete the four-mile race in borrowed kit, carrying 24lb overweight and still won by a sore head. Prince Charles put up 1lb over in his ride at Cheltenham, at 11st 4lb.

In the more than 30 years since, the attention, deference and sheer regard accorded to the Royal family has often seemed light years away from what it was in 1981, but in the early part of the current decade, with the Queen's Diamond Jubilee and Prince William's wedding to Kate Middleton, it was possible to get a very powerful flavour of it. Royals were again waving from the balcony of Buckingham Palace, as the Red Arrows roared overhead with their trails of red, white and blue, with huge crowds cheering below. Back in 1981, three weeks before Prince Charles was lined up to ride at Cheltenham came the announcement of another engagement, the one between him and Lady Diana Spencer. Almost anything he'd done before that point had been the object of major media interest, but with Diana involved as well the media coverage was a frenzy.

On the Monday of Cheltenham race week, the front-page headline in the *Gloucestershire Echo* was 'Four Royals Expected At Festival'. Lady Diana, sadly, would not be among them on raceday but the Queen Mother, as usual, was booked in, as were Prince Charles, Princess Anne and Captain Mark Phillips. A local grocer had presented the Queen Mother with flowers and chocolates for the past 13 years and would again be waiting at the roadside. And as that piece in the paper explained, interest in royal activities on the racecourse itself would this year take on a new dimension: 'Prince Charles and Lady Diana took a look for themselves at Prestbury Park conditions yesterday. After walking the course in the afternoon the Prince announced his attention of partnering Good Prospect tomorrow ... Prince Charles will be the first member of the Royal family ever to have ridden over Prestbury Park's demanding fences, and it is perhaps appropriate that he should set this precedent in the 150th anniversary year of racing there. It is known that to ride at Cheltenham, where Queen Elizabeth the Queen Mother has had six winners as an owner, has been one of Prince Charles's ambitions since he started riding, and that he feels he may never get another opportunity as good as tomorrow's.'

Twenty-eight-year-old Edward Gillespie, in his first year as manager at the racecourse, could hardly believe his luck at the incredible publicity. 'I remember thinking I'm sure football, rugby, cricket and every sport would envy racing for our engagement with the heir to the throne,' he says now, and he also has a vivid memory of Prince Charles walking the course, accompanied by Lady Diana with a small child on her shoulders, and four or five others including Good Prospect's trainer Nick Gaselee and his wife Judy. When the Prince had completed his circuit, reveals Gillespie, 'he did remark to me how well the jumps were painted on the landing side. It's not something that people often say.'

Good Prospect was a 12-year-old and already a dual Festival winner, having taken the Kim Muir one year earlier (among five wins that season) and the Coral Golden Hurdle Final four years before that. He had also won at Wolverhampton in November among nine starts before Cheltenham in the current season but for this Kim Muir, heading the weights, he was a 25-1 shot. 'Charles the rank outsider' was how the *Daily Mirror* put it in their headline on page three, while informing readers that the day before 'he wore an air of dedication as he led out the morning-exercise team from trainer Nick Gaselee's stables at Lambourn.' On their front page they had a photograph of Lady Diana stepping over a puddle, declaring that 'This was how Lady Diana Spencer took a water jump yesterday and cleared it with the finesse of a thoroughbred.'

At The Festival

As the race approached, her husband-to-be avoided some attention by reportedly arriving at the track during Sea Pigeon's Champion Hurdle. What a race to miss. Gillespie recollects that a private place to change was arranged for the Prince, in the same building as the weighing room but in the first aid area. As the final minutes ticked away before the Kim Muir, however, there was no avoiding the close gaze of a quizzical public, because to get from the weighing room to the parade ring in those days, the riders had to walk about 70 yards through the crowd. Once he was mounted, according to the *Echo*, 'hundreds of spectators lined the path from the parade ring to the track to call out, "Good luck, Your Royal Highness," as Prince Charles and Good Prospect made their way to the start.' That I cannot remember but I do recall clearly that, as the Prince was escorted from the weighing room through the massed onlookers, one spectator enquired loudly whether he had brought his UHU. The UHU being a well-known brand of superglue.

~

Prince Charles in the Kim Muir was a long way from being the subject most on my mind that day, but his presence on board Good Prospect undeniably added considerable spice to the occasion and you had to be struck that he wanted to be an active player in it. I was glad he did. That someone in his position was keen to participate was a major positive statement for the sport. Although not about to swap professions, he was clearly bitten by the bug all the same and, in that, his motivation must have been very similar to those of the other riders. But it is still hard not to wonder precisely why he did it and how it came about. What follows, therefore, is a not entirely typical case study of the amateur jockey. I was present at only one of these races and have not seen any recordings of them since, so the story is heavily reliant on reports from the time, as well as the kind assistance of three interviewees who were close eyewitnesses.

Now that he is in his sixties, it is a little strange to remember – and those not alive at the time may find it fairly incredible – that the 32-year-old Prince Charles of 1981 was known in the popular press as 'Action Man'. In that year and the year before, for instance, in a rather muted period by his standards, there were reports of him salmon fishing, playing polo, team show jumping, shooting for the House of Lords rifle team, skiing, trekking in the Himalayan foothills, flying a Tiger Moth, parachuting (not on the same flight), diving to the wreck of the *Mary Rose* (in those days it was still in the Solent) and meeting Miss Australia, and that was just in *The Times*. Tony Morris in *The Sporting Life* affirmed that 'at other times I'm sure I've read how he climbed Everest, swam the length of the Mississippi, and crossed the Atlantic by hang-glider.' Prince Charles's polo was of a good standard and he was a devotee of hunting, reportedly riding with 45 different hunts in Britain by the mid-1980s. There was also already a precedent for him raceriding, albeit on a camel.

When the Prince decided to include riding in horseraces among his activities, 40-year-old Lambourn trainer Nick Gaselee became his chief teacher and racing advisor. When an amateur jockey, Gaselee had ridden more than one hundred winners, including in the Foxhunter as well as the Kim Muir, both in 1967, and had spent five years as assistant trainer to Fulke Walwyn. Explaining how his role in Prince Charles's riding career came about, Gaselee reveals: 'Well, he was a great friend of Andrew Parker Bowles and Andrew thought it would be good for him to get involved in racing.'

Parker Bowles elaborates: 'I think he was staying with myself and my first wife, now his present wife, and we talked about how he enjoyed watching it [jumps racing], but he always much more enjoyed riding than watching, and so I said, "Why don't you give it a try?"'

Neither Parker Bowles nor Gaselee were shocked that he was keen to ride in races because, as the latter puts it, while the Prince was never one to look at the racing pages, 'he loved riding, he loved hunting and he was very active and competitive', and as the former declares, 'he was very brave when he was out hunting, and it didn't surprise me at all.'

Gaselee and Parker Bowles had been friends in the army and also had plenty in common in racing, as Parker Bowles was a nephew of Fulke Walwyn and had been an amateur jockey himself. Having been recommended to the Prince, the trainer was introduced to him at the Parker Bowles home, Bolehyde. Prince Charles had the flu and Gaselee had to go upstairs to see him in bed.

Once plans with the Prince were afoot, the trainer called a staff meeting in the tack room, briefed everyone and said he would like it to be kept as quiet as possible. His head lad, Peter 'Jumbo' Heaney, had severe doubts about the likely efficacy of this request. However, relates Heaney, 'He was riding out for about probably five or six weeks before the press got to know about it. I couldn't believe it. There he was, he was just another face in the string, riding out every morning. He'd ride out maybe two lots three times a week, and he'd be on the Downs, ride back with the string and passing other strings and nobody picked him out.'

The chief initial risk of discovery was provided by Prince Charles himself: 'The first morning he got out of the Range Rover beautifully dressed, with beautiful white gloves and all, and [Heaney laughs at the thought of it] you can't ride out like that and not be recognised, you know. So we had to rough him up a bit.' By this, he means that an old pair of substitute gloves was found and, when the Prince next arrived, he was sporting what Heaney describes as 'one of his old gardening jackets'.

Just how anonymous the Prince looked in his revised garb was tested one morning when coming off the gallops and passing Major Nelson's yard, where 'old Denny' was cutting the hedge. As Heaney narrates it, 'Dave Mooney is just in front of Prince Charles and just when he gets upsides Denny he says, "Denny, the hedge cutters look sharp" and Denny turns round and he just looks straight up at Prince Charles – he hasn't got a clue who he is – and he says, "They're sharp enough to cut your bollocks off." Well Prince Charles nearly fell off laughing, so he did. And Denny was completely oblivious to it all.'

Those hedge cutters were not, of course, the only threat to the Royal line. Jumps racing has inherent dangers and part of Gaselee's job was clearly to minimise them, a responsibility as well as an honour. The trainer reflects that 'When you're younger you don't worry about those things so much. I probably would now.'

Gaselee himself owned an experienced chaser called Sea Swell. Back in November 1977, ridden by Nicky Henderson in an amateur riders' race at Haydock, Sea Swell had provided the trainer with his first chase winner. He was the definition of a safe conveyance but the trainer's task was not just to find a suitable mount, it was also to provide training for the rider, whatever his proficiency might be at other equine sports.

'We would try to teach him the essence of riding in steeplechases and schooling,' outlines Gaselee. 'It's a completely different principle to anything else – eventing or hunting. We had to get him ready to learn to ride shorter and to keep his weight off the saddle, and try and make him a bit more like a jockey really.'

On his way to the gallops one morning in his first week, the pupil was asked to pull up his leathers a notch or two and ride a bit shorter. Gaselee's own horse then whipped round and deposited him on the ground. Among the other riders Prince Charles was one of the most amused, and

Mooney even more so – 'quite understandably,' says Gaselee. 'He was a wonderful lad. All my lads were marvellous'. Mooney was nevertheless instructed to surrender his mount to his boss and go after the trainer's hack on foot.

Over the next three or four months, the Prince got used to the routine of a racing stable, in his case arriving at 7am two or three times a week, tacking up his mount, pulling out with the string at 7.30, then cleaning up the horse and letting it down when they got back. His security men would sometimes video the Prince in action on the Downs and he would study the results with the trainer over breakfast. Washing and grooming his horse after exercise, which he loved to do, there was a moment of surprise for the Prince when one of the lads shouted, "Look at that ******* Charlie washing that horse's legs with his gloves on", but the actual miscreant was future trainer Charlie Egerton in the box next door.

The Prince had no difficulty fitting in with the Gaselee team, as the trainer reports: 'The lads were wonderful, they respected him and were very fond of him.' Confirming that, Jumbo Heaney says: 'He was great, he was absolutely brilliant with all the lads – he knew them all by their first name, and you just called him Sir, and it just flowed. He made you feel at ease and it was never a problem. There was always the worry of the boys getting too familiar with him, that they'd want to tell him the latest joke or whatever. Which he probably wouldn't have minded because he was in the Navy anyway, wasn't he?'

A concerning incident for the trainer on that front came one day returning from the gallops when Mooney and the new recruit were some way ahead of the rest. 'The boss caught the string up and he said, "Where's Prince Charles?"', recalls Heaney, 'and I said that he'd just gone off round the corner there with Mooney. He looked at me and said "I wonder what they're talking about", so I just replied, "Knowing Mooney it will be about sex." He was horrified. The look on his face! So we got Mooney in at breakfast time and asked him, "What were you talking about?" and Mooney said they were talking about politics. He wouldn't have known who was prime minister. It must have been a really interesting conversation the two of them were having.'

With the Prince's limited opportunities to ride out at Lambourn, let alone to gain the fitness that comes from raceriding itself, Gaselee gave him some important homework and inspiring reading in the form of the 1951 John Hislop book *Steeplechasing*.

'It is a sort of Bible about raceriding,' Gaselee explains. 'There's a chapter in it about fitness which you need to read and reread and reread because fitness is an incredibly important part of it. If you're fit you're more confident and if you're confident the horse is confident, so fitness plays a very, very vital role, and we concentrated on fitness, at which he was extremely good. He got himself very fit. He put a tremendous effort into it.'

On page 89 in the 1982 edition of *Steeplechasing*, Hislop spells out the need for fitness in these terms:

'Success cannot be bought. Rich young men (if there are any nowadays) may imagine that all they have to do is to buy a good-class 'chaser to sweep the board in races for soldiers and amateurs, in which their more impecunious opponents are nothing like so well mounted, but such meetings as the Grand Military at Sandown prove, time and again, that a good horse is useless unless his rider can sit on him, is fit enough to control him and offer him no interference, while a moderate horse ridden by a capable rider in good condition will always beat a good horse whose jockey is unfit and unskilled.'

In addition to those on general fitness, Hislop gave other detailed tips, including three on how to condition the all-important thigh muscles. First was to ride a motorcycle on a bumpy road while standing with 'the seat just clear of the saddle … cobbled roads as found in France provide excellent going for this purpose'; second was to ride a bicycle with the saddle far too low and therefore out of use; third was to squat in the position of a Flat-race jockey and hold it, checking one's position in a mirror, and then to lower the buttocks towards the heels and raise them again, while all the while moving the arms as if riding a finish.

Of the one-man motorcycle display team approach there has been no mention, but the Prince did adopt the other two methods. He became a familiar sight pedalling the adapted bicycle along lanes around Lambourn and presumably elsewhere. Several years later, when one of those lanes was turned into a horse track and named Fulke Walwyn Way, Prince Charles came down to open it. In the 1987 book *Prince Charles: Horseman* by Michael Clayton, the Prince revealed that he also used to adopt the jockey posture, before going to bed. Hislop went on to detail exercises for the wrist and hand muscles, and while press-ups were not considered of any value for those muscles in the arm, pull-ups were. These could be conducted 'on a bar, or any convenient place – a stair-landing sometimes presents a possibility'. Of these locations at which to dangle, in my mind's eye at least, the Prince must have been spoiled for choice at venues such as Windsor Castle, Buckingham Palace and other Royal residences.

~

After what Jumbo Heaney reckons was five or six weeks of the Prince coming down to Lambourn to ride out and school, on one morning when he was not due to visit, four or five photographers appeared on the doorstep instead, clamouring for his whereabouts. It was a mere taster, as first became apparent when the Prince fulfilled his first two riding engagements, in early March 1980. Having struck up a good relationship in frequent schooling with

Sea Swell, they were entered for the Duke of Gloucester Memorial Trophy, a hunter chase at Sandown's Grand Military meeting. But to get the Prince some experience of raceriding before he lined up over fences it was decided that he would first contest a 2m Flat race five days earlier, the Madhatters Private Sweepstakes at Plumpton. Having also ridden out at Ian Balding's Kingsclere stables, the Prince would don the famous Paul Mellon colours on Long Wharf. The event was confined to four-year-olds and older horses without a win in any race before January 1 but Long Wharf had won over hurdles since that deadline. Among the 12 opposition riders were three-day-eventing celebrities Lucinda Prior-Palmer and Richard Meade and the Chairman of Playboy in Europe, Victor Lownes. There was ante-post betting and on the morning of the race it was reported that Long Wharf had been backed from 7-2 into 6-4. In the *Sporting Chronicle*'s front-page story, headlined "Madhatter Charles faces 'Long' battle", Hills reported a bet of £200 on him at their Park Lane betting shop, their nearest branch to Buckingham Palace.

Prince Charles advised spectators at Plumpton not to back him. He was sent off 13-8 favourite nevertheless and apparently finished strongly, but too late to catch 14-1 shot (from 20-1) Classified, who won by two lengths. Ian Balding observed: 'The Prince was absolutely thrilled, but possibly let the winner get too far in front. He rode like a jockey and did as I told him by staying on the rails.'

Jim Stanford in the *Daily Mail* pointed out that 'Riding at a comfortable and sensible level of stirrup, Charles was in full control throughout the race – perhaps too much so. … His bad luck was that the race was run over such a tight mile-long circuit. The galloping-actioned Long Wharf was not suited to this type of course.'

It was also somewhat unlucky that he stumbled across Classified, who almost exactly two years later would be runner-up at Cheltenham in the Arkle. Trained by Nicky

Henderson, Classified was ridden by none other than the then BBC sports commentator Derek Thompson. After a few words himself – 'I have accomplished a life's ambition. It's a dream come true' – Tommo presented the microphone to a rather surprised Prince, who said: 'I always thought the BBC had the last word. I would like to say how sorry I am to all those people who put a bit too much money on my horse. I apologise on behalf of the management.'

At Sandown on the Saturday, in a five-runner race, bookmakers attempted to swell their coffers by offering odds about Prince Charles's finishing position and one reported quote was 2-1 against him getting round. The Imperial Cup crowd was swelled by over one hundred photographers who, as *The Sunday Times* phrased it, 'were on hand ready to record the unspoken fear that the Prince might fall.' At 16-1 and after one rival had fallen at the first, Sea Swell avoided the loose horse jumping across him late on the final circuit and, already behind at that point, he completed without mishap as the distant last of four finishers.

As became the trend, reports on the performance of the Prince and his mount had wildly different tones. In a jocular piece in *The Sporting Life*, under the headline 'The riding style of Prince Charles' and alongside four photographs of him and Sea Swell in action, Jeremy Chapman wrote: 'If you were willing to wait long enough, there wasn't much danger of HRH the Prince Of Wales failing to complete – Sea Swell saw to that. The horse took his pre-race publicity as a "safe but slow conveyance for an amateur" so literally that the extra police on hand were entitled to charge him with loitering.'

In the *Sporting Chronicle*, Graham Rock recorded that 'Prince Charles finished a remote fourth and last ... but even if the Archangel Gabriel had ridden Sea Swell, the horse's final placing would not have been improved. Sea Swell was totally unsuited by the going. ... Although Sea Swell and his partner crossed the finishing line a distance behind the winner, the crowd gave him a cheer not heard since the days when Arkle was stamping his name on the Whitbread Gold Cup.'

For Prince Charles and those connected with Sea Swell it was a case of mission accomplished. Heaney has a signed photograph from the rider of the Prince on Sea Swell at Sandown, and Gaselee's wall also has one, on which is written 'To the Instructor. From a grateful pupil. Charles.' Among the favourable reviews of his riding style, Fred Rimell apparently said: 'He has a good style for a new boy, especially when you consider he is in his thirties. On the basis of what we have seen here today he is the type of amateur who could go far.'

~

It may have been not long after this that the story started to get around that the Prince's ambition was to ride in the Grand National. This was not based on the approval of Rimell, trainer of four Grand National winners, but the Prince reportedly made his first visit to Aintree racecourse that spring, soon afterwards he wrote an enthusiastic foreword to a book called *Long Live the National!* and he had also chatted about the race with Andrew Parker Bowles who had himself completed the race, in 1969 on The Fossa. There is a great Pathé News film of that Grand National Day on YouTube. Of his time as an amateur jockey, Parker Bowles stresses how much he enjoyed it but is the opposite of singing his own praises, for instance relating what happened after one race at Cheltenham when Fulke Walwyn told him, 'As you came over the last fence you had 20lb in hand but you still got beaten.'

Of his conversation with Prince Charles about Aintree, Parker Bowles says: 'He asked me about it because I had ridden, rather badly, in the Grand National. I did get round, thanks to the horse really, old Fossa. He asked what it was like and we talked about it, and he said it would be a great excitement to do that, but I don't think much more than that.'

If the Grand National was seriously an aim, Nick Gaselee does not remember it. 'It was all very much a step at a time,' he stresses, 'to have a season's hunter chasing and if all that had gone well, who knows?' In the summer of 1980 the next step was for the Prince to buy a horse of his own, with a view to going hunter chasing early in 1981 before a tilt at the Grand Military Gold Cup. The Queen Mother was patron of the Grand Military meeting and the race is restricted to horses owned and ridden by members of the armed forces, for which Prince Charles with his plethora of ranks and titles could not have been better qualified, but now they had to find him a suitable horse.

The ten-year-old Allibar was bought from Ireland by Tom Cooper. Because there were limited opportunities for the Prince to ride out, the decision was taken for him to focus on riding this one horse. 'We concentrated on his confidence in this horse and he was 200% confident in him,' states Gaselee. 'It wasn't as if he was going to ride lots of other horses [in races]. He wasn't setting out on an amateur career to be leading amateur. He was setting out to have some really good fun in hunter chases on a horse he knew and loved.'

In all these respects Allibar turned out to fit the bill perfectly. 'He adored him and they got on very well together,' remembers Gaselee, and the first chance for horse and rider to show in public what they could do together came at Ludlow in October. To illustrate the sort of timetable he was keeping, Prince Charles commenced the day before the race by riding out Allibar at Lambourn, was then reportedly 15 minutes late for a meeting with the British Deer Society in London, before flying by helicopter into Hampshire to a press conference for the Mounbatten Memorial Trust and then returning to London where he was guest of honour at a charity film premiere of *Breaker Morant*.

Eventually putting up 3lb overweight at 11st 7lb on Allibar in the Clun Handicap Chase for amateur riders, he drifted from 4-1 to 10-1. In a field of 12, they made the running until the fourth fence, dropped back on the far side on the second circuit, then finished strongly. On the run-in he passed three horses but one other rival was beyond recall. Allibar was second, by six lengths. *The Sporting Life* reported that 'Keith the farmer's boy beats Charles', the Keith in question being 17-year-old Keith Reveley who was riding his mother Mary's Hello Louis and recording his first winner.

While characteristically apologetic to the betting public, the Prince was apparently thrilled by the experience and Nick Gaselee was full of praise: 'In another hundred yards he would probably have won. It was an extraordinary performance, to start that late in life and on only your second ride over fences.'

Also clearly impressed, Jack Logan (the nom de plume of former Conservative minister Sir David Llewellyn) in *The Sporting Life* petitioned: 'Now that Prince Charles has ridden such memorable races on Long Wharf, Sea Swell and Allibar, it may be timely to recall the words of Edward III about his son, the Black Prince, at Crécy: "Let the boy win his spurs." As far as racing is concerned – and many other fields of derring-do – the Prince of Wales has long ago earned his. So much so that I suggest, respectfully, that he be persuaded to join the Jockey Club and so bring to its counsels the vigour, imagination and realism brought by his father to the wider world of equestrianism.'

More than 30 years on, Andrew Parker Bowles reaches for a photograph and reads the message on it: 'To Andrew, best wishes, Christmas 1980. From the jockey with the worried expression.' Parker Bowles continues: 'It's a picture of him jumping the fence, perfectly adequately. On the back there's a letter saying "Andrew, I thought you might like to have this photo as a small memento of all your persuasion in the last few years which finally bore fruit in the shape of Allibar, for which many thanks. Charles.'"

In *Prince Charles, Horseman* the Prince offered more detailed thoughts on what had transpired at Ludlow: 'I had ridden Allibar out and schooled him over fences, but of course I did not know what he would be like in a race. He went off in front immediately, and terrified me. I didn't really know what was happening, but suddenly there was a whack down the side of somebody's horse and they all started to overtake me. It was a marvellous experience, but alas I was getting left behind. Then the great thing happened. I asked the old boy to catch up – and he did. He was grand. We had nearly completed the second circuit by then, and had made up some ground. When I kicked him on he picked up speed. On the last run we actually overtook people like Tim Thomson Jones – and came second.'

Reportedly unnoticed in the crowd, until she blew her cover with some energetic support during the closing stages, was the 19-year-old Lady Diana Spencer, accompanied by Camilla Parker Bowles. Not for the last time, in some quarters Lady Diana attracted more attention than the Prince, the next day's *Daily Express* headline for instance reading 'Dark Horse Diana wins with Charles'. She had backed him each-way.

When there was soon no hedging of bets among the press in their coverage of the Royal romance, an understanding was reached between them and a trainer who was in danger of becoming under siege. 'The press were very, very good,' claims Gaselee. 'They came to the yard and everything but they weren't allowed up on the Downs when he was doing work. They were very good and they stuck to that.'

Or almost all of them did. 'There was one old boy who used to work for us, he was called Chris,' reveals Heaney, 'and he went up into the city and he was a journalist for one of the newspapers. He rang me up and quite innocently he just says, "Oh, is Prince Charles down tomorrow?" And I said, "Oh yeah, he is." I never thought any more about it. So the next thing is I hear there's bedlam up on the gallops, there's the security men chasing somebody all over the place in their Range Rovers, and it only turned out to be this Chris. He knew a back way up on to the Downs, you see, that none of the other press boys would have known, and he only gets up on to the Downs trying to take some photograph and the next thing the security boys are after him. I never said a word. I thought I shall have to keep quiet. I'll just have to give him a bollocking the next time I got a hold of him.'

Prince Charles was hell bent on denying the press any photograph of the happy couple before the official snapshots at the announcement of their engagement. The pair would get out of their car separately and on different sides, before walking about 15 to 20 yards apart. 'The only time they would be together would be in the horse's box,' says Heaney. Patience among the press at these tactics was not universal. 'They were up trees, they were in drains, they were every bloody where,' says the head lad of some of the snappers. Attempts were made to bribe the lads, including offering them a camera worth at least £1,000, with instructions just to get the photograph of the two of them, hand over the film and keep the camera.

Having proposed in early February, in the last 16 days before the official announcement of the engagement, Prince Charles and Diana apparently met only once, at the stables when the Prince was to ride out Allibar in preparation for their participation in a hunter chase at Chepstow the following day. It was not a happy reunion. After completing a 7f canter, Allibar collapsed and died of a heart attack. Jumbo Heaney was following Allibar in the string: "The old horse he started to wobble, so he did, and I've seen it happen before, so I just started shouting out at him "Get off, get off" as quickly as I could and he was a bit flustered to start with, he didn't realise what was happening, but the old horse started to stagger and stumble a bit, and lucky enough he just got off him before he went down.'

The Prince was distraught and Lady Diana, who had witnessed it, was in tears. Later that day, with seemingly as many press men as stable lads and other customers in the Lambourn pubs, some tall stories were flying around. One such tale was that Prince Charles had been so besotted with the horse that he used to spend many hours talking to it alone.

Four days after the death of Allibar there was the official engagement jamboree and 17 days after that was the Grand Military Gold Cup. The Prince decided to ride in it if he could find another horse and Good Prospect was purchased from John Edwards' yard. 'There are many who can ride the horses they know adequately but are hopeless as soon as they have to get on anything strange,' wrote John Hislop in *Steeplechasing*. 'It is not of the slightest use sticking to one horse,' he went on. Both Prince Charles and Good Prospect were reported as having made the necessary and hasty adaptations.

Previewing the Grand Military, opinions differed over the Prince's performances so far. Charles Benson, for instance, perceived that he had shown 'admirable horsemanship', while John McCririck described the ride at Ludlow as 'adequate, no more'. A more heated debate, however, was building over whether the Prince should be riding over fences at all. John Junor in the *Sunday Express*, while stressing that nobody doubted the Prince's personal courage, wrote: 'And still he goes on taking quite unnecessary risks. On Friday he will be riding his new horse Good Prospect at Sandown over fences I personally would need a stepladder to climb. After that it is said that he has his sights on the Grand National. Just what is he up to? Is he still trying to prove himself to himself? Whatever the reason, I would respectfully suggest that, for the next few months at least, and even if only for the sake of the British tourist industry he concentrates on arriving at St Paul's on July 29 in the Gold Coach and not in an ambulance.'

In his rebuttal of that argument in *The Sporting Life* on the day of the race, having already pointed out concernedly that 'it's not as if he is the only heir in line to the succession of the British throne', Jack Logan declared that: 'For my part, I am profoundly grateful for the daring of the Prince of Wales, the wisdom of his family and the good sense of our politicians in all parts of the House, which pave the way for his presence in the field today. I cannot help thinking, too, that if it were not for men like him, and other Servicemen of all ranks, the rest of us would not sleep so soundly in our beds. Please accept my thanks, Sir, and may the best horse win.'

Allibar that season had a Timeform rating of 118. Good Prospect's was 137, he was the forecast favourite and went off second favourite. None of which counted for anything when Good Prospect clipped the top of the fence and unseated his rider at the fifth from home. 'Nose Dive !' shouted the front page in the *Daily Express*. 'Jockey Charles falls – and Di can't bear to watch.'

The bloody-nosed rider was interrogated by John McCririck, revealing: 'He didn't quite have the leap in him I thought he had. There's only one way of finding out about a horse and that's it. He isn't very big and just couldn't make it.' Jim Stanford's summary of the drama at fence 18 was that 'the Prince asked his mount for a big jump as they reached it half a stride too soon. The 12-year-old flicked the top, screwing as he came down and ejecting his Royal partner ignobly out of the side door.' Many observers hinted more or less subtly that a more experienced rider would have stayed on board. Although he was sixth and about 15 lengths off the leaders at the time, Good Prospect was apparently just beginning to make his move. John Edwards said he would have won.

In the *Daily Express*, Peter O'Sullevan submitted that 'As it was, the royal rider reckoned he had "learned a lot" from the experience. And it is to be hoped that the old women of both sexes who would have him forgo activity involving risk will not be heeded. The bad luck yesterday was that Prince Charles survived the toughest part when racing in a closely-packed group – showing the courage and dash which he has made his hallmark – only to go at a point where the race was becoming less hazardous.'

'I think he would have gone very, very close,' Gaselee recollects in 2013, 'so if that had happened to a certain extent we'd have got things right. And then we'd maybe have had a chance to look around for something different the following year.'

Instead, from the Grand Military there were to be garnered only what-might-have-beens, and the speculation and frustration along those lines encouraged the connections of Good Prospect to throw their hat in the ring for the following week's Kim Muir. It had not been the original plan, far from it, and it was a harder task for the horse and its jockey, but the latter at least was eager for another crack. After dusting himself down after the Grand Military and allaying Lady Diana's concerns about his welfare, the Prince professed that 'I was so thrilled to be out there and doing it at last.'

～

In Chapter 3 of *Steeplechasing*, entitled 'Rider's seat over fences', John Hislop points out that: 'The first duty of a steeplechase-rider is to get round, which he will not succeed in doing if he falls off. This can easily happen if he is not on his guard when his horse makes a mistake, an eventuality that can come about through no fault of the horse or rider.'

Prince Charles's failure to get round on Good Prospect at Sandown ensured that even more press attention was concentrated on him when he ventured forth at Cheltenham. Jumbo Heaney states that 'Cheltenham on the right horse, it's not a problem. He rode well enough and he picked up the racing side of his riding pretty quick for a guy who'd only done hunting and polo.'

Doubts were growing though about whether Good Prospect (the name attracted inevitable comment) was the right horse. As Gaselee reflects, 'he had this tendency to make the odd mistake and he didn't have the best front on him,' or as his head lad puts it, 'he was a little short-necked bugger and when he hit a fence, he mightn't fall but he would shoot you over his head.'

Prince Charles was not the only one to have been unseated on him, Jim Wilson, no less, having left his company at the second fence at Newbury in January. In *Prince Charles: Horseman* the horse's new partner confided that 'He didn't give you a nice feeling; sometimes you had to push him into a fence. There was nothing of him compared to Allibar, and I realised how good Allibar was because this beastly thing didn't take a hold.'

Only four days after coming down to earth in the Grand Military, which could not have done his confidence much good, Prince Charles was at the starting gate once again. 'He's very brave – he's bloody amazing,' was the pre-race assessment of the then Lieutenant Colonel (and subsequently Brigadier) Parker Bowles, who was there with his wife. Trying to assess how the Prince himself was feeling about his impending role on one of racing's biggest stages, Parker Bowles says now: 'I think he was apprehensive but he'd done parachuting and everything else – he was quite cool about the whole thing.'

Considering the same question, Gaselee thinks back to his own days in the saddle: 'It is a very exciting thing. You get the nerves beforehand, not the nerves that you're going to have a fall or anything, but the adrenaline rush. The adrenaline rush, it's very hard to replace.' Gaselee, himself, was nervous before that Kim Muir because he was always nervous when he had a runner. On this occasion, though, he concedes that he was probably rather more so.

Prince Charles's second-most quoted statement on his riding career under rules, expressed earnestly to Brough Scott of *The Sunday Times* in the aftermath to the Grand Military, is that 'If people could just understand the real thrill, the challenge of steeplechasing. It's part of the great British way of life, and none of the other sports I've done bears any comparison.'

His most quoted statement on the subject, unfortunately, seems to be 'A bloody nuisance' and 'Now I've got to go back and face them all again,' after the Kim Muir had seen him jettisoned by his horse for the second time in five days. Having completed a circuit of Cheltenham and racing in about 14th, well before the race began in earnest, Good Prospect made a blunder and unseated royal at the tenth. The Prince was driven back to the medical room and checked over. With no physical damage done, he left the course not long afterwards and was whisked off to Buckingham Palace for a state reception in honour of President Alhaji Shehu Shagari of Nigeria.

The multiple photographs of Prince Charles about to hit the deck, hitting the deck and just having hit the deck in the next day's papers – the *Gloucestershire Echo*, for instance, had eight on its front page – suggest a large number of photographers at every fence, and the most published photograph was probably that of him beating the ground with his whip in frustration. 'Yes, one would have far preferred a picture of him walking into the winner's enclosure,' confesses his trainer. 'It didn't make good viewing but that's it. We went into it with our eyes open and it's no good whingeing about that afterwards, is it?'

Hopefully all concerned will forgive if I reproduce some of the following day's front-page headlines: 'Down he goes again!' [*Daily Mail*]; 'Prince Falls Again' [*The Daily Telegraph*]; 'Heir we go again!' [*Daily Express*]; 'Another fall for the steeplechase Prince' [*The Times*]; 'Poor prospect' [*Financial Times*]; 'Another fall for Charles' [*The Guardian*]; 'Come off it, Charlie!' [*Daily Star*]; 'Down Again!' [*The Sun*]; and 'On yer bike Charles! It's safer than a horse' [*Daily Mirror*]. Nick Gaselee states, 'I believe he hardly ever reads the papers.'

The chastened rider himself certified that 'It's all my fault.' Gaselee remembers the Prince as 'very, very frustrated' and that 'being a tremendous self critic, he would always rather blame himself than the horse but this was just unfortunate.' Most journalists seemed to concur with the trainer that Good Prospect's mistake gave his rider no chance of maintaining the partnership, but many also ventured that the Prince needed more time to acquire the skills of self-preservation and probably needed a different horse.

Gaselee's post-mortem on the Good Prospect races is that 'the horse makes a mistake and tips him forward on both occasions, but you're better going out of the front door than the back door. You don't want to be seen to be on the buckle end and he wasn't. He rode like a proper jockey and because it takes a long time to learn exactly when you think the horse is going to make a mistake, so you can put your feet forward or do whatever, the horse just lost him on these two occasions.'

~

One person with a good view of the unseat was Chris Cundall on the 7-1 shot Waggoners Walk. 'I was just behind him, literally on his tail when he fell, and I thought if I stand on him I'll be in trouble,' says Cundall. 'But any avoiding action was done by the horse, not me.' While television coverage reverted to pictures of the prostrate Prince, Waggoners Walk was making his move. Trained by Caroline Mason, he had won the previous season's National Hunt Chase at the Festival and in 1981 he had won the Eider at Newcastle.

The rival he needed to catch in the Kim Muir was the Irish challenger Indecision, ridden by Colin Magnier. 'I was about 20 lengths behind him but I was beginning to travel,' recalls Cundall. 'Waggoners Walk was a true stayer, and I was happy where I was. Three out, at that drop fence, I saw that Indecision landed very steep and his hind legs went up very high. I remember thinking to myself if he does the same at the second last he might be on the ground and I might be in with a big chance.'

Indecision fell at the second last and Waggoners Walk was left well clear. 'Up until recently when I saw the video again I hadn't realised how far we'd actually won by – 30 lengths. That was the days of the old unsaddling enclosure and the walk back was absolutely terrific as well. I tried to savour every moment of that – round the back of the grandstand and then it was a cauldron of people. People were stacked up really high all around the enclosure. That day at Cheltenham still ranks as one of the best days of my life. I've got a photograph on the wall of me jumping the last fence. On bad days you come back and look at that and think life isn't so bad really.'

Cundall, a Yorkshire vet, was 27 at the time and had been riding in races since 1972. When I interviewed him early in 2013, he would still have been riding in point-to-points had he not suffered his own rather worse unseat the previous December. He describes what happened and how his medical training was called upon: 'The horse just got spooked by some chickens in the yard. He went round and round in circles, and it was like being on a Waltzer. I fell off the side, in the yard, right on concrete. I was lying on my back and my foot was pointing in the wrong direction, so I realised something might be wrong. Normally I have a glass of whisky, a couple of paracetamol and a hot bath and I'm all right, but this time I decided that remedy wasn't going to work.'

In 1924, his grandmother won at the Sinnington point-to-point in what Cundall believes was one of the first races in Yorkshire open to women riders. One hundred winners was his own target, but his progress slowed after 1991 when he was unconscious in Middlesbrough General hospital for nearly a fortnight after a fall sustained halfway between two fences. For several years Cundall's win tally has been stuck on 98. In 2010 he came close to number 99 but was beaten by his own daughter, Charlotte.

Reflecting on the place that raceriding has had in his life and on what has driven him to do it for all these years, Cundall says: 'It has been very important. I've gone from one season to the next and one race meeting to the next, or one horse to the next. It's a good crack. It's the adrenaline kick really. I like the camaraderie and the banter in the changing room. Obviously out on the course you're at each others' throats but in the changing room you're the best of mates.'

Asked in 2013 whether he intended to return from injury and be back in the saddle for the following season, Cundall stated: 'I do, yes. I don't want to go out on this note.'

I phoned him again in June 2015. Cundall had indeed ridden in points in 2014, and did so again in 2015, by which time he was 61. But he was still stuck on 98 winners and immediately after finishing fourth (annoyed that he did not grab third) at Mordon in May he had announced his retirement. He retired very half-heartedly, but it helped to dismiss any future change of heart that he was presented with a framed photograph to celebrate the occasion before he was even out of his riding silks.

The first reason Cundall gives for his retirement is not his own age, it's that of his horse, but there was also a mounting concern that the jockey might not pass his medical examination the following November. This was because of increasing problems with his eyesight arising from his fall in 1991. To pass his eye test Cundall had lately resorted to memorising the letters from the eye test chart. 'I thought unless I got Alzheimer's I was going to be safe – I was okay as long as the memory was alright and the eyesight wasn't.'

~

Back in 1981, once Prince Charles had had his opportunity to admire again those fences on the landing side and had been retrieved from the track in full working order, with Waggoners Walk and Chris Cundall led into the winners' enclosure, Edward Gillespie was able to review the 1981 Kim Muir very favourably. He says now: 'It drew a lot of publicity to the racecourse. He got home safely, that was all we wanted to happen, and I'm sure it drew attention to the racecourse to people who'd not seen it before. It was all very positive.'

Others found it less so. As was inevitably brought up at the time, 'All men are equal on the turf', but for many the Prince of Wales had now been seen on the turf rather too often. On the following day's back page of *The Daily Telegraph* there was a short news item from Greece about one Joannis Katzouros, depressed mathematics student, who had thrown himself off the walls of the Acropolis and landed in a pine tree, suffering minor injuries, and on his release from hospital had then taken a 150-foot jump, this time ending in some bushes and breaking a leg. The headline read 'Man Survives 2 Suicide Leaps', and in Britain disquiet now seemed to be mounting that Prince Charles was intent on trying something very similar.

Prince Charles rides at Cheltenham

Among a host of historical royal contributions to the sport of horseracing, more than 300 years earlier the latest King Charles – the Second – rode winners at Newmarket. Sixty years before the current Prince Charles had a go, his immediate predecessor as Prince of Wales – later to be Edward VIII, briefly, then the Duke of Windsor – had his first ride as a jumps jockey and he won races in point-to-points and under rules. In the latter sphere at the soon-to-be-defunct Hawthorn Hill he won the Welsh Guards Challenge Cup in 1921 on Pet Dog and followed up the following year on Little Favourite. According to Chris Pitt's superb *A Long Time Gone*, on the first occasion he beat two rivals, who both fell. One year on, Little Favourite prevailed despite having at one point refused. *Cope's Royal Cavalcade Of The Turf* professed that 'all sportsmen were delighted to see his obvious enthusiasm even if his skill left something to be desired.' The Prince had another tilt at the same race in 1928 but fell at the first, which was far from his first early departure and a growing list of blue-blooded injuries persuaded the Prime Minister to intervene.

Of the Prince of Wales 1981 version, Andrew Parker Bowles reportedly declared at Cheltenham that 'Obviously he is going to keep on riding' and Prince Charles did indeed try again, over hurdles. Inked in to contest a hurdle race one day after the Grand Military, only for the horse to be withdrawn with an injury, on May 21 the Prince got another chance over the smaller obstacles, his appearance hugely swelling the normal attendance at Newton Abbot. The soft ground, however, was all against his grandmother's Upton Grey and although they did complete, it was in ninth of ten finishers to the Elsie Mitchell-ridden Narribinni. 'It was great fun,' said the Prince, but the fun was about to come to an end.

Good Prospect won a good handicap chase at Chepstow in October carrying the Prince's colours but the Prince was not in them. In November, Gaselee announced that the horse had been sold back to John Edwards – Good Prospect ended the season, and his career, finishing fourth in the Scottish National – because a variety of commitments would prevent the Prince from riding in that campaign.

'We looked around for another horse for him and we couldn't find it,' says Gaselee, 'and, you know, he just decided he'd done it and that was that. There was no ill feeling or anything like that. Of course he wasn't in the first flush of youth and he was married then.'

Did 'the Palace' also have a role in his not continuing? 'Not as far as I know,' says the trainer. Parker Bowles, however, believes that history had repeated itself and that this Prince of Wales was also encouraged to revise his plans in the saddle: 'I think, roughly, yes. After he'd had two falls, they said that's enough.' Both men describe the Good Prospect experience as inevitably a dispiriting one for the horse's rider. Jumbo Heaney's verdict is that: 'Well he could ride, you could see he had the skills there but he didn't really get a chance to show how good he could be. I'm sure that on old Allibar he would have done.' Allibar's death was, as Gaselee sums it up, 'the undoing of everything.'

That July the Gaselees were in St Paul's Cathedral for the wedding of Prince Charles to Lady Diana, their daughter Sarah-Jane was one of the bridesmaids and Jumbo Heaney was among others from the yard who were present both at the service and a pre-wedding reception at Buckingham Palace.

Reflecting on those 15 months when Prince Charles had been a race rider, Gaselee first of all stresses that no one gave the Prince the credit he deserved, particularly for the ride at Ludlow. But, he goes on, 'It was an amazing experience – to have the privilege of getting to know him and the Princess, of going to the wedding and all sorts of things one would never ever have dreamt of doing otherwise. And he became a very good friend. I don't see him much now but I always love it when I do see him.'

Prince Charles rides at Cheltenham

What of the Prince himself? I can only speculate but, despite his reverses in as full a glare of publicity as it was possible to generate at the time, the others involved in the enterprise certainly believe that he enjoyed it. 'I think he loved it,' declares Parker Bowles, 'but he's a busier man than most and I think probably he had other things to do with his day. It took a lot of his time and as you know you can't just dabble at it.'

Princess Anne, already a European Championship gold medal winner and Sports Personality of the Year for her exploits as an event rider, would enjoy much greater success a few years later when she had her go at racing under rules. However, despite the nadir of his ride at the Cheltenham Festival, it is not hard to appreciate just why her elder brother had been so eager to have a go, and to conclude that he may have derived pleasure from this experience far removed from his normal life, especially when you return to John Hislop's *Steeplechasing*.

When concentrating on his homework some time in 1980 or 1981, Prince Charles would have come across these stirring words from Hislop about the steeplechase rider: 'He will be undeterred by adversity, by the disappointment of losing a race through bad judgement or through falling off … the loss of a favourite horse; the humiliation of being '"jockeyed off" by dissatisfied owners, and the many other blows of fate that can beset him. For a dozen such setbacks one good ride will atone. As he swings into the saddle, his worries slip from his mind as a soldier's pack slides from his back at the end of the long march, leaving in both mind and body a strange feeling of unnatural lightness.

'As he canters down to the post, he will experience the comforting sense of confidence and well-being that a good horse in fine fettle inspires, will seem to gain strength from the symmetrical bulge and sweep of the shoulder and neck-muscles before him, and draw courage from the bold heart that beats beneath him. At the start, he will know that sharp tingle of anticipation in the pit of the stomach that precedes every race, which, once the gate has gone up, is replaced by a glow of exhilaration at the strong, piston-like beat and rhythm of his horse's stride, the leading foot shooting out almost beyond the nose, the stroke of the hind legs wrenching the ground from under them. Every fence is a fresh thrill as it draws nearer and he picks the place at which to jump it, sighting the spot through the resolute, unmoving ears pricked eagerly towards the obstacle and assuring a measured approach made with the confidence of a skilled tradesman, which is justified a second later as the horse leaves the ground, picking up (it may seem) outside the wings but landing safely as far the other side and galloping on without a check.

'In this way fence after fence flicks by, the stands are passed, and groups of spectators out in the country, but these are sensed rather than perceived, as if their world lay on the other side of a thick glass through which form and sounds penetrates but dimly, the only reality being the race itself, which acquires an atmosphere and consciousness peculiar to itself: one in which senses are sharper, but only towards the task on hand, and from which fear and fatigue have unaccountably departed, to be replaced by a glorious exaltation.

'When the race is over there remains a joy mixed with the relief of relaxed muscles and nerves, the pleasant tiredness that follows physical exertion and the knowledge of a task well done. As opposed to material treasures, it is something that can never be lost, which neither wars nor sickness can take away, a memory to bring gladness to times when riding days are over.'

CHAPTER FOUR

1982 CHRISTIES FOXHUNTER CHASE

A Tale of Two Corinthians

AMATEUR RIDERS, AND other amateur sportsmen, are commonly referred to as Corinthians and when they produce notable feats of derring-do or sportsmanship, turn their noses up at financial gain and act as if it is indeed not the winning but the taking part that matters most; this is often described as the Corinthian spirit. When Corinthians are to the fore in horseracing, however, it usually demands a moderation of betting activity. The most reliable source of financial profit from Corinthians that I have known was St Paul's first letter to them, Chapter 13 ('Love is patient and kind; love is not jealous or boastful', etc.), the appearance of which used to represent a solid wager at the majority of wedding services.

So what was it that so characterised the Greek city of Corinth and its citizens that their name is now attached to the practitioners and values of amateur sport? Ancient and classical Greek cities used to have some very individuals traits. It was the Spartans who sent their children to military camps at the age of seven, were not allowed to show any sign of pain and fought to the last man. Corinthian is one of the classical orders of architecture and some would say that an immobile structure adorned with some purely decorative flourishes represents a fair description of many an amateur rider. St Paul was not, though, writing to the Corinthians to put them straight on their architecture. Of more concern to him, Corinth was also famous for its wealth, the beauty of its women and its fondness for worldly pleasures. Its temple of Aphrodite was said to have a thousand sacred prostitutes. There was also one direct connection to sport, as Corinth founded and staged the Isthmian Games, a gathering similar to the more established Olympics, and winners at the Isthmian Games were apparently rewarded with a wreath of celery. This would seem to be an exemplar of amateur sport if ever there was one but, with St Paul's extensive intervention probably guaranteeing it, Corinth's reputation in history seems to have been far more as a place of drunkenness and debauchery.

Moving on over 1,500 years and about 1,500 miles north west to Elizabethan Britain, in Shakespeare's *Henry IV Part I*, Prince Harry reports back on a drinking session with the 'loggerheads' of Eastcheap in which they have spoken warmly of him as 'a Corinthian, a lad of mettle', but while Corinthian could be used to describe his excellence as a drinking companion there was as yet no hint of an association with sport. When Prince Harry had become Henry V, he did not react positively when the Dauphin sent him a box of tennis balls.

Another two hundred years or so later in Regency Britain, drinking continued to figure prominently. One of the labels for a dissolute man about town was 'Corinthian' and many such men also formed an attachment to sports, most notably horseracing and boxing. Perhaps if the dissipated Regency Corinthian had more actively participated in those sports, rather than merely spectated and wagered on them, he would have had little choice but to celebrate maxims such as 'it's not the winning, it's the taking part'.

But when Corinthian later became incorporated into the title of sporting clubs, the loose-living connotations seem to have been replaced. The Corinthians FC, founded in 1882, included many of the best players around. It is said that they would have been well capable of winning editions of the FA Cup in their early years, had the club's constitution not forbidden their participation in any competitions. Perhaps this is where a second look at the people of ancient Corinth took place and the revisionist history concentrated instead on what code of conduct might inspire the quest for a wreath of celery.

~

In 1982, duelling for a Foxhunter Chase first prize of £6,588.20 and tenure of one of the sport's more outlandish trophies, Brod Munro-Wilson and The Drunken Duck and Tony Fowler and Honourable Man were the principal players in a race for amateur riders that I remember above all others, at Cheltenham or any other racecourse.

Fowler was 22 years old and had been assistant to leading trainers Jimmy Fitzgerald and Arthur Stephenson. He left school at Southwell at 16 and had gone straight into racing. Broderick Munro-Wilson was 36 and a merchant banker, an undisguised member of the English upper classes and friend of the royals. The name and the background may conjure up images of Bertie Wooster, Barmy Fotheringay-Phipps, Pongo Twistleton and other members of PG Wodehouse's Drones Club. However, the institution which Munro-Wilson remembers with particular fondness is the Pitt Club, a Cambridge sporting man's equivalent of Oxford University's now-infamous Bullingdon.

The histories of both men and both horses add many new layers to the story of the 1982 Foxhunter and shed some light on what it took to be a 1980s Corinthian, but at the time, and in my memory of it for decades afterwards,

117

one element almost totally eclipsed the others, and that was the riding of Munro-Wilson. His style was unorthodox, perhaps unique, and the 1982 Foxhunter was where it found its ultimate form of expression.

Two distinctive elements in the Munro-Wilson method were his riding with long irons and a torso position that often tended towards the perpendicular, and in that astonishing struggle for the Foxhunter these had an all-action accompaniment from his arms and legs. Or, as he puts it, with 'arms and legs everywhere.'

For Racing UK commentator Steve Mellish that upright posture was reminiscent of the closing scenes in the 1961 film *El Cid*, in which Charlton Heston as the recently deceased Castilian nobleman is fastened to a metal frame and then on to his saddle, the gates of Valencia are opened and the besieging Almoravid army scatters in terror as the Cid on his white steed gallops among them. In *Chasers & Hurdlers 1981/82* there is a tantalising snapshot of the Foxhunter action, an image of the two horses jumping in virtual unison at the final fence but with Fowler crouched low over Honourable Man, his back parallel to that of his mount, while with The Drunken Duck and his rider nearly all the angles appear to be at a 90-degree variance. From foot to shoulder, Munro-Wilson looks to be almost bolt upright.

Timeform's very scrupulous description was that 'The Drunken Duck's owner-rider embodies the spirit of the National Hunt amateur almost to the letter and anything he lacks in style he certainly tries to make up for in enthusiasm – O'Neill or Scudamore couldn't have shown more endeavour on The Drunken Duck at Cheltenham.'

Elsewhere, I have seen Munro-Wilson's stance compared to that of a 17th-century cavalry officer, and his appearance in a finish likened to 'playing the violin', 'a demented Barbirolli' and 'someone trying to put up a deck chair in a gale'. He was a former SAS man and my rather shell-shocked recollection of his performance at Cheltenham was that it had something of the martial arts about it. It was easy to imagine him killing an adversary with one blow. Or maybe with three or four. Many amateurs and inexperienced jockeys attract criticism for their passivity in the saddle when it comes to riding a finish – indeed, this featured in the aftermath to the 1982 Foxhunter – but on the formidable evidence of this race I doubt very much whether Munro-Wilson was ever one of those.

On his basic style, the man himself said that: 'I like to ride like a gentleman, not a monkey on a stick, which is why I rarely take a tumble. Length of leg, that's what it's all about.' Comparing himself to the more orthodox jockey, he says, 'If I stand up properly I am nearly 6ft 1ins. My legs are twice as long. Where do you put your legs? On my point of balance – I've done the Cresta Run, I did seven years in 21 SAS, so I know how to balance myself.'

The 'monkey on a stick' analogy has always seemed a little mysterious to me but Munro-Wilson can rest assured that he did not look like one, or indeed like anything I had previously seen on a racecourse. The uproarious crowd reaction suggested that many others that day at Cheltenham were wholly unprepared for it. Of course, I was very young. I had not then seen much racing for amateur riders. Within two years, though, I was reporting on point-to-point racing for the *Gloucestershire Echo* and another 30 plus years as a follower of horseracing have passed since. It nevertheless seems safe to say now that the Munro-Wilson method never really caught on.

Or perhaps that should be 'never really caught on again.' Writing to the *Racing Post*, Malcom Pannett of Brighton explained that the monkey on a stick (or monkey up a stick) was a reference to a children's toy of yesteryear: 'When the movable part of the toy was pushed fully up the aforementioned monkey resembled the style of riding introduced by, among others, Todd Sloan in the late 1890s.

Utilising short stirrups and crouching over the horse's neck, it is the style we are accustomed to today. Prior to that, gentleman riders, aka amateurs, rode with an upright stance, exemplified in any racing painting from that time. Therefore this method did not need to catch on as it had been the only style in Britain for well over a century.'

Asked whether he had a unique riding style, Munro-Wilson himself at first agrees and then disagrees, but has to go back a further 'ten, 15 or 20 years' to when 'Pat Taaffe and people like that, they rode with a much longer leg.' Whatever the precedents and parallels in his technique, the sight of Munro-Wilson at high revs made a huge impression on me and other onlookers. For a start, he managed to get everyone talking about him rather than a horse called The Drunken Duck.

The name comes not from some half-baked spoonerism, but from an inn at Barngates in the Lake District, near Ambleside, and that establishment gets its name from a local legend. Reputedly, one day in the 19th century the landlady discovered all her ducks laid out dead, so she plucked them ready for cooking. It turned out that they were half-cut rather than kaput, as a barrel had burst in the cellar, drained into their feeding ditch and the ducks had not spent all of their time there merely swimming. When they came round in the nick of time, the chastened landlady knitted them waistcoats until their feathers grew back again.

Listing the initial ingredients that made 'probably one of the most famous amateur races of all time', the horse's big-race partner commences with 'One, you've got a horse called The Drunken Duck – is that a stupid name for a horse or what? Then you've got a guy with a Hollywood name like Broderick Munro-Wilson.'

The two of them began their association in 1979 after The Drunken Duck was knocked down for 8,600 guineas at the Ascot Sales, and that wasn't the first or last time that others had their chance to buy him. Two years earlier he made 1,100 guineas out of David Gandolfo's yard after four runs in juvenile hurdles during which his most notable achievement was at Worcester when, although the form book describes The Drunken Duck as 'tailed off before pulled up three out', in fact he went straight on rather than left when confronted by the turn for home and jumped into the River Severn. He was ridden that day by the former champion jockey Graham Thorner, who observes, quite understandably, that at that stage of his career The Drunken Duck was 'bonkers' and that 'he had no steering whatsoever and I bailed out.' Thorner also reported back to the trainer that the horse appeared to be extremely well named.

However, in the next two seasons with farmer and livery yard owner Alan Smith in Cleveland, The Drunken Duck made a big splash in Northern point-to-points, and it was following a recommendation from Smith at Ascot that Munro-Wilson bought him. The racing journalist Colin Russell describes Smith as 'a genius with difficult horses but very quiet and modest, a real gentleman. He was an unsung master trainer.'

Munro-Wilson's first choice of stable for his new charge, however, was the Dickinsons'. Tony Dickinson was second in the trainers table in 1979/80 and his son Michael was champion in 1981/82, the season of The Drunken Duck's famous race at Cheltenham, but this was one runner who did not contribute to their scores, as he got too worked up around other horses and had to be trained on his own, for which his owner sent him back to Smith (arcane rules at the time meant that the horse was officially recorded as owner-trained). There was another trip to Ascot Sales on the way, though, where this time The Drunken Duck went through the ring for 7,600 guineas but was returned to his owner.

Munro-Wilson explains: 'At one stage [in today's currency] I had about two million quid's worth of horses and my bank manager said to me, "Don't you think we should be cutting down a bit?" I brought about 75 per cent of them back.'

Returned to Smith and united with his owner in hunter chases, there was also some fine-tuning with his tactics. 'This horse could pull like a steam train,' Munro-Wilson explains. 'Traditionally if you were taught to ride in races, the idea was to drop out at the back, switch off and then two from home start moving up. But the only way you could ride this horse was the way I rode him, which was to pop out in front. What we now think of as "Old England" said to my mother, "Well, look here, we like your boy but he's got to be taught to ride properly. He will win good races if he learns to hold horses up," but I don't care if you were Charles Atlas or Sylvester Stallone, you could not hold this horse up. He was not exactly the easiest horse to ride and I learned you can settle in front. A bit of horsemanship was required here which wasn't going to be done by conventional methods.'

~

The Drunken Duck was in perfect hands and all was now set for his march on Cheltenham but one horse, in particular, barred his way. About 50 miles away at Claxton in Yorkshire, Honourable Man was bred, owned, trained and often ridden by Trish, wife of Colin Russell. Her sister Caroline Mason trained Waggoners Walk who won the 1980 National Hunt Chase under Tony Fowler and then, [see Chapter Three], registered a second Festival success in the 1981 Kim Muir. The Russells never had more than three horses and when Edmund Collins, a friend of theirs and a good Irish amateur, rode Honourable Man before he ever ran, he reported back that 'this is the best horse you'll ever have'. He was right. Having won in point-to-point, Honourable Man was sent hunter chasing in 1980/81.

When The Drunken Duck, too, returned to racing under rules in February 1981 for a maiden hunter chase at Stockton, he was co-favourite of three, and one of the others was Honourable Man. The contemporaries finished 20 lengths clear of the rest and Honourable Man was in front by a neck after a photo finish. In the words of *Raceform*, the winner 'led four out, well clear when eased flat', while The Drunken Duck was 'headed four out, ran on flat, just failed'. As the *Sporting Chronicle* reported on this heart-stopping finish, the stewards reminded Honourable Man's rider 'of the severe consequences that can arise through not riding a horse out to the line'.

That rider was Tony Fowler and the task of assessing just how much he and Honourable Man had in hand against their strong-finishing rival had only just begun. On the subsequent evidence that season, the answer was a great deal, because although The Drunken Duck went on to win the Grand Military Gold Cup at Sandown, Honourable Man showed much better form in winning twice more and finishing 12 lengths second to subsequent Grand National winner Grittar in the 1981 Foxhunter.

When The Drunken Duck won that Grand Military Gold Cup, many observers, but definitely not Munro-Wilson, believed it was only because at the second-last fence the leader Colonial Lad (ridden by the Marquis de Cuellar, son of Aintree legend the Duke Of Alburquerque) was carried out by a loose horse. The general feeling that it would also take something along those lines for The Drunken Duck to overturn Honourable Man was not greatly altered when the two of them met again at Newcastle one month before the 1982 Foxhunter. It was on good to soft ground and 5-6 favourite Honourable Man won by a length and a half, The Drunken Duck giving him 4lb but Honourable Man winning 'cleverly'.

Recalling the daunting task that lay ahead for him and his horse at Cheltenham, Munro-Wilson points out that his birthday is the anniversary of the Battle of Waterloo. Warming to his theme, he expounds: 'I'm an expert on the Battle of Waterloo and there's a lot of similarity between Waterloo and the Cheltenham Foxhunter 1982 because, to be frank with you, Napoleon could not lose Waterloo. You know he said afterwards, "Don't give me a clever general, give me a lucky general." Napoleon was in an absolutely brilliant position to win that battle but nobody would carry out his instructions. They all got cold feet – Marshal Ney, Marshal Soult. Napoleon should have finished off Wellington before Blucher even got there. It's a fantastic story. So the answer is you look at the Cheltenham Foxhunter 1982 and you see Honourable Man the very hot favourite – he could not be beaten by The Drunken Duck.'

The latter-day Iron Duke had one further outing on The Drunken Duck before Cheltenham and they won it, battling back in game style at Wetherby. Honourable Man, meanwhile, breezed home at Southwell and then did his final piece of serious work with two horses trained by Mick Easterby, and he worked well. The Easterby horses were Bally-go and Skewsby, who both ran at Cheltenham one day before the Foxhunter in the Coral Golden Hurdle Final (now the Pertemps) and disputed the lead over the final hurdle, finishing second and fourth. If the immediate build-up had gone well for the two horses in the Foxhunter, it also seems to have gone pretty smoothly for one of the jockeys.

'I'd stayed the night before at a minor stately home called Chavenage, which is the seat of the Lowsley-Williams family,' recalls Munro-Wilson happily. 'The ghost of Charles I is meant to walk down the corridor with his head under his arm. I'd done a deal with the butler and said, "Look here, when you've got hold of *The Sporting Life*, shove it under the door as soon as you get it because I want to speak to a friend of mine on the Stock Exchange to put on a bet but I've got to see the paper first." So, there are all the runners and riders but the most important thing is there's been massive rain overnight. Now this horse, The Drunken Duck, could gallop in the soft and heavy ground as if it was good ground. He loved it because of his action – he had a very high knee action – and I opened the paper and it was "soft, heavy in places" and I thought, "This is the ground we like." I rang up my friend on the Stock Exchange and we had a massive each-way bet. My friend, he said, "Brod, I hear bells ringing," so I said, "Right, we'll go for it."'

While Munro-Wilson was tucked up in bed growing increasingly excited as he thumbed through the pages of *The Sporting Life*, but trying not to wake 'Mrs Munro-Wilson Mark II', all was not so comfortable for Tony Fowler, as he explains: 'I rode Cooch Behar at Doncaster the Saturday before the Festival and I got buried. I'd never broken a collarbone before. I didn't feel right and drove up to Ashby [a specialist] and I was all black and blue. I'd missed the Festival the year before. I said, "What's wrong?" and did 40 press-ups. I said, "Will I ride on Thursday?" and he said, "Do you want to ride on Thursday?" I said I did and he said, "You will do."'

When Munro-Wilson had ridden his first winner under rules, on Champers Galore in March 1975, it was with a disguised plaster cast on his left wrist, which had been fractured in a point-to-point two days earlier. In 1981, Fowler had taken a point-to-point fall (on Honourable Man's half-brother Woodwind, backed in from 10-1 to 4-5) that broke his arm and put him out of action for nearly a year. That was eight days before the Cheltenham Festival and cost him the ride on Honourable Man in that year's Foxhunter. Whether Fowler should have been on the sidelines at the 1982 Festival as well was about to become a contentious issue. On Champion Hurdle day, he was at Sedgefield in a bid to prove his fitness, riding Doctor Win into a never-dangerous fourth in a hunter chase.

Two days later at Cheltenham at 2.53 pm, bidding for the top prize in hunter chasing, Honourable Man started 9-4 favourite (from 7-2) and The Drunken Duck was 12-1 (from 14s), in a 19-runner field. Did Fowler feel any pain? He says 'No. It's the buzz, isn't it? If you're apprehensive, as soon as that gate goes up everything floods out.'

~

Watching a recording of the race in 2012, I was the one who felt some trepidation as the gates went up. A gap of thirty years can play tricks with the mind. For all that time, the 1982 Foxhunter had been a cherished memory but I very much doubt whether I had seen the race since the day it happened. When I had the pleasure of meeting Brod Munro-Wilson in 2012 he urged me to try and get my hands on the race video. 'You'll love it,' he said. 'It's hysterical', which was exactly as I remembered it, as well as it being a simply titanic battle. But had the intervening years exaggerated what took place that afternoon? Was the legend in any way a myth?

'I lead from the front,' declares Munro-Wilson, probably more of life in general, and true to his word he sets off in the Foxhunter at a strong pace and quickly sends his mount into a clear lead, making the most of The Drunken Duck's strengths in stamina and jumping. At the third fence comes the first indication that what I am about to watch will not be a disappointment, far from it, as Munro-Wilson calls for a cab in exaggerated style. All that is missing is a cowboy hat in his outstretched hand.

At the next fence, the water jump, the first three horses are stretched out over about a dozen lengths and at the fifth (and later the 15th) Munro-Wilson calls for his cab again. As the early entertainment unfolds, Honourable Man is held up in the last half of the field but Fowler makes a move, from 12th into ninth, just before the field starts to go more steeply downhill; at the 11th he is alongside the big Irish hope Colonel Heather when that horse unseats his rider. Turning away from the stands for the final time, The Drunken Duck leads by six lengths. Always happy with the way his mount was travelling, Munro-Wilson recollects that 'I thought I was going to win by miles' – it did not turn out that way.

Even with a circuit to go, the two eventual principals stand out from the rest. Munro-Wilson you cannot miss, especially as he has just taken the fence in front of the stands in that famous upright stance, while Fowler is at the other extreme and could not be stooping any lower. At the water jump second time round, Honourable Man disputes fourth. He is making a sustained move round the outside but probably does not forfeit much more ground than Munro-Wilson does in extra wind resistance. Two fences later Honourable Man disputes second and the leader's advantage is down to a length. Two fences after that, at the final open ditch, Honourable Man jumps slowly but the duel is only briefly delayed. From that point, Munro-Wilson relates, 'I'm still hanging on there and from the top of the hill Honourable Man and The Drunken Duck pull clear. Within a fence we'd slipped the rest of the field by 20 lengths. It's head and head and neck and neck, head and head and neck and neck. A 20-horse race turned into a two-horse race and we'd jump together, we'd land together'.

For most of what follows, Honourable Man has the lead but it is only slight and rounding the final turn there is a neck in it. That has stretched to a length approaching the second last but is immediately forfeited when Honourable Man goes through the top of the fence and loses momentum. As both jockeys ask their mounts to stretch on, elbows are much in evidence. Approaching the final fence it has already been a fantastic race, an epic, but that was merely the phoney war.

Taking up the story, Munro-Wilson says: 'Galloping flat out at the last I remember thinking two things. First of all, I hope I meet it on a good stride, which I did, otherwise I'd be sitting in the grandstand, and Honourable Man didn't jump it so well but he came back at me. I also thought to myself that there's a fair few bob in this – I mean I am an economist, so I did a little quick maths in my head – and after I'd jumped the last I thought, "Get on with it Brod, there's about 70 grand up for grabs for Pete's sake, so throw the kitchen sink at it."'

Among friends, Munro-Wilson's nickname at the time was the Brodfather. Others later came to call him Force and the run-in for the 1982 Foxhunter is where the full force is unleashed, although its rise to the pinnacle of the Beaufort Scale is not immediate. Six strides after the fence he goes to raise his whip and slaps The Drunken Duck down the neck but although at subsequent points he appears to strike his own right leg and foot, he does not hit his mount behind the saddle. 'I used to carry a stick,' says the rider, 'but I never really used it because I didn't really know how to use it properly.'

On the stands side, meanwhile, Fowler on Honourable Man opts for hands-and-heels encouragement and sticks to it; virtually all the way to the line, he is crouched low with his head down and his hands close together moving up and down like pistons either side of the horse's neck. Between Munro-Wilson's hands, on the other hand, there is a chasm as his left grips the reins and the right embarks on an increasingly animated and roughly circular motion, all the while with him bumping along in the saddle. From Honourable Man having been a neck up on landing, there is nothing between them for most of what follows and the action reaches a mighty crescendo in the last hundred yards. With Fowler feeling the urgency of the situation, and perhaps alarm, he ends up rowing forwards as if in a small boat being pursued by a fast-closing Jaws. At this point, albeit within the confines of hands-and-heels riding, there is no sign of his injury. Both horses give their all, the small Honourable Man up against his rangy, much longer-striding rival, and in his last 20 strides The Drunken Duck is just ahead and his rider in full cry. The right hand goes from shoulder height to head height and higher still. With his white gloves, Munro-Wilson resembles a very busy traffic policeman. As he deals with the vehicles coming at him from every direction he nevertheless keeps The Drunken Duck in front by a head in the photo finish. As the two jockeys pass the post, taking Munro-Wilson as the minute hand of a watch and Fowler as the hour hand, it looks as if the time is about two minutes past three.

For a second opinion on the race finish, here are the observations given almost immediately afterwards by ex-jockey Richard Pitman, as he guided BBC viewers through the replay from the second last: 'But here two contrasting styles; nearest to us Tony Fowler looking like a professional, on the far side Brod Munro-Wilson not looking too bad at the moment but just keep your eye on them. Go to the last, and Tony Fowler and Honourable Man look as if they've clinched it there but now it gets down to the working stage and the stylish one amongst them, Tony Fowler, doesn't actually do very much. Brod Munro-Wilson looks as if he's playing a violin on the far side but it is actually making The Drunken Duck go somewhere. Tony Fowler who is hands and heels and trying to get Honourable Man to go, starting to work now, but Brod Munro-Wilson throwing everything, everywhere, and it seems as if at least he's getting a tune out of The Drunken Duck. He's simply bumping around there and hitting him down the shoulder and throwing everything at the horse's head and I'm sure that Brod Munro-Wilson has been rewarded for his exertions there and he'll get the photo finish.'

~

Brod Munro-Wilson had won one of the biggest trophies in the sport, figuratively, because it is the most coveted prize for amateur riders in steeplechases, and literally, because the silverware for the Foxhunter is absolutely massive. If there is one trophy presentation that is worth turning up to watch it is this one. Lifting the thing is a sporting challenge in itself. No mantelpiece could accommodate it, and not many sideboards. When Munro-Wilson took it back to his Tudor farmhouse in Sussex he stationed it in an alcove where there had once been a fireplace.

The 1982 Foxhunter was, not surprisingly, the highlight of his raceriding career. He is devoted to the military races at Sandown, and Sandown is his favourite course, but he says, 'It has to be the ultimate to win at the Festival. That was the ultimate for a gentleman amateur, to win not just any old race but a race as spectacular as that.'

The race also resulted in a sort of immortality for him, as an incident on another continent helps illustrate. 'I was walking in central Africa,' he recalls, 'and some people I didn't even know came up to me and they said, "It's The Drunken Duck I presume." They were there at Cheltenham and had never forgotten it.' Some ten years after the race, he was out walking again, this time down Hamilton Terrace in London, when a man stopped him and said, 'You're Brod Munro-Wilson, aren't you? I've been waiting to meet you for ten years to thank you.' It was a bookmaker who had been alerted to The Drunken Duck's chance and kept laying Honourable Man.

Victory at the Cheltenham Festival had been achieved despite the fact that he was so obviously not a professional rider. 'You have not got a jockey,' he admits, 'but you have got a proper gentleman amateur with a double-barrelled name who is nowhere near a professional, who is a real foxhunting, polo-playing, sporting amateur.'

He was a merchant banker, at a time before banking had fallen into disrepute, and he continues, 'For a lot of people the feeling is that it inspired a generation. Anthony Fowler wasn't going to inspire anybody because he was a semi-pro but I was the city boy. It pointed out to people that someone like me, buying his own horse with his own money, and with a bit of education and a bit of guts, you could go to Cheltenham and win a race in front of 100,000 people.'

On the other hand, while Munro-Wilson was now commencing his ride on the crest of a wave that never stopped rolling, narrow defeat put Fowler's decision to ride with an injury under immediate critical scrutiny. As the runner-up relates 30 years later: 'I got charged that I got beaten because I could not ride it out but then my style of riding was always quiet. I was called Fairy Fowler.'

He continues: 'People have said you want your head looking at, you had too many knocks on the head, but life is a challenge. Rightly or wrongly, Lord Oaksey said I shouldn't have ridden it but your life as a jockey isn't very long. I was only an amateur. I felt I did the horse justice and rode it how I thought I would. I could never say I wish it hadn't happened, for all the trouble it caused, and that in the end it didn't quite pay off, did it? Was it the hill? Was it me? We'll never know.'

Describing that riding style, he elaborates: 'I never used my whip, I used to flick it. I was always kidology. You've only got to look at the horses I won on. Hands and heels – that was my style. A lot of horses went for me because they thought there was nobody on board.'

Later Fowler was locked in the weighing room at Perth and Hexham for his own safety after controversial rides. Some of the trouble he refers to, caused by his Cheltenham ride, is gauged from the fact that he became the only jockey the Russells ever jocked off. Going into the race he was engaged to Caroline Mason. Shortly afterwards he wasn't.

He therefore had more important things to worry about but when Fowler remembers Lord Oaksey criticising him for taking the ride, he is not wrong. In the *Daily Telegraph* the day after the race, Marlborough (Oaksey) declared: 'Going to the last, anyone with eyes would certainly have laid long odds on Honourable Man to beat Brod Munro-Wilson and The Drunken Duck. The latter had led nearly all the way but his rider is more a sportsman than a stylist and the overwhelming probability seemed to be that the much more experienced Tony Fowler would outride him up the hill. But unknown to me and probably to Honourable Man's many backers, Mr Fowler had badly bruised, if not cracked a shoulder in a recent fall. I am all for courage, daring and willingness to put up with pain; but this was frankly ridiculous. Up the hill Mr Fowler was scarcely able to help his horse at all and, admittedly talking through my pocket, I think he needs both his head and his shoulder carefully examined.'

Under the headline 'Brod's The Boy As Duck Shows His Spirit', *The Sporting Life* reported that for Tony Fowler and Honourable Man 'it was a case of what might have been' and that 'if only he had been 100 per cent then the head verdict just might have gone the other way. Fowler was bitterly upset afterwards but can take some consolation from the fact that he rode a beautiful race throughout and the horse ran an absolute blinder. Fowler, incidentally, never hits Honourable Man as he is convinced the horse gives his all.'

Expressed in the *Sporting Chronicle* – headline 'Honour For Brod As Rivals Take A Ducking' – Mrs Russell's feeling on whether Fowler should have given Honourable Man a strike with his whip was that 'I would have given him just one, close home.'

~

Five days after the Foxhunter, Fowler rode Bachelors Hall into third at Nottingham, and four days after that he won on the same horse by ten lengths in a televised race at Newbury.

A Tale of Two Corinthians

In the 1983 Foxhunter, The Drunken Duck and Munro-Wilson finished 22 lengths fourth to Eliogarty under Caroline Beasley, the first woman to ride a winner at the meeting. The Drunken Duck also ran in the 1984 Grand National but was pulled up. Munro-Wilson rode in the National himself, on Coolishall in 1980, but his luck unquestionably deserted him on this occasion because his iron broke on landing at the third and he was unseated. He also rode in the Maryland Hunt Cup and the Velka Pardubicka.

Honourable Man was prevented from a third bid at the Foxhunter by a virus days before the 1983 renewal and when he did return to the Festival in 1984 it was to finish second yet again, in the Kim Muir. In 1992, the Russells sold their successful pointer Claxton Greene to join Martin Pipe and he started favourite at the Festival in the following year's National Hunt Chase. He was beaten a short head. In 2015, Colin Russell continues as a stalwart of the racing press, a greatly appreciated colleague of mine on the *Racing Post*, someone whose opinion on racing and racehorses always demands respect.

In addition to the one enjoyed on Waggoners Walk, Tony Fowler won a second National Hunt Chase in 1985 on Northern Bay. He was not to ride Honourable Man after that fateful 1982 Foxhunter but he did ride The Drunken Duck. Reading in *Directory Of The Turf 1987* that one of Fowler's retainers was with Mr B. Munro-Wilson, I had first taken this to be a piece of self-deprecating humour but in fact Munro-Wilson believed the reaction to Fowler's ride on Honourable Man, expressed so forcibly by Lord Oaksey, had been unfair, and later in their racing careers the two became friends. At one time Fowler acted as a racehorse scout for him and he was entrusted with the ride on most of The Drunken Duck's starts in 1984/85, including winning from the front at Bangor in March and coming from well behind at Sedgefield that April to lead close home at 4-7 when the horse secured his final win in a hunter chase.

The Drunken Duck raced on until he was 13. It was May 1990, three weeks before his 45th birthday, when Munro-Wilson retired from raceriding but this was by no means a retirement from the saddle. Having joined the Guards Polo Club in 1983 at the behest of Major Ronald Ferguson, who like the rest of us had watched the Cheltenham triumph spellbound, Munro-Wilson eventually fully switched his focus to polo and at one stage owned a string of 35 polo ponies. Playing for his team Rocking Horse he won the European Championship in 1987. Those who felt nostalgic, or intrigued, to get a sight of Munro-Wilson on horseback could still have seen him in action in 2015 in Windsor Great Park playing at Guards, a club in which he had the distinction of being the oldest playing member, and he was showing no signs of relinquishing it. Having just turned 70, however, he admits to struggling slightly to play three days in a row.

The highlights of his professional career came in the Alternative Investment Market, first with flotations connected with North Sea oil and above all in 1984 when orchestrating the flotation of The Body Shop, which became known as 'The shares that defy gravity' when an initial valuation of £5 million turned into one of £658 million when the company was sold to L'Oréal in 2006.

In 1993, however, Munro-Wilson's name was in the papers in a new and unwelcome context when he appeared in Court 13 at the Royal Courts of Justice following an accusation that he had harassed his former fiancée. Munro-Wilson is adamant, and explains in lively terms, that the original charge against him was outrageous and ridiculous (it was eventually dismissed) but concedes that it was unwise to have called the lady in question a 'silly little tart' while he was speaking to a reporter from a tabloid newspaper, who then went and printed it. *That* was not allowed. Opting to defend himself – 'I love these things like *My Cousin Vinny*' – and undertaking the task with some zest before an apparently appreciative gallery, Munro-Wilson 'bollocked everybody' and proclaimed 'I pour scorn on this, and I pour scorn on this and that and the other.'

The judge was not won over: 'I hear it ringing in my ears now,' recollects the defendant. '"You have made disparaging remarks about a woman you once loved, and you, with your background, social standing and education, I would expect you, even now, to behave like a gentleman. You have not. You have behaved like a cad."'

Munro-Wilson received a 14-day jail sentence, immediately suspended.

The press knives seemed to be poised over what they labelled 'Prince Charles's polo playing pal', but he launched a counter-offensive and, in keeping with his racing career, once again threw the kitchen sink at it. Deciding that 'Well, if I'm a cad, okay I'm the King of Cads', Munro-Wilson propelled himself into the media limelight as a sort of Cad's Correspondent. In the centre pages of *The Sun*, he gave his 'Bad Cad Guide' with '20 essential tips from the Bounder in the Boudoir'. TV appearances included *Richard And Judy*, who went on to broadcast a mini-series comprising not only *A Bounder In The Boudoir* but also *A Rogue In Brogue* and *A Toff In Tartan*. He wrote a column in the *Daily Mail*.

~

Comparing the amateur riders of 1982 to those of today, Munro-Wilson believes there has been a massive change in the social demography of those riding. The inspirational effect of his own ride back in 1982 may well have worn off. 'You've got to realise,' he says, 'that in those days the gentleman amateur scene was different to how it is now – it was very, very classy.' Among the participants in one recent edition of the Aintree Fox Hunters, a race he finished third in three times, he detects that there was only one Honourable and two double-barrels, and that the winning rider 'can scarcely speak the Queen's English. There were three what I call old-style traditional gentleman amateurs. They don't do it any more.'

Instead, he has discerned a switch of allegiance from National Hunt racing to polo: 'Everybody who is in the Thames valley, like me, they all play at Guards, they play at Cirencester, they play at Cowdray. Polo is the big, big sport for everybody.'

I am not in a position to assess the scale of this shift but reckon that in most respects Munro-Wilson is surely something of a one-off, and that the same must be true of Tony Fowler, a big clue to which can be gathered from the press he received in 2010 when it was his name that returned to the national newspapers. Having trained racehorses himself into the early 1990s, the former jockey's attentions had shifted to an at-first-glance steadier and less exciting conveyance when he took on one of the longest milkrounds in the country. It takes him 12 hours on a good day; on a bad day it's 15. In addition to delivering milk in Leicestershire, whatever the weather, he became a local hero for embracing a series of crime-fighting and other community-minded activities carried out while on his round. He was Milkman of the Year 2008 and there was a Pride of Britain award as well before in 2010 he was made an MBE in the New Year's Honours List. In 2013, at the Houses of Parliament, he received a Countryside Alliance award as Rural Hero.

The ensuing publicity has helped Fowler in his equally energetic role as fundraiser for charities and he reports he has now raised millions of pounds, a large proportion of which flooded in as a response to his MBE investiture at Buckingham Palace, an event which achieved international coverage. As one of the headlines, in *The Telegraph*, put it: 'Milkman Dressed As Cow Receives MBE. A milkman dressed as a Friesian cow has been given an MBE by the Queen.' Wearing his black and white jacket and tie – but agreeing late on to swap his similarly patterned trousers for a pair of plain black – Fowler asked the Queen whether he would get a job in her private herd at Windsor. 'No,' she replied, 'mine are Jerseys.'

Fowler says: 'The buzz of racing I can never replace but I get my buzz now out of saving somebody's life and foiling somebody up to no good. The biggest buzz was leaving some people stranded when I drove their getaway car. It was hotwired and I'd never been in a hot car. The original intention was to get in the car, take the keys out and leave them stranded. Of course I get in the car and there are no keys there and all of a sudden one of them sees me and they're all running. Well they're not running to shake my hand are they?'

They are men of several obvious outward contrasts, the milkman and the city gent who battled it out up the hill at Cheltenham in 1982. But there are similarities too. 'I love the horse and the horse loves me,' reflects Munro-Wilson. If he sees a rag-and-bone man in London he always has to go up and give the horse a pat. For Fowler, 'the horses always came first'. With animals, he says, 'I've been lucky to be given a gift.'

'I always like a challenge in life,' asserts Fowler, while for Munro-Wilson it is a case of 'I've treated everything as "Well, let's have a go."' Both of these seem to be considerable understatements. 'I've been passionate about it,' continues Munro-Wilson, 'but always done it with a bit of a smile and never taken myself too seriously.' Over the years, 'Corinthian' has signified different things and embraced wildly different behaviour, but if there is anything shared among the amateur-riding Corinthians at Cheltenham, this have-one-hell-of-a-go attitude has to be it and in 1982 the result was a duel that made this renewal of the Foxhunter a Festival legend.

CHAPTER FIVE

1984 ARKLE CHALLENGE TROPHY CHASE

The Two Bankers in One Race

TO FIND OUT who is the best. It is one of the most fundamental desires of anyone who follows sport, from match to match and race to race; and in jumps racing the Cheltenham Festival serves the purpose as well as any meeting can. More literally, this may be a case of who is the best on a certain day, at a certain course and under a certain set of conditions, but with the vast majority of top horses being targeted at the Festival, and with trainers aiming to get them there at their best, this is the meeting at which most of the champions are decided.

In 1992, Desert Orchid's owner Richard Burridge made an observation about the regularly exasperating traffic management on the approaches to Prestbury Park which an awful lot of Festival racegoers will relate to. 'Getting to Cheltenham is easy,' he wrote in *The Grey Horse*. 'Whenever you come to a sign telling you to go one way to the course, you go the other way.' In a more figurative sense as well, it seems that all roads in National Hunt racing lead to Cheltenham.

The Two Bankers in One Race

In this case, though, the sport is big enough that congestion is not a prerequisite of getting there and the roads taken by championship contenders do not necessarily intersect before they arrive at the Festival. When a putative champion from Ireland is due to take on one from Britain the journeys are far enough apart that the form can be hard to equate and the anticipation acute.

From whatever starting point, the route to top honours in steeplechasing is a matter of years and it is seldom easy. Recognising that a horse has the potential to make that journey is usually more of a process but sometimes it can come in a moment.

~

During the 1980/81 season, hopes were building at Eddie Harty's in Ireland that just such a horse resided in their stables. The jockey (now trainer) Pat Murphy was attached to the yard. 'This horse was so good,' declares Murphy, 'we used to have two different horses to work with him – one would have to jump in at halfway.'

In October when the vaunted four-year-old gelding by Deep Run appeared in a maiden hurdle at Fairyhouse for his second race, connections went for 'a massive touch'. Murphy was in the saddle. He passed the post first and lost the race in the stewards' room. Consternation ensued but, with Harty telling him not to worry and that they would get the money back, the jockey's feeling once more turned to a burgeoning confidence. The recovery mission would take place two runs later, in a bumper at Leopardstown on Friday May 8. The horse was made ready, with Murphy riding him in another maiden hurdle, finishing down the field, and in his work at home.

About ten days before Leopardstown, Murphy received a phone call from the trainer Francis Flood. 'He said could I meet him down at the Curragh. There were a few young horses he wants to work and could I sit on one. So I rode this horse work and Jesus he gave me some feel. I knew nothing about it – it was a chestnut horse, that's all I knew. I pulled up and said, "Francis, this is some tool." I said, "Bloody hell, what's this?" and he wouldn't really tell me.'

With his interest more than a little piqued, Murphy offered his opinion that the horse was ready to run, to which Flood replied, "Yes, we're going to run him in the bumper at Leopardstown next Friday."'

Urging the trainer not to did not work. 'I said, "Francis, don't. Don't because you won't win." He said, "The owners are all lined up and I think this is the best horse I've ever had." I said, "He might be the best horse you've ever had but take it from me he is not the best horse in the race."'

Frank Berry was the Flood stable jockey but, with the race confined to amateur riders, he was not on board their horse at Leopardstown. Anthony Powell had that responsibility, with Ted Walsh on the Harty runner, and as Berry says: 'Both camps were up for it, both fancied their horses and both backed them on the day. So it was a real good race.'

They were sent off 2-1 co-favourites in a field of 29. Murphy was a licensed jockey but admits that it was not just the respective owners and trainers who had been lining up a bet. The chance to latch on to a horse of this quality but so little exposure came along very rarely, and yet here were two of them in the same race. Murphy stuck with his original plan, with the horse he knew best, and he describes what happened to it: 'This horse of Francis Flood's, he was a bit keen and ended up making the running. Passing the seven-furlong start on the far side and I'm beginning to panic a little bit because Ted is stuck in a pocket. He can't get out and this thing is getting away in front. Anyway Ted didn't get out until passing the second-last fence. He made up about ten lengths in the straight.'

He made up about ten lengths but was beaten by three.

As Murphy bemoans, 'I've ridden both of them in their last gallops and picked the wrong one.'

The runner-up in that bumper was Half Free and he never did win a race for Harty. That is, however, because he entered the ownership of Sheikh Ali Abu Khamsin before the following season and, trained by Fred Winter, went on to become an institution at Cheltenham where he won eight times including two Mackeson Gold Cups, two Cathcarts and one Mildmay of Flete.

And the Francis Flood horse who beat Half Free at Leopardstown? He was called Bobsline.

~

In Scotland, the four-year-old chestnut Noddy's Ryde completed that 1980/81 season in contrastingly low-key fashion. His trainer Sue Chesmore then retired and Noddy's Ryde made the journey from her Melrose stables to those of Gordon Richards at Greystoke near Penrith. He was not the only one. One evening, a week or ten days after the arrival of the horse, there was a knock at Richards' front door. Standing there was a young Scotsman, unknown to the trainer and unannounced. Martin Todhunter, in the early years of his 18-year stint at Greystoke, recalls that the conversation commenced in a manner which caused the trainer some surprise:

'I've come to do my horse,' declared the visitor.

'Which horse is that?'

'Noddy's Ryde,' stated the stranger. 'Where he goes I go.'

To which the trainer's response was, 'Well, I'd better give you a job then.'

Tom McCormack had looked after Noddy's Ryde during his time at Chesmore's. 'His horse' had had seven races over hurdles that season, often against Richards-trained rivals – finishing second once – but arguably made as large an impression on the wider world at Ayr in his final outing when pulling hard and making some of the running before being brought down two out. On first impressions at Greystoke, Noddy's Ryde was labelled a big, backward type. As Todhunter points out, 'Tom saw the future in him before we did, obviously.'

~

Given the manner of McCormack's arrival at Greystoke, it is not altogether surprising to hear Todhunter, his new colleague, say that: 'He was a great character, Tom. He was probably as mad as a March hare, but he loved his horses. He took no prisoners. He had wild eyes and was an abrupt sort of Scotsman. I don't know whether you know Scotsmen or not, but half the time you think they're arguing with you they're only talking to you, aren't they?'

Confirming that McCormack's opinion of Noddy's Ryde was probably his most forthright, Todhunter says, 'He absolutely adored him. He adored all the horses, but him especially. He was a bit of a loner but a lovely fella and he loved his job.'

To illustrate McCormack's attitude to the job, both Todhunter and the Greystoke jockey Neale Doughty cite an incident one night at the stables when it was pouring with rain. Doughty was returning from the races: 'He was the most dedicated lad who ever looked after a horse. We were driving back into the yard, the lads had all long gone home, and we picked up Tom in the headlights of the car. Gordon said, "Where are you going, Tom?" And he said, "I'm on my way home. I couldn't remember whether I'd picked out my horse's feet or not, so I thought right I'll walk back and check."'

McCormack's digs were a caravan about three miles away. Doughty observes: 'He'd walked back across the fields to check whether he had picked his horse's feet out or not, and he had. But it was bothering him that he hadn't.

He wasn't bothered [about the wasted journey], he was just relieved. He was amazing.'

McCormack's pride and joy was a striking chestnut with a star on his face and four white socks, a tall horse but unfurnished. At his age he did not possess the strength to match his size but that physique offered long-term promise. 'The old man used to have a saying,' recalls Todhunter. 'I'm six foot, just over, and he was pretty small and if he couldn't see me over his wither when we were saddling up he used to say, "This is a proper horse." And that certainly went with Noddy's.'

The concept of a horse growing into its frame is frequently aired – how many horses change hands on that assumption? – but its doing so is not an inevitability. Then, in addition to the physical development of the animal, a trainer also has to deal with the mental side. When asked what Noddy's Ryde was like in his box, Neale Doughty replies: 'From what I can remember he was very kind, but out the door he was an Action Man.'

'You knew he was there,' comments Todhunter, dryly. Both men recall that on some mornings Noddy's Ryde would emerge from his box and scatter the string. Doughty gives more detail: 'As soon as you were legged up on him he'd be sort of sideways down the drive, snorting and prancing. He was like a really red-hot colt when he first came to us. A bit of a lad like. He'd disrupt the string, so we let him lead and let him get off on his own. He would walk quite fast – he did everything in a hurry.'

This attitude carried over to the gallops where Noddy's Ryde could be worked with other horses although it was often wiser not to. 'So that he didn't overdo himself we just worked away on our own with him,' remembers Doughty. 'He was quite competitive.'

With the experience of other would-be partners not proving entirely successful, Doughty and McCormack were virtually the only ones to ride Noddy's Ryde at home. Under Doughty he returned to racecourse action in October and won at Perth by 15 lengths. Completing three runs in the space of a month, he scored at Catterick by seven lengths and Newcastle by three. The last leg of that hat-trick was in the Comedy Of Errors Novices' Hurdle on Fighting Fifth day, and three starts later he appeared on the Scottish Champion Hurdle card. On this occasion, however, Doughty could not renew the partnership: 'I'd broken a collarbone. I think Jonjo [O'Neill] and Ron [Barry] wanted to ride but the old man knew if he put them on he couldn't get them off again. They'd want to be on him all the time. Jonjo wasn't in the yard, Ron was coming round to retirement, he was only going to go on for a year or two, and the old man he wanted me to be a part of him. So he rang John Francome and John said, "Look, I'll only ride him if Neale is definitely hurt. I'm not going to jock the lad off."'

Doughty confirms that he and Francome have remained great friends. The ride at Ayr, however, was not a winning one. 'I've just run into Dick Turpin,' pronounced Francome after Noddy's Ryde passed the post first and was then disqualified for interference.

Much worse was to follow not long afterwards when Noddy's Ryde's owner died. Despite the trainer's entreaties, his children decided the horse would be sold. Three years earlier, as a two-year-old, Noddy's Ryde had gone to the Doncaster August Sales and made 5,000 guineas, among the selling points being that his dam Rydewell had won three times as a juvenile hurdler, including twice at Cheltenham, while one of her earlier foals, Celtic Ryde, had just finished second at the Festival in the Triumph. In the three seasons after that, Celtic Ryde was one of the best hurdlers in Britain before being killed in a fall at Haydock.

With Noddy's Ryde now having advertised himself in that first campaign with Richards, a sizeable sum would this time be required to purchase him but, in what threatened to be most unfortunate timing, the trainer had recently made a considerable outlay on the installation of an all-weather gallop. McCormack might have wondered at whose door he would have to appear next.

'Doughts tipped a load of money on the desk, didn't he?' says Todhunter. 'He offered the old man all his savings to make sure he got him back.'

While the money was not literally deposited on the desk, Doughty confirms: 'I told the old man, "Make sure you come back with this horse." He said, "How much does he mean to you?", and I said, "Well, I've only got 3,000 quid left because I've changed cars, but you can have it – make sure he comes back." If I hadn't changed cars I'd have given him more.'

On the plus side for Noddy's Ryde's prospects of remaining at the yard, they were quietly confident that, away from home, he would not be seen to best effect. This was chiefly because of his temperament. For a horse in demand at the sales, the preliminaries can involve repeated examinations in and out of the box and being paraded up and down.

'He didn't like any of that nonsense,' reports Doughty. 'He was sweating up in his box and all the rest of it. He was a bit of a character and he liked the nice life at home. People going in and feeling him and messing around with him, it drove him mad. We knew of that of course – that was in our favour.'

Noddy's Ryde was led into the sales ring, with Doughty among those watching on: 'There was no interest for a while. We thought we were going to get him back for peanuts and then all of a sudden somebody stepped in and started bidding and then the old man had to jump in.'

Late in the build-up, Richards had found a potential buyer. As Doughty says, 'I always felt that I could trust the old man to get him back.' The sum paid was 24,000 guineas. The new owner of Noddy's Ryde was businessman Peter

Hinchliff, and Noddy's Ryde made the journey back to Greystoke.

~

The owner of Bobsline was Bob Kelsey. As Francis Flood describes him: 'He was a farmer and he was in racing for a very, very long time. He lived right beside the Maze racecourse, Down Royal, that's where he lived. He was the straight-talking man – what you saw was what you got. He trusted you or he didn't, that were the type of man he'd be. If he trusted you he'd believe in you, and if he didn't it would be doubtful.'

Flood first earned Kelsey's trust by training him not a winner but a hopeless loser. 'The first one he brought wasn't a lot of use and he appreciated me telling him that,' says the trainer. Flood's short tenure of the first horse ensured the arrival of a rather more talented animal, a chestnut son of High Line with the unusual markings of a white blaze all the way down his face and three white socks.

The trainer's son, Fran, reports that Bobsline would not have impressed at the trot, because he used to wind his front legs and swing them outwards, but once he was galloping those at his Ballynure stables in County Wicklow knew that this horse was something special.

'We liked him,' recalls Flood senior of his initial impressions, 'but the more we worked him the better we liked him. The owner came down one day and said, "What do you think? Will this horse pay his way?" and I said, "I think he will."'

Kelsey was a Northern Ireland unionist but it was his religion rather than his politics that played a role in his racing life – he did not want to race on a Sunday. On any other day of the week he loved a bet.

The plunge at Leopardstown was Bobsline's only start in a bumper, following two maiden hurdles in which he had been sent off among the '50-1 others'. When Bobsline was a new arrival, Frank Berry remembers that he was 'a little bit quirky and had his own ideas about things'. That settled down after a few months, although 'settling' was not a description that easily fitted Bobsline.

His trainer recalls: 'He was a fine, big, strong horse, about 16.2, but he was inclined to be very, very free in his early days. He used to take a very strong hold.'

The man assigned to look after him was Larry Dunne, Flood's right-hand man for many years, who says: 'When you'd be rubbing him over in the evening he'd try and bite you and that. He was playful. And then when you'd be riding him out he'd pull the arms out of you.' When Bobsline was out of his box, as Dunne describes it, 'he was always jig jogging and showing himself off.'

On both the gallops and races, this outlook could have had seriously negative ramifications had it got out of hand. Copious schooling and the first two runs over hurdles were designed to encourage Bobsline to settle down. Indeed it was not long before he was schooled over fences with the same intentions. 'Always a bit hyper' is one description that Berry has of him, and the jockey continues: 'He was a very short horse in front to ride, he hadn't much front on him, and he could pull hard.'

After his bumper was a case of job done, and he was put away for the summer, Bobsline returned for a hurdling campaign in earnest the following season and won twice in December, the fitting of a new bridle making a big difference as it enabled Berry to exert a little more control. A shoulder problem, however, interrupted Bobsline's season and denied him an appearance in a novice hurdle at the Cheltenham Festival.

In a second full campaign over hurdles, he won three times and was a close fourth under 10st in Ireland's top handicap hurdle, the Sweeps at Leopardstown, in January, although on that occasion he still left Berry rather disappointed and feeling that his mount was not at his best.

～

For Noddy's Ryde, that season was over before Bobsline's had begun. His first race carrying the Hinchliff colours was completed in fine style with victory in a handicap at Cheltenham in October, but one month later on another visit south he was tailed off throughout at Sandown.

'He wasn't right and Doughts looked after him,' reports Todhunter, by now the travelling head lad. With Noddy's Ryde having started favourite, there were repercussions. 'The crowd were going mental and coming up that walk, in front of those rhododendrons, they were throwing plastic bottles at him. Because he never moved on him. Typical of Neale. He didn't give a bollocks about anybody else. He looked after the horse, and that's what made the horse. He could have bottomed the horse and finished him.'

Noddy's Ryde returned from Sandown dehydrated and looking in poor condition. A bug swept the Richards yard and, after an initial plan to get him ready for the Swinton in the spring, the trainer decided to let him be. As Doughty reflects, 'It was the best thing we could have done.'

～

'Father would never overcook them when they were babies, because he was a specialist steeplechase trainer as much as anything, wasn't he?' observes the trainer's son, Nicky Richards.

Todhunter also stresses that his boss would give his horses all the time they needed. Just as Richards liked to find himself next to 'a proper horse', so he also valued 'proper money'. This was a reference to those owners not fixated on swift returns.

The Two Bankers in One Race

Born and raised in Bath, Gordon Richards was sent away from home to commence his life in racing at the age of 11 and apprenticed soon afterwards to leading trainers Jack Waugh then Ivor Anthony. Barely into his teens, when the blood was up during one of his first rides on the Flat and he disobeyed his riding instructions, the punishment from Waugh was to be whipped.

As a 20-year-old, Richards made the move north and his career in the saddle as a jumps jockey lasted until he broke his back in a fall at the age of 29. Five years later he was training and from 1967 he trained on the estate at Greystoke. 'He was a Somerset man but he loved training at Greystoke, and it suited his way of training,' relates Nicky Richards. 'It suited the type of horse that he loved to train, a big chasing sort of horse, be it a two-mile horse like Noddy's Ryde and Little Bay, right through to Lucius and Hallo Dandy.' The last two of those stable stars were the two Gordon Richards-trained winners of the Grand National.

His son continues, 'It suits a steeplechasing horse because there's so much variety here. It's one of the proper old-fashioned training regimes. You've got to take your time with our horses. You'd be out an hour and a quarter, an hour and a half every day, and some days they would never see another horse. You could send him out for a week and he'd never see another horse.'

Neale Doughty joined the yard in 1979/80 and went on to have two sustained periods as the stable's number one jockey. Doughty's description of his boss is that: 'He loved his horses, absolutely loved them. If you went in the yard early in the morning, you'd see the old man in there walking around, checking his horses, feeding horses and doing stuff. He'd be one of the first in the yard and he'd be one of the last to leave as well. He loved the horses' side more than the business side of it, I think. He was a horseman, an old-fashioned horseman.'

Gordon Richards was only the fourth jumps trainer ever to register 100 winners in a season and in 1975/76 no other trainer sent out more winners than he did. On television, I thought that the man who mopped up races in the north but retained his Somerset brogue came across as genial and even a touch eccentric given his winning turn of phrase, but in reality there was nothing folksy about him.

'Well, he was a tough, hard man my father, wasn't he?' says Nicky Richards. 'Very, very hard,' says Todhunter. In John Budden's biography of Richards, *The Boss*, the words 'short fuse' crop up quite a lot, and his son elaborates: 'If he had something to say he wouldn't be too long in coming and telling you – you know what I mean. And he didn't care who it was – jockeys, owners, stewards, stable lads, anybody. They'd soon get a sharp reminder of what he thought. He wasn't too bad really, as long as the game was played his way at Greystoke anyway.'

Among many of those who worked for him, however, Richards inspired great loyalty. Those who stayed at Greystoke usually stayed for a long time, but in Neale Doughty there was another man at the stables who could be strong both in opinions and his expressing of them.

'Him and I fell out on a regular basis,' discloses the jockey. 'I think the press said I was sacked twice – it was probably about 14 or 15 times. We were very, very similar in that we were both quite competitive and wouldn't take any nonsense. And sometimes we just crossed swords.'

Martin Todhunter tells an anecdote that gives a flavour of the dynamic Richards–Doughty partnership and that competitiveness: 'Neale Doughty was a great horseman. A great chase jockey. He took no prisoners. I remember one day at Perth, Richard Dunwoody come up to ride and it was before cameras in those days. Going down the back Dunwoody decided to poke up his inner, and anyway Doughts shut the door on him once; he kept coming and then he shut it again, and the next time he nearly had him over the rails. Dunwoody was champion jockey.

'The old man said to Doughts, "You were a bit hard there, son". And Doughts said, "Well, if they come up here, boss, they've got to learn the rules. They think we're hillbillies."'

The trainer's response to that was, 'You're right, son – you should have put him over the rails.'

As relayed to me, interspersed between these words were others that those of a sensitive disposition might have found perturbing.

~

Bobsline and Noddy's Ryde entered the summer of 1983 as promising, physically scopey horses who had shown plenty of ability. But neither possessed that high a profile for a horse about to graduate to top-class chasing honours. With Timeform, Bobsline had a rating of 146, which put him within striking distance, but Noddy's Ryde was on 121. However, if they were not standout candidates for novice chasing to the wider world, both camps experienced a mounting confidence that they might know better.

At Greystoke, Tom McCormack had not been alone for long with his belief in Noddy's Ryde. The horse was strengthening and maturing all the time and, in Martin Todhunter's words, 'he was a 110 per center at home,' so his capabilities became very evident.

For years the top dog on the Richards gallops had been Little Bay. Two years older than Noddy's Ryde and with a high standing since 1979/80, Little Bay was one of the sport's great jokers on the racecourse, a high-class two-mile chaser who eventually ended his career in 1988 with a win at the age of 13, which took his victory tally to 21 from 81 starts over jumps. But he was better known for those races he could have won and didn't, opting instead to throw them away after hitting the front.

As Timeform put it in 1981/82, 'No horse succeeded in snatching defeat from the jaws of victory more often than Little Bay,' but away from the racecourse the story was very different. On the gallops he was untouchable. 'Little Bay was brilliant at home,' remembers Doughty, 'and if anything could go anywhere near him we knew we had a half-decent horse.'

Early in Noddy's Ryde's second season with Richards, the time arrived for the trainer to find out what his up-and-coming hurdler could do against the gallops star. Doughty was on Noddy's Ryde and Ron Barry was on Little Bay. 'We'd breezed up over a couple of hurdles and we were going to accelerate to the top of the gallop,' recollects Doughty, 'and I don't think Big Ron had been as fast for a long time, I can tell you that now.'

Even 30 years later, it is not hard to gauge the heady and bullish reaction which Doughty experienced from that gallop. From a very early stage it was clear that the younger horse was not just rising to the challenge. 'He just had him and that's it,' states the jockey. As Doughty puts it, Little Bay had never been beaten in a gallop, but he had now, and 'from then on the old man kept them separate because Little Bay couldn't cope with Noddy's. They never went near each other.'

After that, the task with Noddy's Ryde in his work was chiefly one of trying to rein him in. It may not have been apparent to the racing public but the pecking order in the stable string had changed. Not that it was always conceded even at Greystoke. 'His eyes would light up if you mentioned Noddy's Ryde,' says Todhunter, recalling an image of Tom McCormack. 'We used to take the mickey by saying that Little Bay was better.'

~

GOING CHASING

Bobsline and Noddy's Ryde could run, and Noddy's Ryde could run a lot better than the professional handicappers were willing to accept, but of course there is one more vital part of the equation for these graduates to steeplechasing. They were very slick jumpers of a hurdle, but could they jump a fence? Readers may already have guessed that they could.

As the chapter on the 1986 Gold Cup makes very clear, the switch from hurdling to chasing is sometimes not at all smooth, even for the most fluent jumper of a hurdle; but with Bobsline in the summer of 1983 there could be an unusually high level of confidence that he would manage it because this was not by any means his first attempt.

'We schooled him early on over fences,' says Francis Flood, 'even before we ran him over hurdles. He was inclined to be so free, so it was to get him to steady up a bit. To relax a bit. Before he even ran over hurdles we were jumping him over fences. That was very early and we knew he liked it.'

Of Bobsline's return to jumping fences in earnest, Frank Berry recalls: 'When we started back over fences with him he was electric. He was really a very slick jumper.' Berry did most of the schooling and rode Bobsline in nearly all of his races in his first two seasons chasing, but Larry Dunne also partnered him at home. 'He was a natural lepper,' says Dunne.

I remark that it must have been a thrill for him to take Bobsline over fences:

'It was,' he remembers, chuckling. 'It would make the hair stand on your head.'

~

Noddy's Ryde, on the other hand, had never faced up to a fence. When he had been sent to the Doncaster Sales one year earlier and those at Greystoke tested their resolve to bring him back, Gordon Richards asked Neale Doughty whether he was sure the horse would jump a fence and was told, 'Don't worry, he'll fly them.'

The time had now come to find out and Doughty remembers: 'I wasn't nervous at all but Gordon was. There were great expectations for the horse and he just wanted everything to go well.'

The jockey describes what horses at Greystoke would encounter in a schooling session: 'He had a line of three fences and loads of other little obstacles – barrels, telegraph poles, hurdles – and you might go and jump four or five small jumps and then go up over three fences three times. So in a schooling session you might jump nine fences and you might have jumped ten or 15 other small jumps before the bigger ones.'

Gordon Richards was not one of those to make a big thing of a schooling session but in this instance it was impossible to deny a sense of occasion. Todhunter was one of those watching: 'Some mornings the string would be privy to watch the schooling sessions. We'd just walk round on the side, maybe two or three hundred yards away from the fences, and he would pick the ones out to school. We were there that morning.'

Noddy's Ryde set off in company with what Doughty labels an old handicapper, and in no time at all the younger horse was out on his own. 'Neale Doughty always said that when he jumps a fence you'll see the best of him,' reflects Todhunter.

And he was quite right?

'Oh, he was very right.'

Once the session was completed the jockey compared notes with the trainer: 'He said, "What do you think, Neale?", and I said, "He's just amazing, absolutely amazing." He was a fantastic horse and Gordon, he couldn't believe what he was seeing.'

The Two Bankers in One Race

~

It can be argued that the races most crucial to a successful Festival are those that precede it. The same Festival contests from earlier years provide history, heritage and prestige. Other races on the calendar put those at the Festival in context, an exalted one, and those in the same season also provide almost all of the cast list, with copious pre-publicity. In the 1983/84 season, Noddy's Ryde and Bobsline provided reams of it.

First into action in novice chases was Noddy's Ryde, and he swiftly made up for all the frustration of time lost in the previous season. On September 14, he was 8-15 in a five-runner race at Wetherby and led at the eighth of 12 fences to win by ten lengths. Already, Neale Doughty was in no doubt about what he had in his hands, telling the press, 'This fellow is top class and I'm not frightened of anything the Dickinsons might have in their locker.'

Thirty years later, Doughty reflects: 'I can remember him jumping one fence down the back and when they came back in everybody said, "Blooming heck, he passed about three or four in the air," and I said, "Yup. That's him. And when I let him go you won't have seen anything like it."'

That October, Noddy's Ryde added further wins at Ayr by 12 lengths and Cheltenham by 15. Previewing the latter race, *The Sporting Life*'s Man On The Spot described Noddy's Ryde at Ayr as 'extremely impressive, jumping to the front at the fifth and coming home at his leisure while putting in some fabulous leaps.' Faced with the undulations and variety of fences at Cheltenham, in Doughty's words, Noddy's Ryde 'cantered round, never came off the bridle.'

At the start of November, however, there was another fruitless trip to Sandown. 'Torvill and Dean would have felt at ease,' joked Geoff Lester in the *Life*, but Noddy's Ryde was not at his ease, and in a three-runner, one-finisher race he slipped up at 1-3 while attempting to jump the sixth fence. Most unusually, and a mark of the powerful earlier impressions, the post-Sandown headline in *The Sporting Life* was focused on this mid-race faller rather than any of the winners.

Five days later at Punchestown it was the turn of Bobsline to step up and he too launched his chasing career with a win, but the performance was not without blemish. *The Irish Field* reported: 'But for losing ground constantly over the fences, by darting to the left, the otherwise slick jumping Bobsline would have won by more than the head by which he prevailed over Royal Fair.' Bobsline had jumped to his left over hurdles too, but this was more marked.

At the end of the week, Noddy's Ryde was back in action and back at Cheltenham. Just eight days after the Sandown debacle, there might have been a question over his confidence and other possible after-effects, but none were evident as he led at the third in a three-runner race and won easily by ten lengths.

With two rounds of the Old Course at Cheltenham in the autumn, Noddy's Ryde had received valuable practice over the same course and distance as the Arkle Challenge Trophy at the Festival, easily the season's most important prize for two-mile novice chasers. Of course, it was not by accident. Todhunter describes the yard's attitude to Festival challenges: 'We didn't have a lot of runners really. He wouldn't waste running one down there if he didn't think they were good enough.' Asked at what stage those at Greystoke began to think of Noddy's Ryde as an Arkle propect, Todhunter declares: 'As soon as he jumped a fence.'

However, as Gordon Richards told the press after the horse's second stroll around Prestbury Park, there was an important proviso: 'He's all right on good to soft ground, but he's no good if it's bottomless.' In 1983, the official going at the Festival had been good to soft but in 1979, 1980, 1981 and 1982 it had been either soft or heavy. In the face of statistics like that, Richards could not make the Arkle the be-all and end-all of his campaign for Noddy's Ryde. 'It would be great if it happened but it wouldn't be the end of the world if it didn't,' is how Nicky Richards summarises his father's way of thinking.

Bobsline, on the other hand, had proved himself thoroughly on soft going, as he demonstrated again at Naas later in November when winning with a great deal more authority than on his chasing debut, on this occasion dealing nonchalantly with rivals headed by the dual Irish Champion Hurdle and Aintree Hurdle winner Daring Run.

Contrasting ground conditions on either side of the Irish Sea continued as both horses set out their stall in December. Or attempted to. First, Noddy's Ryde slipped up for the second time in a month, this time at Newcastle. Neale Doughty was kicked in the stomach during a fall in the previous race and watched on television in the weighing room as Jonjo O'Neill took his place in the 2m4f Dipper Novices' Chase. For the first time as a chaser, Noddy's Ryde did not start odds on. He did not even start favourite, given that this race was over two and a half miles and he was up against the Dickinson-trained Lettoch, one of the season's top staying novices who would end the season caught on the line by Special Cargo in that most famous of all finishes to the Whitbread. But Noddy's Ryde was challenging Lettoch strongly when he sprawled badly on landing at the second last and came almost to a standstill.

It was a defeat but, against an opponent such as Lettoch and over a trip he would not try again, Noddy's Ryde had enhanced his reputation and two weeks later he did so again in the Freebooter at Doncaster. At 5-4 on, he was ten lengths clear and going easily when his nearest rival fell at the final fence, leaving Noddy's Ryde to win by thirty.

One unmistakable feature of the Doncaster race was that Noddy's Ryde went on at the second fence and was never headed thereafter. In none of his races over hurdles for Richards had Noddy's Ryde made the running. In his six outings earlier over fences, he had gone to the front from an early stage only twice and those were when he was up against just two rivals, but at Doncaster it was against seven. However, such was the impression that Noddy's Ryde made in the Freebooter and subsequent pacesetting performances that he ended the season described as 'a natural front-runner' by Timeform, who also recorded that 'no novice's jumping was so consistently brilliant as Noddy's Ryde's in the latest season.'

The new tactics produced an image that fulfilled every aspiration for a fence jumped at speed. Of that metamorphosis, Neale Doughty records: 'He was easy enough to tuck in. It was just that when he went over fences his jumping was that good – he used to gain that much ground at the fence that we found it easier just to lob along in front. You've got 12 fences and if you can get a length at every one you've won a race without coming off the bit. Which more or less happened most times with him. We decided that because he was such a flamboyant jumper we were going to make it with him. He was relaxed in front, nothing was going to take him on and better still nothing was going to bring him down or put him off at the obstacles.'

Comparing his experience on board Noddy's Ryde to that on other horses, Doughty asserts: 'Riding this horse was just something else. He was like a bullet. You'd come into the wings of a fence and he'd lift out of your hands – gone. He found it very, very easy to get from one side of a fence to the other, and for a big horse he was very, very light on his feet.'

Crucially, that dashing style and jumping technique was by no means dependent on prodigious but uncalculating leaps off a long stride: 'Oh no,' says Doughty. 'He was quick, he was neat, he was accurate – he could do anything.'

'He was electric over a fence. He was that quick,' adds Todhunter. 'He took off and landed and was gone.'

With three months to go before the Festival, Noddy's Ryde was given a midwinter break, while Bobsline built towards his ultimate objective at Cheltenham with his third run over fences. On Boxing Day, or Saint Stephen's Day as it's known in Ireland, he won the Dennys Gold Medal Novice Chase at Leopardstown. A close race was expected judging by the betting as he was up against Ballinacurra Lad, who had been impressive in his previous two starts. After what was described overall as a superb display of jumping, Bobsline jumped to his left at the final fence and made contact with his rival, but Frank Berry's mount was travelling much the stronger at the time and raced clear by four lengths, leaving the jockey to report that 'we were always going easily.' Thirty years on, Berry reflects: 'The day with Ballinacurra Lad, he answered all the questions.'

When his chasing campaign began there could not have been any certainty about Bobsline's main objective, but, as his jockey marvels, 'He improved so much from being a hurdler to a chaser. You couldn't have anticipated it that he would be that good. He'd love jumping, he was very quick away from his fences and he just went from strength to strength.' After the clash with Ballinacurra Lad, Flood confirmed to the press that Bobsline's main objective was the Arkle at Cheltenham.

Both horses would have one more outing before the Festival and it was on the same day, February 18. Neither race could have done more to whet the appetite. Bobsline's was the Arkle Perpetual Challenge Cup at Leopardstown, after which Dave Barker in *The Irish Field* reported that the horse was now 'jumping with almost mechanical accuracy', while also pointing out that he had again 'meandered to the left' at the final fence, his only mistake. Timeform raved that Bobsline justified his odds of 5-4 on 'in effortless fashion, jumping fast and fluently throughout.'

Daring Run had been sent on four out, but Bobsline had no difficulty going with him, mastered him at the second last and swiftly went about 20 lengths clear before being eased down to win by twelve from Larry's Latest, Daring Run having cracked before finishing a well-beaten third.

With maturity, Bobsline had developed into an indisputably top-class prospect and Francis Flood is in full agreement with the praise lavished on his stable star. 'He was really a great jumper over fences, and his speed told,' says the trainer. 'He had great power and could stand a long ways off a fence and he always got there.'

At Nottingham 25 minutes later, Noddy's Ryde lined up in the Nottinghamshire Novices' Chase at 11-8 on against four rivals. Of the decision to run him there after his break, Nicky Richards comments: 'It would have been a brave shout to go straight to Cheltenham from Doncaster.'

'I remember it as clear as day,' says Martin Todhunter of Noddy's Ryde at Nottingham, and included in those memories is an incident in the preliminaries: 'The saddling boxes at Nottingham in them days were pretty low when you got into them and I'm pretty tall. I could see over the top and in the next box a certain northern trainer said to whoever was with him, "All I want to do is beat that effing Noddy's Ryde and shut them lot up." When we got out of the saddling boxes, the old man said to me, "Did you hear that?" and I said, "I did."'

Temporarily, Richards became flustered. He knew that Noddy's Ryde had done little work since his rest and he prepared his excuses. They weren't needed, and the nameless rival was probably not best pleased, therefore, when Noddy's Ryde won by 12 lengths on the bridle. 'In that Nottingham race he was outstanding,' says a spellbound Todhunter, with a major stress on the *outstanding*. 'A flat track, winging his fences, and he was hard held – you know, he never moved on him. You had to be there. It was just one of those days that took your breath away.'

The motionless Neale Doughty records: 'He had 19 days in work and he blitzed up, and then it was all systems go for Cheltenham.'

~

Previewing the Arkle in the week before the race, Dave Barker wrote in *The Irish Field*: 'Francis Flood's Bobsline, just below top class as a hurdler, has blossomed into the complete chaser, at least by novice standards. He jumps beautifully and when asked has an impressive turn of foot which can win a race for him when used anywhere inside the last half mile. He looks good in the Arkle Challenge Trophy Chase in spite of the presence of Noddy's Ryde. At Leopardstown last month he jumped his rivals silly to score by a dozen lengths. In my view, Bobsline has only to put in a clear round to win and I expect it to be in majestic style.'

With such an assertion, Barker seemed merely to be reflecting the national mood and I asked Francis Flood what it was like being the man responsible for an Irish banker at the sport's most important meeting. He replies, 'I didn't feel any pressure whatsoever. You can only do your best and that was the way it was.'

'He would have coped with that, no bother,' agrees Fran Flood. Agreeing that the trainer was temperamentally very well equipped for what others have found an enormous pressure, his stable jockey Frank Berry says: 'He was an easy-going man but a very hard worker.'

Flood and jockey Frank Berry had been a team since 1970. Berry relates: 'I went to him when I came out of my time on the Flat and I just started off with the young horses that year and the next year, but I rode the Gold Cup winner for him two years later and we never looked back. He was a great man to ride for, left things to yourself, and I couldn't speak highly enough of him.'

Having been the champion amateur jockey in Ireland seven times, Flood was the champion trainer in Ireland in 1970, and that Gold Cup winner in 1972 was Glencaraig Lady. In two previous appearances at the Festival, the mare had just taken the lead when falling at the last in the 3m novice chase in 1970 and was also in the lead and going easily three out in the following year's Gold Cup when she fell again.

Flood faced a perennial battle getting Glencaraig Lady to the track, due to a knee injury and tendon problems, and he reveals: 'I would say that she was a better mare in 1971 than '72 – she was four or five lengths clear when she fell. I was lucky that I could get her back again.'

When Cheltenham victory came her way at the third attempt, she got up close home with Royal Toss and The Dikler at her quarters. Two objections for the stewards to consider help to indicate that it was an extraordinarily exciting finish. 'It surely was,' reflects Flood. 'That was her last race as well. She finished slightly lame and never ran again.'

The Gold Cup win, amazingly, was Berry's first ever ride at the Festival. 'I hadn't that much experience,' says the jockey, 'and he was all behind putting me up for the Gold Cup. After being unlucky the two previous years, there was a bit of pressure but he had faith in me. We got on great and I had 18 years there.' In that period, Berry was champion jockey in Ireland ten times.

When Berry speaks of Flood's particular strengths as a trainer, the first on the list has a familiar ring to it: 'Patience. He'd give them big jumping horses plenty of time. And he was a good loser, which was a big thing when you're riding for someone.'

Based at Ballynure Stables at Grangecon in County Wicklow throughout his training career, Flood was born and bred in the area as was Larry Dunne. While Dunne is quiet by nature, all who worked with him sing his praises loudly. 'I couldn't give him enough praise,' says Frank Berry. 'Glencaraig Lady had a bit of a leg problem and he used to do hours and hours of road work with her. This was a top-class man.'

It was no accident, therefore, that Dunne was also assigned Bobsline. Berry affirms: 'They couldn't have been in better hands. They weren't straightforward but he was brilliant at his job.' In Bobsline's case, Dunne used to get along best with him and he would mind him like a baby. Flood senior confirms Dunne's importance at the yard and his dedication, adding, 'There's not very many genuine fellows like him around nowadays with the horses.'

After Glencaraig Lady, patience had also been required in the wait for a horse to come along of comparable quality. Now, in Bobsline, that horse had arrived. However, while the trainer felt no extra pressure because of that, in the last couple of weeks before the Festival all at his yard did experience a major anxiety.

Flood explains: 'He won his four races before the Arkle but in the meantime nearly every fortnight he'd have a problem with corns. A week before Cheltenham we had the same problem and he was pretty lame.' In the run-up to the biggest race of his career so far the affliction seemed particularly severe and to Francis Flood and Larry Dunne Bobsline's participation at Cheltenham was touch and go.

Their farrier had got to know Bobsline extremely well. 'He'd take out the corn and then they'd go again. I used to be saying to the farrier, "Make sure this horse is running in a fortnight. Make sure that you have him right for that day," and then two days before he goes lame again and it would be the corns.'

It was a longstanding issue and Berry could recognise when it was surfacing again because Bobline's tendency to hang would become more marked.

'He was very hard to keep sound,' says Larry Dunne. 'Usually coming up to a race he'd go lame and we'd have a headache trying to get him right.' The corns would flare up on one or other of his front feet, sometimes both. As part of his treatment, Bobsline would be stood in a bucket of hot water for two hours a day and although a rather highly strung racehorse would not seem the ideal candidate for such a regimen, Dunne reports that this one would, in fact, quieten right down and behave like the model patient. Bobsline liked it because he was getting relief.

'I remember one day at Naas we had him standing in water and we didn't put a shoe on until half an hour before the race,' recalls Flood of one occasion the previous season. 'He won it as well.' A poultice would also form part of Bobsline's therapy and then, two or three days before a race, if he was sound again all such treatment on his feet would stop.

Fran Flood was at boarding school at the time, but his mind seems to have been focused more on Bobline's preparation for the Arkle and he knew how his father reacted to this troubled build-up: 'He would have made sure no matter how many hours it took, he was definitely going to do everything he could to get him there – to treat his feet any way he could, to do right by the horse and the owner, that was the way he approached it. He'd have been a perfectionist like that and nothing else would matter.'

Flood's team became used to Bobsline and his corns, and their aim was always to keep riding him out. This time approaching the Arkle, unknown it seems to the wider world, the affliction threatened to get the better of him but, says Flood, 'We got him sound. It took until a couple of days before.'

Bobsline flew over from Ireland with Larry Dunne two days before the race and was stabled at the racecourse. On the night before the race Flood slept well – 'I'm always a good sleeper. You can't do anything about it' – but the trainer was far from carefree on arrival at the racecourse the next day. 'I remember going over on the morning of the race to see how he was, and I wouldn't have been surprised if he was lame because he had been lame a few days earlier.'

Although Dunne had lavished even more attention on Bobsline than usual, trying to take extra care that nothing went wrong, he too was nervous that morning. But when the two men met at Bobsline's box, Flood was assured that their horse 'was flying – the horse was in right order.' Bobsline was ridden out by Frank Berry and Flood's conclusion was that 'I felt he was going to run the race of his life.'

~

To the outside world Bobsline and Noddy's Ryde had been on an unbreakable arc from December onwards to clash at Cheltenham. To those on the inside, enabling Bobsline to fulfil that engagement was too great an undertaking for them to be that concerned about their rival. There was, however, a growing awareness, and then a few days before the race Francis Flood was told by someone just how much Gordon Richards fancied Noddy's Ryde. He was told that Richards thought he could not be beaten.

Nicky Richards reflects: 'When you train a horse like him, you build a bit of a belief up in your horse. No doubt Mr Flood had the belief in his horse. They come along and you believe in them.'

While confirming the faith they had, Fran Flood recalls: 'We were worried about Noddy's Ryde. He had such a reputation. Gordon Richards was so bullish about him as well. Everybody in Ireland believed that Bobsline was going to be so hard to beat but they all respected Noddy's Ryde as well and that a man like Gordon Richards held him in such high regard. We weren't taking anything for granted.'

When asked how worried about him he was, Frank Berry replies, 'You're always worried. I was well aware of what he was doing and he was getting good write-ups. It looked a two-horse race in the last couple of weeks.'

Gordon Richards was fully conversant with what Bobsline had been doing in Ireland. Others at Greystoke had taken note of Bobsline's odds as they contracted in the Arkle betting, and Neale Doughty knew which horse he had to beat: 'There were big reports coming out of Ireland about this exceptional horse of Francis Flood's. Yes, big reports all the time. It set it up for a great Cheltenham, didn't it?'

However, in the days before the race, just as Bobsline's corns were resurfacing and then clearing up, the Noddy's Ryde camp had their own cause for concern. Tom McCormack reported something unusual in the horse's behaviour and Neale Doughty records: 'My confidence was only knocked when the lad said he was worried about him because he'd been lying down in his box at home a lot. It was a worry to the lad because he knew him inside out. I was hoping that, oh well, he has had a busy season, maybe he's starting to relax now as he's maturing.'

Nicky Richards reflects: 'He was a high-class lad and he knew the horse very well, so if he'd seen anything like that, a little change in the habits, it might just give you a little bit of doubt in your mind. But I think if father had had any doubts he wouldn't have run him. He'd had a fantastic season and there was no reason not to run him.'

On the day of the race, Todhunter and McCormack set off with Noddy's Ryde for Cheltenham first thing in the morning and Todhunter recalls 'We were concerned obviously but we still went there with a lot of confidence. We were just upbeat about things.'

~

When the Cheltenham pre-publicity can focus on a prospective head-to-head, the anticipation it engenders knows few bounds. In the months before the Festival, Bobsline and Noddy's Ryde would be described as on 'a collision course', but those words have too negative a ring to them. To some of us this collision had the potential to unleash a fantastic positive energy, the sort of thing that could light up 100,000 homes for decades. Or 100,000 memories of the Cheltenham Festival.

A head-to-head echoes the origins of the sport in a match race, one horse against another, but in the modern day things are nearly always more complicated than the headlines would suggest. When the time comes for the race to be run, those head-to-heads have a nasty habit of failing to materialise and only one head might be pushing on to glory, or neither.

For a start, prospective duels usually do a great disservice to the other horses. While the market leaders have made their stately progress around the lesser meetings, others may have been trained to peak more specifically at Cheltenham; and while a horse may look brilliant in its build-up races, doing the same at the Festival is far more difficult when faced with what is nearly always easily the most competitive race of the season.

As this chapter, and others, will already have made clear, getting to the race in prime condition is not that easy either. It is hard to guarantee that any horse will give its running on a certain day, and much harder when there are two in the equation rather than one. Kauto Star versus Denman was the most frenziedly publicised duel in my racing experience and their four clashes in the Gold Cup were fine races, but I never felt that the two horses were ever at their best on the same day.

Back in 1984, there was not so much at stake with the novice chasers in the Arkle and I do not remember any scarves rolling off the production lines in their respective colours. But Bobsline versus Noddy's Ryde was being talked about by anyone who had an interest in the game and it was billed as a titanic clash. On the front page of *The Sporting Life* that day, the second headline was 'Brilliant Noddy's Ryde will take some catching' and the third headline on the same page read 'Impressive Bobsline should be a banker for Berry'. The headlines acclaimed two bankers in the same race!

While Flood, Dunne and, as one British newspaper reported, a host of Irish racegoers who 'have been yelling the name of Bobsline at us virtually the entire season' were all present at Cheltenham, owner Bob Kelsey remained at home because his wife had had a heart attack. Also remaining on that side of the Irish Sea were Francis Flood's sons Fran and Tom, still at boarding school, the Ballyfin College, Portlaoise. A reception was being held that afternoon in the study hall for members of the Offaly Gaelic Football team and all pupils were instructed to attend. As Fran Flood relates: 'Nobody was allowed out when the presentation was going on but I remember my brother and a few pals of his got up, tapped me on the shoulder and said, "Come on, let's watch the race."'

Bobsline started at 5-4 for the Arkle and Noddy's Ryde 7-4, in an eight-runner field. David Nicholson harboured hopes for his representative, Voice Of Progress, who had won four of his five starts over fences and was sent off at 6-1, with Arthur Moore's The Ellier 16-1 and the rest as outsiders. There were no surprises in the pre-race plans.

'Frank Berry had been riding him in all his races and Frank was a really good judge,' explains Francis Flood. 'He said, "Noddy's Ryde, I won't let him get away too far."'

For Neale Doughty, 'the idea was to hopefully make the running or go at my own pace and if something else took it off me, they took it off me. Then I'd still be there at the bottom of the hill before we turned in. The old man said to me, "Just ride your own race. You know him inside out." He never bothered me with orders and things like that.'

The Two Bankers in One Race

While bowling along in front suited Noddy's Ryde and his rider, it would also be a huge plus for Frank Berry with his efforts to settle Bobsline and not arrive in the firing line too soon. As always, though, Berry was mindful that Bobsline could throw in a jump to his left. As was often the case, to try to combat this tendency Bobsline was fitted with a pricker on the bit on his near side.

When the tapes went up at 2.51 pm, there was immediately something of a surprise when Noddy's Ryde did not make the early running. At 200-1, it was Orp Baltic who set off with the most zeal and he led by a length or two over the first four fences, in front of Noddy's Ryde, with three or four lengths back to the others. 'I didn't make it because I didn't think he was as sprightly as he normally is,' explains Doughty. Behind him, Voice Of Progress was third and Bobsline disputed fourth, rather throwing his big white face around as Berry tried to anchor him.

Completing the turn away from the stands, however, Orp Baltic's moment in the sun was about to end, and the cloud that had eclipsed most predicted images for the race disappeared at the fifth – Noddy's Ryde jumped to his right but he also jumped to the front. After skipping over the water jump, the new leader then met the first open ditch perfectly and emerged from it ahead by seven lengths. The scale of Noddy's Ryde's lead was maintained over the next fence and then Berry asked Bobsline to make his first move.

The vast majority of spectators must have anticipated Noddy's Ryde racing along in front with Bobsline trying to catch him, but when that sight actually materialised it had an electrifying and mesmeric effect. While nearly all of the pursuers rapidly dropped away, Bobsline moved closer. He went into second place, two lengths in front of Voice Of Progress, and as these three went on the others were all tailed off before the fourth last.

Nicky Richards was watching from the house at Greystoke: 'From the top of the hill it was going to be a right old set-to, wasn't it? Two very good horses, two very good novices going at a fantastic gallop and they had a right old go at each other, didn't they? And two very good jockeys I'd have to say as well – two top-class jockeys.'

Crowded around a television at Ballyfin College, the room was now nearly full. The atmosphere as Fran Flood describes it was 'huge' and he was feeling the tension: 'You'd be feeling sick looking at it until it would be over.'

Coming down the hill, both camps had cause for some confidence as their charges were travelling within themselves but next were the downhill fences three out and two out and many a Cheltenham challenge could be wiped out with one false step, or often without one. Glencaraig Lady had lost a Gold Cup at one of those fences on the New Course in 1971. But there was no example in the whole race of Bobsline jumping to his left, not a trace, whereas Noddy's Ryde, who led by three lengths going into the third last, gave away a chunk of that by jumping to the right.

Doughty reports that his mount never jumped to his right at home but did so on the odd occasion at the racecourse. This fence would be one of the most conspicuous examples. Fourteen seconds later they were at the second last and Bobsline had closed to within a length. Almost immediately after landing, Berry gave Bobsline a slap down the shoulder and asked him to join battle. Voice Of Progress was there as well at the second last but the two market leaders were about to surge clear.

Rounding the final turn was where Bobsline and Noddy's Ryde finally, and wonderfully, did go head to head. The momentum seemed to be with the Irish challenger but Noddy's Ryde responded. He had plenty still to give. Jumping the final fence there was a blaze of white as well as chestnut, one white face right next to a white nose.

'I knew I had a bit of horse round the bend, and straightening up for the last I got in a bit close,' says Frank Berry. 'He jumped great but got in a bit tight and landed a little bit steep.'

Alongside him, Noddy's Ryde's partner was also looking for a really good jump at the last but, as Neale Doughty records, he too 'could have done with meeting it on a longer stride. I met it a bit tight but he was still fairly quick over it. He was quick and competitive.'

Neither jockey was able to ask his mount for the prodigious leap he wanted and of which they were capable, but when all the hopes and predictions had been channelled into two miles, twelve fences and nearly four minutes of Festival action, the two protagonists were so closely matched that they landed after the last fence precisely in unison.

Up the run-in it was the same as they matched each other stride for stride a dozen times before Bobsline edged ahead. He drifted right, and Noddy's Ryde never relented with his effort, but at the line Bobsline was in front by just over a length.

Watching from the stable lads' stand, the quiet man Larry Dunne shouted Bobsline home: 'I did, I was hoarse all right. It was the best race that year at Cheltenham. Good, brave horses and good jockeys.'

The post-race celebrations were on a daunting scale but in *The Times* the next day John Karter wrote of Francis Flood's 'soft, lilting tones' and observed that his 'demeanour and sober dress are more evocative of a priest rather than a racehorse trainer and, like Paddy Mullins, he is that comparative rarity – a reticent Irishman.'

Thirty years on, for Flood, 'It was the race of the century nearly, wasn't it?'

~

'We wanted to win the Arkle and we were beaten by a better horse on the day,' states Neale Doughty. 'You've got to take these knocks. You can't have everything, you know. We were disappointed we didn't win. Nobody blamed anybody, and on the day Bobsline was that little bit better than us.'

To the spectators it was the race of the meeting, but could Doughty appreciate that? 'No, I didn't appreciate it. You never do when you get beat, do you?'

Gordon Richards had plaudits for both horses but, as Nicky Richards describes the trainer, 'Father was a very determined man and he didn't really take defeat lying down. You know, you might knock him down but he soon got back up again.'

The Noddy's Ryde camp was eager to see their horse take on Bobsline again. Everyone was. The rematch was a prospect to relish as soon as they passed the post at Cheltenham, but it would never happen.

For the rest of that season, the pair went their separate ways again, with Bobsline winning impressively at Fairyhouse, while Noddy's Ryde did the same at Aintree and then also won at Ayr to make it eight wins from eleven races in the season. Both had confirmed that they were firmly on course for Cheltenham the following March to take on Badsworth Boy, who won the Champion Chase in 1983 and 1984, the latter by ten lengths from Little Bay. When the 1985 renewal arrived, however, there was no runner from Greystoke and in the case of Noddy's Ryde it was for the worst possible of reasons.

'I think Father was looking forward to take the world on,' says Nicky Richards of the anticipation at Greystoke as Noddy's Ryde prepared for his next season. Training in Cumbria, Richards senior did not have runners at racecourses like Devon & Exeter (as it was then known) but, as Martin Todhunter, his travelling head lad, relates: 'The old man always wanted to win the Haldon Gold Cup (Exeter's most prestigious race) because he was from down there, and he's got the horse to do it. He was trained for the race. It was early on in the year but he was trained for it, everything was grand. He travelled well. We had another runner down there, as his companion, and we went down the day before. In the paddock before the race, in front of me, Gordon or Mr Hinchliff was offered a lot of money for him – if my memory serves me right it was a quarter of a million – which was turned down because the owner didn't need the money. He had a very nice horse on his hands.'

The would-be buyer was Sheikh Ali Abu Khamsin, one of whose best horses, Fifty Dollars More, was Noddy's Ryde's only serious rival. At the final fence, Fifty Dollars More was the nearest pursuer to the 1-2 favourite but Noddy's Ryde was a distant speck up ahead of him. As Neale Doughty relates, 'He got up over the fence and as he went to kick to come away his back leg shattered.'

Todhunter remembers: 'We both rushed down, me and Tom. I said to Tom, "I'll hold him" and he said, "You won't." Doughty was inconsolable when we got there. We had one in the last race, which ran. I don't know why we ran it, we should have just come home, but we ran it. He ran poorly.'

'This is one of the most distressing things I have ever seen on a racecourse,' stated Sheikh Ali Abu Khamsin in the aftermath. 'I was devastated, absolutely devastated,' confirms Doughty.

At the end of a terrible afternoon, Doughty and a heartbroken Richards drove back north together. 'It's a very long ride home when they get beat anywhere,' says the jockey, 'but when you lose a good horse like that – he was a once-in-a-lifetime horse wasn't he? It's tragic to lose any horse but when you lose one that you've been looking all your life for, you know what I mean, they are the ones that define your career, aren't they? The lad said to me that the family never seem to last very long. You get a few seasons out of them but they don't have any luck. The lad used to tell me that. He was always terrified because they were exceptional horses.'

Todhunter and McCormack picked up their belongings from where Noddy's Ryde had spent the night before. The journey back to Greystoke is 340 miles. 'I went round the pub and bought a bottle of whisky for Tom, and he drank that all the way home,' confides Todhunter. 'He used to have his flask with his coffee in and he kept pouring the whisky into the flask top. Never said a word. He just drank the whole bottle of whisky, a full bottle of Grouse whisky, and he got out the other end. He was sober as a judge, and away he went.'

~

Having won the Mildmay of Flete at the Festival one day after Bobsline's Arkle, old adversary Half Free scored three times at Cheltenham the following season – including in the Mackeson Gold Cup – and in March he lined up in the Gold Cup itself, finishing a non-staying fifth. Bobsline, too, was back at Prestbury Park, and he started 6-4 on favourite in the Champion Chase, with Badsworth Boy 11-8, the pair of them having scared off all but three other runners.

'I'd say he was a much better horse, a much, much better horse,' says Frank Berry of the Bobsline who went to the Festival in 1985. 'He had a straightforward run to the Champion Chase and he was in marvellous form. He was jumping great and he was cantering all the way down the hill, but he just didn't get out the landing gear. He felt like he'd have won a long way that day.'

Bobsline was caught out by the third last and fell. Worse, he suffered an injury as well, reportedly chipping a bone in a hind leg. It was nothing compared to the sad fate of Noddy's Ryde but Bobsline was never quite the same horse again. Berry's theory is that 'It changed his outlook on jumping a bit. He still was a great lepper – he had a low style of jumping fences, he was very quick into his stride – but from the time he got the fall he always jumped his fences a little bit more careful.'

At the 1986 Festival, Bobsline again started favourite for the Champion but finished fifth, and that was his final visit. Also present at the 1986 meeting was the year-younger Pat Hughes-trained Barrow Line, who, with very similar markings, could not be mistaken for anything other than Bobsline's brother. Incredibly, he had failed to make it to the racecourse until December when he was an eight-year-old due to his physical frailties but he was good enough to start fourth favourite in that season's Sun Alliance Hurdle. Barrow Line was well beaten in that, but then took so well to chasing that he won his first four races before finishing third against top-class opponents in the Irish Gold Cup. He would have been the Irish banker in the 1987 Sun Alliance Chase but for a recurrence of persistent corns.

'That's right,' says Flood. 'Something very similar. It was in the breed.'

Bobsline's problems with corns never got the better of him and, once they had cleared up for good, he was able to enjoy an exceptionally long career. Having been forced to miss the triumph of his horse in the Arkle, Bob Kelsey was present at Cheltenham for the following year's most disappointing loss. When Kelsey died in 1989 he left Bobsline to Francis Flood's wife and the last five of this stable favourite's 26 wins were all registered when, ridden by Fran Flood, he was a teenager.

'The power he had when he'd see a fence was marvellous. He never lost it,' reflects his awestruck partner. 'I think it was a stretch for him to get two and half miles but he'd fight his corner to get it and his jumping was so powerful even to the very, very end.'

Another longstanding feature of Bobsline's jumping remained in evidence and the first of those five wins, at Killarney, is a vivid memory for Flood junior. On the bend past the stands, a rival jockey tried to get up Bobsline's inner, Bobsline's left-hand side. Flood warned him against it. At the third fence down the back straight, the jockey tried again, most ill-advisedly as it turned out because Bobsline jumped left, pushed his opponent through the wings of the fence and there was nothing Flood could do about it. 'My lad was determined to get off the ground first and he was going left and that was it.'

That rival jockey had not done his homework. 'He definitely hadn't,' confirms Flood, 'and he wasn't listening to me either.'

Bobsline's final win came in November as a 14-year-old and he was retired the following year. He spent that retirement at Flood's yard and was stabled close to the house, from which his big, white face could be seen looking out of the stable door.

'You wouldn't forget him in a hurry,' reflects his trainer. When I last spoke with Francis Flood in December 2014 he was 84 years old, his Wicklow accent transmitting great warmth as well as wisdom in his dry sense of humour, and assisted by his son Fran he was still training, 47 years after he first took out a licence.

Larry Dunne worked at the Flood stables for 33 years before a fall, which resulted in a badly broken leg which did not heal properly and prevented his return. Frank Berry retired from the saddle in 1988. After his own training career, he is now the longstanding racing manager to top owner JP McManus.

Eighteen days after Noddy's Ryde came second in the Arkle, Neale Doughty and Gordon Richards had their greatest win together when Hallo Dandy held off Greasepaint in the Grand National. The two men split in 1986 but got back together from 1989 until 1994. 'He wasn't the easiest boss in the world but I miss him and I still wish he was around,' says Doughty in 2014. Richards died in 1998, five months after the Champion Chase triumph and Aintree tragedy of his final stable star, One Man, the last of his five Festival winners. Nicky Richards took over the helm at Greystoke and Martin Todhunter trains about 18 miles away at Orton.

Remembering Noddy's Ryde, Todhunter reveals: 'It is

one of my great regrets. He was the best horse I've ever had anything to do with – in all my times at Greystoke we had some good ones – but I never sat on him. How old was he when he died? Seven? The big horse had just come to himself, and the way the old man trained, he trained for the future.'

And what of Tom McCormack, the man who arrived at Greystoke on the heels of Noddy's Ryde and stayed with him to the end? Todhunter reports that the death of Noddy's Ryde took its toll. McCormack was very quiet for months: 'He looked after some other good horses and he stayed a few years,' continues Todhunter. 'Then he moved to the Midlands somewhere, but where he went after that I don't know.'

Bobsline and Noddy's Ryde ended their Arkle season with Timeform ratings of 161 and 160. The *Chasers & Hurdlers* annuals first covered the 1975/76 season and from then onwards no Arkle winner matched those ratings until Tidal Bay won it by 13 lengths in 2008 to be rated 160 and Sprinter Sacre breezed home seven lengths clear in 2012, earning him a staggering 175. The passage of time has therefore confirmed what those watching the 1984 Arkle must strongly have suspected, that Bobsline and Noddy's Ryde were two of the race's all-time greats. With the novice events at the Cheltenham Festival there is a compelling dual attraction – to find out who is the best (in that division in that particular season) and to find out who could be the best (in future seasons among all horses over that distance). After that race in 1984 which yielded so much and promised even more, the future for Bobsline and Noddy's Ryde could not have been guessed at. The Arkle was their Festival moment.

CHAPTER SIX

1986 DAILY EXPRESS TRIUMPH HURDLE

The Duke's Long Wait

WALKING UP THE par four 13th hole at Cleeve Hill Golf Club is to be treated to one of the greatest views I know in sport. This course was the scene of my first ever birdie (there have not been many) and one of my best-struck but slightly less well-directed approach shots (the sheep was okay), but the view I am talking about has nothing to do with golf, apart from it being from a golf course. At the sight of it, the natural reaction is to forget what you were doing and gaze in wonder.

The 13th is 435 yards long and the fairway lies straight ahead. A hacker such as me could wish for nothing more as, wide and inviting, it climbs steadily uphill and almost due west.

This is a place for skylarks as well as golfers. The green is out of sight but about two-thirds of the way, in the middle of the fairway, there is a marker post on the horizon, and in striding towards it that horizon alters and the eyes will start to shift their focus: having travelled the distance of one duffed tee shot, console yourself by looking north west some 16 miles away to the Malvern Hills; nearly halfway to the Malverns, the 12th-century tower of Tewkesbury Abbey climbs 150 feet out of the Severn Vale; walk another 80 yards and Gloucester comes into view, 11 miles away and dead ahead, and beyond that rise the Brecon Beacons and the Black Mountains. According to a nearby trig point, the Black Mountains are 77 miles away. Turning towards the south, it is said that on a clear day you can see 90 miles to Exmoor.

For those looking back to see whether there are other, less distracted golfers queuing to be waved through, about two and a half miles past the 13th tee rest the Cotswold stones of one of the area's most ancient towns, Winchcombe, and next to it, in its pastoral idyll, lies Sudeley Castle where Catherine Parr celebrated her survival as the sixth and last wife of Henry VIII. Closer is a neolithic monument, the long barrow of Belas Knap.

Relocating to the present and turning again at the fairway marker, the green ahead is protected by the diving ditch and soaring bank of an Iron Age hill fort, which the golf club claims are 'probably the oldest man-made golfing hazards in the world'. Men and women have lived on these hills for at least ten thousand years. They have fought too: down in the valley, on May 4, 1471, eleven thousand men met just outside Tewkesbury in one bloody phase of the Wars of the Roses, to seal the death of a king and his heir.

When the chipping and putting is done and dusted, on the far side of the 13th green there is a bench, one that I imagine is very well used. We are much closer to the Cotswold escarpment; the view into the valley stretches out over pretty much 180 degrees; Cheltenham is there now, with the village of Prestbury next to it, and lying about 240 metres beneath our feet is the Racecourse. The lives of many generations of my family have been played out in the Severn Vale. To gaze over this expanse from this vantage point, I know where I came from and believe I know where I belong.

At The Festival

~

One other person to whom, I feel certain, this view meant a great deal was David Nicholson. I don't know how keen he was on golf, but it would be a surprise if anyone had a greater passion for Cheltenham Racecourse and the sport that enjoys so many of its greatest days there. He would have known this view intimately because about half a mile further along the escarpment is where, every day, the horses trained by his father Herbert 'Frenchie' Nicholson would emerge for exercise; or rather for more of it, because the greater part of their labours came from just getting up there. On leaving Prestbury, the Nicholson horses had to snake up the escarpment like a mule train. It took about 40 minutes. Once at the summit on a summer's morning it must have seemed like heaven, and Frenchie would proclaim to his lads that other less fortunate people would pay good money to be doing this. In the winter, few places can have seemed more exposed. When it was cold and wet, restraining the horses in a slow canter could be hellishly difficult, and when it was foggy to restrain them was a mortal necessity. From a very young age, already bent on being a jockey, David Nicholson would have had his opportunity, the fog and cloud line permitting, to survey the Severn Valley every morning with both first and second lot. At one period he would have been up there in the afternoons as well, helping his father's apprentices pick up stones from the gallops.

From infancy until he was married, his home was never more than a furlong from Cheltenham Racecourse. Next to Frenchie's stables there was a field, then the racecourse, and Richard Nicholson, David's younger brother by four years, describes the sort of thing that might be seen at the bottom of that field on a raceday. 'When I was very, very small,' he relates, 'I remember leaning across the stile, overlooking the racecourse. It would be the late '40s, my father was still riding then and as he went past he said, "Hello son, how you doing?"' The Nicholson schooling fences and hurdles were laid out in that field alongside the course, roughly adjacent to where the water jump is now, and David Nicholson was riding schooling sessions over those hurdles before he was a teenager.

From whichever vantage point, the views of Prestbury and the racecourse meant much more to him than mere familiarity, and the family's ties to the racecourse did not begin with his father. From 1819 until 1830, Cheltenham's first race meetings were on Cleeve Hill (50,000 people were said to have attended in 1825) and David Nicholson's family had been integral to the local racing community for almost as long. Frenchie himself moved to Prestbury in 1939, with his wife Diana and the infant David, removed from Epsom by the onset of war, but Diana's great grandfather William Holman had settled in Prestbury in 1834. The Grand Annual Chase, still contested at the Festival, was then the most important race in the calendar and Holman rode the winner five times. He also trained the winners of three Grand Nationals. Under Holman's sons the family's involvement in the sport was embedded and extended, and once steeplechasing had finally settled at Prestbury Park, it was one of those sons, Alfred Holman, who had designed and built the course when the first Cheltenham National Hunt Race Meeting (the Cheltenham Festival) took place in 1911.

In David Nicholson's home there are two plaques made by his grandmother to display horseshoes from William Holman's famous victories, and there are more such trophies spread around the family because there was no shortage of these victories. 'He was Cheltenham in his day,' David used to proclaim, and somewhere along the line there grew in him an ambition for something very similar. When I was stepping out in racing at the onset of the 1980s,

Frenchie Nicholson was a legend in Gloucestershire and David Nicholson was the area's biggest racing personality. Between a legend and a personality there is a big difference. David Nicholson's attempts to bridge the gap amounted to an epic quest and anyone with half an interest in the sport was left with no choice but to take notice of it.

~

Personality is something that David Nicholson was never short of and a large part of it seemed to be summed up by his nickname, 'The Duke'. Very few followers of racing familiar with his behaviour and bearing can have wondered why he was given that aristocratic label, but the story of exactly how he got it has a surprise twist. Tracing the 'Frenchie' in Frenchie Nicholson is straightforward – it came from his years in France, where he was apprenticed at the age of 12 when his father worked as a huntsman near Pau – but the derivation of The Duke is more complicated.

According to David Nicholson's excellent autobiography, entitled *The Duke*, it was one of his father's stable lads, Chris Middleton, who came up with the badge that fitted so well, when the boss's son returned one day from Haileybury School. Nicholson wrote: 'Unimpressed with the haughty way I strolled into the yard at the end of term he observed, "Here comes the bloody Duke."'

Speaking to me in 2013, however, Middleton confirms he was responsible for the nickname but has a different memory of its origin. As Middleton recalls, 'David was in the yard one morning with Frenchie, sparring, boxing with one another, and Frenchie just said to me, "Who does he remind you of?" and I said, "The Duke". The Duke was an old fella who used to be around here years ago, tall like David and upright. He used to have a few greyhounds.' The nickname was conceived because of a resemblance to another local personality.

As well as personality David Nicholson possessed character and alongside that stood ambition and belief. He was the son of a racehorse trainer but to forge his own life in racing, initially as a jockey, Nicholson had first to combat asthma and a huge list of allergies – there were scores of them and one was an allergy to horses. His physique was another obvious issue. The journalist Shaun Usher once described him memorably as 'a big man with a face built on Easter Island statue lines' and, in terms of his height and natural weight, at 6 foot 1 inch The Duke was not the ideal model for a jockey.

To pursue his career in racing, Nicholson had to live up to the history of achievement on both sides of his family and his father's example would have been foremost, as a jockey and a trainer but also as a man. In 1984, my mentor Ray Gould wrote in the *Gloucestershire Echo* that 'Frenchie Nicholson had the enviable reputation of being one of the most stylish and courageous riders of the period. With a tremendously powerful finish, he often snatched victories from seemingly hopeless situations.' As well as numerous finishes in the top four in the jockeys' championship, and in 1944/45 a share of the title, he won the Champion Hurdle in 1936 (on Victor Norman) and the Gold Cup in 1942 (Medoc II).

When he concentrated on training instead of riding, Frenchie became a trainer of men as well as of horses and in the end he would be far better known as a trainer of men. Paul Cook, Pat Eddery, Richard Fox and Walter Swinburn were among a host of jockeys who learned their trade with him on the Flat, while his own son, Michael Dickinson, Mouse Morris and Brough Scott were among those under his tutelage who made their careers in jumps racing. Brough Scott's godfather was Ian Fleming, the James Bond author, but Frenchie Nicholson was Scott's inspiration.

'He was the person I listened to,' Scott explains. 'He was just wonderful as a person who would tell you what to do.

He was a captivating man because he never lost the child's eye. He was a better jockey than he was a trainer and he was a better trainer of people than of horses because he was actually too hard on himself and a bit too hard on his horses. He would work all the time, so he was a terrific example to jockeys. He was very inspirational. It was my ultimate good fortune that here was a man who was a proper trainer and he liked talking about riding.

'He would tease David Nicholson, who was by then a quite considerable jockey but rather serious, and the lads used to laugh at him being childish but they knew he'd work harder than them and they also knew he had been a great rider. His great insistence was on the basic orthodoxy. You had to get the orthodox right to begin with. He had this boyish enthusiasm and he was sort of reliving his jockey's days through others but he was also tough and he would spot things. Most people just complained if you got beat but he would say, "you did X right there and X wrong". He was wonderful, he was really wonderful and I could absolutely see how he lit up those apprentices, a string of them.'

Was Frenchie Nicholson a hard act for his son to follow? David's wife Dinah believes so: 'Yes. It's a word which everybody uses too much but Frenchie was a legend. He was a cracking jockey. Everybody said he was a much better jockey than David ever was, all his old cronies did.'

To the son, the father's achievements and reputation were a spur, not a millstone, and, setting off on his own path in racing, David Nicholson was also fuelled by a larger than normal degree of self-confidence. 'The belief just shone out of him,' is how Scott has described their first meeting, and, elaborating on the man he came to know extremely well, 'His gift, throughout his life, was to make you want to be on his team. Naturally he had to be captain, to open the bowling, to control the schooling, to order pals, princesses, employees and everyone else to do his bidding. But we all

184

put up with it because there was something inspirationally addictive in such apparent self-belief.'

This self-belief certainly came across in Nicholson's public persona and this man of strong opinions was not shy about expressing them. Considering whether her husband was a very self-confident person, Dinah Nicholson concedes: 'I think he came over that way. I think he had quite a lot of self-confidence or eldest-child arrogance.'

David Nicholson the jockey registered 583 British winners under National Hunt rules, including the 1967 Whitbread on Mill House and five wins at the Festival, in the 1962 Cathcart, 1963 Grand Annual, 1971 Totalisator Champion Novices' Chase and in 1972 the Gloucestershire Hurdle and the County Hurdle.

Of those at the Cheltenham Festival, the brace in 1973 almost certainly meant the most to him. He kicked off the first day in the Gloucestershire Hurdle (now the Supreme Novices') with King Pele, and this was a triumph that in one important respect would set the template for his Festival experience for decades to come. David Minton was responsible for buying and syndicating King Pele, and Gavin Pritchard-Gordon trained him. Both men stayed at the Nicholson home for the meeting and, updating this text in 2015, they are still doing so.

Pritchard-Gordon's happy recollection of what unfolded that night when the inebriated King Pele contingent left the racecourse car park at 11 o'clock and wondered where they could find something to eat, is that Nicholson – 'The Duke being The Duke, obviously being a good customer' – rang the Unicorn in Stow-on-the-Wold only to find that the landlord was going to bed and the kitchen staff had been released an hour earlier. Nevertheless he managed to secure a table for ten for dinner and they did not leave until 4 o'clock in the morning.

Those celebrations sound as if they may have taken some getting over but when the last race of the meeting came round two days later, the County Hurdle was won by David Nicholson on Current Romance, trained by his father. Frenchie had sent out Buckingham to win the 1957 Birdlip Handicap Hurdle in the days when he trained for Dorothy Paget and this was his first Festival success since. The owner's wife stood up past the winning post waiting for Current Romance to come in, having had a premonition that he was going to win. The *Timeform Black Book* describes the 20-1 shot 'leading after the fifth and fighting off numerous challenges from the second last', on his way to winning by a head.

Frenchie Nicholson was not there to see the triumph but the celebration was brought to him, as Dinah Nicholson describes: 'Frenchie wasn't there because he was in bed with flu. Afterwards we all decided we had to call round and see him and as usual the traffic getting out of the track was impossible, so we took a route that took us down the side of the course, which you could do then, right down to the far end where there was a big iron gate which we carefully took off its hinges; we went through that gate and it took us straight into Prestbury. David's brother Richard had had to go off and get a bottle of champagne from the local pub because Frenchie didn't keep much drink in his house and he wasn't feeling much up to it, but he did cheer up a bit.'

David Minton, also in that car, remembers that Richard Nicholson must already have been to the Royal Oak by the time they successfully applied that bit of local knowledge, because 'we drove up to Frenchie's house and Frenchie was in his dressing gown and pyjamas with a bottle of champagne in his hand.'

In *The Sporting Life* the following day, Len Thomas reported on the County Hurdle, saying that 'It was touch-and-go all the way up the run-in, David Nicholson riding one of his strongest finishes … Incidentally, I was surprised to hear that Nicholson had not ridden a hurdles winner at this meeting until King Pele won the final event on Tuesday, the Gloucestershire Hurdle.'

~

More surprising to the racing world, in a developing saga that came to be played out season after season, was the time it took for David Nicholson to appear again in the Festival winner's enclosure, this time as a trainer. At the time of the 1973 meeting he was already in his fifth season sending out runners as well as riding them. Instant success as a Festival trainer is not to be expected but the 1973 Gloucestershire Hurdle had shown that it was possible and it might reasonably have given Nicholson some encouragement that he would not have to wait too long, seeing as his role in King Pele's triumph was more than that of just a jockey.

Gavin Pritchard-Gordon tells the story of how he first met The Duke and what followed: 'My first year's training was 1972 and I had a winner called Harbrook at Wolverhampton on the August bank holiday. I was meant to have Brian Taylor riding and Brian, God bless him, was a great friend but he was a bit vague about things when he wasn't in the saddle and he actually took Harry Wragg, the veteran trainer, for whom he was also riding, to Doncaster instead of Wolverhampton and was rather surprised when about half an hour before racing there was no other car in the car park.

'Anyway, the result was that he was too late to partner Harbrook, who was ridden by one of Frenchie Nicholson's apprentices. We had a lot to drink, dare I say, to celebrate and in the bar was Frenchie Nicholson and of course he was delighted because it was his apprentice. Frenchie said to me, "Gavin, well done" and we were chatting away and he said, "You should have some jumpers." I said, "Mr Nicholson, I've only just started training Flat racehorses. I don't know how I would train jumpers." And he replied,

"It's very, very simple. That tall fellow over there, he'll give you a hand." So David came over and gave his usual crunching handshake and he just said, "When do you want me to come up and school them?" That's all he said. So I replied, "Why don't you come on Wednesday?" and that's exactly what happened.'

Pritchard-Gordon had absolutely nothing in mind among his string which might make a suitable hurdler, but after Nicholson had stayed the night – 'We had a wonderful evening, as one does with the Nicholsons' – five horses were assembled the next morning and the bleary-eyed collection of new-found friends repositioned some railway sleepers before The Duke climbed on board and found out whether they could jump. Three of the five went on to win seven races between them over hurdles that season.

'I didn't know anything about jumping,' confesses Pritchard-Gordon. 'David came and schooled them and he basically told me how to train them. It was not as though King Pele was a brilliant horse on the Flat. He was a reasonably good-looking horse, his form was just middling form, but he was a seriously good jumper. And well done The Duke because there was nobody better for schooling horses than David. I willingly admit that all I had to do was just to keep the horses fresh, well, fed and happy and the rest of it David did.'

When the 1973 meeting drew to a close, its success had been such that Nicholson's house guests in Festival week were booked in for the rest of time. The name of his first Festival winner as a trainer was slower to reveal itself. Based at Condicote near Stow-on-the-Wold, Nicholson had accomplished win tallies in single figures in the first four campaigns as a trainer and that increased to 24 in 1972/73. Fair Catch was his first Festival runner, pulled up at 50-1 in the 1970 Totalisator Champion Novices' Chase, and three further outsiders failed to make an impact at that year's meeting. One more in 1971, plus two in both 1972 and

1973 followed the same trajectory. On the final day of the 1973 meeting, however, Inaudible was fourth at 20-1 in the Triumph Hurdle. Things were looking up.

Nicholson's first runner at the 1974 Festival yielded another fourth – 33-1 shot Tudor Dance in the Champion Chase, admittedly as the last of four finishers – and then came his Mildmay of Flete candidate What A Buck; at 15-8 favourite he was the trainer's first Festival runner to start at less than 20-1. To help his cause, I'm Happy fell at the last and brought down Sonny Somers, in a seven-runner race. Although What A Buck was beaten 15 lengths into second, Dinah Nicholson remembers that 'We were all delighted. He was a much better horse right-handed.' On the final day, there was a 50-1 also-ran in the Triumph. Bidding to repeat the previous season's heroics, Frenchie Nicholson's Current Romance led two out in the County Hurdle but finished sixth. It was the final ride at the Festival for his son, who retired from the saddle the following month.

'He was totally dedicated to his raceriding and whatever he did,' says Dinah Nicholson of her husband, and this dedication was transferred seamlessly into his quest for winners as a trainer. Richard Nicholson elaborates: 'His onward drive to succeed would have been ever present in his life and having a Festival winner would have been at the forefront of his ambitions. He wouldn't necessarily go around shouting about it and he wanted to succeed at whatever he was doing but winners at Cheltenham would have been top of the list.'

In his first campaign as just a trainer, Nicholson had a good shout in the 1975 Coral Golden Hurdle when Shinto was third, beaten 2½ lengths. He was also represented that year by a Festival winner but it was not a Festival winner for him. Willie Wumpkins had taken the 1973 Aldsworth Hurdle and would have second, third and fourth Festival comings in the 1979, 1980 and 1981 Coral Golden Hurdle Finals, but when he lined up in the 1975 Lloyds Bank Hurdle in his sole season with Nicholson, he trailed in eighth at 33-1. At the same odds, two other Nicholson runners that year did not fare any better in their engagements.

What A Buck, a half-brother to the Gold Cup and Grand National winner L'Escargot, was a smart chaser and a great favourite at the yard, going on to be Nicholson's hack. He was pulled up at 16-1 in the 1976 Gold Cup. Shinto weakened into seventh when co-second favourite in the Joe Coral Golden Hurdle Final, but No Gypsy managed a great deal better than his 50-1 suggested in the Sun Alliance Chase, beaten 2½ lengths into second by Tied Cottage.

At this point, therefore, Nicholson had sent out 20 Festival runners over seven seasons for two seconds, a third and two fourths. Only three of those runners had started at 10-1 or less while 15 had been 20-1 or longer. Anyone with an involvement in jumps racing wants a winner at the Festival and with his historical ties to the track, the example of his family and his sheer proprietorial attitude to the place – 'he always thought Cheltenham belonged to him really,' concedes his wife – it is easy to appreciate why David Nicholson would want that winner more than most.

He had twice come within two and a half lengths of one. To somebody dedicated to his job and to his sport, bridging those two and a half lengths was naturally an imperative, but to understand the full scale of his determination and why this developing quest against the Festival fates became so out of the ordinary, it is necessary to return once more to his complicated and powerful personality, one element of which was an extreme competitiveness.

The Duke's son John describes that drive in his father and how it manifested itself when John became old enough to join his father on visits to the local pub: 'Everything had to be won, whether it was cricket, whether it was playing Spoof in the pub. We'd always Spoof for a drink.' They ended up playing for crisps because if his son lost when

Spoofing for the drinks round, it was The Duke who ended up paying anyway.

Nicholson's attitude to Spoof was one thing; the way he played sports other than racing was something else. *The Duke* contains an amusing, if rather frightening, chapter entitled Playing To Win, in which he described his similarly uncompromising approach in these spheres. In football, for instance, as a 'no-nonsense defender', this resulted in regular hefty challenges and altercations with the opposition. When playing against a TV All Stars team, The Duke was felled by a punch when one of the opposition forwards, comedian Bernie Winters, failed to see the funny side.

Nicholson was captain of the jockeys' football and cricket teams although that title seems not to come remotely close to describing the authority he exercised over the cricket XI.

Although he was not one of those to retain his jockey's shape following retirement from the saddle, it is nevertheless not too hard to picture the player described by his son, John: 'Scary. In his 20s and early 30s he was a quick bowler. He'd come in off a long run and he'd come all arms flailing – he'd frighten a lot of batsmen. Batting-wise he was a lower-order big hitter – it was long handle with Dad really, straight back over the bowler. Every now and then he'd come up against some pretty good bowlers and he wouldn't step back. He'd wear a few. He would wind a few of the bowlers up as well.'

Such players are not so unusual, but some of the tactics to which Nicholson resorted in search of victory do raise the eyebrows. 'The umpire's word is always final' does not seem to have been his team motto. John Nicholson laughs and shakes his head at the same time as he recollects one match, against Newmarket, when he and his brother were sat on the edge of the pitch watching the Newmarket run chase and the young boys were instructed by their father to subtly move the boundary markers back. On another occasion, in a charity match at Cheltenham College, The Duke assisted his own pursuit of the opposition total as time ran out by getting someone to stop the clock. Apparently his team won off the last available ball.

In his autobiography, David Nicholson stated: 'People might think I take my sport too seriously but that is the way I have always been. I am just the same playing dominoes, darts or skittles and make no apology for it. Sport mirrors life and I would rather be a winner than a loser.'

~

Back on the racetrack, in 1977 the strength of the Nicholson Festival team improved markedly, in numerical terms, but his 11 runners (one of them Flitgrove, a 3-1 joint favourite in the Arkle) came away with nothing. The 1978 and 1979 Festivals saw 14 have a go but Prehibas (three lengths third in the 1978 Mildmay of Flete) was the only one to finish in the first four; eight of those runners started at 50-1 or longer.

In the 1979 National Hunt Chase 50-1 shots Westberry Lodge and Lizandon both came a cropper when beaten at the second last but it nevertheless represented a highly significant point in the stable's history because Westberry Lodge was ridden by Peter Scudamore. Two of the sport's most driven personalities had joined forces at the Festival for the first time.

An 18-year-old amateur, Scudamore was having his third ride at the meeting. In May 1962, he had been pageboy at the Nicholsons' wedding. At the start of the 1979/80 season he was working full time for The Duke and in 1981/82 he would be champion jump jockey for the first time, jointly. After an injury which stopped Scudamore riding John Francome declined any other rides once he had matched Scudamore's total.

The Duke's Long Wait

Of his time with The Duke, the jockey later stated: 'He taught me all the basics. I learned to do things correctly, and it's stood me in good stead ever since.' Scudamore went on to become champion jockey eight times. Which, of course, did not guarantee that the equally motivated Nicholson would now get off the mark as a Festival trainer or that Scudamore would do so as a jockey. Scudamore was injured and missed the 1980 meeting – when Nicholson's four runners were all 50-1 or longer, with Aingers Green at least managing fourth in the Sun Alliance Hurdle – but after that both men would have to suffer together.

The year of chief suffering was undoubtedly 1981. Nicholson had only five runners, all ridden by Scudamore, with not that much expected of Sailor's Return or Great Developer, but rather more of Collars And Cuffs (20 lengths third in the Mildmay of Flete) and Highway Patt (unseated when second favourite in the Ritz Club Handicap Chase) and Broadsword in the Triumph Hurdle carrying absolutely huge hopes.

Useful on the Flat for John Dunlop, Broadsword soon looked a good deal better than that as a hurdler. Once he found the key to jumping he became seriously good at it and won six of his seven hurdling starts before the Festival. Writing about that year in his autobiography *Scu*, Peter Scudamore said: 'Throughout my riding career I tried to cultivate tunnel vision as far as racing was concerned. I didn't want to be distracted, either by pressure at home or on the course, or by expectations from the press … Yet in March, with the Festival inexorably approaching, it was very difficult not to share in the general increase in tension and anticipation.' A good deal of that anticipation was centred on Broadsword and, as Nicholson later related, 'I had been waiting 13 years so far for my first winner at the Festival as a trainer and really did believe Broadsword was the one to break my duck.' The horse also carried major public confidence and was sent off the 7-4 favourite, despite a field of 29 and heavy going.

A big-field Triumph can be a phenomenally rough race but there were no problems of that sort for Broadsword who was produced to take the lead approaching the final flight. 'I remember thinking going to the last that I'd done my job,' says his jockey.

The race was about to provide a breakthrough success for one of the sport's big-name trainers but it wasn't for David Nicholson. There were only three horses anywhere near Broadsword. Two of them were weakening but the third was the Martin Pipe-trained 66-1 shot Baron Blakeney, a grey, who stayed on much more strongly than the favourite up the hill and got to him just before the line.

When Broadsword passed the place where Nicholson was standing in front of the grandstand, he was in a clear lead. 'I turned and ran off the lawn, shouting, "He's won, he's won," the trainer wrote in *The Duke*. He and the owner hugged each other in celebration and when his sister Josie told him that she thought Broadsword had been beaten, he assumed that she had made a mistake. When the numbers appeared in the frame, he thought that was a mistake too.

Speaking more than 30 years later, Dinah Nicholson recalls the aftermath of that defeat. 'He just could not believe it,' she says. 'I never saw him so totally deflated. We were taken out to dinner with Broadsword's owner Lord Northampton and David ended up not going. He was a very good loser, normally, but this just absolutely annihilated him. He couldn't take it at all.'

The Nicholsons had never heard of Martin Pipe before that day and when asked whether they felt a particular competitiveness with Pipe in later seasons, Dinah Nicholson replies, with a laugh: 'I think we hated him! At the start, but we got on perfectly well afterwards. We hated him for Broadsword. That was the biggest disappointment of all time.'

Nicholson blamed the defeat on a loose horse which went clear of the favourite on the run-in, concluding that

Broadsword 'thought he was beaten. You could almost sense the resolve draining out of him.' Scudamore, in later years to reap a spectacular harvest in winners when he was the Pipe stable jockey, has concluded on the other hand that under those conditions Broadsword was not good enough: 'Baron Blakeney outstayed me. I didn't even miss the last, we jumped the last fantastic. The joke was that whenever I went into Martin Pipe's I used to look up at that picture in his hallway, and they'd be pulling my leg about it, about Baron Blakeney and Paul Leach just outstaying me.'

Broadsword's defeat was on March 19. It was Nicholson's 42nd birthday. Reviewing the week's action in the *Sunday Telegraph*, John Oaksey wrote: 'In a life quite a lot of which has been spent playing one sort of game or another, I have never met anyone more wholeheartedly competitive than David Nicholson. Whether he was playing tiddlywinks or Russian roulette, no one in my experience could like winning more or losing less. ... So when Baron Blakeney and Broadsword came into the winners' enclosure and David Nicholson walked straight up to congratulate the winning trainer, Martin Pipe, I reckon that any Duke who happened to be present would have been proud to share his title.'

~

A Festival win had been snatched from their grasp but overall the fortunes of the Nicholson team were a major consolation, and in the next two seasons there was a better class of horse in the stable and marked improvement in their seasonal totals: 47 wins in 1980/81 had itself set a new best for the yard and that increased to 67 in 1981/82. There were 64 in 1982/83. Back at the Festival, however, the Nicholson win total continued to stick resolutely at zero, the small consolation being an increase in the number of placed returns. Broadsword ran in two Champion Hurdles, finishing second and fourth.

Scudamore remembers with regret what happened on Broadsword's run following the first of those Champion Hurdles, in which they had finished seven lengths adrift of the 40-1 shot For Auction: 'I fell on him at Aintree at the last and I drove him into the ground. I suppose that was pressure. I'd got beat on him in the Champion Hurdle and I was so determined to win. I was going to the last and I just whacked him up and the poor old thing turned over.'

At that 1982 Festival, none of the rest of the Condicote team (nine horses) finished better than eighth. In 1983, in addition to Broadsword's fourth, Goldspun was 1¼ lengths third in the Stayers' Hurdle and Gainsay was a 50-1 fourth in the Triumph, but nine others were all among the also-rans.

'We still celebrated,' says Dinah Nicholson. 'It was no excuse for not having a party.'

Gavin Pritchard-Gordon concurs that the years – and they were mounting – in which Nicholson was frozen out of the winners' enclosure did not affect the après-ski proceedings on top of the Cotswolds. 'David was so looking forward to every Cheltenham,' he says. 'He didn't get down despite the fact he might have been disappointed not to have a winner. It never stopped him smiling and having fun and partying. He just was so thrilled when Cheltenham came because the whole thing was the highlight of his year. All right, it sounds strange if you don't have a winner but it still was – with his passion for the sport and his passion for the place, he just looked forward to Cheltenham as being the highlight. Cheltenham was his spiritual home.'

At his actual home during Festival week, the evening ambience was apparently pretty raucous. His sons were employed topping up the drinks and, perhaps after watching some piggy-back races around the sitting room, they might then have had to lend some assistance to the participants by trying to help them – or 'pour' them – upstairs to bed. The Duke had generally retired some time earlier but to arrive at their bedrooms everyone else had to make their way past his. Many shushing noises resulted, somewhat counterproductively. When most of the house rose the next morning, as John Nicholson puts it, 'they generally didn't make first lot.'

In 1984, three Nicholson-trained longshots were well beaten but third-favourite Voice Of Progress was third in the Arkle and Goldpsun (Stayers' Hurdle), Captain Dynamo (Mildmay of Flete) and Connaught River (Cathcart) all finished second, at 20-1, 10-1 and 25-1 respectively. Goldspun had every chance on the run-in and was beaten one and a half lengths, but Captain Dynamo went even closer, and in trying circumstances for his trainer. Nicholson was a stickler about the right way to behave in defeat. As the 1981 Triumph aftermath illustrated, when beaten into second he would always try to be the first to shake the hand of the winning connections. By now he must have been pretty good at it and one of the most frequent in the very wide variety of descriptions applied to him is that he was a very good loser. But when one fellow trainer attempted to take the mickey out of him following Captain Dynamo's narrow loss, the guard apparently slipped somewhat. The Duke made it known that this comment was not appreciated. When I asked John Nicholson in another context whether his father was an emotional person, his first reaction is to say, 'Oh yeah, he'd lose his rag.'

That Captain Dynamo race would certainly have been a test. With four horses still in serious contention, Captain Dynamo led at the last but blundered badly (in the process hampering Classified who eventually finished fourth) before going down by half a length to that great Cheltenham specialist Half Free. It was the closest a Nicholson runner had come to a Festival win since Broadsword. In this instance, though, it is frightening to imagine what would have transpired had he finished that half a length closer, because in a stewards' inquiry Captain Dynamo was demoted to fourth.

Speculating on how much worse the situation would have been, including perhaps for the colleague who attempted the joke at her husband's expense, had Captain Dynamo finished first past the post before getting moved down, Dinah Nicholson observes 'that would have been cruel, cruel justice wouldn't it?'

On April 27, 1984, Frenchie Nicholson passed away after a long illness. Sixteen seasons with a training licence had now passed without his son training a Festival winner.

~

'I think we just forgot the previous meeting and said, "Right, let's go for the next,"' reports Mrs Nicholson. 'It was always in the trainer's mind that we look towards Cheltenham. We were always looking for a horse to win at Cheltenham, looking to buy a horse with Cheltenham potential.'

While experience – repeated experience – must have tempered any expectations come the day about specific horses succeeding at the meeting, the trainer's overall optimism that the elusive win was bound to come in the end remained unaffected. In general, optimists seem far better suited to the emotional trials of life as a trainer, and the belief remained strong in David Nicholson.

Regarding his father's training, John Nicholson says: 'I think he always trusted his own ability because of the results he got outside the Festival. He was always happy with his own ability, confident of his own ability.'

For the majority of his training career, that confidence would indeed have found plenty of support from results away from the Festival, which after all was not the be all and end all, but in the 1984/85 season that comfort was savagely removed. The total number of Nicholson winners slumped to just 17. It was the effect of a virus, but the problems behind the scenes at Condicote were far worse than that. The trainer was on the edge of bankruptcy. On one occasion Peter Scudamore stepped in to pay the lads' wages and in the autumn of 1984 a group of friends and supporters rallied round to refinance the training operation and transform its organisation under the new banner of David Nicholson Racing Ltd. In *The Duke*, the trainer confessed that 'Had they been unable to bail me out, it was the end of D. Nicholson as a person and a racehorse trainer.'

Results at the 1985 Festival were remarkably good in the circumstances, although still without a winner of course. Eight of his 13 runners started at 33-1 or longer but two of those – Against The Grain in the Triumph and the mercurial Connaught River in the Cathcart – finished strongly to go down by just a length in second, and another – Lulav – was fourth in the Grand Annual. Among the five shorter-priced representatives, Very Promising was third when second favourite in the Arkle and Goldspun fourth in the Stayers'. Charter Party fell when third favourite for the Kim Muir. In *The Times*, John Karter's report on Very Promising's Arkle bid took on a not untypical hue when he talked of a Festival 'jinx' and said that for Nicholson the meeting 'has become a perennial nightmare'.

In 17 seasons as a trainer, Nicholson had now sent out 96 runners at the Festival for no wins but 22 in the first four, and it was not only the trainer who could be excused for feeling the frustration of it. Having first ridden there in 1978, Scudamore had by this time taken 64 Festival rides for no wins and 21 in the first four, of which 12 plus the demoted Captain Dynamo had finished second. Forty-one of the Scudamore rides had been for Nicholson, 23 of them at 20-1 or longer, including nine of his 11 Nicholson runners in 1985. His rides for other yards had yielded seconds for High Prospect (in the 1979 Kim Muir), Chinrullah (the 1982 Champion Chase and Cathcart), Artifice (1983 Champion

Chase), Cima (1984 Champion Hurdle) and Bajan Sunshine (1984 Sun Alliance Hurdle) plus a third on Artifice (1984 Champion Chase).

'You can't be a top trainer without training a winner at Cheltenham, or a top jockey without riding a winner at Cheltenham,' is how Scudamore felt, yet Nicholson's unmistakable and burning ambition was not just to have a Festival winner, it was to be recognised in the top rank of trainers. His jockey's summary of their position at that time was that 'we were still the Second Division club trying to be a First Division club.' At first Scudamore had been delighted to have any rides at the Festival but that would no longer suffice. His secret nightmare was that 'supposing there were two in the race and I rode the wrong one, or if he [Nicholson] won an amateur race'. In time, there was also frustration that many of those rides were on outsiders.

'He put a big front on, didn't he?' reflects Scudamore in 2012. 'Everything was aimed at Cheltenham whether they were good enough or not. I had tremendous admiration for him when he did turn it round but a lot of what The Duke did he did as a front, and this was almost part of that front. It was this image, this image of a big trainer, so everything went to bloody Cheltenham.'

'Typical Duke, all done half in show,' he says when relating how the horses would be trained normally until the Festival was just around the corner and then the team's final preparations saw them sent up special gallops, the most exacting of which was a local landmark called Arkle's Bank.

Of course, the lack of Festival success for both men was not private knowledge and Scudamore's recollection of a big evening function at about this time makes it clear how this predicament could sometimes demand the most stoic of responses.

'I remember going to a dinner and John Francome got up and told a joke,' relates Scudamore. That section of Francome's speech went something like this: "There are three trainers – Jim Old, Mercy Rimell and David Nicholson – and they all asked God a question. Jim Old said, "When will I train a winner at the Cheltenham Festival?" and God got his scroll out and said, "Jim, you'll train a winner at the Cheltenham Festival in five years' time." Mercy said, "God, when will I train another winner at the Cheltenham Festival?" God looked further down his scroll and replied, "Mercy, in ten years' time you'll train a winner at Cheltenham," to which she groaned "Bloody hell. I'll be dead by then." And The Duke asked, "When will I train a winner at the Festival?" So God kept going down his scroll, he kept going down his scroll, and then he said, "By that time it's me who'll be dead.""

Francome would have given his joke a considerably more polished delivery but you get the idea. Nicholson was present at that dinner and his jockey believes that the lack of a Festival winner was by this time causing a lot of pain. At the very least, as Scudamore observes, 'The Duke didn't have a lot of time for John's sense of humour.'

Each year when March approached, there must have been a lot of extra pressure in store, as well as the extra pleasure described by Gavin Pritchard-Gordon, thanks to Nicholson's favourite meeting. The trainer Alastair Lidderdale, who worked for him at the time, does not remember this being reflected in the atmosphere at Condicote or in the boss's behaviour in front of his staff.

'He didn't come across to me as someone who was twitchy,' says Lidderdale. 'I'm sure he got excited and on edge but I didn't see it. Of all the people I've worked for he was probably the best "people" man. He was good with people, he was good with his lads and it was a great place to work.' Frenchie Nicholson inspired a generation of racing professionals that worked with him, and his son did the same.

Behind the scenes, however, Mrs Nicholson confirms that her husband was not resting easily. It may not have helped that by this time his domestic refuge had also become the residence of a very loud and disaffected parrot called 'Inspector Clouseau'. At the time of his purchase in 1982, it was claimed by the shopkeeper that this Mealy Amazon (who commonly live for 70 years) was on the verge of learning to talk. Perhaps it is just as well he never did, because with his antisocial demeanour he would probably only have squawked something along the lines of 'Who's trained a Festival winner? Who's trained a Festival winner?'

Nicholson admitted in *The Duke* that: 'my long-held ambition to train a winner at the Cheltenham Festival was close to becoming an obsession. Each year I tried to train with the Festival as the focal point of my programme, but it just did not seem to work.' According to his wife, their lack of success at Cheltenham in March was preying on his mind. She believes he felt 'he was letting the side down a bit'.

Mrs Nicholson reflects: 'Probably if you'd asked him he'd have said yes I'm in a state about it. But he wasn't one for talking about things very much. He didn't actually like to bring things out into the open an awful lot. Well, not with me anyway!'

The leading trainer Alan King, one of those people The Duke inspired, joined the yard for the 1985/86 season and during his many years as the trainer's assistant he would get to see just how worked up Nicholson could become before a day's racing. But with the Festival, Mrs Nicholson testifies, her husband would get especially on edge:

'He was very twitchy running up to the meeting and to get through the meeting I'd end up giving him large doses of Rescue Remedy. It's a sort of herbal thing. I give it to the dogs as well. I don't know if it does any good at all really but he used to think it did him good. It's supposed to help you settle down. Anybody who stayed would remember the Rescue Remedy.'

The Duke's Long Wait

David Minton recalls that the odd glass of Fernet Branca (involving 27 herbs from five continents; either way it's strong stuff) also played a pretty prominent role but, when casting an eye down the list of ingredients in the original Bach Rescue Remedy on their website in 2012, it was possible to appreciate why The Duke may have considered it worth adding to the copious medicines he already had to take for all his allergies and asthma:

> *Impatiens: For those who act and think quickly, and have no patience for what they see as the slowness of others ... Teaches empathy and understanding of and patience with others. We've found it very fast-acting in alleviating an impatient attitude and lowering stress.*

> *Star of Bethlehem: For trauma and shock, whether experienced recently or in the past. Teaches the ability to recover from traumas and to integrate them into the present life.*

> *Cherry Plum: For those who fear losing control of their thoughts and actions and doing things they know are bad for them or which they consider wrong. Teaches trust in one's spontaneous wisdom and the courage to follow one's path.*

The 1986 squad for Cheltenham comprised nine horses. On the first day there was French Union at 33-1 in the Arkle, with Against The Grain and Goldspun both 50-1 in the Stayers'. Against The Grain outran his odds to finish third, albeit beaten 17½ lengths. Peter Scudamore was not on board Against The Grain but he did ride the Rimell-trained Gaye Brief, runner-up to seven-length winner See You Then in the Champion Hurdle.

On the Wednesday, Nicholson saddled Tickite Boo at 14-1 in the Sun Alliance Novices' Hurdle, a landmark runner for the trainer, but only because he was sending out his 100th Cheltenham Festival runner. Tickite Boo finished fourteenth. Thirty-five minutes later Very Promising was 11-2 third favourite for the Champion Chase, and approaching the second last he was on the heels of the leader Buck House. In a long and honourable career, Very Promising deserved many plaudits for his jumping but at this fence he blundered, and his usual very game response at the finish could only reduce Buck House's advantage to three lengths. Including Captain Dynamo, this was a tenth second-place Festival finisher for Nicholson and a 15th for Peter Scudamore.

To round off the day, in the Mildmay of Flete, Connaught River was a Festival outsider once more but this time the odds proved an entirely reliable guide to his performance. Having ridden Connaught River at the previous three Festivals, Scudamore did not attempt to make it fourth time lucky, appearing instead on the Fred Winter-trained second favourite Fifty Dollars More. He too was well beaten but the outside ride which caused the jockey real anguish that day was on 5-2 favourite Bolands Cross in the Sun Alliance Chase. For this horse, Scudamore had got his hopes up. 'I thought that he couldn't get beat,' he remembers. 'I'd made lots of excuses before of why I hadn't ridden a winner at Cheltenham but this couldn't get beat and I fell off him at the ditch.'

He was disputing third at the time, alongside the eventual winner Cross Master. Thirty runners had started the race and the form book lists five casualties at that 16th fence, four from home – four as fallers and one brought down. Bolands Cross was actually an unseat. He hit the fence so hard that he almost came to a stop but there was no consolation in that for his erstwhile rider and although he reports a deal of black humour shortly afterwards among the pile of jockeys who found themselves on top of one another, the suspicion is that he wasn't laughing overmuch at that either.

Reviewing all his 74 Festival rides up to and including that Wednesday, Scudamore says: 'There was nothing I remember thinking I should have won on – until that day and the horse that fell in the Sun Alliance, Bolands Cross. Then it got to me.'

His immediate reaction was to think that he would never ride a winner at the Festival: 'I was as low as you could get.'

~

When the Festival reconvened the following day, Nicholson and Scudamore came back for more. First came the Daily Express Triumph Hurdle, their representative this time coming in the unassuming shape of Solar Cloud. The physical description accorded him that season by Timeform was 'short-coupled, light-framed colt'. The Triumph is for the youngest category of horse allowed to contest jumps races in Britain and most in those days were bred with the primary purpose of racing in preceding years on the Flat. Under some criteria it could be argued that Solar Cloud's heyday had been even earlier, when he made 210,000 guineas at the yearling sales. His pedigree was full of good winners on the Flat in North America but although he showed plenty of ability himself in that sphere in Ireland he had never translated it into a win. As the 1985 Flat season was drawing to a close, David and Dinah Nicholson made a trip to Ireland looking at other would-be purchases, without success, but on their way home they were diverted to Con Collins' stable to examine what Mrs Nicholson describes as 'a flashy little chestnut', one originally supposed to be sold on to the United States. The colt would be owned by a group of Nicholson's most loyal owners. 'His form was okay and the price was okay so we ended up with him,' she says.

What was not okay, however, as soon became evident, was Solar Cloud's temperament for racing. At home he worked well and jumped well. He was assigned to Lidderdale, who describes him as 'quite a monkey – a typical colt, bit of a boy. He was not a difficult ride but he was a fun horse to look after I suppose. He had a bit of character about him.'

There were positives on the racecourse too, as Solar Cloud won two of his first four races over hurdles, at Worcester and Kempton in what Timeform described as 'run-of-the-mill juvenile events', but having observed the manner in which Solar Cloud accomplished it his trainer came to this conclusion, that 'he was still a maiden on the Flat because he did not try very hard.' On the strength of those first four races for him, Nicholson said, 'He was, in short, a rascal, would hang badly either way and try anything to avoid having to win.' In passing the post first at Kempton, on his final start before the Triumph, Solar Cloud veered theatrically off a straight line once in front and, as Mrs Nicholson puts it, he resembled a sidewinder snake.

A visor would go on Solar Cloud for the Triumph but Scudamore tried to get off him. On his way to a second jockeys' championship, he was offered the ride on two other horses in the race, one being Tangognat, on whom he had already won twice at Cheltenham. Going for the hat-trick, this is the one Scudamore wanted to be on board. 'I'd been champion jockey,' he states, 'now I wanted Cheltenham winners and I didn't want to be going there just pretending.'

A discussion took place between Scudamore and his sometimes volcanic employer, whose view was that the stable jockey should be on Solar Cloud. One hesitates to ask how that discussion went. 'Of course it gets tense,' remembers Scudamore. 'I was getting big enough then that I could have made my own mind up but he was pretty good. I don't think he thought Tangognat would win to be perfectly honest.'

Tangognat's wins had been on soft and good to soft but when the Festival arrived it was top-of-the-ground, firmer than the official good. 'I didn't give him any chance,' states the jockey about Solar Cloud, and the trainer was hardly raving about him either, far from it, but there was not a big argument and it was agreed that Scudamore would ride the stable's representative.

In a field of 28, the favourite was Roark, an on-the-bridle winner of his only hurdles start and trained by Martin Pipe. He was 9-2, Tangognat 12-1 and Solar Cloud 40-1. As Dinah Nicholson details, her husband's instructions to Scudamore were to 'sit, sit, sit and sit and to come with one quick run if he was in a suitable position.' The jockey's firm belief was that this policy of not coming too soon was most unlikely to present him with the slightest problem, because the leaders would go off at a strong pace and Solar Cloud would not be good enough to get near them anyway. And then something strange happened.

Scudamore describes the first two-thirds of the race: 'So I got off handy, travelled nicely and I got to the top of the hill and I was still going well.' The upshot having just jumped the third last was that Solar Cloud, on the inside throughout, was now disputing the lead. 'Usually when you rode for The Duke you did as you were told,' Scudamore divulges. Now, however, without kicking on as such, the jockey allowed his mount to stride ahead. 'I don't know why I did it to this day. Because I thought he'd got no chance, I suppose I thought "Go for it, nothing to lose" and away we went.'

Turning left and downhill, Solar Cloud was two lengths up and going further clear, while in second place The Musical Priest was himself at least that far ahead of the others. Watching by the lawn near the Arkle Bar was David Minton, standing by Solar Cloud's trainer, and the observations Minton made down there are that 'there was all hell let loose', 'The Duke stamped his feet a bit' and 'one or two expletives came out.'

Just as things were well and truly hotting up in the race as well, one of those horses prominent in the chasing group broke down and was pulled up. It was Roark. Of course, Scudamore did not know that and neither did he know by how far he was surging clear. Putting in another rapid leap at the second last, as The Musical Priest faltered badly and Son Of Ivor commenced his effort, Solar Cloud's lead was very quickly up to eight lengths. 'You don't really sense how far clear you go,' says the jockey. 'You sense how the horse is going. I sensed that I had not really gone for him but I had let him run along. Because he was a shit I knew that even if I challenged from behind, as soon as I went for him he'd stop, so I let him run without ever asking him. It was all about rhythm; I was trying to keep rhythm – jump, run, rhythm, jump – and you know that it makes everything else have to come to you. So you're not conscious of how far in front you are, you're conscious of rhythm and conscious of never – it's a terrible term – putting the gun to his head, always asking him and never telling him.'

Thus far it was certainly working, and when Solar Cloud turned for home he had a quite extraordinary lead for this stage in a Festival hurdle race. 'I'm still in front going to the last,' relates Scudamore, 'and I thought, "Well, this has run bloody well, much better than I could ever hope or think."' As anyone who has ever watched a day's racing at Prestbury Park will know, let alone David Nicholson who had surveyed hundreds of them, Cheltenham does not yield its prizes easily. Its most obviously formidable obstacle, the final hill, lay ahead and, as Peter O'Sullevan's television commentary intimated, fortunes were about to turn: 'Running down now towards the final flight it's a long run to it but Solar Cloud and Peter Scudamore are a long way clear and Peter Scudamore and David Nicholson must be thinking that finally their luck is going to change at Cheltenham now as Solar Cloud is well clear of Son Of Ivor, who's second. Racing into the closing stages now, coming to the last flight, is Solar Cloud weakening? Son Of Ivor is certainly gaining.'

Jumping the last, Solar Cloud's lead was down to two and a half lengths. A classic Cheltenham finish was in the making, with a faltering leader, the closest pursuer gaining on him inexorably and another horse bearing down rapidly on them both. The latter was Brunico, owned by the famously unrestrained gambler Terry Ramsden, who had already won £1 million at the meeting when another of his horses, Motivator, justified favouritism in the previous day's Coral Golden Hurdle Final and was apparently looking to add £5 million or £6 million more after doubling Brunico with the Gold Cup favourite Dawn Run. Brunico was halfway back in the field starting down the hill and he was sixth turning for home, about 20 lengths behind Solar Cloud. Making minor gains approaching the final flight, after it he cut down the leaders' advantage dramatically. Brunico was a grey. John Nicholson describes his father as having an almost photographic memory, which is possibly a mixed blessing when you have trained 102 Festival losers, and the trainer later confirmed that he had visions from five years earlier of Broadsword and his grey pursuer Baron Blakeney on the run-in.

On Solar Cloud, Scudamore was not looking round to check on any dangers. There were enough of them in front because he was positioned on the far rail, very conscious both of Solar Cloud's previous errant behaviour and that this particular rail, on the outside of the chase course, was about to run out halfway to the finishing post. 'I could use my stick in the left hand and I knew that he'd dive off the rail as soon as it disappeared,' says the jockey. Just before this critical point he gave Solar Cloud a crack with the whip in his left hand and soon afterwards one of the legendary

Scudamore finishes was in full swing. 'It wasn't until the last few hundred yards that I really had to ask him,' he recollects. 'I could make his mind up for a short running until he thought about pain and how hard it was for him.' Solar Cloud carried his head awkwardly and wandered, the immediate threat in the shape of Son Of Ivor was not going away and Brunico flashed home between them.

Solar Cloud's jockey describes the final strides: 'Dermot Browne was on Brunico, wasn't he and he came from the next county. We flashed past the line and Dermot says, "I've won! I've won!" and I thought I'm in for a good bollocking. You usually have an idea but I cannot remember thinking I've won or I've lost, because Dermot came at me so fast.'

As he relates this in 2012 Scudamore is laughing, of course. The three horses ended up spread almost right across the track and they were finishing at very different speeds, so the result was hard to assess. But the judge's verdict on the final margins was three-quarters of a length and a short head, with ten lengths back to the fourth. Son Of Ivor had finished third. Brunico had finished second and Solar Cloud had won. Peter Scudamore had won at the Festival. David Nicholson had won at the Festival.

~

For those connected to Solar Cloud, the commonest reaction by a long way seems to have been disbelief; huge disbelief that this particular horse had won. As Alan King testifies, of all the horses the stable ran at Cheltenham that week, Solar Cloud was the least expected by them to win. But perhaps also there was a measure of stunned disbelief among Scudamore and the Nicholsons that they too were finally on the Festival roll of honour. A couple of hours later Nicholson gave his jockey the leg up again on Charter Party in the National Hunt Handicap Chase and, in Scudamore's words, 'I relaxed and on Charter Party I jumped him off,

Top left: The author meets the foal who became Birds Nest
Right: Further early introductions, with George Morris holding the dam Fair Sabrina

Bottom: Birds Nest launches his challenge for the 1976 Champion Hurdle, in pursuit of
Night Nurse at the final flight (Bernard Parkin)

Top: Night Nurse and Peter Easterby, after the 1977 Champion Hurdle

*Bottom: Monksfield and Des McDonogh at early-morning exercise at Cheltenham
Racecourse in 1980 (Bernard Parkin)*

Top: 1980 Champion Hurdle – Jonjo O'Neill delays Sea Pigeon's challenge to Monksfield a little longer (George Selwyn)

Bottom: 1981, and John Francome leaves it later still; Pollardstown and Daring Run lead, but the veteran Sea Pigeon is about to unleash one of the most famous finishes in Festival history (Bernard Parkin)

1981 Stayers' Hurdle – Derring Rose is about to sprint 30 lengths clear (Alec Russell)

Jockey John Francome and the legendary trainer Fred Winter (both Cranhams)

Derring Rose

b. 1975 by Derring-Do – Bandi Rosa by Relko
A BRILLIANT HURDLER WITH A SUPERB PEDIGREE

Won 2 flat races and 8 hurdle races, £62,941, inc.

Flat
WON Prix de Saint-Denis, Maisons-Laffitte, 12f.
WON Aston Park Stakes, Newbury 13f.
3rd Newbury Autumn Cup, carr. 9-7, beating Valentinian, Another Sam, etc.

Hurdles
WON Waterford Crystal Stayers Hurdle, by 30 l, from Celtic Isle, beating, Richdee, Prominent King, etc.
WON Colt Car Corinium Hurdle, by 3l, from Heighlin, beating Connaught Ranger, Lumen (all rec 8 lb.), etc.
WON Rendlesham Hurdle, by 7 l, from Celtic Isle (rec. 6 lb.).
WON Long Walk Hurdle, by 5 l, from John Cherry (rec 14 lb.).
WON Rendlesham Hurdle, by 8 l, beating John Cherry.
WON Berni Inns Long Distance Hurdle, by 3 l, beating Mountrivers.
WON Monksfield Handicap Hurdle.

Chasers and Hurdlers 1980/81 "gave an astonishing performance in the Waterford Crystal Stayers Hurdle at Cheltenham in March, one that really had to be seen to be believed . . . produced such extraordinary acceleration that he put thirty lengths between himself and the runner-up Celtic Isle, from the time he flew into the lead going to the last to the time he galloped strongly past the post . . . in this form . . . unquestionably the best three mile hurdler in training" Rated **164**.

Sire
DERRING-DO, won Gr. II Queen Elizabeth II Stakes, A leading sire of classic and group-winners, including HIGH TOP (sire of Top Ville, Cut Above, Circus Ring, etc.), ROLAND GARDENS, HUNTERCOMBE, PELEID, DOMINION (a leading young sire).
FIRST CROP YEARLINGS IN 1984.

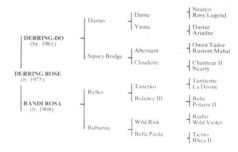

			Nearco
		Dante	Rosy Legend
	Darius		Dastur
		Yasna	Ariadne
DERRING-DO (br. 1961)			Owen Tudor
		Abernant	Rustom Mahal
	Sipsey Bridge		Chanteur II
		Claudette	Nearly
DERRING ROSE (b. 1975)			Tantieme
		Tanerko	La Divine
	Relko		Relic
		Relance III	Polaire II
BANDI ROSA (b. 1968)			Rialto
		Wild Risk	Wild Violet
	Bubunia		Ticino
		Bella Paola	Rhea II

Dam
BANDI ROSA (by RELKO, sire of top N.H. performers BEACON LIGHT, TRUE SONG, ANGELO SALVINI, etc.). Dam of 3 winners. She is half-sister to RAMANOUCHE (Gr. III Prix Eclipse).
Grandam
BUBUNIA (by Wild Risk, Champion Hurdler; Champion Sire under both rules in France). Winner of 3 group races, and half-sister to group winners POLA BELLA (Champion 2-year-old, Gr. I French 2000 Guineas; grandam of 1983 Group winner VALIYAR, European Champion VAYRANN and PERSEPOLIS, Gr. I Prix Lupin, 1982), BEAU PERSAN and POLINA, and stakes-winner POLLY GIRL (dam of Gr. I winner TOP COMMAND; outstanding young sire in U.S.A. and STRAIGHT AND TRUE, Champion Steeplechaser in U.S.A.)

One side of Derring Rose, as presented in Sires For '84

Top: 1981 Kim Muir Memorial Challenge Cup – Good Prospect and HRH Prince of Wales on their way to the start (Cranhams)

Bottom: Negotiating one of the early fences (Bernard Parkin)

Charles completes double

Over the tenth fence and heading for a fall.   Prince Charles and Good Prospect part company.   The fallen Prince amid the pounding hooves.   Another rider about to join the Prince.   Charles beats the ground with his whip in frustration.

'Grudge' blaze man jailed

Gunman in siege drama

FATAL COLLAPSE AT RACES

U.S. JETS CAUSING 'MENTAL STRESS' APPEAL TO COURT

NOISE FROM the KC-135 Stratotankers of the U.S. Air Force at Fairford was causing mental frustration and anguish to people living nearby, a Valuation Court was told at Cirencester yesterday.

In addition, said farmer Bruce Arkell, the noise and vibration made normal conversation impossible, and meant he could not use his phone or her his radio or television set while the aircraft were taxi-ing or taking off.

Disturbance

Five tankers

Training

Mother is killed in collision

A 25-YEAR-OLD mother Mrs. Sarah Coleridge died in a head-on collision on the Cheltenham to

Naughty . . . a streaker showed bare-faced effrontery when he revealed all to startled passers-by in the centre of Cheltenham today.

'All my fault' says the shaken Prince

THE CHEERS of excited Cheltenham racegoers turned to groans yesterday as Prince Charles took his second tumble in five days. The disappointed Prince blamed himself for the fall.

DROPPED BACK

The Queen Mother and Prince Charles being greeted by Capt. Miles Gosling, chairman of the Steeplechase Company (Cheltenham) Ltd.

His frustration turns to laughter.

A helping hand from a St. John Ambulance man.

The Prince of Wales on his feet again.

Royal bonus for Festival racegoers

THERE WAS a bonus for Cheltenham racegoers this afternoon as the Queen Mother was unexpectedly accompanied by Prince Charles on her visit to the National Hunt Festival.

Jobs shock

THE AMERICAN owned Caterpillar Tractor Company is planning to cut production at its Uddingston plant, near Glasgow, and put the entire 2,200 workforce on short-time from June.

SUPER SNATCH
— See Page 3

Andrews & partners

Top: Honourable Man and Tony Fowler set off up the hill with a slight lead over The Drunken Duck and Brod Munro-Wilson in the 1982 Foxhunter Chase (Bernard Parkin)

Bottom: The extraordinary photo finish

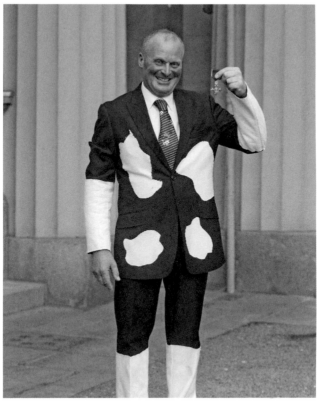

Top: Brod Munro-Wilson holds aloft one section of the Foxhunter trophy (Bernard Parkin)

Bottom: Tony Fowler at Buckingham Palace in 2010 after receiving his MBE (Press Association)

Top: 1984 Arkle Challenge Trophy, the final fence – Bobsline (left) and Noddy's Ryde land
precisely in unison (Bernard Parkin)

Bottom: Bobsline's trainer Francis Flood (Healyracing), and Gordon Richards, trainer of
Noddy's Ryde (Cranhams)

Top: An early setback for David Nicholson at the Festival, as he returns to the weighing room with his father after a fall in 1956 (Bernard Parkin)

Bottom: 'That was the biggest disappointment of all time' – Dinah Nicholson. Broadsword has gone clear in the 1981 Triumph but the grey Baron Blakeney is getting closer (Cranhams)

Top: 1986 Triumph Hurdle – Solar Cloud and Peter Scudamore are also in front at the final flight (Bernard Parkin)

Bottom: The Duke at Cheltenham, pictured in the immediate aftermath of his win in the 1988 Gold Cup with Charter Party

Top: Dawn Run and Charmian Hill parade at Tramore in May 1984 (Caroline Norris)

Bottom: 'If it came to correcting herself going into a hurdle, or a fence later in life, she wasn't great at it' – Tony Mullins. Here, Dawn Run takes the final flight under Jonjo O'Neill in the 1984 Champion Hurdle (Cranhams)

Top: Tony Mullins is all smiles as Dawn Run goes to post before her chasing debut
(Caroline Norris)

Bottom: Wayward Lad sets off up the run-in with the 1986 Gold Cup seemingly in his
grasp; Forgive'n Forget is in second, the pair having moved past the front-runners Dawn
Run and Run And Skip (Cranhams)

Top: But at the finish, it's Jonjo O'Neill on Dawn Run who is punching the air in triumph (Getty Images)

Bottom: Dawn Run and Jonjo O'Neill are led through an excited parade ring and into the winner's enclosure, by owners Charmian Hill and Oliver Hill. Edward Gillespie (next to Oliver Hill) attempts to keep the crowd at bay (Action Images)

Top: Galmoy and Tommy Carmody jump the final flight clear on St Patrick's Day in the 1987 Stayers' Hurdle (Cranhams)

Bottom: John Mulhern's famous silks are sported by the man himself, going out to ride in a point-to-point

Top: Gold Cup day, 1989 – on the track at 11.30 that morning (Bernard Parkin)

Bottom: Two and three-quarter hours later, in the Triumph Hurdle, the leaders (out of picture) have already jumped the last but they are tiring badly and Ikdam is gaining fast (Bernard Parkin)

Top: Richard Holder, trainer of Ikdam (Cranhams)

Bottom: David Elsworth and Desert Orchid (Cranhams)

Top: Ten Plus (Kevin Mooney up) at Newbury in February 1989 (Bernard Parkin)

*Bottom: December 31, 1988 and Cath Walwyn presents the trophy for the Mandarin Chase
to the winning owner Basil Thwaites, alongside Ten Plus's trainer Fulke Walwyn*

'Jumping – that was the problem all his life'. Jim Dreaper's rising star Carvill's Hill hardly rises at all at the final fence of the Dennys Gold Medal Novices' Chase at Leopardstown in December 1988 (Caroline Norris)

Top: Desert Orchid leads Ten Plus and Yahoo after a circuit in the 1989 Gold Cup (Caroline Norris)

Bottom: Yahoo is in front on the run-in but Desert Orchid has begun his fightback (Cranhams)

Top: 1990 Gold Cup – Desert Orchid is beaten this time and Norton's Coin has Toby Tobias in his sights (Bernard Parkin)

Bottom: Sirrell Griffiths bows before receiving the Gold Cup from Queen Elizabeth the Queen Mother (Bernard Parkin)

Top: Sirrell Griffiths and Norton's Coin at Nantgaredig (Bernard Parkin)

Bottom: Sirrell Griffiths and his wife Joyce, Gold Cup winners (Bernard Parkin)

Top: 1991 County Hurdle – 33-1 shots Winnie The Witch and David Bridgwater are on their way to a seven-length victory (Bernard Parkin)

Bottom: In the winner's enclosure, from left to right, are Mary Bridgwater, Ken Bridgwater junior, Winnie The Witch, David Bridgwater, Gary Bridgwater and trainer Ken Bridgwater (Bernard Parkin)

never moved on him and the less I moved on him the better he was going and the further he won.'

Charter Party was prone to jumping errors, many of them major – for instance falling under Tim Thomson Jones in the previous year's Kim Muir – but he did not make any errors on this day in 1986. Festival win number two was in the bag.

If the Nicholsons' guests thought they knew all about partying at Condicote, they were about to learn something different, and not just because the Princess Royal dropped in having cooked up a couple of puddings.

In all, Nicholson won only 22 races that season, still less than one-third of the total four years earlier, but those two at the Festival marked a turning of the tide and gave it serious momentum. Scudamore was not a part of the successful navigation. Within one month of the Festival, provoking an acrimonious response from The Duke, he decided that the following season he would take up the offer to be stable jockey to Fred Winter. In 1988 he went on to join forces with Martin Pipe. In all, he was champion jockey eight times and won a further 11 races at the Festival, including the 1987 Champion Chase on Pearlyman, the 1988 Champion Hurdle on Celtic Shot and the 1993 Champion Hurdle on Granville Again. By the time of his retirement in April 1993, Peter Scudamore had ridden 1,678 winners over jumps in Britain.

Nicholson too was about to enter the most glorious phase of his career, although it was not in respect of sartorial elegance. The sheepskin overcoat was already an institution on racedays and, if that wasn't enough, a pair of bright red socks also took up permanent residence. Gavin Pritchard-Gordon's wife Coral had pondered what to give The Duke as a present that week in 1986 and the result of those deliberations had their first outing on the Thursday.

'She bought these red socks as a birthday present,' says Dinah Nicholson, 'and said you've got to wear these whether you like it or not, because he'd always been a bit conservative about things like socks. So he did and that was it, he never wore anything else afterwards.' With his attachment to these good luck garments very hard to miss, his wife confirms that in future years opening the sock drawer was not for the faint-hearted: 'Every present that he got from anybody was red socks.'

That aside, did all The Duke's defeats at the Festival make victory, when it finally arrived, all the sweeter? 'Yes, I'm sure it did,' says his wife. 'But then you start expecting it, don't you?'

Not with Solar Cloud, of course. He ran 20 more times for Nicholson, winning two novice chases, but was eventually awarded a Timeform squiggle and the epithet 'faint-hearted' before he was sold out of the yard in 1989. With his new connections, he demonstrated toughness of a different type, racing on a further 49 times and in the process winning four handicap chases and a point-to-point, the last of those in 1995 when he was a 13-year-old.

There is an overwhelming consensus that Solar Cloud's Triumph win was primarily a result of the ride he was given. For his trainer, though, success at the Festival in 1986 did not prove a fluke and the sort of hopes to which the Nicholsons had inured themselves over so many previous seasons could now be entertained. By the time he retired in 1999, David Nicholson had trained the winners of 1,499 races and 17 were at the Festival, including the Gold Cup with Charter Party in 1988 and the Champion Chase with Viking Flagship in 1994 and 1995, the latter when he sent out three Festival winners on one day. In an era when the trainers' table came to be dominated by Martin Pipe, Nicholson had realised the need for change in the type of horse he trained and the way that he trained them, and he changed his methods more than most. One enabling factor was his move in 1992 from Condicote to Jackdaws Castle, a short journey in terms of mileage but a major leap in terms of the facilities at his disposal. He was the first trainer at the state-of-the-art training complex and he made the most of it, becoming the champion trainer in 1993/94 and 1994/95.

Successfully ensconced in his new headquarters, he voiced a regret to his wife, as she relates: 'I can always remember him saying when we'd been at Jackdaws Castle for a couple of years, that he wished he'd had Broadsword there because he was a big gross horse and he could have worked him so much more.' It might have saved a lot of bother.

David Nicholson died in 2006 at the age of 67. His ashes were spread in two places; on What A Buck's grave where the two of them used to survey his string at the top of his old gallops at Condicote, and at Cheltenham Racecourse between the last fences on the Old and New courses, which had become his favourite place from which to watch.

When a new contest was introduced to the Festival programme in 2008, it was registered as the David Nicholson Mares' Hurdle. The metamorphosis had been completed years before, the process commencing on that afternoon of March 13, 1986, but this was confirmation that the personality had indeed become the legend. David Nicholson's relationship with the Cheltenham Festival was ultimately a story of monumental success. This is where he belonged and when deeds, as well as words, eventually spoke as loud as The Duke's did, the place was always going to remember him.

CHAPTER SEVEN

1986 TOTE CHELTENHAM GOLD CUP

The Greatest Race

TO THOSE NOT that conversant with the sport, the difference between a race of two miles over hurdles and one of three and a quarter miles over fences may not sound great. That, in bald terms, is the difference between the Champion Hurdle and the Gold Cup. The Gold Cup, as we know it, was first run in 1924, the Champion Hurdle in 1927. As a measure, however, of the extreme difficulty involved in one horse winning both races in its career, the record books do not lie. It would be wrong to say that a single horse conquering these twin pinnacles of the Festival has been some sort of Holy Grail or cherished dream in the sport, because to set out for such success with almost any horse is beyond imagining. Isn't it way beyond the limits of sensible ambition? To win one of those races is hard enough and in most cases it is enough.

The career path, if there is one, is nearly always from the Champion to the Gold Cup and the first to try it was already a pioneer. The name hardly betrayed his origins but Sir Ken was one of the prototype French-bred horses that have excelled in British racing. He won the Champion in 1952 and 1953 in the course of 16 straight wins over hurdles. That set a record for the longest winning sequence in jumps racing, one that stood until Big Buck's came to dominate the staying hurdle division 60 years later. In 1954 Sir Ken won the Champion again, becoming the second of five horses who have won the race three times.

During that final Champion Hurdle-winning season the description given him by his trainer Willie Stephenson was that 'He was getting a bit of an old man and his legs weren't so good either.' Sir Ken returned to the Festival a further three times though. First was another tilt at the Champion in 1955, finishing fourth, but in 1956 as a nine-year-old it was as a chaser. Having been among the entries for the Gold Cup, a disappointing show in his final race before Cheltenham saw him diverted to the Cotswold Chase (now the Arkle) and he won it. The following year, when he was a ten-year-old, was when he became the first Champion Hurdle winner to line up for the Gold Cup but Sir Ken's time over fences ended in a flurry of falls and this was one of them, at the fifteenth.

To win a Gold Cup, 22 fences have to be safely negotiated. It was too long ago for a forensic analysis to be conducted of how Sir Ken's jumping technique affected his Gold Cup challenge but some difficulties in that department would not have been a surprise given the time he spent hurdling. It is generally much easier for horses to learn something new at a young age, and Sir Ken was not young. At that stage of his career he would have had every excuse for being past his best anyway.

Some horses can adapt without a problem, but adaptation is needed. Given the size of fences compared to hurdles, a new arc is required to get over them and, given the different construction, whereas speed is the essence of good hurdling, the prime requirement when taking on fences is probably to give them some respect. A horse can hit a hurdle and learn how to retain its balance but that is not recommended for chasers. Many believe that the best preparation is not to run over hurdles at all but to gain an education in the hunting field and point-to-points.

Thankfully that was not the path for either Bula or Lanzarote. If it had been, two of the best hurdlers ever – in 2015 they still figured in Timeform's top 11 for hurdles ratings – would have been missing. They became the next two Champion Hurdle winners to bid for the Gold Cup.

The trainer with the decisions to make for both horses was Fred Winter, who won the Gold Cup as a jockey in 1961 on Saffron Tartan and 1962 on Mandarin, the former requiring a mention in this context because he had also been five lengths third in the 1960 Champion Hurdle.

Saffron Tartan's progress from one race to the other was not orthodox, as he had already been favourite for the 1959 Gold Cup as an eight-year-old but was withdrawn after coughing on the morning of the race. When he finally did get a crack at it and won, that was not straightforward either because, in Winter's words, quoted in his biography *Fred*, by Alan Lee: '50 yards from the last fence my horse almost collapsed with tiredness … a stride after passing the winning post he was down to a walk.'

Questions of stamina would be just as acute with the two Winter-trained Champion Hurdle winners. Bula took the hurdling crown by four lengths in 1971 and by eight in 1972, when aged six and seven, and he was fifth in 1973, so he, like Sir Ken, turned nine during his first chasing season. He had five wins and a fall from six starts over fences in 1973/74, a campaign that ended before the Festival. In 1974/75 he won three of four before the meeting and proved he stayed three miles in his race before Cheltenham, but he never did prove that he stayed three and a quarter.

With the ability in his two-mile hurdling days to rush to the front late on from well off the pace, Bula and his turn of foot were not the most obvious combination to succeed in the grind of an extra mile and a quarter at Cheltenham, and in the 1975 Gold Cup the weather conspired to make it all but impossible.

Starting 5-1 co-third favourite, Bula turned for home narrowly behind Ten Up and in front of Soothsayer. With John Francome yet to go for everything, this snapshot might have conjured up the heady image of a Gold Cup victory and when Bula jumped the second last better than Ten Up he went into a narrow lead. It was relinquished a dozen strides later, and at the final fence he failed to lift himself anything like high enough, an impact that threatened to bring him to a standstill. As Bula staggered up the hill, Ten Up was left to go on and win by six and a half lengths, with Soothsayer getting back up to deny Bula second.

Asked whether he thought Bula had a chance of winning on entering the straight, Francome states, 'No. He'd run out of petrol a long time ago.'

On better ground, would he have had any chance of coming up the hill first?

'Probably not. He wasn't an out-and-out stayer. His class got him through but with three and a quarter miles around Cheltenham you've got to stay and stay really well. He jumped adequately in the Gold Cup – by that stage he had his own way of getting from one side to the other – but whereas he was adequate, Ten Up and Soothsayer would go and take a length off him every time they got to a fence.'

In 1976, Bula had firm ground instead of heavy in the Gold Cup and started 6-4 favourite, but he was an 11-year-old and, for whatever reason, he trailed in a well-beaten sixth. 'He was never going to win a Gold Cup,' says Francome in summary. 'He had quite a few miles on the clock.'

There was no shortage of racing for Lanzarote either. After a Flat career at two and three before he was ever sent to Winter, there was a sustained and enthralling rivalry with Comedy Of Errors as a hurdler before both, in their turn, were swept away by the even more brilliant generation headed by Night Nurse. Having won the 1974 Champion aged six, Lanzarote finished seventh in 1975 and fifth in 1976, but as he had won the Long Walk Hurdle over three and a quarter miles at Ascot there was more hope at Fred Winter's that this second candidate could make a serious Gold Cup horse.

'Yes, much more,' states Francome. 'He looked much more as though he was going to stay than Bula ever did.'

Stamina, though, was only one part of the equation. Of this second graduate, Francome says, 'Lanzarote was very quick over his fences but when you got in close he just parted the birch halfway up.'

The jockey's view is that he was still a better jumper than Bula: 'I've got a photo of Bula going through a fence at Newbury and his front feet are literally an inch above the frame at the back of the fence. At least Lanzarote, because he was less robust, he had to make a bit more effort.'

Like Sir Ken and Bula, Lanzarote was sent chasing as an eight-year-old, but only just. At the start of the 1976/77 season he ran twice over hurdles and it was not until November 27 that he made his debut over fences, over the American variety in the Colonial Cup. Beaten by just three lengths in Carolina, Lanzarote then impressed in winning three novice chases back in England, at odds of 4-7, 4-7 and 4-9. When he took the three-mile Reynoldstown at Ascot by 25 lengths it made Lanzarote many people's idea of the Gold Cup winner, even though Cheltenham was less than four months on from his chasing debut. He started the 7-2 second favourite.

Fred Winter had sent out the market leader for the Gold Cup in five of the previous six seasons, twice at odds on, yet he had still to come away with his first win in the race as a trainer. Lanzarote proved the saddest loss of all. *The Sporting Life* reported that he 'got over the ninth fence, seemed to falter and then crumpled to the ground ...

Lanzarote was found to have broken his near hind and had to be destroyed.'

He had given a solid display of jumping up to that point but according to Francome 'I'm sure what damage he did he did through hitting the fence.' In a wretched meeting for the Winter yard, the 12-year-old Bula, the winner of 13 steeplechases as well as 21 hurdle races, had already fallen in the two-mile Champion Chase and sustained a shoulder injury so bad that he had to be put down eight weeks later.

Bula and Lanzarote won good races over fences but Francome concludes: 'They were both pretty much set in their ways by the time they went chasing. Both suffered from the same problem – they were really good hurdlers but they couldn't round their backs at all over a fence. The fact that they were so good, they got away with plenty until it came to the biggest test of all. If you're a Gold Cup winner you've got to be able to gallop and jump, and those two were good gallopers but they weren't jumpers.'

~

NIGHT NURSE

In September 1978, 18 months after Lanzarote's Gold Cup bid, the highest-rated hurdler of all time was asked to try his hand at chasing. Like Sir Ken, Bula and Lanzarote, Night Nurse was switched only when his reign as champion hurdler had clearly come to an end. Incredibly, considering what had gone before, his final campaign over hurdles yielded just one win from ten starts. He was, however, switching codes one year earlier than those three predecessors.

Market Rasen was the venue, the course that four years earlier witnessed the birth of his stellar hurdling career. At 2-1 on, Night Nurse went straight into his customary lead over the first three fences. The horse also got safely over the fourth, but in the words of Raceform, Night Nurse 'jumped big and left', while Jonjo O'Neill seemingly went big and straight on. The jockey was deposited on the turf.

It was just a hiccup. O'Neill, who broke an arm in another spill not long afterwards, was not able to benefit, but under Ian Watkinson Night Nurse had another five runs before the end of December and won them all. His jumping over fences had swiftly proved a huge strength, just as it had been over hurdles.

'He was a natural jumper over anything,' says his trainer Peter Easterby. 'He enjoyed jumping. We just schooled him and kicked on.'

Jonjo adds, 'You would be surprised if he didn't, because he was such a fine, big, scopey horse.' When weighing up the factors that can make for a successful transition to chasing, O'Neill emphasises the importance of the horse's physique, but also the right attitude. 'That's the top and bottom of it really. If they want to do it they'll love it.'

For the last two legs in Night Nurse's five-timer, O'Neill was available but Watkinson retained the ride. Just under two weeks before the Festival, the Easterby stars Night Nurse and Alverton ran at Haydock, with the former under Watkinson losing an epic duel with Silver Buck on the Friday and Alverton under O'Neill easily winning a top handicap on the Saturday. Despite his novice status, Night Nurse was given the green light to go for the Gold Cup but six days before the race Watkinson's career was ended by a fall at Towcester. O'Neill was left with the choice of Gold Cup rides and he stayed loyal to Alverton. He says now that the decision was mainly one of stable politics.

The man called up for Night Nurse's Gold Cup bid was Graham Thorner, whose delight at the prospect was not lessened when he gave the horse a canter on the morning of the race. At the off, Alverton was 5-1 joint favourite, Night Nurse 6-1 joint third favourite, and Alverton played his part in one of the most debated Gold Cup finishes, disputing the lead at the last and left clear by the fall of Tied Cottage. Night Nurse was nowhere near them.

'Going to the first he felt dead,' says Thorner, who describes what followed as like driving a high-performance car that possessed four plugs but was firing on only one.

'He was absolutely listless but I carried on through sheer pride. I thought, "I cannot pull up a champion hurdler. I cannot disgrace him."' Night Nurse's bid to become the first Champion Hurdle and Gold Cup winner ended as a totally uncharacteristic tailed-off seventh.

That was not the final Gold Cup opportunity for Night Nurse but he could not contest it in 1980, his season ending in November with a tendon injury that led to him being fired on both forelegs. Such an injury could inspire legitimate concern about future prospects but when Night Nurse returned over a year later his chase form did not deteriorate, it improved. With O'Neill injured for most of the season, Alan Brown took the ride on all but one of his starts that campaign.

For Champion Hurdle winners, the King George VI Chase at Kempton over Christmas had been as unbreachable as the Gold Cup, but just one week after his successful reappearance Night Nurse attempted to put that right. Champion Hurdle horses did have some sort of history in the race. In 1960/61, Saffron Tartan built on his Champion third by winning the King George and the Gold Cup. Captain Christy came third in the 1973 Champion and won the following season's Gold Cup as a novice, belying his falls on two previous visits to Britain over fences. He went on to win the 1974 and 1975 King Georges, and on the second occasion it was with Bula in second, albeit beaten 30 lengths.

Night Nurse's bid for King George glory was a lot more potent than that of Bula. 'Turning in he was absolutely flying and I thought I was going to win,' recalls Brown, 'but going to the third last he just stood off a full stride too soon and I think he came down before the fence.'

Of this mistake, the jockey theorises that it would have stopped an elephant. It very nearly stopped Night Nurse but coming to the final fence he had almost fought his way back to Silver Buck's quarters. 'I'm adamant I would have won,' says Brown, 'but I think he gave himself a bit of a fright at the third last and he's just lost his confidence. It was a King George, you had to go for him, but he got into the bottom of it and he didn't know what to do.' What chance Night Nurse had of creating history was this time forfeited completely, because Brown was comprehensively unseated.

Night Nurse was now better over three miles than shorter. Going into the 1981 Gold Cup he also looked in excellent form, but Silver Buck was there again and so was Night Nurse's stablemate Little Owl, to be ridden by his part-owner, the leading amateur Jim Wilson.

'I knew they both had a good chance. And two good chances is better than one, isn't it?' says Easterby. 'Obviously the guvnor had them both spot on,' says Brown. 'We couldn't really split them at home.' Neither could they be split in the betting, both going off at 6-1 to Silver Buck's 7-2.

Night Nurse could not get to the front in the early stages but he was up there soon after the sixth fence and, as Brown relates, 'We just went a real good gallop, turned down the back second time jumping really well and we just turned the tap on a bit.' This was not something that could have been countenanced with the previous Champion Hurdle winners who ran in the race, but Brown had every confidence in Night Nurse's stamina. He recalls a moment at the top of the hill, when Jim Wilson on Little Owl moved into closer proximity. 'He shouts across to me, "How you going Al?" and I said, "I'd be going a lot better if you weren't there."'

'It was a fair race,' states Peter Easterby of what followed, with a large dose of Yorkshire understatement. 'The only time I started getting worried was when they started coming down that hill and I thought, "Christ, they can't both fall, surely?"'

Easterby does not have a high opinion of that downhill fence at Cheltenham. On this occasion, however, it proved no stumbling block to the leaders. Brown recalls that Night Nurse produced two or three unbelievable leaps in that round of jumping and one of them was at the third last, keeping him in contention after Silver Buck and Little Owl had moved up, both going much more smoothly.

After the three turned for home line abreast, however, 'he just went a bit short with me,' says Night Nurse's concerned jockey. 'I felt he wasn't 100 per cent going to the second last. He just sort of changed his legs, but then he squared himself up and got galloping again. His stamina kicked in between the last two and he just ran right to the line.'

Silver Buck was reeled in just after the final fence; Little Owl was still two and a half lengths ahead and Night Nurse started to gain on him too. 'I thought Night Nurse would catch him,' recalls their trainer.

'I didn't know whether I'd have enough time to,' says Brown, 'but all I knew was he was really staying on and giving everything. Whether Little Owl was idling a little bit in front I wouldn't know, but I think we were only beaten a length and a half.'

Brown's memory of that day and Night Nurse's previous race at Sandown was that the crowd cheered him back into the winner's enclosure as if he had won rather than finished second. Summing up his experience with Night Nurse, Brown says, 'The guts of the horse was unbelievable. Especially at that stage of his career because he'd had some really hard races.'

Although Easterby describes his feelings when watching that Gold Cup finish as 'First and second'll do. I wasn't that bothered which way round,' he admits that he was rooting for a Night Nurse win, both for the chance to make history and because Little Owl was three years younger.

Alas, the future Gold Cup challenges that were envisaged for Little Owl never appeared. 'One hell of a horse that, you know,' says Easterby, 'but he got a very bad virus. I mean a bad 'un. Blood vessels the lot. That was the end of him.' Night Nurse, however, did make it back in 1982, aged 11, and showed enough in the build-up to be sent off 11-4 favourite in a field of 22.

This time, finally, O'Neill was able to take the ride. In his autobiography *Jonjo* he wrote: 'My confidence was sky high until I asked Night Nurse to take up his starting position … I persuaded Night Nurse to start against the rails but he did not like being enclosed on the inside and started to sulk.' Even Timeform described Night Nurse as putting up a moody display and he was eventually pulled up. O'Neill says now: 'Yes, but that wouldn't be him. That was him on the day, so there was obviously something wrong with him.'

The horse was retired midway through the following season. When I interviewed him, Jonjo O'Neill's memories of Night Nurse returned unsolicited to a race at the turn of the year in the 1981/82 season: 'I was lucky enough to have a few fantastic spins on him over fences. I'll never forget one day around Newbury, in the Mandarin, and *what* a ride I got off him, he was fantastic. That was something you'd pay a lot of money for. I'm sure it was like getting a spin to space in the space shuttle. It was unbelievable. So exciting. It was the thrill of a lifetime. I can still feel it. You never forget it.'

In his autobiography, published in 1985, O'Neill wrote: 'That bleak January afternoon Night Nurse gave me the greatest thrill I have ever had on a horse.' I asked him in 2013 whether that still held true and his reply was, 'Yes, I think that would be right. Oh yes.' In the short period between those initial words being written and O'Neill's retirement as a jockey, there was one race in particular that must have complicated that decision.

~

DAWN RUN

The first sight British racegoers had of Dawn Run was on the second day of the 1983 Festival, for which she was contesting the Sun Alliance Novices' Hurdle. The same season that saw Night Nurse's career draw to a close was Dawn Run's first as a hurdler and by the end of it she was a phenomenon.

Her trainer was Paddy Mullins from Doninga at Goresbridge in County Kilkenny. When he retired at the age of 86 in 2005, having won an Irish Oaks in 2003, nearly 52 years had passed since Mullins first sent out a winner and he was one of the most revered individuals in Irish racing, the founder of a racing dynasty.

Tony Mullins, one of the trainer's four children, describes his father: 'He never worked anywhere else and he died there in his nineties. So he was completely self-taught and self-made as a trainer, and a fantastic father to us all. All along he provided the horses to ride and the opportunities that made our lives what they are.

'As he said himself many times, he was very lucky to earn a living at his pastime. He just loved training horses and developing young horses and anything to do with horses. He was definitely dedicated, spending many hours out with the horses late at night – every night he spent at least two hours out on his own going through them individually. I don't think he ever trained more than 50, which would be nowadays quite a small string.'

To the outside world, Paddy Mullins was chiefly a man of few words and those words would usually be very quietly spoken. Usually but not always. His son remembers, 'We often laugh at home that even though he was quiet, cool and collected, he could get very excited if staff weren't doing the right thing in the yard I can tell you. You wouldn't refer to him as the quiet man some mornings.'

Dawn Run's owner was Mrs Charmian Hill. Since the early '70s she had had horses at Doninga and it was a partnership between two of Irish racing's great characters. This was not the type of owner usual to racing under rules. Of Mrs Hill's relationship with her horses in training, as Anne Holland wrote in her book *Dawn Run*, 'to proffer a sugar lump was not enough'. She needed to ride them, and not just at home but in races too, and that was despite the fact that, when Dawn Run first raced, Mrs Hill was aged 63.

How important were horses to her? Her eldest son Jeremy says: 'In a way they were her life. When she grew up, horses were still working the farm here, although the tractors were coming, so at a very early age she was out with the work horses, handling them, learning about them, talking about them. Her grandmother Adela Orpen was born in Kansas, in 1855, and grew up on the plains of Kansas riding horses; at the age of eight she was able to saddle a team of four on to a cart and she was able to drive it into town. Almost certainly she would have encouraged my mother.'

The pioneer spirit present in the grandmother was passed on to the grandchild without diminution. Just the second woman in Ireland to achieve a degree in agriculture, at Trinity College, Mrs Hill was interested in everything and widely read – 'in a conversation with her you needed to know what you were talking about,' says her son – but above all it seems that she was interested in the outdoor life. Swimming, tennis, hill walking, mountain climbing, skiing, she loved them all, but she was addicted to horses. As a child she was totally dedicated to hunting and eventually in her married life with Eddie Hill, a doctor, she was able to resurrect that interest, and take it to surprising levels.

Jeremy remembers her winning a paper chase and wonders whether that might have been what fired her competitive spirit. Whatever the spur was, if it was ever needed, Charmian Hill took up raceriding in point-to-points when she turned 40. There were no queries or qualms from her children because it seemed a perfectly natural extension of what she was doing already. Besides, as her second son Oliver relates: 'We had no say in the matter; she was just going to do it anyway. She was a very determined lady and that's what she wanted to do.'

Many accidents and injuries followed, but that was nothing new either. In 1955, the Hill children had been told at boarding school that their mother was going to die following a fall when out hunting in which she had broken her skull. If anything, after that accident her determination to ride as much as possible was strengthened.

Eccentric and formidable are two words that crop up in descriptions of Mrs Hill, and hard is another. Of the side he saw, Jeremy says: 'She was always great fun and had a ball. She was a terrific whiskey drinker; she was the last one standing, she never had a hangover and she'd be the first one up in the morning.'

He also tells how she encouraged her children to ride, but not all of them did so: 'I was the only one who didn't learn to ride. I was thrown off a horse when I was five and my mother said to get back up immediately and I said, "No, I'm not getting up", and she said, I remember it very well, she said, "You are a pathetic little boy." I just said, "Well, I'm not getting up on it," and I never did.'

The late Valentine Lamb, the editor of *The Irish Field* from 1970 to 2003, knew Mrs Hill well and his summary of her character is that 'The expression is "singular". She did her thing and that was it. Nothing would waver from it.'

Given her exploits in point-to-points, Mrs Hill was

already well known in Ireland as the Galloping Granny when the authorities first permitted women to ride against men under rules. Landing what must have been very short odds, Charmian Hill became the first woman to do so. In a bumper at Fairyhouse on January 1, 1973, at the age of 54, she came third on Sundancer at 33-1.

Bumpers, hurdle races and chases – Mrs Hill went on to ride winners in all three disciplines under rules. Showing that she did not completely reject more traditional grandmotherly pursuits she knitted her own riding colours, of red with a black hoop. Later, in the Dawn Run days, she would always be seen wearing a red coat with a black belt.

When she donned those colours in racecourse competition, it was a striking spectacle. Jockeys do tend to be on the short side but Mrs Hill was minute and extremely light with it. Her accident in 1955 played a part, because, as Jeremy explains, 'After that fall she'd lost her sense of taste and smell, and she really had very little appetite. So all her life she was like a sparrow. She had to have a special saddle made to do the 12 stone in a bumper. She had about three stone of copper coins apart from the lead and she had to fill her pockets to make the weights. So it was difficult and awkward to ride, and she wasn't strong enough to hold a fully fit horse.'

Oliver recollects watching her in action: 'A couple of times she was unable to control the horse going down to the start, which was always kind of embarrassing but it didn't seem to faze her in any way.'

Jeremy describes what might transpire when the race commenced: 'Look, she wasn't a great jockey. If you ever see a video or you see any reports, the horse has gone out and she can't hold it. It's not out of control but she never held a horse back, and the funny thing was that they all said, "Oh, that's only Mrs Hill. We'll get her," but very often they didn't. She never did showjumping, and so all she had to do was sit on a horse and go and that's what she liked –

she loved the speed. The faster the horse went the better as far as she was concerned. She didn't have a fast car but she drove fast and she just enjoyed speed.'

The other riders in her races did not intentionally give her any concessions, quite the contrary, and Jeremy describes one other consequence of her very light weight – in one point-to-point two jockeys arrived on either side of her and lifted her out of the saddle. Naively, I asked whether they put her back.

'She was absolutely fearless on a horse, fearless. They did all the tricks. They were very, very dirty and really rough with her,' says Jeremy. Of the lifting incident, he continues, 'She whipped the two of them across the face the next time they tried it. Really hit them hard, so that was the end of that one.'

~

In November 1980, Mrs Hill was airlifted from the track having been crushed in a fall in a hurdle race at Thurles, breaking her neck (among other bones) and suffering kidney failure, but only a year later, having recovered sufficiently to ride one winner in a bumper, she was at the Ballsbridge Sales with her son Oliver on the look-out for another horse to ride.

'The reason that I was even involved,' says Oliver, 'was because I had borrowed some money from my mother and then I got the money to pay her back and said, "Look, rather than giving you the money, why don't we buy a horse together?"'

This was the sort of offer that held some appeal and, going perilously close to their intended budget, Mrs Hill purchased an unnamed three-year-old daughter of Deep Run out of Twilight Slave for 5,800 guineas. The filly had a good jumping pedigree and made a huge impression on her purchaser as soon as she set foot outside her box to be viewed. Oliver Hill's Wednesday night card school in Dublin happened to include the owner of For Auction, winner of the 1982 Champion Hurdle, and on the same night that Dawn Run was purchased Hill bullishly predicted to his poker chum that he had just bought a horse to put For Auction in the shade. It turned out he was not bluffing.

The filly was barely broken in but Mrs Hill rode her at her home and took her over a fence. The two got on well together and initially Mrs Hill became concerned that Dawn Run might be too placid to make a successful racehorse.

Ownership is usually the least engaging element in a racehorse's story, an account of how one wealthy individual chooses to spend their money. I have a friend who used to try and spice it up by shouting 'Well owned!' when it came to their turn in the presentation ceremonies. In jumps racing in particular, however, things can sometimes be a little different. To what degree she was 'well owned' would become a bone of contention in some quarters but her ownership was indisputably an integral, and not at all passive, part in the story that was about to unfold with Dawn Run.

On being sent to Doninga, Dawn Run immediately made a big impression. 'She was a big, masculine-looking individual, a very imposing filly,' says Tony Mullins. 'She stood out in a crowd.' And on closer inspection, 'her conformation was as near to perfect as you would get.

'At that time Deep Run fillies had a reputation of being very fiery and after a couple of days I remember she refused to go on to the gallop. We all said, "Another typical Deep Run filly". It was just really pure greenness, that she didn't know what was being asked of her. But when the penny dropped, she was the quickest learner nearly I ever saw.'

The care of Dawn Run had been entrusted to John Clarke, a 15-year-old who had joined the stable only a month before she did. The reason he was allotted to her was that the other lads did not want the task. Denis Walsh has written in the *Sunday Times* that Mrs Hill was 'fair and correct, but short on gifts'. Valentine Lamb remembered affectionately that on her visit to the yard after one of Dawn Run's big wins the lads were waiting expectantly and found out that 'she'd baked them a pie or a cake. She wasn't being deliberately mean, that was her.'

For Paddy Mullins, the task of training Dawn Run was different for him from start to finish. As Tony observes: 'She wasn't trained like the normal owner's horse that would be trained to win first time out. She was trained to make her suitable for Mrs Hill to ride in a bumper. You're talking about a senior lady in age, so it was very important that the filly didn't take off in the parade ring or run away going to the start and that, so as opposed to buzzing them up to be ready to win, it was important that Mrs Hill and Dawn Run stayed together.'

Dawn Run was consequently not tested at home before she ran. On her racecourse debut at Clonmel in May 1982 she came eighth. Most may have missed it. At Thurles on her second start, however, Dawn Run and Mrs Hill made up an eyecatching amount of ground late on to finish fourth. Five days later they went to Tralee and made most to win. There was a powerful, added incentive for Mrs Hill in that race because she had just been informed by a letter from the Irish Turf Club that they had decided not to renew the 63-year-old's riding licence.

'We had to deal with her fury,' says her son Jeremy. 'She was absolutely furious because she'd won on Dawn Run and she was still winning races. As far as she was concerned she was still perfectly fit and she just didn't get the point that a licensed jockey couldn't ride after 60. They'd never thought to ask her her age. She wrote all sorts of letters and appealed to the Turf Club and appealed to all the people she knew but it was no good. It was futile.'

It has been speculated that Mrs Hill wanted to ride Dawn Run herself throughout her career and that it was only this intervention of the Turf Club that prevented her. Undoubtedly she found it very hard to accept that her competitive riding days were over.

Jeremy Hill's view is that: 'It wouldn't have cost her a thought to saddle up for the Gold Cup if that's what somebody said go and do. She would absolutely have loved to have done it, but that was never going to happen. She would have wanted to have ridden her over hurdles, but whether she would have actually argued her way into the saddle I don't know. I'd have my doubts because she was smart enough to realise that this horse was special and that's what she would have cared about. That would have been the priority.'

When Dawn Run returned to action at the Galway Festival in July and Tralee in September it was under Paddy Mullins' youngest son Tom and she won both races. The latter was the prestigious Haversnack Flat Race and Tom's brother Tony, the stable professional jockey, was watching in the wings, waiting for Dawn Run's switch to hurdles. It was a revelatory performance. 'My father was champion trainer at the time so he knew she was a nice filly, but that day he said to me, "We haven't had the likes of this one for a long, long time."'

Tony Mullins' experience of raceriding on the horse of a lifetime was about to commence, and he got the leg up on Dawn Run's second run over hurdles. 'My first time to ride her over hurdles was in Navan just a couple of days before Christmas and she won easily,' he relates. 'It didn't strike me as anything special on the day; obviously a nice filly, but then I rode her eight days after that in what was a big novice hurdle at Leopardstown and it was unbelievable the difference. I knew then that I had never sat on anything like this before. The speed she went – I remember thinking shortly after halfway that she's going to have to be quite good to keep up this gallop and then around the third last, when I gave her a kick, she just quickened as if she had only been walking, and she just quickened and quickened all the way to the line. I remember passing the post and thinking to myself, "By God, I've never sat on anything like this."'

In her next start Mrs Hill requested that Dawn Run be held up, an experiment which would not be repeated, and then she won at Punchestown and was a good third in a handicap at Fairyhouse where she made a late mistake. Tony Mullins had now ridden her for her last five starts but one morning, after riding out at Doninga, Mrs Hill asked if she could have a word with the trainer. Dawn Run was heading to the Cheltenham Festival but Mrs Hill requested that the trainer engage someone else to ride her.

As Paddy Mullins related in his authorised biography *The Master Of Doninga*, Mrs Hill's 'mind was made up. She didn't want Tony riding the mare in Cheltenham. It was a bit of a shock to me. She said to me, "Can you get another jockey?" and I said that I could. I didn't debate the matter with her. It was her prerogative.'

Mrs Hill insisted that the replacement had to be an Irishman. After careful thought, Mullins came up with Ron Barry as his chosen alternative and Mrs Hill agreed. Of his reaction to being jocked off, Tony says: 'I was very disappointed but at that stage I suppose I had been just conditional champion the year before so I accepted that she wanted someone with more experience.'

The Hill family has had a long association with Cheltenham. Dr Hill went to school there, at Dean Close, where he listened to sermons warning of the sport's moral dangers. All three of his sons also went to Dean Close and while Jeremy did not manage to see any horseracing at Prestbury Park, as a member of the cross-country team he did race at the track himself. 'It's a bloody big climb,' remembers the erstwhile runner.

Brother Oliver was more fortunate and sneaked out of school to attend the 1962 Champion Hurdle. As a family, the Hills became regular attendees at the Festival and always stayed at the Cotswold Grange Hotel.

The Sun Alliance Novices' Hurdle, in which Dawn Run made her first appearance at the Festival, is a race her half-brother Even Dawn had won at 40-1 in 1972. At 11-1, Dawn Run was sixth in the betting with three other Irish horses in front of her. But hopes among her connections were very high. In the parade ring she was always going to be noticed. The majority of mares are insubstantial individuals in physique compared to the males and only a few get to be competitive in top-class jumps racing but Dawn Run bore no resemblance to a normal mare. The field also contained the subsequent Grand National hero West Tip, a strapping specimen if ever there was one, so it is not possible to say that Dawn Run was the most substantial horse in the race, but she not only looked in a different league from the usual mare, she easily overshadowed most of the males.

Dawn Run and Barry were soon striding out in front but, speaking in 2014, the jockey's verdict is that 'I didn't go fast enough. I thought I was flat to the boards but she wasn't. She had a really high cruising speed and I should have been going faster.'

The four-year-old Sabin Du Loir (receiving 13lb weight for age) vied with Dawn Run on the far side and went past her at the second last, but she came back at him on the run-in before her Michael Dickinson-trained rival went on again to win by three lengths.

Dawn Run was beaten fair and square. Barry says 'there was no aggro' from any of her connections afterwards, but when she appeared at Aintree some three weeks later, Tony Mullins was back in the saddle. In the Sun Templegate Hurdle (now the Aintree Hurdle) one rival again went on from her late on, but this time when Dawn Run rallied it was even more strongly and she was doing so against the previous month's Champion Hurdle winner Gaye Brief. The margin between them was just a length. That was on the Saturday. On the Friday, Dawn Run had warmed up by hammering handicap rivals over the same course and distance.

If her Cheltenham performance had been an eye-opener, this near double strike had the racing world agog, but Tony professes that 'We weren't surprised at that stage. We knew before Cheltenham that she was in that league. It didn't surprise us but that's when the public became aware that she was the real one.'

For a novice, Dawn Run's run against Gaye Brief was unsurprisingly the best form seen all season and that sort of standard has been seen perhaps only half a dozen times since.

~

1984 CHAMPION HURDLE SEASON

Commencing her second campaign as a hurdler, Dawn Run had a Flat race in October and returned to the day job at Down Royal at the start of November. At 5-2 on and ridden by Tony Mullins she won easily by ten lengths, the same margin with which they had also despatched a very strong field of novice hurdlers, including the Supreme Novices' winner Buck House, over two miles at Punchestown in May. On coming back to the winner's enclosure at Down Royal, the jockey was greeted by a stern-looking Mrs Hill:

'I jumped down in the number 1 and Mrs Hill said to me, "Well done, but it looks like we have a Champion Hurdle mare now, so you will not be riding her for the rest of the season," Now *that* day I was devastated. I'll never forget it. I couldn't believe it.'

I suggest to Mullins that it must have been a long walk back to the weighing room. 'It surely was. People kept on saying well done to me and I was sick as a pig.'

The jockey did not tell anybody about what had transpired, hoping that Mrs Hill's declaration was a spur-of-the-moment decision that might be reversed, but a surprised Jonjo O'Neill received a phone call from Paddy Mullins a few days later to sound him out about taking over on the mare. The news was made public. At the time, Tony Mullins was quoted as saying, 'It's no disgrace to lose the ride to someone as good as Jonjo,' which was taking it with good grace, but his feelings, and those of his family, ran deeply.

While admitting the scale of his disappointment, Mullins elaborates, 'It was an awkward situation as well because I didn't want to cause any friction that might cost my father the training of the mare. We never discussed it. It was a contentious issue and we knew that not much could be done about it.'

For a second time, Paddy Mullins conceded that the decision was Mrs Hill's prerogative and, while she was aware of his feelings on the matter, he did not argue with her. Jonjo O'Neill observes, 'She was the kind of a lady that you listened to rather than took her on.'

Although it was not officially registered, Oliver Hill had a quarter share in Dawn Run but he explains that 'The understanding was that she [his mother] had the complete rights to any decision in relation to the mare.'

While Mrs Hill had taken the initiative to remove Tony Mullins from the saddle, Oliver Hill says, 'Certainly I approved of the whole idea. Jonjo was suggested and I was very, very happy with that arrangement and told my mother that as far as I was concerned we can't do any better.'

Owners who come to prefer one jockey over another and decide to act on it are not at all unusual. Indeed it would be far stranger were it the other way around, but with the sort of prominence that Dawn Run would achieve, Mrs Hill's preferences have become some of the most famous in racing history.

Jonjo's residency on Dawn Run nearly commenced with a defeat, and at 3-1 on. Over 2m4f on firm ground at Ascot in November, they got home in front from Amarach by just a short head, but Mrs Hill believed that very few other jockeys could have rallied the mare to get back in front that day and that Dawn Run would learn a good deal from the experience. The partnership was beaten at Naas next time but it was a solid performance in a handicap and on her next two outings it became unmistakable that she was Champion Hurdle class. First, in the Christmas Hurdle at Kempton, Dawn Run and Gaye Brief let fly at the last hurdle and the front-running mare held off the reigning champion by a neck. That was in receipt of 5lb but in the Wessel Cable Champion Hurdle at Leopardstown she won by five lengths and she was giving weight not receiving it.

'The public probably thought that she was getting better and better,' says Tony Mullins, 'but we knew what she was capable of and my father had a plan for the long season. He was keeping a little in the locker all the time.'

In assessing the Christmas Hurdle, it seemed that 2m over that sharp track was never going to see Dawn Run at her best but nevertheless Gaye Brief maintained favouritism for Cheltenham with Mercy Rimell having revealed ('rather late in the day' observed Timeform) that her charge had suffered an interrupted preparation for Kempton following a very small crack in a cannon bone. Indeed, Gaye Brief was odds on for the Champion in the week before the Festival, until torn ligaments in his back put paid to his participation.

After that, the Champion Hurdle was all about Dawn Run and there was clearly quite a story for the media to latch on to. The image of Mrs Hill on board her mare at Doninga transfixed all those who saw it. Of the concept of such a small and apparently frail woman, of senior years, trying to control a horse like that on the gallops, Jonjo O'Neill exclaims: 'You've got to be mad, haven't you? I'm not trying to be disrespectful to her but this was a big, strong mare and she could gallop. I'm sure when she used to go round the fields, Paddy must have been closing his eyes.'

Two journalists who kept their eyes open as Dawn Run and her owner stepped out at Doninga were John Oaksey and Brough Scott, and the image lingered with both. Oaksey wrote of 'the great mare and her diminutive, well-over-sixty owner storming up Paddy Mullins's gallops with the trainer murmuring philosophically, "Well, they both enjoy it, you see ..."'

Scott, who once described Mrs Hill memorably as 'a lady so small and frail-looking that you want to keep the grandchildren off her at teatime,' has stated that his greatest memory of Paddy Mullins was of the trainer watching Dawn Run and Mrs Hill 'lapping alarmingly fast round an equally tight training circle', at which Mullins remarked, 'Ah, it will do the old girl good.' Scott wondered which old girl the trainer was referring to.

Jeremy Hill acknowledges: 'She was a hands-on owner. She wanted to be absolutely hands on. She had huge regard for Paddy, of course, and she listened to him, but she wanted to know for herself; that's why she wanted to sit in the saddle. She wanted to come down and say what she thought.'

Of her qualifications to do so, her son states, 'There was nothing that woman didn't know about horses and hadn't had first-hand experience of. There are very, very few owners who had the experience of horses that my mother had.'

I asked Tony Mullins whether his father had any qualms about having Mrs Hill ride her. 'Well, obviously, it was a worry but he realised that it was her mare, so it was part of the deal. He definitely would be anxious but it was never a contentious issue.'

As Dawn Run's career blossomed, Mullins senior took care not to risk any dangers that were avoidable. Whereas, in normal circumstances, there might often be ten experienced horses together along with three 'breakers', young horses with older ones to learn their trade, the 'breakers' were not brought out in the same lot as Dawn Run.

Mrs Hill described her ride: 'She's got a lovely temperament, really lovely. She'll take a fierce hold but she'll never do you down: she'll always go where you tell her and no matter how fresh she is I can always pull her up. If I have to, I can, she never goes mad.'

Tony Mullins explains that Dawn Run knew when Mrs Hill was riding her and was well used to her, and this was one of the areas in which Dawn Run's intelligence manifested itself. 'When Mrs Hill rode her she was completely a passenger when the mare got up and educated,' he says, 'but the mare never did her any harm and Mrs Hill never did the mare any harm.'

When Mrs Hill rode out, Dawn Run always strode out in front. With other riders the mare could follow another horse, and of those sessions Tony Mullins says of Dawn Run: 'She worked with two other horses at a time. There'd be a lead horse and I'd be upsides the other one and, of course, needless to say, when you pressed the button that was the end of that, she'd be on her own.'

In the Champion Hurdle, Dawn Run was on her own in the betting and started 4-5 favourite in a 14-runner field. There had been shorter-priced favourites in the race, including Comedy Of Errors in 1974 at 4-6; Bula had been 8-11 in 1972 and 5-6 in 1973. In all of those instances, though, other horses had been prominent in the betting. Against Dawn Run, the nearest was the prolific novice Desert Orchid at 7-1, making it the most one-sided betting for a Champion Hurdle since Sir Ken was sent off at 4-9 in 1954.

It was chiefly history that seemed to be lined up against Dawn Run as the only mare to have won the Champion was African Sister in 1939. The only ones to have been placed were African Sister, a year after her victory, and Ivy Green 19 years later. Between 1969 and 1984, only one mare (a 500-1 shot) had even run in the race. In Dawn Run's favour, however, was that a 5lb allowance had been introduced in the 1983/84 season for mares in all races for which they were eligible under National Hunt rules.

In the 1984 Champion Hurdle, Dawn Run went into a clear lead jumping the first flight and only three horses mustered serious attempts to challenge her thereafter. Desert Orchid did so by narrowly assuming his normal front-running role on the far side of the course but he was done with as soon as the field turned downhill. Buck House, with Tommy Carmody on board, was the only one near the mare at the second last and the two horses bumped just before jumping it, after which Buck House quickly cracked. Approaching the last, though, one final threat emerged from an unexpected quarter. Peter Scudamore had tried to keep the 66-1 shot Cima in his comfort zone to achieve the best he could and it now became clear that his best was vastly better than most had imagined.

'All of a sudden, I've gone to the last,' relates Scudamore, 'Dawn Run's hanging about in front and I've winged it, I've landed running and I got to Dawn Run's girth.' Cima's cause seemed to be helped when Dawn Run took the last very awkwardly and lost momentum. But it was soon regathered and, although drifting to her right, Dawn Run never looked like relinquishing the lead. 'Of course she's come across,' continues Scudamore, 'but she'd have won a neck if the winning post had been in the middle of Cheltenham.' In the event, Dawn Run won by three-quarters of a length.

Confirming the presence of a formidable competitive spirit, Jonjo asserts that 'Once you got her on the move and she was in front, trains wouldn't have passed her.'

In his autobiography O'Neill wrote: 'For me the most worrying part of the 1984 Champion Hurdle was trying to reach the weighing room.' Which may make the race sound entirely routine until it is remembered that regaining the weighing room afterwards may well have qualified as the 13th labour of Hercules. Here was very tangible evidence that the Dawn Run phenomenon had gained a wild momentum in the hearts of Irish racegoers, hundreds of whom attempted to celebrate with connections in the winner's enclosure. And many succeeded. In the rolling maul through which Jonjo eventually made his way to weigh in, he had to resist particularly determined attempts to wrench away the number cloth and breastgirth.

In this heady aftermath, living up to her reputation for risking life and limb, Mrs Hill agreed to being given 'the bumps' in the winner's enclosure, being thrown into the air and caught again, the sort of thing that more usually attends a youthful birthday celebration. Thankfully on this occasion the number of times she was propelled skywards did not correspond to her years of age.

Among those there to watch her rise and fall, Tony Mullins felt able to join in the other celebrations: 'The Champion Hurdle was I suppose the first real championship race that my father had won at Cheltenham. Now he had trained winners at Cheltenham before but this was one of the big three, so it was a very big day for our family and I put my own personal thoughts behind me and we enjoyed it as a family. I was elated that our family and our business had produced a champion hurdler.'

Less than three weeks later, Dawn Run lined up for the Aintree Hurdle but O'Neill was not there with her. Two days earlier, in what is now the Topham Chase, his mount fell at the first and the jockey's way of describing the physical consequences is that 'I split my head open and I couldn't get my helmet on, so they wouldn't let me ride – it was too swollen.' In hospital awaiting treatment after this latest in a long succession of injuries, he considered retirement.

At the racecourse, Mrs Hill too had a decision to make and Tony Mullins recalls how it was resolved: 'My father went to her and said, "Who's going to ride the mare on Saturday?" and she turned to him and said, "I'm not that mean. I will put Tony back up on her."'

With all the shenanigans of getting on, off, on, off and on again, the restored rider might have been excused for feeling a little pressure when setting forth on Dawn Run at Aintree, but he asserts, 'Just to get my backside back in the saddle I knew I was on a winner. There was no pressure because I knew unless I did something silly like fall off her, there was just nothing around that could beat her. And I was utmostly confident of that long before I left the weighing room, every time I rode her.'

At Aintree, confidence in Dawn Run could not have been more justified and, notwithstanding her starting price of 6-4 on, what followed was a performance of rare dominance for one of the calendar's top hurdle races. Very Promising managed to be ten lengths off her at the finish. It was a further twenty back to the third home in an eight-runner race and Dawn Run, in a clear lead throughout, appeared not to be asked a serious question. O'Neill missed three winning rides on that Grand National card, watching at home on what he called his blackest day of the season. Described in desolate terms in his autobiography, he took it for granted that Mullins would stay on her.

In fact, when Dawn Run was next sighted on a racecourse it was under Mrs Hill, and what a sight it was. The occasion was the Punchestown Festival at which the conquering heroines were due to take the applause of an appreciative crowd and, instead of merely parading in front of them, the Champion Hurdle winner and her owner took an unscheduled gallop down the middle of the course.

'I'd say she ran a bit free with her now,' comments Tony Mullins, 'but people made a bit of a meal of it. Mrs Hill was quite well able to control her and Dawn Run knew she had Mrs Hill on her back. She might have gone faster than she should have but there was never any danger of either getting hurt.'

The additional unorthodox element of this incident was that Dawn Run was still in training. Paddy Mullins had indeed hatched plans for a long season for her, with two more races still to be contested in a campaign that would end almost at the end of June. Dawn Run had won the Champion Hurdles in Ireland and England and now the trainer had his eye on the French version.

The Grande Course de Haies d'Auteuil is actually the French version only in so far as it is the most important hurdle race in France. It is staged over a very different distance – three miles, one and a half furlongs – to the Champion and Irish Champion, as well as over the different, French brand of hurdles, which bear more of a resemblance to mini fences. Dawn Run's warm-up race, the Prix La Barka, was a very serious test against some of France's best hurdlers but, as had become familiar closer to home, she was never headed. This was despite giving weight all round. At only weight for age in the Grande Course itself, an additional six furlongs proved no impediment and Dawn Run's superiority received no serious challenges as she breezed home in front by six lengths, the first ever winner of the race from Britain or Ireland.

In the saddle for both legs of this French adventure was Tony Mullins. At this stage, was he thinking that he had the ride for good unless something went badly wrong? 'Yes, I did think that.'

~

GOING CHASING

'If you've owned horses, and you've raced horses, you know exactly what it's like – just a land of unpredictability,' states Jeremy Hill. 'Everything has to go your way to win a race, no matter what the race. You can't allow yourself to say, "This is great, we're going to win today"'.

With eight wins from nine starts, spanning an unheard of variety of top races, Dawn Run's Champion Hurdle-winning campaign was almost a procession but her chasing career would show that she was prone to the vagaries of fortune as much as any other horse. For her there was only one goal, but even to bring it within range was anything but straightforward.

As described earlier, a chasing career was not the primary objective for the previous Champion Hurdle winners who attempted metamorphosis into Gold Cup winners. Considering whether Fred Winter had high hopes when they switched to chasing that either Bula or Lanzarote could emerge as Gold Cup winners, John Francome concludes: 'No, not in his heart of hearts. I think that he felt he'd got the best out of both of them and it was just one more avenue. He achieved Plan A with both of them.' Plan A had been to win the Champion Hurdle. Schooling from an earlier age to jump in a manner that was more conducive to chasing would have prejudiced their prospects over hurdles.

Sir Ken, Bula and Lanzarote all had their attentions turned to chasing as eight-year-olds. Night Nurse was seven but, even with him, when asked whether he regrets not sending the horse over fences earlier Peter Easterby replies, 'Oh yes, absolutely.'

For Dawn Run, a switch to chasing was also deferred, but only at the end of her first season hurdling, when her potential to win a Champion Hurdle could not be passed over. Once that was accomplished, at the age of six, while Paddy Mullins found the idea of another Champion Hurdle challenge fairly alluring, Mrs Hill was having none of it and was entirely focused on the greater challenge.

Jeremy Hill reflects: 'By the time she was heading to Cheltenham for the Champion Hurdle I'm absolutely sure it was in the back of her mind. She might have said if she wins the Champion Hurdle then we can dream about the next one, but I'm sure she lay in bed at night saying this horse is a chaser not a hurdler.'

Mrs Hill would later confirm that the Gold Cup was always her objective for Dawn Run and that she would far rather win the Gold Cup than the Champion. When the Champion was safely in the bag Mrs Hill predicted that the Gold Cup could be won in another two years.

For stamina at least, Dawn Run looked well equipped, having kidded no one that 2m was her best trip, excelled in two Aintree Hurdles when stepped up in distance and then won the Grande Course de Haies d'Auteuil over almost as far as the Gold Cup. But could there also be confidence in her jumping?

Mrs Hill had thought so from a very early stage, telling RTE television: 'I always was sure that she'd make a good chaser. She's very, very big and I put her over a fence here before she went to Paddy's and she just did it like a natural. She's a natural jumper and I was always determined that she'd go chasing. She had a bit of speed and she could stay and she could jump.'

In Dawn Run's Champion Hurdle-winning season, however, she made last-flight mistakes at Down Royal, Naas, Cheltenham and Aintree, and she was not foot perfect at Auteuil either.

Tony Mullins elaborates: 'She was so big that she could stand back unbelievable distances and she overcame a lot of little things with her sheer size and ability to let fly at one, but if it came to correcting herself going into a hurdle, or a fence later in life, she wasn't great at it.'

After two racecourse schooling sessions, all was set for her competitive chase debut at Navan in November, over 2m and with rivals including the familiar white blaze of

Buck House who had already won over fences. Dawn Run won by ten lengths with, as was usually the case in her races, the field well strung out.

'She was such a bold jumper,' eulogises Tony Mullins of that chasing debut. 'You've probably seen the picture of her winning that day – she broke the breastgirth. She had such a stretch and when she met the last ditch I suppose she took off all of 15 feet before. For a handicapper to do it would be unbelievable but she just took it in her stride and she broke the breastgirth she stretched so far for it. And riding her it didn't feel like she stretched. She was unreal.'

After that, Dawn Run was quoted at 6-1 'with a run' for the Gold Cup but Paddy Mullins cautioned that she was being aimed at the Sun Alliance Chase for novices instead. About a month later, that plan had to be torn up when Dawn Run strained a ligament. She was put away for the season and her campaign in novice chases, during which she was supposed to gain the nous and experience to equip her for the far greater challenges ahead, had amounted to just one race.

Her recuperation included probably the longest time she ever spent at the Hills' house, Belmont, near Waterford, punctuated by one 12-hour period near the end of her stay in which the highest-profile racehorse in Ireland went awol and not just from her paddock.

'The gates were fitted so that you could lean down and just push a catch when you're on the horse, and she just might have worked that out, you don't know, but anyway she was gone,' says Oliver Hill. A phone call was received at the house from someone saying, 'I think your mare is walking up the road' and, as Oliver describes it, 'she did go up the road, up the little boreen that led down to the house, and then she went out on to the main Dunmore East road and just kept going.'

Dawn Run was in the company of two other horses and they were tracked down a couple of miles away in a housing estate in Waterford. Mrs Hill enlisted the help of some women and children, exhorting them to be brave and wave their arms in a bid to stop the horses and collar them. Similar attempts will have been seen many times at the races when there is a loose horse. It does not seem to work that often. In this instance Dawn Run kicked Mrs Hill in the thigh and they got loose again, but later on that night someone was able to shut the three miscreants in their garden and Mrs Hill collected them the next morning.

Confirming that Dawn Run was not always the easiest to deal with, Oliver recalls another incident at Belmont: 'She was always the boss of the other horses there and she got a bit wilder as time went on. She got more and more stroppy. I remember going down one time to have a look at her and she put her ears back and bared her teeth and I said, "Mmm, I'm not too keen on this kind of attitude." The horse didn't know me so I decided to back off and then she started coming towards me and I had to get in behind a tree to avoid her. So she was a well arrogant madam when she wanted to be.'

~

THE 1986 GOLD CUP SEASON

Safely back in the care of Paddy Mullins and recovered from her injury, Dawn Run made her reappearance in a 2m4f chase at Punchestown in mid-December. Ireland held its breath, and then it could let out an almighty cheer. For most of the race, reported Michael Clower in *The Sporting Life*, 'Dawn Run's fans were stunned into a disbelieving silence' at the sight of the mare even more imperious than ever, but from the last fence to the line 'there was prolonged cheering and clapping, the like of which has not been heard on an Irish racecourse since the days of Arkle. And nor can I recall an instance when the crowd broke into the sort of spontaneous applause that Dawn Run met with as she was led away from the winner's enclosure back to the racecourse stables.'

Tony Mullins was on board for that win, and he recalls: 'She was a little ring rusty but still won well. Then she went to meet Buck House in Leopardstown at Christmas and by God was she sharp. That was an unbelievable day. There are six fences down the back and I'll never forget it. We were just coming near the end of the back straight and we had jumped maybe five of them and Tommy Carmody turned to me and he said, "I don't know if we're getting enough money to be going this speed" and he laughed. I actually thought we were going quite a good pace but I knew from the way he said that that he was nearly flat-out so I knew I had him. She was just unreal that day and I pulled her up a long way before the line.'

Clower recorded that 'Buck House, a truly brilliant jumper, not only tried to match strides with her in the Sean Graham Chase but attempted to find her out by repeatedly quickening at his fences and taking off half a length in front. Far from forcing Dawn Run into making mistakes, Tommy Carmody often found himself outjumped – and, when the crunch came, it was his mount who had nothing left.'

It was not a foot-perfect round at Leopardstown, though, as Dawn Run had a disagreement with the last fence and was knocked sideways before still being able to coast home, and there had also been an issue with the last fence at Punchestown. Connections decided that a trip to Cheltenham would be ideal to further the mare's education. There she would encounter harder fences that she could not brush through with impunity and, as there are no water jumps in Ireland, as Tony Mullins puts it, 'we didn't want her first run over a water fence in the middle of a Gold Cup.'

Paddy Mullins was famous for never giving riding instructions but even the most verbose of trainers might not have covered the set of circumstances that prevailed during Dawn Run's first taste of the fences at Cheltenham. As she was sent off at 4-9, most backers may have thought they were due to cheer an exhibition round and what followed was indeed an effervescent display of front-running and bold jumping ... as far as it went. This is a transcript of Julian Wilson's BBC commentary. The capital letters indicate where the pitch and volume of Wilson's voice rises dramatically:

'Dawn Run cruising, coasting in the lead. 18 wins behind her. It's two years since she's been beaten. And this only her fourth race over fences but certainly her best performance of jumping so far and this is the last open ditch and she's a bit CLOSE AND SHE'S GONE, SHE'S GONE. Dawn Run has unseated her rider and Tony Mullins has landed on his feet and the mare has stopped and he has caught the mare but the others are away.'

Her jettisoned jockey recalls: 'We were jumping well, brilliantly, and then she met that ditch just a little bit wrong, she got confused, she bellied into the middle of it. She lost two shoes when she hit the fence and that takes a fair mistake to pull off two shoes.'

That, however, was not the end of either Dawn Run's race or Mullins' very public examination. 'Now, I don't know whether it was right or wrong,' he explains, 'but when I hit the ground that day I said to myself, "Well, we're here for a school, that's what we're here for," and I wanted to re-bolster her confidence after making the mistake so I decided to jump the last five fences.'

It must have been a lonely experience. and in the course of it one thought inevitably occurred: 'I jumped the last and I remember thinking to myself, just as I cantered up to the line, well, the owner has the excuse to jock me off again now.'

Literally, very graphically and for the foreseeable future in races, in that incident at the final open ditch at the top of the hill he did indeed lose the ride. A stunned Mrs Hill had been watching with her son and co-owner Oliver, and by the time their plane landed back at Dublin airport, while no decision had been made about who would ride Dawn Run in future, what had been decided is that it would not be Tony Mullins.

'I said, "As far as I'm concerned he's off,"' reveals Oliver Hill. 'My mother had a bit of a dilemma because she had such an attachment to the Mullinses. But to be quite honest with you I was absolutely insistent – no way.'

In a documentary on RTE, Mrs Hill later confirmed that she blamed Mullins for the unseat at Cheltenham, saying that 'He let her jump too free all the way. She should never have been allowed to jump so free.' Of the decision to replace him she explained, 'I'd been thinking of it for quite a while' and said that the issue that confronted her was 'What chance have you twice in a lifetime to win a Gold Cup?'

For several days, Tony Mullins remained uncertain of his status, but fully aware from previous experience that he was hardly set in stone as Dawn Run's jockey and also that he was now the centre of a vehement debate conducted in the press. Those days, he says, felt like 'a long time when you were trying to ride a horse that was going to win the Gold Cup.'

After Mrs Hill's next visit to Doninga, the news was delivered: 'It was right at the back door, between Dawn Run's stable and the back door. I remember it well. My father told me. I think he just said, "She wants to change again," I nodded my head and we never spoke about it after.'

Comparing this to his previous removal from the Champion Hurdle ride, Mullins says, 'I expected it after what happened at Cheltenham. But it didn't make it any easier to take.'

Jonjo O'Neill was riding at Cheltenham that afternoon in January, but not in Dawn Run's race, and says he had no inkling that Tony Mullins' travails might have any implications for him. On February 4, however, it was announced that O'Neill had been recalled. Mrs Hill said, 'Every jockey has a different way of riding. Jonjo's experience is really what I went for more than anything else.'

The deposed rider says that the decision was something never discussed in the Mullins family but that it was a raw issue for them for many years. He also says, however, that 'I don't think she did it out of malice, I think she did what she believed was best for her horse. So from that point of view I'm more disappointed than sour.'

Of his relationship with Mrs Hill after that, he reports: 'We were polite. We weren't friendly. We did a pretty good job of avoiding each other.'

In *The Sporting Life* on February 4, Michael Clower's Report From Ireland included 'An open letter to Tony Mullins'. It gives an impression of how high the passions were running on this issue:

'If you become bitter and twisted and stay that way for the rest of your life, nobody could in all honesty blame you – but I know you will not. However, you have gone on record as saying you will not change your style, no matter how much criticism is heaped upon you. You must think again, but don't lengthen your leathers or shorten your reins. The former suits you and the latter, which plays such a key part in getting your mounts to relax, is one of your strongest points. And don't be tempted to use your whip more in a finish. Nobody who saw you throw everything at Hungary Hur at Fairyhouse last Saturday need ever doubt that you have a talent – unfortunately rare amongst your rivals in Ireland – for getting your mounts to give their all without hammering hell out of them. No, Tony what you must do is improve on those areas where you are at fault.

'Your habit of calling a cab is unnecessary, undignified and unbefitting a man who is entitled to call himself a champion. Also concentrate on going the shortest way round. By all means let your mounts have their head but keep them on the rails. And, if you can bear it, look upon the bright side. It's Jonjo O'Neill who is on trial now. Remember how Dawn Run was always all out to win with him on her back, remember how she never really seemed at ease with him in the plate? We will not let Charmian Hill forget that and, if Dawn Run does not run for him as sweetly as she has always done for you, you will be back where I for one sincerely believe you still have a right to be.'

I do not know whether Jonjo O'Neill read that piece or felt on trial, but with Dawn Run due to run at Punchestown towards the end of February, O'Neill was engaged, but he had not been asked to ride her in the Gold Cup. Before Punchestown, he received his first chance to ride Dawn Run over fences when she went for a racecourse school at Gowran Park.

I asked him how it went. 'Bad,' Jonjo groans. 'That one went desperate.'

'We set off to school her on her own and I was only supposed to go round once but she was so bad the first time, I couldn't even get her to go and see the first fence. She wouldn't even trot up to it. And of course Mrs Hill is there and so on. Eventually I got her over the first, and she honestly trotted through it. I thought, "Will I pull up, or will I go back or what will I do?" Anyway I decided that if I go back she'll do the same again, so I might as well try and keep going. I could only barely get her to canter by the second fence and she did the same thing again – trotted straight over it. And then the ditch down the hill in the back straight, I got her over that, just, and I'm only literally cantering. So when I thought I was out of view, I picked her up and gave her a belt, I gave her a belt or two – well, she pulled up and walked with me! I thought that wasn't the right thing to do. So I got her going and I jumped another couple down into the straight and I thought, "Christ, there's no way I'm going to pull up here, I'll just keep going all the way round and get her going." I went to the fence down the back where she stopped with me before and she nearly pulled up to a trot with me again. Oh, she was so moody, honestly. Anyway, I kept going and she got a bit better. And I just came back and I said to Mrs Hill and to Paddy, I said, "That was grand. I was delighted with that," and Paddy looked at me as if I had three heads. It was funny – funny looking back on it. She was favourite for the Gold Cup and I thought not only that she shouldn't be favourite, she shouldn't even be running in it.'

'I can imagine that Jonjo wasn't that excited,' comments Tony Mullins. As far as her Gold Cup chance was concerned, though, the Mullins team at least were unperturbed. The mare was lackadaisical when schooling at home, a totally different proposition when racing and not one to be fooled that this was the real thing when she was taken to be schooled on a racecourse. Paddy Mullins also pointed out that she had never been to Gowran Park before and had found it 'a bit strange'.

One week later, when the O'Neill–Dawn Run partnership was due to be reunited in a race context, Punchestown was abandoned. In its place, another schooling session was arranged for the same track one week before the Gold Cup, this time in the company of a stablemate, Lantern Lodge, ridden by Tony Mullins.

When that session was completed at a steady pace in front of the press as well as connections, O'Neill was characteristically 'all smiles' and again professed himself 'delighted'. When he reported that 'she went a lot better than she did at Gowran Park' he was on safe ground, of course, but in adding that 'going smoothly over the lot wouldn't have taught her anything' it is not hard to think he was looking on the bright side.

While there was marked improvement, Dawn Run had not jumped with any great élan, and Michael Clower, for one, found that his doubts about the mare's Gold Cup prospects had increased: 'The difference in style between O'Neill and Mullins was very marked as they rode round. O'Neill rides with a much shorter rein and Dawn Run does not like it.'

Clower was not won over by O'Neill's words of reassurance when the jockey asserted that 'Dawn Run is not a mare you can get up on and tell her what to do. You have to let her do it the way she wants and I'm not going to change her method of racing.'

Reaction to the change of jockey on Dawn Run seemed to be divided along national lines, with the Irish press supportive of Mullins while the British recognised the controversy in the change, and had no hesitation in latching on to it, but largely felt that there was no controversy in Mrs Hill's preference for O'Neill. In some Irish quarters the owner was also lambasted for having caved in to pressure from the British press, a notion scoffed at by Valentine Lamb, who wrote in *The Irish Field*: 'The wind from the wings of a butterfly would have about as much chance of blowing over a pyramid as anyone, especially journalists, would of changing her mind once it is made up.'

Debated constantly in the papers and no doubt in the conversations of almost anyone who had an interest in racing, the furore over Dawn Run's jockey added strain on Paddy Mullins, who already had the responsibility of getting his nation's most cherished sporting icon to Cheltenham in prime condition.

'My father, who was always quite cool, he felt the pressure going into that race,' recalls Tony. 'He was anxious every day. You could see him relaxing when she was ridden and put back in her stable – that another day was gone by without injury.'

Mullins elaborates on the task in hand. 'It was trying to do something that had never been done before and then, with the 20 per cent difference in currencies, there were very few good horses left in Ireland, so the whole weight of Ireland was on her going into the race. With the recession in Ireland and that, a lot of people clung onto Dawn Run and it was a very, very big thing at the time. I've seen a lot of very good horses since and they've never had the same impact that Dawn Run had. I wasn't old enough to remember Arkle at his height, so I can't tell you in comparison to Arkle but it was certainly way bigger than anything I've seen since.'

The Hills too were fully aware of Dawn Run's wider popularity and, as Oliver says: 'It was almost as if Dawn Run wasn't ours. It was as if Dawn Run belonged to the Irish racing fraternity.'

Whatever the view on Mrs Hill's choice of jockey, Irish confidence in a Dawn Run victory seemed to be snowballing. Tony Mullins' view on whether Dawn Run was going to win was that 'I knew there was no horse could beat her' but that there was an issue with her novice -like jumping.

The mind on which that jumping issue probably preyed most of all, though, was that of O'Neill, who sums up his thoughts then as 'She was favourite and everybody was backing her. No one had seen the background shots that I had seen. I'm thinking the whole of Ireland thinks she's going to win and I think she's no chance!'

Perhaps there is some comic exaggeration in that statement, but O'Neill had been the man on board when a Champion Hurdle winner last made a bid for the Gold Cup, and when asked to compare the way Night Nurse adapted to jumping fences to the way that Dawn Run did it, he replies, laughing again:

'Big difference. She wasn't a natural really, you know – she was clever and she always found a leg but she wasn't a natural. She didn't weigh the job up like he did. Even though she was a fine big mare – and that is probably why she got away with it. Even over hurdles she'd run through them. You never saw him run through a hurdle but she would. And that was the same with the fences really. When she was good she was good but when she was wrong [he pauses, then says the next three words slowly and with emphasis] *she was wrong. ...* And you just hoped.'

~

WAYWARD LAD

For a serious Gold Cup challenger Dawn Run was extremely inexperienced over fences. She had run in just four chases. Only Roman Hackle (1940) and Mont Tremblant (1952) had done that prior to winning the Gold Cup, with Golden Miller and Mill House the only ones to have done so after five previous attempts.

In addition to that inexperience, the opposition to Dawn Run in the Gold Cup was far stronger than that in her Champion Hurdle, and that despite one major absentee. Burrough Hill Lad had won the Gold Cup in 1984 and was in a class of his own among the entire chasing division the following season, only to be ruled out of the 1985 Gold Cup with an injury sustained the week before. Returning to action two weeks before Dawn Run did so, he was much slower than her to show his old flair and a heavy defeat behind Wayward Lad in the King George saw him cede Gold Cup favouritism to the mare.

The response of Burrough Hill Lad's owner has a familiar ring to it – he decided to replace the horse's regular jockey. Phil Tuck made way for Peter Scudamore. Burrough Hill Lad's runaway triumph next time out suggested he was back to his brilliant best and he regained Gold Cup favouritism. But then, for the second year running, injury intervened.

In his absence, Dawn Run still faced the 1985 Gold Cup winner Forgive'n Forget. He had suffered a copper deficiency in January, but had been trained all season to peak in the Gold Cup and his superb trainer Jimmy Fitzgerald was entirely capable of doing that. Forgive'n Forget started second favourite to Dawn Run, just in front of Combs Ditch, who had won three of his four starts that season and gone down narrowly for the second year running, in the King George. Run And Skip had emerged from the ranks of handicappers and, ominously for Dawn Run, he too was firmly set in the mould of a front-runner, and a very determined one at that. The promising Easterby-trained Cybrandian was another seen to best advantage when racing at the front. The 1985 Gold Cup runner-up Righthand Man was trying again, but thought vulnerable on fast ground, and also trained by Monica Dickinson at Harewood in Yorkshire was Wayward Lad.

At 11, Wayward Lad was the joint oldest in the party, older than any Gold Cup winner since 1969. As that longevity was accompanied by top-class form and unusual panache, Wayward Lad had long been a toast of the racing public. He possessed everything that Dawn Run lacked in terms of experience, skilful jumping and a long list of major chasing prizes, including a then record three King George VI Chases at Kempton, but whereas this Gold Cup threatened to come too early for Dawn Run, it looked to be too late for him. Third in 1983 was easily the best he had managed in three previous attempts.

Tony Dickinson, Michael Dickinson and Monica Dickinson each held the training licence during Wayward Lad's career and the esteem with which he was held in the wider racing world was more than matched by those who had day-to-day contact with him. 'My parents and I and all our boys at Harewood thought the world of Wayward Lad,' affirms Michael Dickinson. 'A very kind horse, one of the best movers I've ever seen, brilliant over fences. It was a pleasure, a privilege and an honour to train him. Wayward Lad was a medium-sized horse, not big not small, beautifully balanced and a ride from heaven.'

In addition to his sheer class, Wayward Lad's most shining attribute was his rapid and accurate jumping, but even with him that proficiency was not immediately gained. Most of the Dickinson horses were affected by a virus when he trailed in ninth as second favourite in his Sun Alliance Chase, but jumping errors were a regular feature in that novice season. Michael Dickinson outlines the cure:

'Some people who did not know blamed Tommy Carmody but this was wrong. Before his next season, Wayward Lad was treated by Siegfried Farnon, yes the vet from *All Creatures Great And Small*, who in real life was called Donald Sinclair, who injected his back and after that his jumping was always perfect. One person estimated in the 1983 Gold Cup he gained a dozen lengths in the air over the fences.'

That momentous race was the one in which Dickinson sent out the first, second, third, fourth and fifth – Bregawn, Captain John, Wayward Lad, Silver Buck and Ashley House – the most lauded of his many spectacular achievements during a brief but trail-blazing career as a trainer in National Hunt racing. But remembering that astonishing result hits a discordant note with him in one respect.

'For almost the whole of the month of February, Wayward Lad had been lame with a hock problem,' the trainer explains. 'We gave him one gallop at home and then took him for a gallop on the flat after racing at Catterick in a vain attempt to try and get him fit. It was obvious after the work he wasn't fit but Jonjo rode him, didn't have a ride in the Gold Cup and persuaded me to run him. I still feel guilt that I asked him to go into battle less than 100 per cent fit but it was only the horse's class and courage which got him into third place.'

Dickinson believes that if Wayward Lad had been 100 per cent fit in the 1983 Gold Cup, the horse to have led home his 'Famous Five' would not have been Bregawn. It would have been Wayward Lad.

In the 1984 renewal, Wayward Lad was 6-4 favourite but pulled up, his jockey reporting that he was never moving well and made a gurgling noise at the top of the hill on the second circuit. At 8-1 in 1985 he was a well-beaten eighth. His form elsewhere was good enough to win a Gold Cup and some believed passionately that he deserved to win one, to gain the level of recognition that only this race can impart. But many had now written him off as a viable Gold Cup contender.

With his record at Cheltenham contrasting so sharply with the one he had established over 3m on the much sharper King George course at Kempton, allied to his performance in the 1983 Gold Cup, questions were inevitably asked whether Wayward Lad could come up the hill over the additional two furlongs of the Gold Cup. Some posited that Wayward Lad was fundamentally unsuited to showing his best when faced with the race's particular demands. Michael Dickinson will have none of it.

In 1986, however, another factor threatened to derail Wayward Lad's Gold Cup challenge. At 12-1 in a five-runner field, he had already staged one revival to register his third King George victory but thereafter the weather prevented him from running in any other race before the Festival and severely restricted his training. One indication of the widespread snow and frost is that between February 6 and March 4 not a single race was run in Britain. When racegoers arrived at the Festival, they found that the weather had so affected turf management on the track that the grass was not green but brown.

For Wayward Lad, the upshot of all the bad weather was that the first work on grass he could be given in preparation for the Gold Cup was when he worked over fences at Wetherby with Forgive'n Forget eight days before the race. With Michael having set forth for pastures new on the Flat, Monica Dickinson was now in charge at Harewood and, as well as Dawn Run and her 5lb allowance, she knew that lack of fitness would present a problem. As he had in 1985, Wayward Lad started 8-1 fifth favourite.

~

1986 GOLD CUP

'I didn't go into the parade ring but I was down at the saddling enclosure,' says Tony Mullins. 'I think that there was a silence and nervousness before the race which I thought was surprising with such experienced men, but it was a very high-tension time.'

In the parade ring, the instructions from Paddy Mullins to his jockey were the same as usual – he did not give any. 'All you wanted to hear from Paddy was "She's right today,"' says Jonjo. 'That's all you needed to hear.'

Mrs Hill asked the jockey what his plan was for the mare, to which he replied that he would try to be up there with the leaders if he could. Those gathered around might have been shocked had the jockey said anything else, but this was not O'Neill's first conception of how he might ride the 15-8 favourite:

'I thought, well, she's won a Champion Hurdle and there were three or four front-runners in the Gold Cup, so she doesn't need to make it – I'll drop her in last and pick them up. But I went and schooled her at Punchestown, with only one other horse in the school, and she was not going a yard until I got her head in front of the other horse. I realised there's no way I can be dropping this in, because I'll never get her going again. So we had to get a good start.'

Going down to post, the crowd acclaimed Dawn Run already. Mrs Hill said later that this was the one moment when a tear came to her eye. As the field lined up for the standing start, O'Neill could not get on the inside so he allowed Dawn Run to stand side-on and asked the starter to bring them in again. When the starter acceded to this request, the jockey made sure that he gained the position he wanted. In the failed footsteps of Sir Ken, Bula, Lanzarote and Night Nurse, Dawn Run stood ready in her bid to become the first horse to be victorious in the Gold Cup and the Champion Hurdle.

The man on her back says, 'My main concern was getting over the first because I thought we'll be going so bloody fast and if she doesn't get a leg out, well, we're gone. And I'd be lynched because I'd be right among the crowd at the first fence.'

Although his confidence in her jumping was shaky to say the least, O'Neill believed that, when presented with an unmistakably bona-fide racecourse assignment, Dawn Run would at least show a lot more dash than she had in either of her recent racecourse workouts. In this, the jockey was not disappointed: 'We were trapping I tell you. We're going like two-year-olds out of the stalls going to the first and she's not the best at getting the height.'

In a great many staying chases the first circuit lacks any real statement of intent. The participants basically form an orderly queue, leaving it to the fences to sort them out, but the 1986 Gold Cup was a race as soon as the tapes went up and it never slackened. While Dawn Run set off with a purpose, Run And Skip under Steve Smith Eccles was even quicker out of the blocks. Catching him fast, Dawn Run clipped the fence and nodded on landing. Suffering nothing more untoward, however, her jockey thought, 'We're halfway round now anyway.'

Dawn Run was usually a front-runner but the concept of an 'easy lead' was alien to her. Making the pace was not about sneaking a tactical advantage, it was what her extreme competitive spirit demanded, and given that a turn of foot was not one of her strengths it was also about battering the resistance from her rivals. In the Gold Cup she had to deal with one rival determined to do exactly the same thing and the lead could not have come any harder.

At the first fence the pair of them led already by maybe four lengths. At the second they were going even faster and Dawn Run leapt into a narrow lead. Cybrandian was often a front-runner but he never got near them before his race ended with a broken stirrup leather after the sixth. Run And Skip made a bad blunder at the third but was back on terms by the seventh and had the lead over the next three fences before Dawn Run wrested it from him again turning for home for the first time. Coming down the hill and for that rapid completion of the first circuit, Dawn Run and Run And Skip were ten or twelve lengths clear.

Going out again, Run And Skip made a mistake at the same fence as first time round but surged forward going into the water jump, and that obstacle was where Dawn Run's race started to look like a losing battle. She was literally on the back foot when splashing alarmingly and she was metaphorically on the back foot throughout almost everything that followed.

Jonjo was concerned: 'I was trying to give her a breather and she left her hind legs in the water. That put me behind Run And Skip and I knew I had to get up in front with her again.'

She was almost level at the very next fence, eight from home, and two fences later, at the final ditch, where her previous visit to Cheltenham had met with such an indignity, there was no indecision as Dawn Run and Run And Skip once more jumped together. Up to this point the race had been all about two horses. Now, however, you did not have to scan nearly so far back to see the pursuers and at their head was Wayward Lad. Along with Righthand Man and Forgive'n Forget, they were not just in touch, they were well in touch and closing.

Dawn Run had a difference of opinion with Jonjo at the fifth last, clouted the next, and between the fences for nearly all of the second circuit she generally looked to be going as fast as she could. All the while, Wayward Lad and

Forgive'n Forget were travelling relatively smoothly, and at the fourth last Wayward Lad had almost caught up.

Dawn Run's mistakes over those two fences handed the initiative to Run And Skip by a couple of lengths and forced Jonjo into repositioning her to try to challenge him, first on his outside and then on his inner. Three out she was only a fraction behind Run And Skip but now Wayward Lad and Forgive'n Forget were on them. Hearing that pair coming up behind him caused consternation for Dawn Run's jockey – 'We've gone some gallop here I thought. We'd been winging it from the first fence' – and it was not long before he also had the dispiriting sight to contend with.

In line for home and from right to left as racegoers looked at them, Dawn Run, Run And Skip, Wayward Lad and Forgive'n Forget took the second last almost in unison. Then Run And Skip finally cracked, going from first to fourth in three strides. O'Neill determined: 'If I don't fly the second last I ain't going to win anything, you know, so I gave her a slap down the shoulder and she flew the second last – and they passed me as if I was standing still!'

Up in the grandstand, among her family and recorded by at least two film crews, even Dawn Run's most ardent supporter lost hope – probably for the first time in years. After guarded comments – 'A long way to go yet' – and quiet entreaties – 'Now watch this one, there's a drop; watch it girl' – earlier in the race had given way to roars of 'Come on the girl!' and 'Come on the mare!' approaching the second last, Mrs Hill's voice quietened and a dozen strides before the final fence she muttered 'No. No,' almost as if conceding defeat. The crowd hushed with her as Dawn Run lost a length and a half on the new leaders.

Wayward Lad was the first to go on from her, but Forgive'n Forget nosed ahead just before the last and looked to be going the better. He did not take it as fluently as Wayward Lad, though, and it was the Dickinson veteran, having been under very hard right-hand driving from Graham Bradley's whip well before the second last even, who was now propelled to the front again. Forgive'n Forget drifted further right and Wayward Lad went two lengths clear.

It looked like further from the stands and on television, but that was an optical illusion because, almost as soon as Wayward Lad moved himself within touching distance of the Gold Cup, he started to drift left towards the far rail. To many of those watching, his place in Cheltenham history looked there for the taking nevertheless, but instead, halfway up the run-in, incredibly, Dawn Run was challenging again and suddenly galloping on much the stronger. Mrs Hill was in full cry and I doubt whether Pavarotti could have hit a note for so long that conveyed such passion. And most of the crowd was now in full voice with her.

Jonjo describes the resurrection of Dawn Run's challenge: 'Once they'd gone past me I thought, "Well, I'm beat" for a few seconds, but then I felt her ribs, she took a right old breather, and I thought, "Now we're in business." She started picking up and I kept slapping her down the shoulder all the way down to the last and she winged the last. She was motoring at the last. I saw Brad in front of me was hanging into the rails, so I thought let him hang in there and I'll go the other side, and when she saw open air she just flew up the hill, as if she'd just jumped in at the last.'

Half a dozen strides before the line, Wayward Lad's bid for the Gold Cup was over as Dawn Run was driven to the front. The lead in the race had changed a dozen times. Dawn Run had it for the fifth time and Jonjo was able to pass the post with his right arm aloft as Dawn Run won by a length. Forgive'n Forget was another two and a half lengths away in third, with Run And Skip a length behind him. All horses returned safe.

I asked Michael Dickinson whether, as Wayward Lad set off up the run-in, he thought that his favourite was at last going to win the Gold Cup? He replies, 'No.' His reaction was: 'I thought my mother trained him brilliantly. He was 11 years old and had missed a lot of training. It is a wonder that he ran as well as he did and it just goes to prove that Mrs D was a brilliant trainer.'

Dickinson sums up the horse's two placings in the Gold Cup thus: 'Wayward Lad was not beaten by the Cheltenham hill, nor was he beaten by the three miles and two furlongs, he was not beaten by Bregawn and Dawn Run, he was beaten by lack of fitness on both occasions. On each occasion his class, courage and brilliant jumping enabled him to finish closer than any normal horse under similar conditions.'

From the winning camp, away from the heat of the battle, O'Neill reckons: 'They were probably stopping and made her look faster than she was. I felt I was going to win going down to the last. I had to get that breather into her and I couldn't get it into her when I wanted. But it worked out well in the end.'

Jeremy Hill pinpoints Dawn Run's jump at the second last: 'It just galvanised her and put her back in the race. That's where that race was won. It was an extraordinary race. Jonjo gets that phenomenal jump at the second last, absolutely phenomenal, and the whole mindset of the mare changed. Her destiny was to win the Gold Cup and she was fortunate to win the Champion Hurdle on the way because she was a chaser really.'

Every winner at the Festival has won a place in racing history, so big is the event, but Dawn Run had now wrenched and wrought a place out of that Cheltenham hill that was all her own. For those who witnessed it, the likelihood is that she will be remembered far less for the completion of this unique feat than for the way she did it.

～

'I was aware of nothing until I'd passed the post,' says Jonjo of what was going on around the participants on that most famous run-in. 'You pull up and you're kind of in a state of shock. When you've got past the line you hear the whole place go mad and see the hats flying.'

When John Clarke reached Dawn Run, the groom found that the man on board her was still 'roaring and shouting'. O'Neill was far from alone in that, as these were the early stages of a victory celebration that is unprecedented in my experience. The walkway from the track to the parade ring filled with celebrants. 'I started to walk her along and at first it was like going into a tunnel,' Clarke reported in the *Sunday Times*, 'like before the FA Cup final. After a while I couldn't see a thing. I couldn't see my feet below me.'

So disdainful of most human contact, Dawn Run was now the centre of attention like almost no horse before her. While O'Neill shook so many hands he could have outdone any politician at an election rally, the mare received innumerable pats and slaps in exuberant congratulation.

Clarke could not possibly have seen the way ahead as he led them back but Dawn Run somehow maintained her unbreakable arc towards the Gold Cup winner's enclosure. Once entry to that had been secured, the numbers around her became more manageable, but not for long. This was a rapture that could not be confined.

'I don't know how the mare didn't kill someone that day,' Clarke recalled. 'At home if you stood behind her and patted her on the rear you'd have ended up 30 yards down the road with a kick. Probably the only reason nothing happened was that she hadn't the room to lift her hind legs.'

Jonjo's memory of it is that 'we nearly got carried into the weighing room, horse and all. There were so many people in there and the poor mare was in the state of shock I'd imagine. You never see that many people. She was hardly able to breathe.'

Also in the thick of the celebration party was Tony Mullins, and he was very much in the spirit of it. When Jonjo re-emerged from the weighing room for the presentation ceremony he carried Tony up on to the podium on his shoulders.

'I would imagine that for anyone that was there it was the greatest aftermath in the 1-2-3 that was ever seen,' says Mullins. 'A lot of my good friends had been backing her all year ante-post. A lot of people were very excited and lots of people commiserated with me. There were mixed emotions but overridden by the delight of winning it. I remember thinking to myself if she was beaten what use is it to anybody? I went with the win more than feeling sorry for myself, and at that stage I honestly believed that I'd win two or three Gold Cups. I probably was so young and naïve I didn't realise how hard it was to win one.'

While Dawn Run was winning hers, Tony Mullins watched it from the front lawn but had been accompanied there by two men from the British non-racing press. 'They stuck a microphone in my face as the horses passed the post and said, "Are you sick you've missed the Gold Cup winner?" And I turned to them with a smile on my face – I didn't feel like smiling – and said, "My family has just won the Gold Cup, I'm delighted," and I walked away and that was it. It annoyed me a lot. They tried to get a sour grapes quote, if they could, for a headline.'

It did not spoil his enjoyment of the race finish. After the last fence he thought that Dawn Run was beaten but, in the mass of racegoers and with no big screen in those days, the horses went out of his sight in the last 50 yards. Mullins turned to look at the crowd in the grandstand. He could see which among them were her Irish supporters and he knew that Dawn Run had got back up.

Of the presentation ceremony, Jonjo says: 'We were going up to receive the prize and I took Tony up with me because I thought he deserved to be there.' O'Neill has also said many times since that he believes Dawn Run went more sweetly for Mullins than for him, and he says it again to me:

'I used to have to motivate her a bit to get her going while Tony used to just sit up and drop his hands and away she'd go. I found her very moody and you had to get her motivated and get her carrying you. I'd say she used to run sweeter for him but I was the lucky one to ride her in the right races.'

Mullins replies, 'Well, it's nice of him to say that but he still won the Champion Hurdle and the Gold Cup on her. He knocked a bloody good tune out of her, there's no doubt on that, and you don't win the Champion Hurdle or Gold Cups by making mistakes. He was a great jockey and we remained friends throughout it all as well. He understood the awkwardness of it and my disappointment, but we all just got on with what we had to do.

'She used to win by further distances for me but you have to remember that Jonjo rode her in a Champion Hurdle and the Gold Cup, which are the ultimate races, where the opposition are at their peak as well, so while I like to hear it I don't believe that it's a certain fact. It's nice to think that I rode her as well as Jonjo, but I don't think that she went any better for me than him.'

For much of the Dawn Run years, and incessantly in the months that surrounded the Gold Cup, the younger jockey's riding was discussed in depth in the media and he describes one effect of that experience: 'At the time I was only 24. I think it did affect my riding. Up to that I didn't care what anyone thought, I went out to win every race, then I found myself with all this scrutiny in the papers and I found myself going out to make sure I didn't give them fodder as opposed to what I always did, going out to win a race. I was going out to make sure that they couldn't knock me.'

On its arrival back in Ireland, the Gold Cup and nearly all those connected with its capture went on an extensive, unofficial victory tour that amazed the new centres of attention as they took the trophy to different pubs, clubs, hotels and other venues intoxicated with the triumph. Thanks and congratulations for Dawn Run were given from the pulpit. 'The party went on for a month,' says Tony Mullins. 'It was exciting, very exciting, and even more so now when I look back and knowing how hard it is to win a Gold Cup. It was one that the whole country was behind and backed it.'

~

One absentee on these many laps of honour was Dawn Run herself. She remained in training. Her next start was at Aintree three weeks later, where O'Neill believes the price was paid for the zealous celebrations that went on around her at Cheltenham.

'She was wired to the moon when she heard the crowd going to the start. They were all giving her a cheer and she took off with me, so I had no steering or nothing, she was totally out of control. And then when we jumped off to the first we were flying and she galloped straight through it and turned upside down.'

Dawn Run and her jockey were uninjured, but it was the last time O'Neill rode her. Fifteen days later he was unseated from Nohalmdun in the Scottish Champion Hurdle and after yet another visit to his orthopaedic surgeon Hugh Barber he was kept in hospital overnight.

'The next morning the nurse came in the white uniform and I just decided then and there to pack up,' O'Neill recalls. 'I just had lost the heart. I'd had 15 years riding and three years out of the saddle with injuries. I'd just had enough of it really and lo and behold then I got bloody cancer, didn't I? They didn't diagnose it for another six or eight weeks, but I'd say I was suffering it on Gold Cup day. All that year I was feeling a bit tired to be honest, from Christmas on. But you think that happens to somebody else, you don't ever think it happens to you.'

Five days after Jonjo's last tumble, Dawn Run and Tony Mullins were therefore reunited on the racetrack at Punchestown. It was also a reunion between Dawn Run and Buck House. Dawn Run had already met her contemporary four times over hurdles, twice over fences and she had won them all, but in the meantime Buck House had tasted his own Cheltenham Festival success, by three lengths in the 2m Champion Chase, and the Punchestown race was over 2m2f. Compared to the Gold Cup, Dawn Run was being asked to compete at one mile less and at level weights.

Organised by Vincent O'Brien, the race was a match, the first in Ireland for more than 20 years, for which the owners traditionally provided the prize money but did so for only IR £5,000 of the IR £25,000 in this instance, with Mrs Hill declining to contribute any of it. The race had not been her idea. 'I think she thought the odds were that she wouldn't win it,' says her son Jeremy.

The investment by the racecourse authorities proved a spectacular winner. 'It ended up probably being the biggest day's Irish racing in modern history,' recalls Tony Mullins. And Dawn Run won again.

'Yes, I'd seen her backside so many times,' confirms Buck House's jockey Tommy Carmody. 'He was never good enough to beat her, so I had to try and think of different ways, this that and the other, but I always came up second or third or fourth. Even at the Punchestown Festival, I done everything possible and I still couldn't beat her over a trip maybe a shade too far for my horse but a good bit short of her best trip as well.'

Buck House was head to head with Dawn Run at the third last. The second last was followed very closely by a right-hand turn but Dawn Run jumped out to the left, whereas Buck House cut the corner very sharply. For the first time in their extensive rivalry, Carmody thought that he was going to emerge on top – Dawn Run rallied to win well.

'She was just an out-and-out battler,' says Carmody. 'She just didn't know what it was like to give up. She was just an exceptionally top-class individual. The best I'll ever see of her kind anyway and her sex.'

Dawn Run had won her 21st race and, with a purse nearly half that which she had taken home in the Gold Cup, she moved further clear in the then all-time list of first-prize money earnings by British- or Irish-based jumps horses, having taken that position at Cheltenham, from Wayward Lad. Two years before, in her last full campaign, Dawn Run had rounded things off nicely by winning twice more in France and, at some stage after the Gold Cup, Paddy Mullins was asked in a television interview whether another bid for the Grande Course de Haies d'Auteuil was a possibility.

He replied: 'I don't think we'd like to go back there. I don't think it would be a good thing to do … Having been a hurdler and then being taught how to jump fences I imagine that it wouldn't be fair to revert back to the smaller obstacles.'

Jumping fences proficiently had not come naturally to Dawn Run and Mullins believed that there was a danger of confusing her. But not everyone in the Dawn Run camp was agreed.

'Mrs Hill never interfered with the training of the horse. It has to be said that. She just interfered with me riding her, that's all,' says Tony Mullins. But at this juncture the owner was once again determined to have her way. Mrs Hill was adamant that the horse would return to France.

'Yes,' comments Mullins. 'You see, I think Mrs Hill unfortunately at that stage had begun to believe that the mare was infallible. I think she just didn't realise she was still only a horse.'

As in 1984, Dawn Run first contested the Prix La Barka but this time she was beaten three lengths and was in receipt of 7lb from the winner Le Rheusois. 'I came back in and I jumped down and I said to my father that there was no hard luck. That horse beat us fair and square,' says the jockey. 'I said her speed that was all there in her younger days over hurdles has gone, and if you come back this horse is going to do the same again to you. They relayed it to Mrs Hill and she said, "If he hasn't the confidence to ride her to win, we'll get someone who has," and I was jocked off again.'

This time, the fourth, Mullins was expecting it but his reaction was very different: 'I didn't mind you see because I didn't think she'd win, which was unbelievable. That had never happened with her before.'

No one could have predicted what did happen in the Grande Course, though for the first time since the Prix La Barka in 1984 she did not start favourite. On the day of the race, Jonjo O'Neill and Tony Mullins were both casting their eye over prospective new bloodstock in Ireland.

'I was at the Derby Sale in Ballsbridge in Dublin,' relates Mullins, 'and Ros Easom, who was Michael Hourigan's travelling head girl, she came in to where I was in the stable and said to me, "Dawn Run fell" and I laughed. She said to me, "Have you no feelings?" or something. When she said she fell I had no idea that she had been killed and I remember the shock as she said to me, "She's dead." I had imagined her getting beat and I was expecting her to get beaten, and it didn't surprise me when she fell, given the way myself and my father had discussed jumping back over hurdles again, but I had *never* dreamt of her getting killed and it was a massive shock. It was like a death of a human.'

Just four years and four weeks after Mrs Hill had first ridden her into eighth at Clonmel, the Dawn Run story was over. In that very limited timescale the mare had run at three Cheltenham Festivals, been beaten there by only one horse and won the two biggest races at the meeting, easily the two most important championship races over jumps on the whole Racing Calendar. Earlier in June 1986, Buck House too had died but in very different circumstances, as a result of colic not long after he had been put out to grass.

It was reported that Dawn Run (ridden by the highly experienced French jockey Michel Chirol) broke her neck in her fall at the fifth from home when in serious contention, but Jeremy Hill says, 'My opinion is she had a heart attack. She never rose at that fence.'

Of his mother's reaction, he says, 'She was shattered. And it was compounded by the cruelty of the public comments.'

Unsurprisingly, Tony Mullins reports that all connected with the mare took it 'very, very hard. We went from flying the most exciting kite that we had ever known to suddenly, bang in five seconds, we had nothing, only a bridle. It was a massive shock. The buzz around the yard was gone for a long, long time.'

At Doninga, as they always did in such circumstances, they put another horse into her box straightaway. Mullins says, 'We never leave a box, even for lesser horses. It's just horrible to go back the next morning looking at an empty stable.'

This horse, though, was simply not replaceable.

∼

Gaye Brief also ran in that 1986 Grand Course at Auteuil. He fell at the trial hurdle before the race and did so again in the contest itself, at the tenth, but he was able to continue his career in Britain. Until the David Pipe-trained Un Temps Pour Tout won it in 2015, Mullins had remained the only name among British- or Irish-based trainers to have won the Grande Course and it featured on that roll of honour five times because Paddy's eldest son Willie, in addition to his record number of Cheltenham triumphs for an Irish trainer, has won four renewals of the Grande Course.

For the 1987 Gold Cup, it was Wayward Lad who returned, now aged 12 and making his fifth attempt on the summit. Chasing the leader into the home straight and over the last two fences, he threatened once again initially on the run-in but this time quickly faltered and finished fifth behind The Thinker. At Aintree the following month, though, he was retired on a win. Or so it appeared at the time but the following month a dispute among his owners led to the unedifying spectacle of this hero being led round the sales ring, at Doncaster. The bidding went to 42,000 guineas before he was knocked down to Tony Dickinson, his retirement confirmed and ownership secured.

Asked how important that was for his family, Michael Dickinson says: 'Absolutely essential.' Dickinson was by that stage training in the United States and explains: 'He was bought by two good friends of mine, Joy and Rusty Carrier, and he resided on their farm in Pennsylvania. He hunted for eight seasons which he really enjoyed, then his final few years he was in a field with King Spruce, winner of the Irish Grand National, and Tom Bob, winner of the Maryland Hunt Cup. You can imagine those three horses would be able to share a lot of stories.'

Despite living in the United States, Dickinson has missed only the odd Festival and, writing in 2014, none in the previous ten years. When there he usually lunches at least once with Mrs Maureen Mullins, Paddy's widow, and he wants to stress that the Dickinsons have always had great respect for the Mullins family.

Paddy Mullins did not train another Festival winner after Dawn Run and in his biography and interviews given at the time of the publication of *Paddy Mullins: The Master Of Doninga* by Peter O'Neil and Sean Boyne it is clear that the trainer's experience of the 1986 Gold Cup, which all those looking on from a distance must have credited as his greatest achievement, was deeply tarnished. One quote in the book is that: 'My feeling after the Gold Cup was one of absolute numbness. I would not have minded so badly only I had stuck Tony in to get a fall off the mare when schooling her around Cheltenham for the Gold Cup. That was the part that really got to me. I sacrificed him. Mrs Hill was only waiting for something to happen.'

When the trainer's prize was presented that day at Cheltenham, his wife Maureen received it on his behalf. Paddy chose to absent himself, checking on Dawn Run. He continued to train for Mrs Hill, though, even after the mare's death, and also did so for her son Jeremy. In July 1986, the month after Dawn Run's death, Mrs Hill and Paddy Mullins won one of the most prestigious races in Ireland, the Galway Plate, with Boro Quarter.

In March 1987, in the week after Mrs Hill had helped unveil a statue to Dawn Run at Cheltenham, she was riding Boro Quarter at Doninga when at the age of 68 she fell, broke a leg in two places and badly fractured her hip. Paddy Mullins was absent at a Trainers Association meeting and in his biography he said: 'I feel that if I had been home that day, the accident would not have happened. I would not have allowed Mrs Hill to do what she was doing. She was riding Boro Quarter around a gallop and the animal was a bit strong for her. She was so tired she fell off. Tom was the only one here that day and he said he could not stop her.'

In 1985, in between Dawn Run's two wins at Cheltenham, Mrs Hill had been hit hard by the death of her husband. Now her riding days were over. Having later survived one stroke, Mrs Hill had another at Christmas 1989 and died on January 11, 1990, her death announced over the public address system at Punchestown racecourse.

Since Dawn Run, seven Champion Hurdle winners have tried their hands at chasing. Celtic Shot did best, matching his form over hurdles, and after wining the January trial at Cheltenham he started 5-2 favourite in the Gold Cup itself in 1991 as a nine-year-old. Three out he was travelling like the winner too, but he blundered and faded to be seventh of eight finishers. He also flopped that season in the King George and at Aintree and after that the best of him was not seen again. Beech Road, who famously and bruisingly had a go at chasing before he won the Champion Hurdle, made it to the 1995 Gold Cup but only as a 13-year-old and at 100-1 he finished a well-beaten seventh.

~

Tony Mullins was fourth on Clusheen in the 1987 County Hurdle, third on Grabel in the 1987 Triumph and second on Minorettes Girl in the 1991 Sun Alliance Novices' Hurdle, but he never did ride a winner at the Cheltenham Festival. He has joked that the closest he got to doing so was being perched on the shoulders of Jonjo O'Neill.

Mullins was joint champion jockey in Ireland in 1984. The championship was calculated on a January 1 to January 1 basis in those days and he came top of that list outright in 1989. He was presented with the trophy too, but with a new championship awarded on a seasonal basis being instigated in 1989–90, that second Mullins win seems to have disappeared from the records. In 1990 in Kentucky he won the world's then richest ever hurdle race, on Grabel, and was by that stage combining riding with his own training career. But his days as a jockey were on the verge of coming to an enforced end with a back injury. In 2007 the Tony Mullins-trained Pedrobob won the County Hurdle.

Talking with Tony Mullins about Dawn Run, the strongest impression I am left with is of his pleasure in the role he did play with her and of the sheer thrill and exhilaration he experienced when riding her in a race. There is a great photograph in his book of Dawn Run going to the start before her chasing debut and the laughing smile on Mullins' face is a mile wide.

The Greatest Race

Among his tributes to her, Mullins states: 'What people forget is that on the flat she won her three bumpers; over hurdles she won on hard ground, soft ground, right-handed, left-handed two miles, three miles and two and a half miles; when she went over fences, she won over two, she won the Gold Cup at three and a quarter, she went back and won the match at two miles. No horse could beat her. She did it at every distance over every type of obstacle and on the flat – she just never failed. She won the three Champion Hurdles [in a season] which was never done before; she won the Gold Cup and the Champion Hurdle which was never done before. Obviously Arkle was the greatest chaser of all time but for me Dawn Run was the greatest National Hunt horse of all time.'

In terms of ratings, Dawn Run achieved higher figures in other races and as she had the 5lb allowance – the handicappers in jumps racing equate 1lb to roughly one length – she cannot be rated the best horse in the race judged on the results of either her Champion Hurdle or Gold Cup.

That is not the foremost impression of her, though, and while I was dismayed to read the depth of hurt felt by Paddy Mullins about the Gold Cup, that is not what I remember first or last about that race either.

Call it her will to win, her bloody-mindedness, her strength of stamina or her mares' 5lb allowance, but as I remember it Dawn Run could dig deep to mine resources other horses did not possess or kept out of reach. In the 1948 *Racehorses* annual there is a horse called Solway, who sticks in the mind because he was described as "8 cwt of cowardice". Dawn Run does so because she was the polar opposite. Is this character assessment hugely coloured by the memory of what happened in one race? I admit it, and consider it only natural because Dawn Run's unstoppable effort in the 1986 Gold Cup was the most vital element – with Wayward Lad's not far behind it – that made this the best race I have ever witnessed.

In the aftermath that day at Cheltenham Racecourse it was immediately obvious that I was not the only one thinking along those lines. In the midst of it, I found myself standing next to an emotional Tony Dickinson on the weighing room steps and offered my commiserations. In the parade ring and winner's enclosure just in front of us, emotions were running far higher and we watched that pitch invasion by hundreds of people, as thousands of others looked on, who all acclaimed Dawn Run, Jonjo and the greatest race.

CHAPTER EIGHT

1987 AND 1988 WATERFORD CRYSTAL STAYERS' HURDLE

The Hopes of a Nation

WHEN I BEGIN my interview with Peter Easterby about Night Nurse and Sea Pigeon, he quickly interrupts me. There are two points he wants to make. 'First of all, it is the greatest show on earth, Cheltenham,' he asserts, 'and it isn't just us that makes Cheltenham, it's the Irish as well.'

In 1981, the year that I attended the Festival for the first time and Easterby won the Champion Hurdle and Gold Cup, the Tuesday of the meeting just happened to be on March 17 – St Patrick's Day. A 15-year-old schoolboy, I was highly aware of the integral role the Irish played within the British racing industry as well as their own, and recognised Ireland as the birthplace of so many racing legends, equine and human. With Arkle and Vincent O'Brien, perhaps it had nurtured the greatest of them all. I knew that the Irish had an unquenchable enthusiasm for the Cheltenham Festival and that they would be at the racecourse in large numbers. I was told that there would be priests present, and there were priests. However, when an Irishman approached me after one of the races and asked, 'What was third?' I admit that his unfamiliar pronunciation of the word 'third' took me by surprise.

Accents were not the only difference. The scatological consequence of one man's silent 'h' stayed in my memory, but in later years when Irish racegoers in their thousands shouted for Dawn Run, Danoli or Istabraq the reverberating sound of it lodged in my soul. There may be no proof that the Irish feel more passion than the British about Festival victory, but they are undoubtedly a lot more successful at showing it.

Edward Gillespie, chief executive at the Racecourse for more than 30 years, has stated that 'Cheltenham without the Irish would be nothing.' Even for this most energetic of administrators, however, Cheltenham with the Irish has had its testing moments and when they wanted to celebrate Festival victory by an Irish hero or heroine even his management powers could be stretched. As the preceding chapter made clear, the greetings for Dawn Run after her Champion Hurdle and Gold Cup reached levels of legendary exuberance. For Gillespie, even those parties were not the biggest.

'It was fair pandemonium,' he recalls, of Dawn Run's Gold Cup, 'but I think there are other ones that have been as pandemonious.' Top of his list is what transpired when Ireland registered another Gold Cup win, ten years later, with Imperial Call. The following year Gillespie tried in vain to hold back the hordes following Istabraq's win in the Royal Sun Alliance Novices' Hurdle and when he attempted to evict one of the celebrants from the winner's enclosure it turned out to be the winning trainer. Aidan O'Brien may not have experienced that too often since and Gillespie was reported to be 'anxious' about the prospect of an Irish victory in the following day's Gold Cup, for which Imperial Call started favourite and Irish folk hero Danoli was the co-second favourite.

Victory in that race went instead to the 20-1 shot Mr Mulligan, trained in Lambourn, which must have soothed Gillespie's nerves but even that result provides an excellent illustration of Ireland's far-reaching role within the sport. This may not have been greeted by the average Irish racegoer as a win for one of their own but judged on a lot of criteria it could have been, because Mr Mulligan himself was bred in Ireland and had run in Irish point-to-points, he was trained by Dublin-born Noel Chance (who had spent two seasons training in Ireland) and ridden by Tony McCoy, who was raised in Moneyglass, County Antrim.

L'Escargot, Captain Christy, Tied Cottage, Anaglogs Daughter, Chinrullah, Monksfield – all names that chime loudly in my childhood memories. They were celebrities in Britain as well as their native Ireland but there was a mystique too at the Festival that came with the sizeable number of horses who travelled over for the first time. To the British racegoer they were largely unknown quantities. Up until 1961, *The Times* used to print 'Ireland' where the trainer's name should have been, next to Irish-trained runners on their Festival racecards, which really was leaving its British readers in the dark, but even in the 1970s and early 1980s there had to be something enigmatic and inscrutable about most of the Irish challengers before they were first revealed to their British audience. We could read their (recent) results in the papers but anything beyond the bare facts was absent from those staccato form guides and of Irish racing on our television coverage there was only a fleeting glimpse. When they walked into the parade ring it was the first chance to assess with our own eyes the competitors we had heard discussed or whispered about or had never heard of at all on the racing grapevine.

Inspired gambles could be involved with the Irish at Cheltenham, and talk of inspired gambles when there weren't any. The first race I ever saw at the Festival set a powerful tone. Hartstown was the heavily backed 2-1 favourite in the Supreme Novices', having shown his first worthwhile form over hurdles only 13 days earlier when justifying favouritism in a 19-runner race at Leopardstown on his first start for Mick O'Toole.

Recalling that Cheltenham gamble, O'Toole says: 'I put it together, or however you want to put it. I trained an awful lot of winners, but I was always a punter all my life.' Passing the stands with a circuit to go, Hartstown was last of the 16 runners in a very slowly run race, and turning down the hill he was still last, after serious interference; to a rapturous greeting from the crowd, he hit the front with only a dozen strides to go and won by two lengths.

Having triumphed in that opener, there were only two more Irish-trained winners at the 1981 Festival: Anaglogs Daughter was sent off at odds of 10-11 in the Champion Chase but Drumgora, a compatriot at 25-1, beat her; in the County Hurdle, Staplestown easily landed the gamble from 14-1 into 11-2 favourite.

In the first 40 years after the Second World War, those three wins were only a fraction beneath the annual average. The highest Irish scores in that period were eight in 1958 and seven in 1977, and it was not until 2005 and 2006, aided in part by the introduction of a four-day Festival, that they moved up to nine and then ten; Irish-trained horses won 12 of the 27 races in 2014, 13 in 2011 and 2015, and they took 14 in 2013.

With their form going into the 1980s, expectations for the Irish overall, if not for individuals, were at a far more muted level than they are now but as that decade drew to a close even those expectations were not met. Dawn Run was gone. A new Irish flagbearer emerged from an unconventional, extrovert and sometimes controversial source.

~

Just as many Irish challengers arrived for the Festival surrounded by an air of mystery, something similar would sometimes attend those runners in their own country who were trained by John Mulhern. In conspicuous fashion, the issue was alluded to by his own racing colours: 'Red, white question mark on back and front, red and white quartered cap'.

In those days levels of prize money were low. Landing gambles could pay as many bills as the prize money and Stephen McCarthy, who worked for Mulhern for more than 30 years, elucidates: 'There was always a question mark when we had a runner – of what the story was; whether it was D-Day or not. There was a big question mark. And they were fantastic colours, very lucky for us over the years.'

British racegoers would also have seen those colours. In fact they could not have missed them at the 1981 Festival when John Francome and Friendly Alliance answered the question by coasting home 15 lengths clear in the Grand Annual. That bookended the day neatly with Hartstown's win in the Supreme Novices' because Mulhern and Mick O'Toole were old friends, having met when Mulhern was still at school. Asked whether there was any sort of joint celebration of their Festival success, O'Toole says: 'There'd be a celebration with us in those days whether they won or lost. That's the sort of guy he was.'

One of the obvious questions on this occasion was why the Mulhern-owned Friendly Alliance was trained by Fred Winter. I have read both that there was a more suitable programme of races for the horse in Britain and that it was thought better not to have him travel over from Ireland for the Festival as he had in 1980. Also, of course, although the horse had previously been in his own care, Mulhern was then in his early years as a trainer. Before that he was a serious follower of point-to-points and had ridden in them. O'Toole remembers him riding a couple of winners. Mulhern's first training licence was in 1975 and when Stephen McCarthy first worked for him they were based at Castletown House in Celbridge, County Kildare.

'When we started in Castletown House we were a very small team, with polo ponies and a few so-called racehorses,' recalls McCarthy, who was still at school when he made his first appearances there and would later become the trainer's assistant. In those early days the racehorses were outnumbered by the polo ponies, choice Argentinian-bred animals on whom Mulhern used to play the sport religiously every Sunday at the Phoenix Park.

While the racehorses trained by the man himself were small in number, however, an indeterminate number of other animals were also in his ownership or part-ownership. Mulhern would include his staff when it came to celebrating his winning gambles but, McCarthy reports, 'He'd say, "We had a touch today" and you wouldn't know anything about it. You didn't know whose name they could be in or whose colours.'

In 1984 Festival racegoers were similarly unaware when scrutinising their racecards for the National Hunt Chase but for a different reason, and Mulhern was celebrating again. Macks Friendly was listed as being owned by W [Willie] Mullins and trained by his father Paddy but in the event he ran in the colours of Mulhern. The sale was agreed the day before but concluded on only the day of the race because the superstitious buyer would not finalise it on the 13th. I am not sure whether it was Mullins or Mulhern who initiated the deal but both must have been ecstatic when Macks Friendly led two out under his erstwhile owner and won by five lengths. Landing a gamble.

Mulhern's father had been president of the Dublin Stock Exchange, but this was a family in which racing played an important part and the young Mulhern's interest in it was burnished mightily during his time at University College Dublin. The veterinary student sometimes pawned textbooks and instruments in order to boost his betting reserves. Racing and betting seemed to go hand in hand. He made his first visit to the Cheltenham Festival on the final day in 1961 and, thanks to the Paddy Sleator-trained Sparkling Flame in the Spa Hurdle, that visit was short and sweet, as Mulhern related in Raymond Smith's highly instructive 1992 book *The High Rollers Of The Turf*:

'Before the horses had moved out from the parade ring for the next race, I had left the meeting and was already en route to a lecture in Earlsfort Terrace [in the centre of Dublin], counting the readies into neat bundles in the taxi as I winged my way from Prestbury Park.'

The Spa Hurdle was the first race of the day – racing and betting may indeed have gone hand in hand, but sometimes for Mulhern it was betting that showed him the way.

He was a well-known owner for a long while before he made a serious mark as a trainer, and he was a well-known businessman well before that. At one stage he owned betting shops, but most notably he was the boss, then owner, of Clayton Love Distribution. Eimear Mulhern, who married him in 1988, describes the first key step to his business success: 'Clayton Love senior sent John to Harvard to do a business course and when he came back he said the future is frozen food.'

Others' scepticism on that front allowed Mulhern to take the initiative and make his fortune in the distribution of frozen foods in Ireland. With fish fingers in the vanguard, it helped that the Catholic Church had a fish-only policy on Friday – oven-ready chips later took up the initiative on other days of the week – and as a racehorse trainer Mulhern's nickname in the stable was 'The Captain', after Captain Birdseye.

~

In the mid-1980s, perhaps even more enlivened and emboldened by his two Festival successes as an owner, The Captain sought to give his own training operation some major impetus, and one critical step in the process took place at the end of 1984. On December 5, McCarthy travelled to Naas for a bumper in which Mulhern was running a young horse who had shown plenty of ability at home. He was quietly fancied. Or was he?

'We weren't quite sure,' recalls McCarthy. 'The question mark came into it again. I remember Mr Mulhern saying, "I'll see you at the races. If I'm late don't worry about it."'

But when the time came for their horse to be saddled Mulhern was still not present. McCarthy continues: 'I tacked him up. A good amateur was riding him and I told him to go down, jump out mid-division and just enjoy himself, teach him something and don't be hard on him, finish as close as you can and we'll be delighted. So that was grand.'

McCarthy took his place in the stand: 'There was no sign of the boss anywhere and then all of a sudden somebody with binoculars had seen him down at the start. He was down there having a serious chat with the jockey and all of a sudden there's a pile of money for our horse on the racetrack.'

Charlie Lucky, the medium of this late market interest, was slashed from 33-1 to 10-1 only to finish eighth. But in the long term the result of that bumper turned out to be one of the most rewarding of John Mulhern's life in racing. Also present in the 27-runner field was a five-year-old ridden by Ted Walsh and trained by Joe Canty, and this horse attracted even more interest in the betting, backed from 10-1 into 5-2. It won by 12 lengths.

'Galmoy annihilated them, absolutely,' McCarthy enthuses. 'This horse had to be something special, so I think he went and bought him maybe within the week. He paid big money for him.'

It is no wonder that John Mulhern was spotted down at the start that day at Naas, because by then he was already an instantly recognisable figure. 'He'd have had all the clobber,' confirms McCarthy. On major racedays the clobber included a long, fur-collared, woollen overcoat, one of a series he used to bring back from trips to Canada. On normal racedays in Ireland, such as the one at Naas, the overcoat was replaced by a long, very bright red, Puffa-style jacket that stood out like his racing colours, along with a trilby, a pair of enormous spectacles and the almost ever-present, chimney-sized Havana cigar.

When Mulhern died in 2010, the *Sunday Independent* described the man familiar to Irish racing in the early 1980s. He was, it said, 'Debonair, charming and fond of the good life.' Seemingly adapting the title of George Lambton's classic 1924 autobiography, *Men And Horses I Have Known*, Mulhern reportedly claimed that if he were to write such a book it would have to be 'Horses I Knew And The Women I Came Across.' I have read elsewhere that the title of that Mulhern version was 'The Horses I Knew And The Woman I Came Across'. The latter spelling I took to be a misprint.

The *Sunday Independent* went on: 'A dapper bachelor, he was a familiar figure around the racecourses, the Horseshoe Bar in the Shelbourne Hotel and Le Coq Hardi restaurant with a string of beautiful women.'

'I remember once or twice, before he was with Eimear, we went racing and he had various different types of machinery on his arm,' confirms McCarthy, who relates what transpired on one such visit to the racecourse. It was at Fairyhouse and Mulhern was with someone whose charms particularly caught the eye. She caught the eye of racegoers. Perhaps she might do the same even with the stony-hearted, clear-thinking bookmakers and serious punters who normally have eyes only for the form-book? When it came to the race in which Mulhern trained the second favourite he sent his companion down to have a bet.

'He'd do it so that he'd be noticed,' details McCarthy. 'He'd hand her a wad of notes in front of everyone, including in the parade ring, and they followed her down to see what she was doing, to see whether she was backing one of his horses. She went down and backed the favourite, so they all lumped on to the favourite and ours drifted.'

However, it was the Mulhern-trained horse who won and, while the bookmakers were therefore not treated to any further interaction with his glamorous companion, the trainer landed a nice bet with a previously arranged investment on his own horse at starting price.

'He was a gambler early on in his life and then he became a select gambler,' relates Mrs Mulhern. 'He wouldn't be betting on every race, no way, but he might have a horse of his own that he'd have ready for some race. He'd have a serious bet on one horse every so often. He loved to have a good betting coup, he did love that, and had many a one really.'

~

After Galmoy's purchase was rapidly agreed in the aftermath of the bumper at Naas, he won another bumper at Fairyhouse on New Year's Day in the ownership of Mrs Canty before thereafter sporting the colours of Deborah Threadwell, daughter of Mulhern's great friend Stan Threadwell. Still representing Canty, he won hurdle races at Navan and Leopardstown with great ease. They were over 2m3f and 2m6f but he then dropped down to 2m for the important Jameson Gold Cup at Fairyhouse in April and won that as well. He narrowly lost his unbeaten record at Punchestown but Galmoy was unquestionably one of the leading novice hurdlers in Ireland.

In the aftermath of the Fairyhouse race, Mulhern (speaking on behalf of Miss Threadwell) was asked whether Galmoy would be trained for the Champion Hurdle but he dismissed the notion, saying, 'No, no, no. This horse is made for chasing.' Apparently Galmoy had originally been destined to join Jimmy Fitzgerald in England. It was also said that he might stay with Joe Canty. When Galmoy reappeared in the autumn, though, he was now in training with John Mulhern.

Another stage in the evolution of Mulhern's racing career was to upgrade to a new training establishment, and he and his right-hand man set out from Celbridge to cast their eye over a yard at the Curragh. McCarthy was instructed to say nothing as they were shown the property, while Mulhern produced a series of discouraging noises: 'He kept saying, "This is not for us, Stephen. No, it is too barren, there's not enough land" and so on and so forth. On the way home we discussed it and he says, "We'll put in a bid for this place."'

Thus the move was made to Rathbride Stables and it was from that base that Mulhern enjoyed the most famous successes of his training career. McCarthy would take on the role of assistant trainer.

'Stephen was like the son he didn't have in many ways, and they were together through thick and thin,' says Eimear Mulhern. 'He was his right arm at all times and thoroughly trusted with the horses and you couldn't have a better person looking after them. If there was anybody who loved the horses more than John it was Stephen. They both of them were pretty hopeless cases.'

McCarthy would eventually take on a far greater responsibility than the average assistant, having learned how to train from his boss. In Mulhern's book, long-term planning was the cornerstone of their strategy. Cutting corners and taking short cuts would have been the cardinal sins.

Mrs Mulhern describes another aspect of his training methods: 'He was very anti antibiotics; he hated giving them anything. He liked to keep them as natural and as pure as he could. He reluctantly gave them their flu vac.'

His assistant elaborates: 'He had a phobia about injections for himself and horses. He was a great believer in the old-fashioned remedies, as in hosing horses' legs for hours on end. Numerous times we used to spend hours hosing horses' legs and joints. He relied on the old-fashioned ways which the horses benefit from; they last longer, they have a longer shelf life.' At Rathbride Stables, those hours with the hose were a rite of passage.

Galmoy's first season with Mulhern began with a switch to chasing. 'He won his first chase and he won it well now and I was chuffed to bits with him,' relates Tommy Carmody, already Galmoy's regular jockey. 'Potentially he had the ability to be a Gold Cup horse.'

His step up in grade, however, came over 2m at Leopardstown over Christmas and this time, in the jockey's words, 'He was on his head the whole way. He just wasn't happy and they were going a stride too quick for him because he wasn't a two-miler.'

Carmody reported back, and he details the trainer's response: 'He just said, "That's it – no more chasing for him" and when he made his mind up that was it.'

McCarthy agreed with the decision: 'We decided there's no point in persevering here and disheartening the poor old bugger. By the time he got home he was going back to hurdling and that was it. There was no Gold Cup horse. If someone else had him maybe they would have kept persevering but he said he was too good a horse to get injured or jump into himself or do something stupid, or to lose heart in the racing game. It could have happened. You had to sweeten him up and try to get him to enjoy himself again.'

There was an encouraging sign back over hurdles four days later when Galmoy finished second under Frank Berry, Carmody having been booked for one of his rivals. Mulhern later reported that he had then strongly fancied the horse for that year's Stayers' Hurdle at Cheltenham but that a nail pricked Galmoy's foot and the wound turned septic. So when Galmoy was next seen it was at Punchestown in April and the sweetening-up period had clearly worked.

'I'll tell you something now and you'll have a little laugh to yourself,' says Carmody, 'but I would say to this day that this was his best performance ever, the one at Punchestown.' Galmoy carried top weight of 12 stone in that 3m handicap and he won it by 12 lengths. That summer came evidence of just how much the jockey had been impressed when, at the Moyglare Manor one evening, Mulhern could have been spotted having dinner not with one of his beautiful female friends but with Tommy Carmody, and the upshot, announced at the end of July, was that the jockey would end his retainer with Mouse Morris to ride instead for Galmoy's owner Deborah Threadwell.

As quoted in *The Irish Field*, Mulhern explained: 'Tommy was either going to ride Galmoy all the time, or not at all. He's been very lucky for the owner but you only make your own luck by giving horses the best possible chance and we think Tommy would give them that.' Carmody had to all intents and purposes become Mulhern's stable jockey.

'We had some great innings,' says McCarthy. 'Tommy was a great guy. He was always around and if you wanted anything Tommy would be there to do it for you. He didn't have to because all he was paid to do was ride racing and ride out in the morning for a few hours, but he always came back and he was a true professional. He was a good man.'

When he joined the yard in that summer of 1986, Carmody was the reigning champion jockey but in the 1986 jumps trainers' table, headed by Paddy Mullins with 48 wins, Mouse Morris had 20 wins, Mulhern only three. Mathematics aside, Tony O'Hehir would later write in the *Racing Post* that 'Collective wisdom deemed Carmody ill-advised to get involved with the flamboyant businessman-turned-trainer'. Three months before the announcement of his new job, the jockey received a possible clue as to just what it was the collective wisdom might be getting at.

'Ballinrobe is a four- or five-hour drive, a long way to go,' says McCarthy, and Carmody was there to ride a Mulhern-trained horse called Wolf Of Badenoch. One year later Wolf Of Badenoch would be established as one of the top novice hurdlers in Ireland. As Galmoy had done, he would win the Jameson Gold Cup at Fairyhouse. He then developed into one of Ireland's best chasers. That day at Ballinrobe, however, he was having his first run both under rules and for the stable.

Carmody goes on: 'It was just an ordinary maiden hurdle and he [Mulhern] says to me in the parade ring, "I want you to get this horse beat." I looked at him and I said "You're having a laugh." He says, "No. I want this horse to be beat." So I went out and anyway I got him beat.' McCarthy remembers that Wolf Of Badenoch and Carmody were going so fast at the end of the race that they jumped two extra hurdles. 'Ballinrobe is a small course and I nearly went a full circuit around to pull him up,' confirms the man on board.

He continues, 'So the stipendiary stewards had us in. He [Mulhern] says, "You'll be alright" and I said, "You're having a laugh" to him again. It was there for everybody to see that he wasn't trying.'

Mulhern's attempt to lay the groundwork quietly for a gamble at some future date had gone wrong. 'Way, way wrong,' says the stable jockey.

Given Wolf Of Badenoch's temperament and earlier misdemeanours in the point-to-point field, from which he was purchased after running out twice in the space of two days, the trainer may have had his reasons for not going to Ballinrobe with him all guns blazing, but, as his assistant states bluntly, 'It doesn't make any difference – you don't do that on the racecourse.'

The stewards were not satisfied with the explanations of either trainer or jockey and both were fined £200. After another race in December Mulhern was fined £500, with Carmody and his mount Dromoland Lad suspended for two weeks.

So Mr Mulhern crossed swords with the authorities a few times? 'Plenty,' certifies his assistant, 'and he absolutely loved it, thrived on it. He got a kick actually about going in front of the stewards. Because he just loved a verbal challenge. Half the time I think they were afraid to call him in because they knew they'd be in for a blasting as well as him.'

As further evidence of what might transpire when the authorities attempted to place Mulhern 'on the mat', McCarthy describes the aftermath of a race at the Curragh in which another Mulhern runner, 'hard held', caught the stewards' eye. It was the last race of the day and the trainer was due to gallop some of his horses after racing. The announcement 'Would Mr Mulhern please come to the weighing room' was heard over the public address system.

'He said, "Listen, you go up there and tell them I'm busy. You sort it out." So I went up and said, "I'm representing Mr Mulhern and he just told me to tell you that he's too busy, with working after racing."'

Having pronounced that this was not a very good start to the proceedings, the stewards showed McCarthy the video of the race and asked him what the jockey was doing. Alternative views must have been discussed and then … 'after about ten or 15 minutes there was a knock on the door and in charges Mr Mulhern. "We haven't time for this. We've got work to do, not like you lot sitting on your arse all day." He ushered me out of the room and we were referred to the appeals committee.'

McCarthy offers this description of his boss: 'He was a very well-spoken man and he had plenty to say.'

'A lot of it was theatre,' explains Mrs Mulhern. In this connection, though, the suspicion arises that her husband did not in general have a high opinion of the stewards. 'He thought they didn't know anything about racing,' McCarthy verifies.

'He thought half of them had never sat on a horse, that they didn't know anything about a horse, and he said why should we listen to this? There were some he respected. The majority he didn't. Most people go in there, "Yes sir, no sir, three bags full," but he wouldn't tolerate that.'

~

With Galmoy and now Carmody on the team, Mulhern had the horse and jockey to take his training operation to another level, and after his Punchestown win the ambitions for Galmoy did not revolve around handicap marks and betting coups. The assistant trainer confirms: 'Whenever he went to the races there would be no messing around – he was doing his best.'

The decision was taken to plan Galmoy's second season with Mulhern entirely around a challenge for the Stayers' Hurdle, and one run beforehand would be sufficient to get him there in peak fitness. Mulhern would later tell the press at Cheltenham that 'They only run this once a year. We would not want to bring a tired horse over here.'

'He wouldn't be the sort of horse you'd look twice at,' asserts Tommy Carmody. Stephen McCarthy expands on the point: 'He was not over tall, but a big, long, rangy type of horse. Very long. He wouldn't be any oil painting. You wouldn't walk into a yard and pick him out straightaway, and to ride him you'd say the same.'

Riding and handling him at different stages of the season presented different challenges. The stable jockey describes the first: 'When he was getting ready for his season, when he'd be back in off the grass, he'd be a very hard horse to ride, a very fresh horse. You just had to be on your guard with him.'

The first phase of bringing Galmoy back to fitness was a sequence of long canters. Perhaps four or five times a week, Galmoy would canter for five or six miles. At the Curragh they had the space to do it. 'And it worked with the big, strong, National Hunt horses – they were able to take it,' says McCarthy, who does not believe that the typical stock seen in the modern era are nearly so hardy. 'We'd go for miles and miles cantering away and the odd time coming home we'd quicken up for a couple of furlongs sharply, just to inject a little bit of pace there.'

And then, as Galmoy's fitness built up under this regime, there would be a change in his demeanour. 'After maybe six or eight weeks doing that, all of a sudden it would be taking nothing out of him, and taking the saddle off him he'd be trying to tear the arm off you, or something like that. And you knew – he's back. This horse is well now, really well.'

When Galmoy graduated to faster work, McCarthy says it would be barely once a week. Being a very clear-winded individual he didn't need more, and these gallops were not serious tests: 'We'd maybe use one of the younger horses to sail away in front there until we'd pick them up in the latter stages. To give him the confidence to go by something. We never let something really go by him. We'd always build his confidence to let him think he was the king.'

Having returned to his stables, however, Galmoy was not just a king, he was a despot. They used to have a few dogs around but when Galmoy was approaching race fitness they, and others, were well advised to keep their distance. 'Savage' is one word used to describe Galmoy in his stable and a 'bullet-proof jacket' would have been the clothing of choice.

As his lad, Alan Beale must have borne the brunt of this tyrannical rule but McCarthy can still boast a couple of scars and the stable jockey was by no means exempt, as Carmody confirms: 'There's a few of us he left bruises on. By God he would, especially when you'd be tacking him up. You'd know well what he'd be capable of but before you know it he'd be taking a piece out of your side. He would absolutely eat you he would, in the stable.'

For those who had to suffer them, what made these eating habits and unsocial stable manners good news is that this was the way in which Galmoy's well-being would be revealed. 'He'd never impress in his homework, never did,' records Carmody, 'but you'd always know when he was bang on – he ate you.'

In the winter of 1986/87, all appeared to be going smoothly with Galmoy's Cheltenham preparation and those painful dietary supplements – until he actually raced again. The Boyne Hurdle over 2m6f at Navan in late February saw his comeback and Galmoy was beaten by the Paddy Mullins-trained Welcome Pin, a novice receiving just 2lb. *The Sporting Life* reported that 'an apparently distraught Mulhern promptly declared: "Galmoy should have been able to beat a novice on those terms."' He also predicted that he would not be sending a runner to the Festival.

The trainer's distress at the prospect can be understood when his wife says: 'Cheltenham was the Mecca. He absolutely geared everything towards Cheltenham.'

However, giving what had transpired in the Boyne some further thought, Mulhern modified his conclusions and for a reported six-figure sum bought Welcome Pin. The front two at Navan had drawn 12 lengths clear and with the trainer now feeling more at ease about the performance, Galmoy was back on course to run at Cheltenham.

In Mulhern, the Festival had one of its greatest devotees. As first evinced in his student days, with that fleeting visit for the Spa Hurdle, betting was undoubtedly part of the attraction. In subsequent years too, as McCarthy reports: 'The boss man himself, he used to have a good few quid on him when he went to Cheltenham alright, because he'd say they take money over there. You could go into the ring and have a bet. In Ireland there would be very few who would take a good bet, but at Cheltenham they love to take the Irish money.'

But the Festival for Mulhern had become vastly more than that. Mulhern's friend JC Savage used to call it 'The Big Picture'. It was the very best their sport had to offer and, like so many, Mulhern was part of a group that made its way there year after year to celebrate the fact. Together with Savage and Peter Costello, Mulhern had a tried-and-tested routine of travelling over from Ireland, joining up with Stan Threadwell and heading to Gloucestershire.

'Cheltenham was such a one-off; it was like a pilgrimage they went on every year,' remembers Deborah Woodmansee (then Deborah Threadwell). 'And they came back after a week totally, absolutely shattered but had had the best time, particularly if they'd had some good bets along the way.'

Additions to that core group, in the Threadwells' case anyway, were not contemplated: 'That wasn't on the agenda. That was Dad's thing and no one questioned that. Mum never went to Cheltenham. That was his domain. He shared so much with us but no one would ever have said I'm insisting I come. Nobody would have done that ever.'

Stan Threadwell, an Englishman from Felixstowe, was a former Flat jockey who had made a success of a second career in the leisure industry, including the ownership of several piers. Having met Mulhern racing, as Threadwell's daughter reports, 'It was a firm friendship all their lives. They had this love of horses and love of life, and a deep connection.'

Threadwell was no stranger to racehorse ownership, most notably with Jupiter Island, whose Flat career in the early 1980s had the sort of longevity and following normally reserved for a jumps horse. Deborah Threadwell went sometimes with her father to see Jupiter Island run and, she says, 'for some reason whenever I went the horse used to win. They used to call me lucky, that I was a lucky person to have around, and that's when my dad said, "I think we'll put a horse in your name."'

The first horse to carry Miss Threadwell's chosen colours of 'red, pink diamond and sleeves, and white cap' was Galmoy. However, by April 1986, as *The Irish Field* revealed, while the good luck attached to her colours now seemed firmly established, the owner's own such status regarding Galmoy had undergone a dramatic shift. They recorded: 'Deborah Threadwell, who is noticeable by her absence on the racecourse, has every intention of continuing to stay away if it means that her luck holds.' Apparently she had seen Galmoy run only once, when he was beaten.

While the daughter preferred to stay in the background anyway, a fair dose of the father's superstition had rubbed off on her. After that initial loss, she would not risk any possibility of becoming Galmoy's jinx. And that was not the end of the complications: 'John was very, very superstitious,' adds Eimear Mulhern, 'so when Galmoy ran in Deborah's colours they all ran in Deborah's colours after that because obviously he thought that Deborah was very lucky. So at one point I think she was the leading owner in Ireland and hardly anybody had ever seen her.'

Mulhern, Stan Threadwell, Savage, Costello and Galmoy were going to Cheltenham but Galmoy's official owner would not be joining them.

~

1987 STAYERS' HURDLE

Up until declaration time, there was also a major doubt over the presence of the horse who appeared to be Galmoy's most serious opponent. Aonoch had won the previous season's Aintree Hurdle over 2m5f. Earlier in the 1986/87 campaign he had shown his versatility by stepping down to 2m for two wins and stepping up to 3m for two more, and the last of those wins, in the Rendlesham at Kempton, was hugely impressive. The Champion Hurdle was still a very serious alternative option for Aonoch's owner Henry Oliver and trainer Sally Oliver, his wife, but when good ground prevailed the feeling was that he had far better prospects in the longer race.

The Hopes of a Nation

The Olivers' choice of engagement was uncontroversial. What attracted more attention was their choice of jockey. Daughter Jacqui had owned Aonoch the previous season and, a 7lb claimer, had ridden him initially in that campaign, alternating with the more experienced Jimmy Duggan in 1986/87. She would take the ride in the Stayers' and, as part of the conditions for a race of this stature, she would not be able to take off the 7lb.

Aonoch had been third in the 1985 Stayers' but was a far better horse in his run-up to the 1987 version. In the *Racing Post* selection box, 11 of the 14 tipsters went for Aonoch and one for Galmoy. The pair started 2-1 and 9-2; the locally trained Model Pupil (on a four-timer) was 6-1, in front of Out Of The Gloom on 7-1 from 10-1, with the 1982 and 1986 Stayers' winner Crimson Embers 9-1 in a 14-runner field in which Galmoy was the sole Irish challenger.

'Nerves were playing a big part now,' says McCarthy, 'especially with the boss when it came very close to the occasion. He'd rather not saddle up. He would have been pacing up and down or chewing on his cigar.'

Tommy Carmody on the other hand was an experienced big-race jockey – in 1978 his first two rides at the Festival were winners – and he knew exactly what he intended to do on board Galmoy: 'I would ride all horses more or less the same, whether it was two miles or three miles or four miles. I would always give horses time to find themselves, warm up and if they were good enough to go on and win I would just arrive down at the last hurdle or fence. Because I've seen so many races lost with people sending horses on at the second last, and then you'd always hear the cliché "I probably hit the front too soon." I rode him [Galmoy] out most days and I rode him in all his hurdle wins prior to that and I just knew what he was capable of. It's a bit of common sense – if you're still going well at the second last you don't panic; you assess what's around you and you see what's happening, and then you can either say, "Well, I'd better get a bit closer" or I can sit still and just work my way along.'

When the tapes went up, the 1987 Stayers' brought tactical complications. The pair who disputed the lead were the 50-1 and 300-1 outsiders Dad's Gamble and Malford Lad, and if this was a duel up front it was of the most anaemic variety because the pace was slow. Carmody closed on the leaders at the eighth of 13 flights. 'An out-and-out stayer he was,' records Galmoy's jockey. 'He had a great bit of speed but his forte was staying.' Asking him to make up ground late on in a falsely-run race would be too dangerous. Oliver, on Aonoch, left her move until later but as the leaders jumped the second last, with Dad's Gamble about to capitulate, it was Galmoy and Aonoch who took over.

The race was between the two market principals. The difference between the jockeys was graphic but, even so, what happened when they rounded the home turn was fairly startling. Side by side, the two contenders were not exactly close enough to shake hands but suddenly there was a chasm between them as Aonoch, on the outer, wandered off dramatically towards the stands side. He then had a partial change of heart and moved somewhat to his left again before jumping the final flight, but Galmoy now led by about two lengths. A good portion of it had been handed to Galmoy on a plate and he was not the sort to relinquish his gift. So with Carmody pushing him out, looking over his right shoulder several times and presumably highly pleased with what he saw, Galmoy passed the post in front by six lengths. Aonoch was ahead of Model Pupil by four.

Much of the coverage afterwards was fixated on issues of jockeyship. In more measured tones in their subsequent essay on Aonoch in *Chasers & Hurdlers 1986/87*, Timeform would write: 'The practice of putting up a claimer unable to claim in preference to a fully-fledged jockey in a top race isn't to be recommended.' They thought that in different circumstances, but in particular it seemed with a different jockey, Aonoch might have won (with the same jockey, he justified favouritism in his second Aintree Hurdle the following month). I cannot see it myself. Galmoy had just taken a narrow advantage when Aonoch commenced his meanderings and Galmoy looked as if he could gallop on for ever.

'He was the type of horse who always had a lot in reserve for you,' states Carmody. McCarthy's description of this horse-and-jockey combination rings very true: 'He was a very, very hard horse to get by once he got his head in front; when he was running down to the second last or the last he just kept grinding and grinding and grinding. That was him. He never lay down. Tommy wouldn't let him lie down anyway. Tommy was as ruthless as he was and the two of them were well suited. To be fair to Tommy, you'd have to be so fit on the horse and he was. He was a super jockey as you know and he was just so determined.'

If there was an element of controversy, or at least rarity, about the closing stages of that 1987 Stayers' Hurdle it did not perturb the winning connections. 'The horse wins and your head was just in the clouds,' remembers McCarthy. 'It came and went so quickly. It was just a huge sigh of relief.'

For others in the Mulhern party, the celebratory feeling was in no way a fleeting one. John Mulhern had revealed beforehand that he was lying awake at night at the thought of having a Festival winner and, with the race safely won, there still was not a lot of sleep to be had. His assistant trainer relates, 'they made a handsome night of it that lasted well into the following day.' For McCarthy himself the night was contrastingly tame. He was still at the racecourse with responsibility for seeing their horse back to Ireland the next day and 'someone had to half have their wits about them to face the early-morning call from the boss about the well-being of his horse.'

At The Festival

On the Saturday before the 1987 Festival, one of the *The Sporting Life*'s chief British reporters, fresh from testing the waters, and perhaps other liquids, on a trip to Ireland, had warned readers to have 'Shamrocks at the ready and stand by for an Irish riot at next week's Cheltenham Festival. Numerically, the challenge from across the water may be the lowest for several years but I confidently predict that their winners-to-runners ratio will be the highest since the halcyon days of the late 70s.'

When the Festival ended, however, Galmoy had won but that was it for Ireland. There were six thirds (and a fourth in the County Hurdle) but Galmoy had been the only Irish-trained horse to finish in the first two. From 41 runners and five favourites or co-favourites, it was their lowest number of wins since 1967.

As Galmoy's win came in only the fourth race of the meeting, there had not been any looming threat that they would draw a Festival blank. Irish racegoers leaving the course on Thursday evening may have done so despondently but the Irish training fraternity is made up of individual establishments and each now had to regather their resources and work towards the next Festival.

∼

Eleven days after their Stayers' win, Mulhern was fined £500 over the running of Rent Or Buy on the Flat, with Carmody and the horse handed a punishment of more biblical proportions, banished to the wilderness (banned from racing) for four weeks.

Galmoy was also by then on his holidays but a more extensive campaign was in store for him than in 1986/87. Confidence was high that there was nothing to be afraid of in the likely 1988 Stayers' opposition and that they could therefore risk him not being absolutely at his best. Galmoy had six races, fit enough this time to win the

Boyne Hurdle in his immediate race before Cheltenham but also successful from a notable rival in The Illiad over 2m at Naas in December. In between the two was an inexplicably poor display in the Findus Anniversary Hurdle at Leopardstown, a race Mulhern would have been very keen to win given his business associations and for which Galmoy was odds on. McCarthy recalls: 'He just didn't show up. We got him scoped and blood sampled afterwards and there was nothing wrong with him. I rode him out two days later and he was perfect.'

If that race was a surprise, however, it paled in comparison with what happened 11 days later. John Mulhern got married.

'When we got married I wanted my own racing colours to have an exclamation mark,' recalls his wife, but the authorities were less amused at the prospect.

'He was always adamant that he'd stay single,' says McCarthy, and when the trainer changed his mind he insisted that the event be very low key. But with Mulhern even low key could be done flamboyantly – the wedding took place in virtual secrecy.

'It was in my parents' house but we didn't tell anybody,' relates Eimear Mulhern. 'He went to the races that day and had a horse running. In fact one of my bridesmaids, he made her go to the races because he said that if she didn't show up people would know that we were getting married. I don't know where he got that from. He just didn't want it in the papers or anything.'

The trainer's bride was already a highly respected figure in the bloodstock industry and has been Chairman of Goffs Bloodstock Sales since 2005, but to understand something of Mulhern's concerns it may help to know that before she became Eimear Mulhern she was Eimear Haughey.

'My father was Prime Minister at the time and it would have been a bit of a palaver. So everything was to go as normal and John went to Leopardstown and he had a horse running that day that was called Hungary Hur which was supposed to win and get the price of the honeymoon [he didn't]. We got married at 6 o'clock after racing.'

The couple took a week's honeymoon in the Caribbean and Mrs Mulhern relates, 'He was speaking to Stephen [McCarthy] each day. His first call in the morning was Stephen and the last call in the evening would be Stephen. But when you're married to a trainer, that's life. That's what you sign up for.'

Galmoy and his well-being, on the back of the disconcerting performance at Leopardstown, figured prominently in those transatlantic conversations. Even following the restoration of his status as Stayers' favourite with victory in the Boyne, Galmoy would never have been far from the trainer's thoughts as the clock ticked down towards Cheltenham.

The trainer's wife gives an insight into how Mulhern coped with the pressure of taking Ireland's saviour back to the Festival: 'Oh don't talk to me – he'd be a basket case. He was a basket case before every race. Just because he wanted the horses to come home in one piece.'

Mulhern's consumption of cigars increased, though his precise intake was shrouded in the smog.

'What it was and what he told me were always two completely different things,' comments Mrs Mulhern. 'They helped to relax him, or he thought they did. I'm not sure. He always used to be very hyper; he'd get pretty wound up about it all. Just because he cared so much.'

The demeanour of Mulhern the trainer could be in huge contrast to that of Mulhern the gambler. In the latter role, as Mick O'Toole remembers, 'He was a big punter and he was a fearless punter too.' In the former, as his assistant corroborates, 'He'd be chewing cigars and he used to get himself worked up. For a high-profile businessman who'd be used to high-pressure jobs and high-pressure decisions, it was amazing – when it came to racing the nerves just kicked in.'

The key to understanding this split-screen personality seems to be his love for the horses. The Captain would give nicknames to all of those in his stable: Friendly Alliance was Big Al, Galmoy was Barney, Wolf Of Badenoch was The Wolf, and Flashing Steel was Lofty. 'John would be absolutely hyper about the horses. Because he actually loved his horses, it wasn't just the winning. He absolutely adored them.' Those words are Mrs Mulhern's but the general tenor is a recurring theme.

In 1988, Tommy Carmody told the *Racing Post*: 'If I was reincarnated there's only one thing I'd want to be – a horse trained by John Mulhern.'

~

1988 STAYERS' HURDLE

After the 1987 Stayers', as quoted in the *Racing Post*, Eimear Haughey's description of viewing the closing stages from the grandstand had been that 'I jumped up and down so much I broke my seat!' Back at Cheltenham in 1988 as Eimear Mulhern she watched the race from the lawn in front of the grandstand, as did her husband.

'He had his lucky spot,' she records. But quite where that lucky spot is located she does not know. 'He was completely superstitious. He wore the same tie, he wore the same everything; whatever he wore when the horse won, he'd wear the same thing when he ran again and he'd always watch on his own. He always went away on his own and he was best left on his own to watch the race. To be honest, if you stood near him it wasn't a good place to stand because he actually rode the race himself.'

Spirited vocal interjections were not the end of it. 'He'd be accidentally digging people in the ribs,' Mrs Mulhern elaborates, 'and it was just not a good place to stand.'

Positioning himself on his own also gave Mulhern some time to compose himself if things went wrong. In the 1988 Stayers', Galmoy was faced by 15 rivals and he was one of only two runners back from the 1987 renewal, the other being a rank outsider, Malford Lad. The Stayers' Hurdle in that era had nothing like the stature it does now, when as the World Hurdle it attracts very few, if any, runners from around the world but nearly always features a mouth-watering cast from Britain and Ireland. Reviewing the 1988 field there are nevertheless some famous names: Gaye Brief, Corporal Clinger and Bonanza Boy; third favourite was the previous season's star novice hurdler Ten Plus, on a recovery mission after a crashing end to his campaign as a chaser; second favourite, however, was the vastly improved mare Miss Nero.

In a similar situation to Aonoch the previous year, except with more fanfare, the Mullins-trained Cloughtaney had had a choice of engagements and was reported the previous Thursday as being far more likely to run in the Stayers' than the Champion, unless there was rain. The prospect of a sound surface, such as that which prevailed in 1987, was worrying Irish supporters. But rain there was. Cloughtaney ran in the Champion, starting second favourite, and he finished tenth. When it came to post time for the Stayers', Irish horses had still not won any race at the Festival since Galmoy in 1987 but on that Tuesday in 1988 they had finished second in the three preceding races. Galmoy was returning as Ireland's best hope of the week and, backed as such, he was in to 2-1 favouritism. The weight of expectation had got to his trainer. Would his jockey also have felt that sort of pressure?

'No I didn't,' reports Tommy Carmody, 'because everything was right with him. We couldn't find any faults in him. Everything was good.'

In the race, Galmoy gave Carmody sustained cause to change his mind: 'He gave me such a hard time, as regards pushing and kicking. I must have pushed him for the second circuit, because he just got into a lull. He thought "I'll just do what I have to do."'

The ground was soft and, in heavy rain, getting softer. Mulhern had to don a raincoat in addition to his usual outfit. After the first circuit, for those watching in the stands, confidence in the favourite was probably a lot less steadfast than it had been three or four minutes earlier. However, with the pace at which Ten Plus had embarked, leading over the first nine hurdles, a right slog was in the offing.

'They go very fast in England,' continues Galmoy's jockey, 'and that would bring out his best, horses going flat out. He always would only just do enough, and do enough and do enough, and then once you got stuck into him it was go, go, go for him.'

From a mile out Carmody's exertions became more visible as Galmoy kept responding, at the same time as virtually all those around him dropped away. Two horses made a move from the front, setting off on a race of their own, Miss Nero leading Galmoy down the hill. Ten Plus pulled up at the back of the field at the third last, where way ahead Galmoy had just jumped past Miss Nero and into the lead.

Galmoy's go-go-go phase had arrived.

'The next thing you could see were hats going in the air,' recalls Mrs Mulhern. 'I could hardly see the finish because people are screaming and roaring and throwing hats in the air and dancing around.'

Approaching two out, it was indeed all over bar the jumping and the hat throwing. Rounding the final turn, Galmoy led Miss Nero by about ten lengths, with Bonanza Boy another 25 lengths or so adrift, having just passed Gaye Brief for third, with another huge margin to the fifth and sixth.

'It was just "Oh my God!"' relates the trainer's wife, laughing. 'Living with it beforehand was a nightmare and then afterwards it was just brilliant.'

'He just put his head down and kept going,' testifies McCarthy in praise of the winning horse, and for most of the race, before Galmoy's superiority asserted itself in such unanswerable fashion, much the same could be said of the man on board. 'You had to be forceful on the likes of Galmoy. It was hard to get to the bottom of him. Tommy was very fit but you'd have to be because you could be riding him for two miles in a three-mile race, and all of a sudden he'd be going as fast in the last half-mile as he would have been in the first.'

For the last ten strides Carmody could ease off, flick Galmoy's ears and, as he had done in 1987, pat him down the neck. With the principals easing down, Galmoy passed the line ahead by seven lengths, with Miss Nero in front of Bonanza Boy by 12.

'To win in Cheltenham is just an unbelievable experience,' says Mrs Mulhern, 'because not only do you have all your friends that are there supporting you, you have the whole country there supporting you. It's just an unbelievable feeling because people that you never knew are hugging you and grabbing you and kissing you and leading in the horse and all, which makes it all absolutely fantastic. It is an experience like no other.'

The feeling she describes is one of 'the excitement and the passion and the angst and the worry and the absolute joy unconfined.'

In the first minutes following that triumph she may not have been with her husband but she could easily guess what his reaction had been. 'John was terribly emotional, he was a terribly emotional person, so if they won he used to cry like a baby.'

∼

When that emotional response calmed, which tended to take a fair while, the trainer's chief feeling apparently was relief that the horse had returned safely and the job was done. His wife elaborates: 'It was the whole horsemanship and the horses that he loved, rather than the honour and glory. That was incidental to John. It was the whole game, picking the horses and buying the horses and placing them; the whole game of racing was really what he was passionate about. It wasn't the success and getting the prize.'

That did not prevent Galmoy's connections from repairing to the Fosse Manor at Stow-on-the-Wold and having 'the best party of all times'. It seemed as if anyone who had ever known Mulhern, Threadwell or the rest of their entourage had all turned up.

By the end of the week, however, for the wider constituency of Irish racing the celebrations had swiftly run dry. After Tuesday's three seconds and a win there was no other Irish-trained winner at the meeting and only one placed horse, in the Triumph Hurdle. That was one of three Irish horses who headed the betting in their respective races, from 37 Irish runners in all.

Eimear Mulhern recalls some of the reaction to Galmoy's win once the wider context had become clear: 'They would say, "John, you saved the day," there was a lot of that, and "Oh thanks be to God we got out" and all this sort of thing. Of course the Irish are terribly patriotic so they always seem to let their heart slightly rule their head at Cheltenham and they all wade in to the Irish horses. So they were getting fairly cleaned out. I don't know how much he saved for them but at least he saved them something. It was seen as a lean one when there was only the one winner alright but at least he kept our head above water.'

There is a difficulty in commenting about how the Irish have felt at Cheltenham, which is that I am not Irish. John Scally, however, has written an enthralling book detailing the exploits of many an Irish challenger at Cheltenham and he titled it *Them and Us*. Observing the emotions of an Irish punter at the Festival, Scally wrote: 'Racing was not just sport for him, it was also about nationalism. The historical relationship between Ireland and Britain had always been one of inequality. Ireland had always had to play second fiddle, but on the racing track the position was reversed. These horses were not simply animals, they were Irish heroes … When they bet on an Irish horse at Cheltenham, Irish fans are betting on national property, investing emotional as well as tangible currency. When a fancied Irish horse loses, the loss is more than just monetary. Any Irish win precipitates a show of national identity. Punters brush aside gatemen and crowd on their way to the winners' enclosure to roar every Irish victory as if each one somehow confers glory on them, personally submerging their individuality in the name of patriotism.'

John Mulhern's take on patriotism at the Festival, as quoted by Liam Collins in the *Sunday Independent*, was contained in advice he gave to Irish punters: 'Your patriotic duty is not to bet on Irish horses – your patriotic duty is to bet on winners and take money from bookies.'

According to his wife, the camaraderie at the event appealed to Mulhern more than the patriotism. His love of Cheltenham always made it a friendly battle and his love of Cheltenham is hard to overstate. At one stage before Galmoy's time, Mulhern purchased a property near Cheltenham and believed that his future as a trainer lay there and not in Ireland.

'Yes,' says his assistant trainer. 'We had our bags packed and all. We were going to cross the Irish Sea.' It never happened, though, the practicalities of setting up as a trainer in Britain while attending to business matters in Ireland proving too problematic.

~

Returning to England as visitors for the 1989 Festival, there was concern within the Mulhern camp that one of their number might not be putting his best foot forward. Putting it like that sounds incredibly unfair. Galmoy had been the hero of two pitched battles at the Festival, the only Irish victor two years running, but he required an increasing amount of persuasion from the saddle before he would join the fray. As McCarthy puts it, 'he was a bit backwards about going forwards in his races'. And in taking a relaxed approach to racing he ended up giving himself a harder race. Tommy Carmody, the man tasked with eliciting Galmoy's effort, observes: 'He was such a laid-back horse. That was just his nature. He gave his all but you had to absolutely drill him or drive him.'

Carmody believed he knew the remedy – blinkers. Mulhern, however, would have none of it. He hated one of his horses having a hard race but at that stage he seemed to feel that such a resort to blinkers would mark a failure in his training.

'He had this thing in his head that he just didn't like blinkers on horses,' comments his assistant. 'If he couldn't train one without blinkers it kind of defeated his purpose in training horses.'

The Stayers' Hurdle was instituted only in 1972 but Galmoy was the first to win it two years in a row. He was only the second horse to win it twice, after Crimson Embers, and none had won it three times (it was not until the new century that there was another double winner, in Baracouda; Inglis Drever has since won it three times and Big Buck's four). Going for the first hat-trick, Galmoy was 7-2 favourite in a 21-runner field. Connections had reverted to a light campaign but when he made his customary pre-Cheltenham appearance in the Boyne Hurdle he fell, returning battered and bruised. On raceday, though, Mulhern reported in *The Sporting Life* that 'he is starting to kick again and take the odd bite'.

Setting off downhill on the final circuit Galmoy was chasing the third-favourite Miss Nero and second-favourite

Rustle, but he was under the whip. At the third last, where he'd come to the fore in 1988, Galmoy had dropped back to fifth. He was fourth two out and fought back further to dispute second with Miss Nero at the last, but Rustle was on his own up ahead. Galmoy ended up beating Miss Nero by eight lengths but was himself beaten by 12 and the improved performance from Rustle was widely attributed to his being equipped with headgear – in his case a visor – for the first time.

Carmody and McCarthy still entertain thoughts of what might have been. Galmoy's jockey reflects: 'They'd say blinkers wouldn't have made the difference on that occasion – it was 12 lengths – but believe me it would have done.'

Galmoy was now a ten-year-old. Aged 11 and 12, he returned for his fourth and fifth Stayers' Hurdles but was past his best and finished well beaten in 11th of 22 (wearing a visor) and fifth of 15. No matter. 'He was just a great, great horse,' says his jockey. Stephen McCarthy sums up the opinion held by John Mulhern and doubtless by many of his countrymen: 'Galmoy was the apple of his eye, a superhero.'

~

Summoning up the spirit of that time to describe the reaction to Irish Festival winners, Eimear Mulhern says: 'Now we have ten or twelve but back then if an Irish horse won it was *such* an achievement, because it was just *so* hard to do. England had all the ammunition. It was really David and Goliath, so of course when one did manage to win it was such a celebration and such a great success – the lesser force coming over and winning against all the power and might that was in training in the UK.'

The 1988/89 season brought the first Irish runner in the Gold Cup since Dawn Run, but there were only 31 Irish runners at the meeting, seven of them in the Supreme Novices', and Galmoy was the only favourite. Along with Trapper John, second in the Sun Alliance Novices' Hurdle, he was the only Irish-trained horse who managed a place – Ireland had failed to register a win for the first time since 1947. Over the three years 1987, 1988 and 1989 only one Irish-trained horse had won at the Festival.

The Irish Field that Saturday had a front-page headline in big, red, capital letters that shouted "IRISH HOPES TAKE DIVE" adjacent to a photograph of a horse hitting the turf headfirst and seemingly at the vertical. An envious mention was given to those Irish racegoers who had booked their passage on that Monday morning's Dun Laoghaire to Holyhead ferry only to find that it was cancelled due to rough seas.

Through the vast majority of my years at the Festival I have always wanted to see and celebrate the best horses, regardless of where they were trained, but when Ireland was reduced to such meagre returns it felt like an affront to the natural order.

In the aftermath of the 1987 Festival, the *Racing Post's* bloodstock correspondent Tony Morris reminded readers that 'In fact, all the meeting proved was that England's Irish horses did better than Ireland's Irish horses. Cheltenham was, as usual, a flop for the native English-bred ... No fewer than 12 of the 17 English-trained winners played for England only by dint of residential qualification.'

He continued, 'Irish jumping breeders are guardians and upholders of a national tradition, with rich resources of carefully nurtured stock representing their passport to a prosperous future. By contrast, their counterparts here ... operate in an environment which just tends to emphasise the "hit-and-miss" nature of the business.'

Writing in 2015, Irish-trained runners at the Festival have never tasted more success than in recent years, albeit with French-bred horses featuring prominently among their most successful representatives, and with Willie Mullins' yard they can boast the sport's most powerful stable. In 2014 there were 123 Irish-trained runners at the Festival, 36 trained by Mullins. Gathering pace, in 2015 there were 148 Irish-trained runners, of whom Mullins trained 54, including a record eight winners. The two most powerful owners in the sport, with gargantuan strings, are the Irishmen JP McManus and Michael O'Leary.

Money talks, just as it did in the 1980s when Ireland's lack of Festival success was not due just to a lack of those very big players but also a reflection of the country's depressed economic situation. 'I think it was the fact that every horse was for sale,' reflects Eimear Mulhern.

Not quite every one. I ask Stephen McCarthy whether anyone ever put in an offer for Galmoy. His reply – 'They wouldn't dare.' Mulhern was one person who could afford to say no and nearly all of the other owners in his yard were his close friends.

Deborah Woodmansee (née Threadwell) is the proud owner of a beautiful set of Waterford Crystal glass courtesy of Galmoy in the Stayers' Hurdle but she never did see her horse run at Cheltenham. She says now: 'I loved my dad so much and to see him so excited about something, that was mostly the thrill really, to see my dad so happy.'

Mulhern used to write letters to her telling her about the horses, how they were and how they were performing, and he would send newspaper cuttings from Ireland. 'He was wonderful,' says Mrs Woodmansee. 'I've never met anybody like him and I don't suppose I ever will. Him and my dad were very good, close friends and I just loved him. He was a character, he was funny, he was warm, he was loving, he was outrageous and he loved horses.'

Asked what his boss's strengths were as a trainer, McCarthy's answer is the same as that accorded to many of the trainers mentioned in this book – 'He was very, very patient.'

McCarthy continues, 'He would see probably a year into the future, even two years. It wouldn't make any difference to him. He was in the position that he didn't have to be rushed; there weren't owners pressurising him. He could do it in his own time, which he did.

'He had a great understanding of horses. In the early stages I couldn't. I'd think, "How could he say that? How could he be thinking that? Where does it come from?" But he knew what he was doing. He was a gifted man and the horses loved him too, you know. The moment he came into the yard every one of the horses' heads would be out. He'd be going round and petting them and every single one, regardless of whether they were a Galmoy or just ordinary point-to-pointers. And they all got the best of everything. Whether they were good or no good, they got everything they wanted.'

All at Rathbride had looked forward to Galmoy having a long retirement with them but health issues intervened and it did not prove possible. John Mulhern died in March 2010 after a long illness. His last win came that January when Puyol carried the red with a white question mark at Leopardstown in Ireland's biggest handicap hurdle, and that was also Mulhern's last runner. He had to watch it from his hospital bed but McCarthy remembers: 'He rang me, I'd say a minute after the race. He was just so excited and he said, "Great, great. I'm absolutely delighted. I'm glad I'm still around for this."'

Mulhern did not train another Cheltenham Festival winner after Galmoy but he did send out Flashing Steel to win the 1995 Irish Grand National in the ownership of his father-in-law Charles Haughey.

Mulhern also never lost his eye for a flamboyant gamble. They were rarer than previously but the bookmakers were still well advised to beware. Big meetings – with lots of money in the ring, longer odds on offer and people prepared to lay them – were the preferred venues for these bets and, as his wife divulges, 'He always used to try and have one really big gamble every year which he said would pay for the horse feed for the year ahead.'

Mulhern's last winner on the Flat was a filly called Few Are Chosen, who made her handicap debut in a 16-runner race at the Galway Festival in 2009. The trainer was present with a very longstanding friend of his from Dublin and as the card got underway he engaged his friend to place a bet for him. It was the first in what turned out to be a series of bets. McCarthy takes up the story:

'Gerry was going up and Muller was giving him 500 quid to go and have a bet on a total duff.'

The same happened before the next race, and the next, but with Mulhern adding a new, more theatrical element to his instructions.

'Mr Mulhern kept saying to him, "Now, as you are going doing your bets, just let on that you are getting a bit unsteady on your feet, that you're getting a bit wobbly and you've had a few drinks." I remember Gerry telling me afterwards that he had a lovely Burberry mackintosh on. He liked to dress well did Gerry and they were in the bar and Muller was having a glass of Guinness and he tipped part of his Guinness on Gerry's lovely Burberry jacket. Gerry lost the plot and said, "What the .... is this? What's going on here?" and Mr Mulhern says, "Don't worry about it, Gerry. You'll be able to buy plenty of those when the day is done."'

So the day progressed, with one persistent but supposedly very worse-for-wear punter having the most terrible of betting days. The sixth race was at 7.55 and Mulhern's friend ventured forth for the sixth time.

'He was told, "You just pretend now that you're well tuned, well oiled", and the bookies said, "Oh, here he comes again. This is money for jam here," and Gerry says, "I'll get me money back off you! I'll have 500 on Few Are Chosen!" and he was doing the line, the boys were laughing and thinking this is great, and then they realised, "Oh .... now – there's something going on here" and she won apologising. So Gerry had the last laugh. It was a lovely touch. They didn't all come up trumps but the ones that did you really do remember.'

Different people will have seen different sides to John Mulhern. None could have failed to notice him. Stephen McCarthy talks of the man he knew so well: 'Mr Mulhern, you either liked him or you didn't like him, and a lot of people probably didn't know him. If you knew him you'd like him. If you got to know him you'd see a different type of man – lovely natured, very intelligent, a great character, and a very, very generous and loyal man who liked the good things in life.'

One very good thing in life is the Festival. 'John lived for Cheltenham,' says Eimear Mulhern. 'He was a businessman who trained horses on the side but in his way of thinking that got a bit skewed.'

In 1987 and 1988, all of Ireland must have given thanks for it.

CHAPTER NINE

1989 DAILY EXPRESS TRIUMPH HURDLE

Splashing through the Standing Water

THE GROUND. IT can be a contentious issue. On individual horses and their ideal ground conditions, there has probably been more misinformation than on any other subject in the sport. Independent analysts regularly beg to differ about official going descriptions, and for nearly 40 years form books have carried alternative assessments on the state of the ground.

Here is another assertion that many are bound to disagree with. Of all the changes that have taken place at the Cheltenham Festival in the more than 30 years since I started attending, my belief is that the most telling has been in the state of the ground.

In 1981, 'Cheltenham ground' meant the mud and, taking its cue from the horse who won four times at the Festival, including in the Coral Golden Hurdle Final on soft or heavy going when he was 11, 12 and 13, there was also 'Willie Wumpkins weather'. On the 25 days' racing (another two were abandoned) at the meeting between 1974 and 1982, the official ground description was heavy on 12 occasions, soft (on either the hurdles or chase course) on eight, good on two and firm on three.

For some informed observers, passionate about racing at Cheltenham, the prevailing conditions threatened to demean the meeting, and tribulations, which repeatedly accompanied the build-up, became beyond a joke. My mentor Ray Gould, correspondent for the *Gloucestershire Echo* and *Sporting Chronicle*, wrote on the Saturday before the 1981 Festival: 'As jumping enthusiasts wait, with fingers crossed, this weekend to learn whether the highlight of their season will fall victim once again to the elements, many will be asking has the time not arrived for it to be allocated a new date in the calendar.'

Outlining some of the problems of the Festival in March, Ray continued, 'It is not just inconvenience and cost. There must be a danger that the sport's acknowledged championship events, decided at the Festival, will lose some of their prestige if they continue year after year as simply a test of staying power.' After another deluge, the case for moving the National Hunt meeting to Cheltenham's April fixture was taken up the following year by the *Sporting Chronicle*'s editor Tom Kelly.

Most fundamentally, when soft and heavy going are the norm it runs the risk of racing not going ahead at all. Giving a flavour of the perpetual crisis that seemed to surround prospects of Cheltenham's premier fixture being staged, in the run-up to the 1981 meeting one *Gloucestershire Echo* front-page headline read 'Choppers stand by to help save Festival'. The helicopters did not just stand by, they were deployed, hovering low over the track to try to force off standing water.

Before the 1975 Festival, Prestbury trainer Frenchie Nicholson was asked to test the turf with one of his horses to see whether the ground was fit to race on. His son Richard elaborates: 'So, being a good racing man, my father got one that liked soft ground, galloped up the course and said that it was perfectly alright.' The first day was eventually lost to waterlogged ground, however, and on the third day, immediately after the Gold Cup, the officials finally conceded defeat to the elements.

At the time of that Festival, I was nine years old, and watching on television as Ten Up ploughed his way through dire conditions to beat Soothsayer and Bula in the Gold Cup. It has been an abiding image. One of those horses who found conditions less congenial, the previous year's winner Captain Christy, was said not to have been pulled up but to have pulled himself up.

Understandably, some connections also wondered whether it was worth bothering. News reports about the Festival in those recurrent wet years were not just about whether the meeting would go ahead and who might win, they were also heavily concerned with soul-searching trainers asking themselves whether their horses should even run.

While marvelling at how slowly the leaders were going in that 1975 Gold Cup, I think I knew even then that this variation on 'survival of the fittest' – or survival of the slowest, as some would label it – was very far from being the best spectacle that steeplechasing had to offer. Indeed, it may sound like heresy, but many have believed that the King George VI Chase at Kempton got a lot closer to that. Stamina and fortitude are the core elements of jumps racing but there must also be a place for speed and flamboyance, particularly in races that seek to anoint the sport's champions.

Cheltenham in March was not witnessing something unusual, as tired and sometimes exhausted horses struggling to the finish are a common sight through the winter, but repetition of it can be wearying and disillusioning for the spectator, let alone the participants. Race distances designed to be stamina tests even on good ground on a flat track can seem like marathons when they take place on soft or heavy and those still going at Cheltenham also have to make their way up that stiff run-in.

The Festival stayed in March, but after 1982 something did change. There was a whiff of it in 1983 – the official going was good to soft on all three days. From 1984 to 1987 came the revelation, though, when the fixture was dominated by good ground. That is if the official descriptions were to be believed, and in reality there were plenty of instances, such as in 1986, when race times revealed that the ground was firmer than that.

With the further passage of time, good ground at the Festival has come to be regarded as something usual rather than an aberration. The question has shifted from whether the course drainage is adequate to whether it is too efficient. Altered conditions have called for different qualities in the horse. The finishing climb at Cheltenham remains one of the sternest challenges but the sight of participants negotiating that hill like ramblers rather than racehorses has almost disappeared. Comparing the Festival of 1981 to those in the current century, it seems that the term 'Cheltenham ground' has not just changed. It now stands for almost the complete opposite.

∼

About 35 miles south of Cheltenham, at Portbury near Bristol, Richard Holder's Racecourse Farm underwent its own transformation in the 1980s. In the 1980 edition of *Horses In Training*, a publication that lists the names of each horse in training at different stables at the start of the year, there were only two names listed under Holder's entry. He was a permit holder, training his own horses, the numbers of which swelled to three in 1981.

Born in 1932, Holder had a passion for racing, but until he was in his late 40s a serious involvement in the sport was his unreachable dream. He had four children, Louise, Paul, Katie and Mark. Perhaps having been brought up at an establishment called Racecourse Farm, adjoining Horse Race Lane, might have planted something in his imagination.

Positioned in an oval bowl set in rolling hills, with the modern-day gallops running alongside a steep, limestone outcrop, the farm was common land 500 years ago, land from which the local nobility, the Berkeley family, used periodically to clear the grazing animals in order to stage their horseracing. Holder's eldest daughter Louise Nikou describes how her own family re-established a bond between the farm and the sport: 'I think my grandfather came here in about 1911. We were tenant farmers originally. My father worked with his father on the farm and when you're just at home with your father you need some sort of get-out, so his get-out was going racing. Whenever he had a day off he went racing.'

Richard Holder rode in point-to-points as a teenager and his children are doubtful whether he ever rode a winner. More familiar was the story of how one ride ended with a blow to the head and he was unconscious for ten minutes. On returning home with heavy concussion he swore all those who knew about it to silence, in case his parents found out and forbade him from trying again.

There was usually a broodmare on the farm in those days and Holder first had a go at training horses under rules in the mid-1950s as a permit holder. On April 22, 1957, Easter Monday, his Pink Notes won the Abloom Selling Handicap Hurdle at Wincanton, but appearances in *Horses In Training* with just two horses in the 1955 and 1956 editions were his last entries in that book until 1980.

December 1977, more than 20 years after the win for Pink Notes, may have been when Holder's ambitions were reignited. Jock's Bond, whom he had in training with his friend Roddy Armytage, justified well-backed favouritism in a selling hurdle at Taunton, and the following season Holder decided to take out another permit and train the horse himself. In September 1979 Jock's Bond won a novice chase at Newton Abbot.

Holder's next winner did not come until April 1981 but it was delivered by easily the most important horse of his career. Of that 6,500 guineas purchase from the 1981 Goffs February Sales, Paul Holder recalls: 'Father had gone with some friends of his from the pub over to Ireland for the weekend and they came back with this horse.' His elder sister says: 'I can remember him coming back and telling me he'd bought a little chestnut mare. He just liked the way she walked.'

The untrumpeted winner of a bumper and maiden hurdle for Dessie Hughes, that six-year-old mare was called Mayotte. 'She was just an unassuming type,' continues Louise. 'There was nothing outstanding about her to look at but she was quite athletic in the way that she moved. From the day she got back here I don't think anybody else ever rode her. I rode her all the time and she didn't pull, she didn't bat an eyelid at anything. She was just a dream. Although she was a chestnut mare she wasn't a typical chestnut mare in any way. There was nothing bad about her. She was just a lovely, lovely mare. I never fell off her, ever. She didn't do anything wrong.'

Among the first things Mayotte did right was win five races in 1981/82, Holder's first season with the public licence he had taken out so that she could also run on the Flat. At the turn of the year that season his string was up to eight, from three one year earlier, and they ended the season with 11 wins, the other contributors being Johns Present, who won three times as a juvenile hurdler, and Jock's Bond, who won three staying chases. The first win for Jock's Bond that season was the first winner all told for the then 19-year-old amateur jockey Paul Nicholls. Representing the trainer, his daughters spent the fuel money on champagne and had to be retrieved when the horsebox ran out of petrol on the way home.

Mayotte, though, was the unquestioned star of the Portbury show, her five wins including three at Cheltenham, and although she underperformed in the Stayers' Hurdle at that season's Festival, she ended the campaign rated by Timeform just 9lb behind the Stayers' winner Crimson Embers.

Paul Holder's recollection is that the only person Mayotte let into her stable was his sister, but Louise says that this impression would not have been inspired by any temperamental issues on behalf of the mare. It was because she, Louise, allowed nobody else to go anywhere near Mayotte.

'I was very possessive,' she admits. 'One day somebody from Lambourn came to ride out and I think Dad was a bit impressed that he'd ridden out for all sorts of big trainers. Dad said, "Well, you ride Mayotte," because she was the best one we had, and I sulked for about a week afterwards because I didn't like anybody going near her. It was a Sunday morning and I can visualise it now – I was not happy, at all. Nobody rode my mare.'

On the racecourse, though, Mayotte soon became public property, belying her size and, as a liver chestnut, her sometimes unprepossessing appearance. As well as winning two further races over hurdles and five on the Flat, she was second and fourth in the next two editions of the Stayers' Hurdle, on the first occasion beaten just three-quarters of a length in a three-way battle after she had to be switched on the run-in.

'To have a top-class horse made us feel we were terribly fortunate,' says Louise. 'We weren't a racing stable in any way. We were a farm and we didn't have top-class gallops – we used our fields and banks. We were stockmen, farmers who knew about animals and knew how to look after animals. I think it made us aware that really you didn't need to have the flamboyant and extravagant surroundings to train a good horse, as long as they're being looked after and fed properly. I think Tim Forster once said you can train a good horse up a main road, and you can.'

Training on the roads around Racecourse Farm, however, would have become a hazardous business, because those roads soon seemed to be full of owners beating a track to Holder with new horses. According to *Horses In Training*, from that starting point of two inmates in 1980, the number in the yard increased in eight of the next ten years: 37 were listed in the 1984 edition, 49 in 1985, 58 in 1988 and 75 in 1990.

Louise relates, 'The landlord wasn't really liking it very much, that we were having more and more horses and less and less cows, so we were offered the chance to buy the farm and Dad bought it, relatively cheaply because we had been sitting tenants. So then we went to converting every cowshed, any nook and cranny – we had horses absolutely everywhere. At one time we had 70 horses on the books but only 60 stables, so they were farmed out. Ones that were having a rest were anywhere and everywhere, with anybody who could lend us a stable.'

Although a small beef herd and some sheep were retained, the dairy cows made way for the burgeoning training establishment, as did 40 acres of potatoes. The main potato field was turned into an all-weather gallop. Some of the land was sold to fund developments. As well as the cowsheds, the milking parlour was converted into stables. The hay barn and tool sheds were converted into stables as were a coal shed and pigsty.

Mayotte and Jock's Bond, who spent their retirements together and lived to ripe old ages, resided in that former pigsty. Of their successors as Holder representatives on the racecourse, nothing eclipsed Mayotte and most inevitably proved relatively undemonstrative flagbearers. Louise says: 'I think that with the more and more success Dad had, we had more and more horses, but they weren't necessarily any better horses. We seemed to get everybody else's castoffs. He'd worked some magic with a few of them, so therefore they thought he could work the magic with everybody's.'

In the six seasons from 1982/83 to 1987/88, the stable's jumping scores were settled at between 15 and 20 per season but Flat racing proved more than a useful sideline with totals not far behind those over jumps, and in among the castoffs Holder always seemed to come up with several much more notable runners who kept the stable in the public esteem.

Of his father as a racehorse trainer, Paul Holder says: 'He had an amazing, amazing way with animals, the old man. He had a brilliant eye as well. He had a gift and he was just one of those that probably didn't realise it. Lots of people have gifts but sometimes the gifts and the chance to use them never coincide. He was a very gifted man. He just knew instinctively when things were right and when they weren't. He knew instinctively when horses were well and when they weren't. It wasn't a Martin Pipe approach with everything scientific.'

One element of the training process to which Holder would apply himself with the relish of a Pipe or a Sir Mark Prescott was the placing of his horses. As we shall see, it would be hasty to say that the form book was Holder's greatest passion but it was certainly one of them. He was thumbing through the pages of *Raceform* many years before he became a trainer, albeit with some difficulty in keeping up payments on all of the instalments, which resulted in plenty of his editions being incomplete. According to those volumes, the jumps season tended to end in March.

Mark Holder describes how in his training days his father would sit down, most usually at the kitchen table, with the form book and *Racing Calendar*: 'His routine would be to sit down after tea at about 5.30 every evening and probably read it for two and a half hours before he went to the pub, at which point I would take it.' Mark

Holder in 2015 is a professional punter who also advises private clients.

Of how his father's 'absolute love of the form book' was translated into running plans, Mark says, 'He just wanted to be successful, so he always started running his horses in the lowest possible grade. He just wanted to win races.'

It cannot be said that in planning for future wins, Holder's intention was always to run those horses in races, or in a manner, that would always see them to best effect along the way. Mayotte was far from typical in terms of the material she provided for campaign planning, but Holder's approach to deploying the mare was not so out of the ordinary for him. 'In the early days,' says Mark, 'to keep everything going it was about punting. Mayotte was a horse that was bought really to land a gamble and who turned out to be hugely better than we anticipated.'

Having already been good enough over hurdles to contest her first Stayers', Mayotte had her attentions turned to the Flat in 1982, starting with three conditions events over 1m4f or 1m6f, at 100-1, 200-1 and 33-1, on the third occasion eliciting some strained expressions when she came from out the back under Louise Holder at Chepstow to finish third, rather closer to the winner than had been anticipated. Notwithstanding that prominent finish, Mayotte was then stepped up to 2m and won three handicaps in a row in just under four weeks.

One huge influence on Holder's ability to understand the form book and put its study to productive effect was the professional gambler Billy Baugh, whom Holder met in about 1980 at Wincanton races. Baugh is described by Paul Holder as 'an absolute genius with the form book' and he would drive down from Birmingham to go racing at the likes of Wincanton, Taunton and Newton Abbot. Then, as now, the M5 south of Bristol was no guarantee of a rapid journey, so Richard Holder used to meet Baugh at the Gordano Services and they would go racing together,

Holder using his old short cuts across the Mendip Hills. They became great friends.

~

Friends are a key part of the Richard Holder story. When attracting owners is the only way to get horses, making friends could be viewed as public relations and good business practice on a trainer's part, and that is how it turned out, but for Holder it does not seem to have been anything other than completely natural.

Chris Scott first appeared in the rapidly increasing list of Holder's patrons in *Horses In Training 1983*. Scott reflects: 'He was a tremendous guy. Richard Holder was my way into racing. I had a great relationship with him, used to travel everywhere with him and he was a great guy, a lovable character and a real genuine chap. He was always happy, always smiling.'

Paul Holder says, 'Dad had one motto when he was training horses. He said however the horse has run the owners must have a good time. So if a horse ran badly they'd still think that they'd had a really good day at the races. If the horse won, then they'd have an extra good day. They seemed to celebrate regardless.'

In the aftermath of one such winner, the trainer and owners stopped off on the way home at a large and well-appointed hotel. After a few drinks – presumably – Holder was bet that he would not ride a bicycle down the hotel staircase and into the main foyer. To someone also imbued in the thrills and spills of jump racing, it may not have seemed such a great challenge, but when Holder had negotiated the stairs and alighted in the foyer still on the bicycle he then collided full on with a suit of armour.

'They were left with the bike on the bottom, then father, and the suit of armour on the top,' summarises Paul. When asked whether it was a different experience having horses with Holder than with other trainers, Chris Scott says, 'Without any doubt.'

Socialising, whether it was in Bristol, a London club or with a suit of armour, was something at which Holder excelled, and it held all the more appeal for him if a touch of betting was thrown in for good measure. For one relatively minor example, Scott cites: 'Richard loved to spoof. Whenever he went racing, sat down for a meal, anything like that, Richard would always have to spoof. Oh yes, he was a gambler.'

'Father was an addicted gambler,' states Paul Holder, more bluntly. Of earlier days, he recalls, 'Sometimes he'd come home and mother would look out and say, "You've lost the car again." He was a card player, father. He used to say that he was an international playboy but that most of his life he'd only had the finances of a parish playboy. He maintained that at all times.'

As a young man, Richard Holder was a regular punter with friends at greyhound races, financing his share of the betting fund by taking 20 bags of potatoes from the farm and selling them in Bristol, a practice to which his father turned a blind eye. Eastville dog track, his old stomping ground, is now a branch of Ikea but I suspect that there are Bristolians who still remember Holder's gambling exploits there and elsewhere in the city. He became well known in the city's casinos and card rooms, and at one stage in the 1970s Holder had a share in a betting shop. In that period he used to milk the cows, go in to Bristol to run the betting shop and return home to milk the cows again. His more usual routine as a farmer, though, comprised farming during the day and gambling during the evening.

On Derby Day he was a regular at Epsom racecourse, borrowing a friend's licence to make a book on the Downs. He was not there to make the most of a money-making opportunity. 'Oh no, it was a big meeting, wasn't it,' says Paul. 'I think if he was Irish he would be best described as constantly seeking the craic. Father would do anything that sounded a bit different and good fun and where there was a gambling edge to it as well.'

Everything his children say about Richard Holder is suffused with deep affection but one phrase that regularly crops up in their descriptions of him is 'constantly skint'. One indicator is that at the local prep school (two fields away) the headmaster used to keep a chart, on one side of which were recorded the price of school fees and on the other what Holder could offer in return. 'Mark and I had our education paid by bartering from farm products,' says Paul. The farmer and the headmaster used to thrash out deals in which Holder would provide 'potatoes, swedes, eggs, straw for the fete, pretty well anything that he could swap that didn't involve cash.'

Mark adds, 'Dad was dreadful with money. He was awful with money, totally, totally irresponsible with it, but I think he became more responsible when he became a racehorse trainer.'

That was too late for Holder's marriage, but Paul continues, 'We, as children, had been given the choice – did we want to go and live with Mother in Bristol or did we want to stay on the farm with Father? There was no chance that any of us would go and live with Mother. Living on the farm was far more exciting. We could do whatever we wanted to. My sister tried to keep some sort of control in the family and Mark and I ran wild. Father used to come in smiling, which meant he'd probably had a half too much to drink or he'd won. About three weeks after Mother moved out, Dad said, "Is it alright if you stay up a bit later tonight? I want you to serve the drinks." I said, "What do you mean?" He said, "Well, they're coming back after the pub to play poker." That was a Monday night thing. You'd get paid for making the drinks and they'd play poker in the front room.'

Paul Holder's summary – 'It was a proper childhood.'

Splashing through the Standing Water

If you go down Horse Race Lane from Racecourse Farm and turn left, the second building you come to is the Failand Inn. Surveying the photo gallery on their website in 2013, it strikes me that the Failand Inn is populated by an awfully large number of dining tables, but it used to be more of a pub, a racing pub, and Richard Holder had his own corner there. Chris Scott relates: 'Wherever you went Richard loved port and brandy. Port and brandy with ice. He was extremely good company. He loved socialising and on a Sunday if we went down to the stables we would go back to the Failand Inn and have a few drinks and play crib.'

If Holder's social diary is beginning to sound a little crowded, the impression is not misleading. 'I don't think he spent one single night in the house, ever,' states Paul. 'That's including the day when he got thrown through the hedge at the top end of the gallop, spent the afternoon in the hospital, came back with a neck brace on and we all thought this would be the first night we could ever remember him not going to the pub. We looked at each other and thought there's no way he'll be going to the pub tonight. It was impossible. And then two of his friends came, put him in the back of a Land Rover and took him up to the Failand Inn. It was quite amazing.'

Of the same incident, Mark states: 'He was completely crocked. He couldn't get upstairs to go to the toilet but he could get to the pub. I can remember going round to a friend's house when I was about 12 and their father was sat watching television. I said, "What's your father doing in?" Because my father never ever stayed in one single night.'

'And he always got up early,' says Paul Holder of his father. 'Irritatingly, he could come in at 5 o'clock in the morning and still get up for half six.'

~

There was a lot to get up for at Racecourse Farm in the 1980s and into the 1990s. The shift from cows to horses brought useful representatives over jumps such as Sea Spice, Star Season, Western Counties and Windbound Lass, while on the Flat Hello Cuddles was second in the 1984 Stewards' Cup, Star Of A Gunner won the Lincoln in 1987 and was fourth in it in 1988, Sonilla won four races in 1989, Red Ruffian was a very speedy two-year-old in 1991 and Bertie Wooster ran well in a host of notable sprint handicaps.

Richard O'Brien, my friend and former Timeform colleague, who has made his living betting on racehorses, is one on whom the Holder yard made a big impression: 'It was the mid-1980s that I was first getting into betting seriously. I kept records and made a profit, and a big part of that was down to getting to know how a trainer campaigned his horses, and in my view at that time Richard Holder was top of the pile. He was my favourite trainer to follow, and as I scanned down the list of runners he was the first trainer I looked for.'

In 1984, Louise Holder married the jumps jockey Pat Murphy and by the end of that decade, with Murphy retired from the saddle, they were the ones who had chief responsibility for day-to-day care of the Holder horses. But her father, who remarried in 1990, was still firmly in charge of their race planning and caring for the owners.

The Cheltenham Festival figured prominently in the consciousness of everyone who worked at Racecourse Farm, as it does for anyone with an interest in jumps racing. After all, Cheltenham was just up the road, albeit with that road being the M5. But for them as a racing yard, the Festival had very few practical implications. Very, very few horses at Racecourse Farm could ever have Festival hopes entertained for them.

Much as Richard Holder relished placing his horses, trying to place horses of their calibre at the Festival would have been a fruitless exercise. Mayotte had got the stable off to a spectacular start but, after her, Holder runners there were thin on the ground and usually among the outsiders: Wonder Wood still managed fifth in the 1984 Sun Alliance Novices' Hurdle, as did The Thirsty Farmer in the 1987 National Hunt Chase and Capa in the 1987 County Hurdle. Then in 1988 the stable had its first placed horse at the meeting since Mayotte when modest Flat maiden Wahiba belied odds of 66-1 in the Triumph Hurdle and proved easily best of the 25 runners who took on the winner Kribensis, running him to three lengths.

That thrilled all connected with the horse, but the Wednesday of the 1989 Festival got underway in what may have been rather galling fashion. Sayfar's Lad won the Sun Alliance Hurdle and he was trained by Martin Pipe. But the previous season he had been at Racecourse Farm.

'He was like four pegs, he was so weak and narrow, and a bit flighty,' says Pat Murphy of Sayfar's Lad, 'but I said this horse really does need looking after and I thought he was going to be a future star. I fed him up the whole summer and he came in looking absolutely fantastic and would you believe it, we'd done the first two months of work with him when the owner took him to Pipe's.'

The owner's son had been working for Holder but moved to Martin Pipe, and so did the horse.

The following season, 1989/90, Racecourse Farm had charge of a bumper horse called Ruling. In the next two campaigns he was placed in the Champion Hurdle but his Cheltenham exploits also came for another yard. 'If ever there was a horse that was a nightmare it was him. A full horse, chronic box walker and a bit of a savage, and he wouldn't go into the stalls – that's how we ended up with him.' Murphy describes Ruling thus, but they won two out of three bumpers with him and he was an unlucky second in the other at the Aintree Grand National meeting. Exploiting a French rule which, if connections requested it, allowed a horse to enter the stalls last if it took the outside stall, Ruling was also fifth for them on his debut under Flat rules in the Group 1 Prix du Cadran.

'In September that year I was at Bath races,' relates Murphy, 'and Fulke Johnson Houghton's travelling head lad came up to me and said, "What's this Ruling like?" I said, "A nightmare. Why?" "Because I've got to pick him up tomorrow," and that was the first we heard about not having him back.'

Sayfar's Lad and Ruling were not the only Festival stars who got away. In 1997, Hanakham, winner of the Royal SunAlliance Chase and trained by Ron Hodges, was another horse who had been at Racecourse Farm the season before. On this occasion, though, the parting of the ways was a blessed relief for Murphy. Hanakham was very highly regarded but, of the owner, Murphy comments, 'I couldn't cope with him and I had to say to him, "Listen, just take yourself and your horse and go."'

What will have helped, briefly, to smooth any regret incurred at Hanakham's Sun Alliance, is that the following day Shooting Light representing Racecourse Farm was 7-1 third favourite for the Triumph. After Mayotte, Shooting Light was their only representative at the Festival to be sent off at shorter than 16-1. Under what Murphy describes as 'a diabolical ride' from Richard Dunwoody, Shooting Light finished third.

Had Racecourse Farm never sent out a winner at the Cheltenham Festival, they could certainly have reflected on their share of stories of what might have been. But that is to be hypothetical.

~

On the morning of Thursday March 16, 1989, those surveying the *Racing Post* weather forecast were assured that 'It will be bright and sunny in most areas apart from a few scattered showers. Temperatures mild.'

Splashing through the Standing Water

The Sporting Life reported that Irish hope Carvill's Hill could be pulled out of the Gold Cup because of the drying ground, and its weather news was that those in the Cheltenham region would find it 'dry with sunny spells.' Weather forecasting is one of the few professions which provides predictions held in the same low repute as those of racing tipsters.

The following day's *Racing Post* gave a drip-by-drip account of what actually transpired that Thursday morning: 'The rains came with a steady drizzle at 6.30 am. Half an hour later the downpour was incessant: there was hail by 9.30 and the first snow flurries arrived within 15 minutes.'

Richard Burridge, Desert Orchid's owner, described in *The Grey Horse* how he drove into the car park at about ten o'clock and sat in his car for ten minutes before stepping out and straight into a large puddle, a puddle that had not been there when he pulled up.

The then Cheltenham managing director Edward Gillespie admits, 'I think you could say without any doubt that had it been any day other than a Festival day, and probably any day other than the Gold Cup day, to be honest we wouldn't have raced. Because the ground was so wet. It was atrocious, atrocious weather.'

Major Philip Arkwright, the then Clerk of the Course, seems to remember the situation rather differently and has written that 'The inevitable gloom mongers were anticipating abandonment, but in fact there was never any danger to racing going ahead ... having walked the course with the senior steward of the day we were satisfied that the course was perfectly safe and that racing would go ahead as scheduled.'

Either way, the racecourse authorities were definitely in emergency mode, and before the course inspections were completed the extraordinary weather called for an innovative response. A fire appliance was on the premises – 'it was sitting there doing nothing, waiting for a fire to break out,' says Gillespie – and was moved into action, pumping water off the track. One area thus treated was the overflowing water jump, but easily the greatest point of concern was by the second-last fence and the last hurdle. Drains from a wider area were funnelling water there and the infrastructure found the task overwhelming. Station Officer Martin Burford, present with his fire crew, reported that he had been at the spot since eight o'clock and would continue until racing started.

At Racecourse Farm, the rain had also had its effect. Their gallops were flooded, for what seemed like the umpteenth time that season. Those horses due to be doing fast work had to be boxed up and taken to another training establishment at Colerne, near Bath. Two other horses were made ready to go to Cheltenham to run in the Triumph Hurdle but overall the day's work was hours behind schedule.

One knock-on effect was that only two people could be spared to go to Cheltenham – Richard Holder himself and the stable's conditional rider Nick Mann. Louise and Pat Murphy stayed behind. The trainer drove the horsebox.

The two horses in it were Ikdam and Sandhurst Park, available for the Triumph at 100-1 and 500-1 respectively with the major bookmaking firms that morning. Pat Murphy describes the shorter priced of the pair: 'Ikdam was a really good-looking bay colt. He wasn't big, he was probably 16.1, but he was all there, great shoulder on him and a powerful backend. He had the most super temperament, ideally suited for a horse to go jumping in that everything seemed to come easy to him. He never did worry about anything. If you fed him and exercised him, he was always happy.'

Louise remembers him as 'one of those gentlemen of horses, that anybody could ride. He never took off with anybody. He was just an absolute star.'

On the Flat, Ikdam had fair form. A 58,000 guineas

yearling, he carried the colours of Sheikh Hamdan Al Maktoum and was trained by Peter Walwyn, registering a very quick hat-trick in handicaps in May/June as a three-year-old, the first leg of which was over nearly 1m7f. Holder liked to have stamina in a hurdling prospect and that was not going to be a problem for Ikdam, whom he bought at the Newmarket July Sales for 31,000 guineas, the trainer having an order from a syndicate in Bristol for a dual-purpose horse, one that might end up at Cheltenham in March. A very expensive purchase by Holder's standards, Ikdam did not make his promise for a hurdling career immediately apparent, however, because in a Flat race at Doncaster that October he stumbled and unseated his rider on leaving the stalls. The owners partied in Bristol nevertheless, with Holder fielding jokes about his skills at picking out a prospective jumper.

In fact, their new purchase had taken to hurdling extremely well. 'He jumped great from day one and absolutely loved his schooling,' says Murphy. The conventional policy with recruits from the Flat is to geld them but, with Ikdam physically looking set in his frame and mentally showing all the traits of a model pupil, 'once we got him we knew very, very quickly that there was no need to geld this horse.'

For further encouragement, on paper at least, his dam was a half-sister to the high-class hurdler Gay George. On his hurdling debut at Newbury in October he started second favourite but that and his next two starts went by without success (on the third occasion he was brought down). For the fourth, Ikdam was sent to Uttoxeter in December and won by eight lengths. That race was over 2m4f, as opposed to the usual 2m in juvenile races, and on testing ground. Holder reported afterwards that 'He is a possible Triumph horse. I was worried about the heavy ground but he definitely does not want it firm.'

In four starts between Uttoxeter and the Festival, Ikdam was campaigned like a good horse but did not show he was one. The three main shareholders in him were Roland Tanner, Ron Craig and John White, under the name LBI Law (873) Ltd, who displayed their connections with and allegiance to Bristol Rovers by choosing their colours of royal blue and white quarters. Chris Scott was one of those who held smaller shares.

Holder liked a wager, the owners liked a wager, but it was hard to believe with any conviction that Ikdam in the Triumph Hurdle was a promising betting medium. Twelve days before the Triumph, Scott travelled to Haydock where Ikdam was contesting the Victor Ludorum Hurdle and was told that his horse was 100-1 for Cheltenham. On phoning William Hill himself, he was told that the price was 66-1. Scott put down the phone, and when Ikdam finished only fourth at Haydock felt extremely glad he had not taken either price.

Ikdam's prospects in the Triumph, however, were still the subject of lingering hope for those at Racecourse Farm. The possibility, however slim, of heavy ground had been one source of sustenance, although it had also been heavy at Haydock. Cheltenham's much stiffer track would definitely play more to Ikdam's strength in stamina. If it was good ground, then a strong pace would be virtually guaranteed and that would also offer Ikdam some assistance.

Of Ikdam's build-up to Cheltenham, Pat Murphy observes: 'These races, they'd all turn out a little bit tactical. The pace mightn't be that strong, you'd get done for a bit of toe at the crucial point, but the one thing he was always doing was finishing off his races. He was always doing his best work at the end.'

Mark Holder remembers that in the week before the Festival, with the rain staying away, 'One of the owners rang up my father and said, "Richard, Ikdam is 100-1 for next week. Do you want a bet?" I think my father had £50 each-way and it was more to appease the owner.'

At the end of that week, Ikdam was taken to Newbury racecourse for his last piece of serious work before the

338

big race. He impressed, with Pat Murphy riding him and Nigel Coleman on the previous year's Triumph runner-up Wahiba. After which, Murphy relates, 'We were at a sporting club dinner on the Monday night and some of the owners were there plus one person who'd had the option to be in the syndicate but chose not to be. I was telling everybody how much of a big chance I thought the horse had in the Triumph Hurdle, to which he thought that I was absolutely daft, so I asked him to put his money where his mouth was and he offered me 100-1.' Murphy had a tenner on with him and would also back Ikdam with a bookmaker.

In Cheltenham week, the Murphys had two friends over from Ireland to stay with them. Pat advised them strongly to back Ikdam each-way and they too thought of sending for the men in white coats. Unswayed by Murphy's counsel, they set off for the races that Thursday with their bet of the week running in the Triumph alright, but it went by the name of Highland Bud.

One person who was not at the yard that morning was stable jockey Nigel Coleman, who would be riding Ikdam. Having been with David Nicholson, Coleman had joined the Holder stable as a conditional jockey in the 1983/84 season. For several years he lived at the yard with the Holders. He was very much involved with the yard day to day, but that morning he was in Torquay, having stayed at his parents' house the night before, and when he was ready to leave for Cheltenham his car would not start. Forced to switch vehicles and borrow his parents' much less powerful conveyance, Coleman's first race of the day was to get to Cheltenham in time and he was not at all confident that their old Rover would be up to it.

Much further up the M5, on Racecourse Farm the rising hopes for Ikdam were that as much rain as possible would fall without the meeting being called off. 'Cheltenham was flooded,' says Murphy, 'but I personally was quite happy in the knowledge that Desert Orchid was running in the Gold

339

At The Festival

Cup so that Cheltenham were going to move heaven and earth to get the race meeting on.'

Cheltenham may not have moved heaven and earth but they did move one hell of a lot of water, and racing was given the go-ahead. Sitting in the racecourse restaurant, Chris Scott recanted his post-Haydock opinion of Ikdam and decided to back him. He went down to the bookmakers and placed £100 each-way at 100-1. On returning to the restaurant, that bet became somewhat diluted.

Scott recalls: 'My pal John White said, "I'll have a tenner of that – no I'll have £20 each-way." So I gave him £20 each-way. My other pal Pat Murphy [not the assistant trainer] had paid for supper the night before and it was my turn to pay, so he said, "Scotty, you owe me 30 quid from supper last night, the Chinese, so I'll have 30 quid."'

I do not know whether Richard Holder backed Ikdam again, but his later comments suggested that, peering through the windscreen wipers as he drove his horsebox up the M5, his spirits were rising. As Pat Murphy relates, 'The one thing Richard and the yard had was massive confidence in the horse running his race, that whatever happens he was going to be going forwards at the finish and that he was not going there as a no-hoper. We were pretty confident that he was the right sort of horse that would give his owners a big thrill and probably finish in the first half dozen.'

~

1989 TRIUMPH HURDLE

Arriving at Prestbury Park with my friend Pete Holdaway, we were descending a flight of stairs to the racecourse entrance when we were stopped in our tracks by a crusty old racegoer making his way in the other direction. 'Hello there! Which one are you riding today?' he demanded of

340

Peter, who, to the best of my knowledge, had never sat on a horse in his life. On being told that Pete would not be riding that day, the racegoer's reaction was shock, dismay. 'What?! Three and a quarter miles, 20 fences, amateur riders – the race is made for you!' Informed that Pete had retired from the saddle, the bewildered racegoer shuffled off, shaking his head.

One race before the Foxhunter, the contest to which this gentleman was presumably alluding, problems of identification and suitability for the challenge would both also play a big part in the Triumph. Twenty-seven of the 30 declared runners stood their ground, or were in danger of sinking into it, and this was a strong field. To illustrate the point, it is worth mentioning what some of them would go on to achieve.

The 1988 Cesarewitch winner on the Flat, Nomadic Way, was second in the next two Champion Hurdles and won the Stayers' in 1992; Highland Bud was sold in the summer to race in the United States and won the Breeders' Cup Chase that October, the first of his two wins in that race; he was second in another; Royal Derbi won the big juvenile hurdle at Punchestown in April and went on to contest three Champion Hurdles, finishing runner-up in it in 1992; Vayrua won the big juvenile hurdle at Aintree three weeks after the Triumph; Kiichi was second in the 1990 Arkle and won the Galway Plate; Moody Man was the 1990 County Hurdle winner; Wonder Man won a stack of races, was second in an Arkle and fourth in a Champion Chase; Martin Pipe had multiple winners Enemy Action and Liadett among the first six in the Triumph betting, and a third string in Voyage Sans Retour, who took fifth in the 1991 Champion.

Racegoers at Cheltenham, who must have been either soaked or sheltering from the elements, could not have been unaware that there had been a major change in conditions. There were also, therefore, changes in the Triumph betting.

Morning favourite Highland Bud doubled in price; Enemy Action and Nomadic Way were backed into co-favouritism; but there was no surge of interest for Ikdam. In the morning he had been as short as 40-1 (with Coral) and as long as 100-1 (with William Hill) and he settled at a starting price of 66-1. On the Tote screens, Ikdam's odds were a great deal longer than that and his returned price with them was 143.7-1. Pete Holdaway and I decided to have a small bet on him each-way.

Paul Holder was at the course in a professional capacity, working with some Bristol bookmakers in the Silver Ring, in the centre of the track. Did he take particular care not to lay Ikdam? 'It was not a dilemma in any shape or form,' he confesses. 'There wasn't a penny for him.'

Crucially, though, Ikdam's rider believed that they could be competitive and he managed to arrive at the racecourse in time. 'Nigel was a fantastic hurdles jockey,' says Pat Murphy. 'He had great determination, he loved the horse and he had the confidence that the horse would run a big race, and that was important. Nigel's instructions were pretty simple – to travel as well as you can, to try and keep the horse within his comfort zone, but obviously if you were on the bridle, they are going too slow, simple as, so then you are going to have to be very much more prominent.'

The stable's long-term projections for what might swing a Triumph in Ikdam's favour were either heavy going or a strong pace. In the event they had both. Royal Derbi and Hywel Davies set off at a dash, closely attended by plenty of others. There was no question of Ikdam racing either prominently or on the bridle. Approaching the second flight, for about eight strides the runners were running through water, not just mud, and completing the turn away from the stands into the back straight, four of them were already threatening to tail off, including the Racecourse Farm representative Sandhurst Park who was, eventually, the last of 24 to finish. Ikdam, having started off in the middle of the field, now had eight horses behind him and that was almost the last that was seen of him.

On a very murky day, with a mass of runners and mud beginning to turn some of the colours an entirely different hue, it was hard to work out exactly who was who and what was happening, except that Royal Derbi continued to lead. Nomadic Way, Urizen, Take Issue, Wagon Load, Wonder Man, Chief Mole, Enemy Action, Liadett, Don Valentino – nearly all of the market principals, and more, seemed to figure at one point or another just behind the leader. Highland Bud started to get a lot closer after the third last.

Turning downhill, the field was far more strung out and Take Issue was trying to match strides with Royal Derbi, two lengths ahead of Don Valentino and Wonder Man, who were two lengths ahead of Highland Bud. The first eight had a gap on the rest. After two out, Take Issue could harry Royal Derbi no longer and was replaced by Don Valentino.

Two dozen strides before the last hurdle, the leaders were splashing their way onwards again and before jumping it the front two had a four-length lead over easily their nearest pursuer, who was Highland Bud. Royal Derbi began drifting to his left and, just as he was getting upsides, Don Valentino started to drift left as well, then to his right. They were buckling. Highland Bud was getting a lot closer and then, suddenly alongside him on the stands rails, there was Ikdam.

Standing close to the rails about 50 yards uphill from the final hurdle, I saw the leaders stagger past towards the far side and, as another set of colours I had lost sight of for the last half mile flashed by much closer to me, there was a very loud moment of recognition.

Paul Holder was watching from the inside of the course: 'I was in the bookmakers' stand, so I was probably three big stools up, way above the crowd. I clicked about 300 yards out and couldn't stop cheering.'

Chris Scott spotted Ikdam for the first time about 100 yards from the post. 'He came up the rail,' the owner recalls excitedly, 'I shall never forget it, and we almost jumped over the bloody stands.' His Chinese meal the night before was about to cost him £3,750.

Racecourse Farm, where the Murphys and a group of their staff were gathered to watch the race in Holder's kitchen, erupted. On the BBC television coverage, in a race lasting 4 minutes, 18.8 seconds, commentator Peter O'Sullevan made his first mention of Ikdam six and a half seconds before he passed the post. It gave an accurate picture of what had happened.

Highland Bud did indeed pass Royal Derbi, then Don Valentino, just, but Ikdam was finishing much more strongly and won by one and a half lengths. The Murphys' two houseguests began thumbing through their racecards to check the colours and see who had beaten their bet of the week. They had, however, taken the small precaution of having £2 each-way on the winner. The doubting Thomas who laid the Ikdam bet to Pat Murphy at the sporting dinner had also decided it might be prudent to have something on himself.

With the benefit of the race video and a lot more composure, Ikdam's path to Triumph victory can be traced more accurately, although this race still gets my heartbeat racing. After the turn away from the stands and for most of what followed, while not under heavy pressure, Ikdam gave a strong impression that he was going as fast as he could. Between the fourth and fifth flights, he started to pass horses and although he took the next, the third last, stickily he moved into tenth. Turning downhill he was passed by Kiichi and they were still disputing tenth place at the second last, but Ikdam responded to two smacks with the whip soon afterwards and, jumping the last, had moved into fourth, albeit with seven lengths still to find.

When their first Festival winner was past the post, Paul Holder abandoned his pitch and his bookmaking colleagues in the Silver Ring by scaling a set of gates – 'the sort of gates you would imagine on a scrap yard or a car compound' – and found himself in the crowd of horses pulling up, before then managing to get to the winner's enclosure to see Ikdam and his father coming in.

Mark Holder was also in the winner's enclosure and he records: 'My father wasn't the sort of person who was going to take his trilby off and wave it to the crowd, that just wasn't him, he was very reserved, but he was shaking. He was shocked, in absolute shock.'

Pat Murphy describes the immediate aftermath back at Portbury: 'There was the initial cheering and shouting, we were absolutely raising the roof, and then when he'd gone past the line it was almost silence. There was almost a moment of shock. You just had to check that that actually did happen, didn't it?' Even at that stage we still had horses to ride out but it wouldn't have mattered what it was doing out of the sky, it really wouldn't have mattered.'

For the gathering at Racecourse Farm, there was only one metaphorical cloud on the horizon – Richard Holder still had to drive the horsebox back to Portbury and moderating celebrations at the racecourse may not have been his first instinct. That and the drive were both safely negotiated, however, before the trainer returned home and celebrated quietly with just his close family. Actually no, he didn't. He went to the Failand Inn and 'that was one hell of a night in there,' says Mark Holder. 'It was a long and boozy night.'

~

'The horse himself didn't give a damn, did he?' says Pat Murphy. 'He just came home that night, he ate up, he didn't know what all the fuss was about.' The following season Ikdam won twice. The Stayers' Hurdle rather than the Champion was always going to be his main aim and he put up a performance of Mayotte-like proportions when running on from well off the pace to take fourth at 33-1 under Nick Mann, beaten two and three-quarter lengths.

By that stage, though, Ikdam had a physical problem which brought his racing career to an end that December. He had quarter cracks – where 'the outside quarter of the hoof used to crack away down from the coronet band,' says Murphy – which the stable and the farrier had managed in his first season hurdling but became increasingly difficult in his second.

'Nowadays it's quite simple,' comments Murphy. 'They have made a thing which you can basically glue on to the hoof which helps it and protects it. Back then we didn't have that privilege. He was really becoming lame every day. He'd still come out bucking and kicking even though he was lame, but we just couldn't keep going with him.' As an entire horse, Ikdam was retired to stud duties but he did not make much impact, the best of his runners being the useful chaser Odagh Odyssey.

Two days after Ikdam's Triumph, Mark Holder was with his father. 'I'll never forget this,' confides Mark. 'On the Saturday morning he was opening up the *Racing Post*, he looked in the back and he said, "We're up to 20th in the trainers list."' The next three jumps seasons yielded the most winners (33, 29 and 31) Holder ever had as a trainer before the career he loved was cut short. He fell critically ill in 1992 with hydrocephalus (water on the brain) and the training licence at Racecourse Farm had to be transferred to son-in-law Pat Murphy. Richard Holder died in March 1994, aged 61.

For Murphy, Tomahawk in the Lanzarote Hurdle at Kempton was among his first winners but the importance of Holder's personal contacts revealed itself starkly as the number of horses in the yard shrunk severely. So many of the owners had been Holder's good friends and that is why they had horses in training with him. Two of them, Jim Neville and Malcolm Saunders, went on to take out training licences themselves.

The best horse at Portbury under Murphy's name was Shooting Light, who showed high-class form as a hurdler over several seasons for the yard. Supreme Glory took most of his steps towards his 2001 Welsh National win from Portbury but by the time of that success Murphy was training elsewhere. There has not been a runner sent out from Racecourse Farm since early 2001, following the death of Pat and Louise Murphy's 14-year-old daughter Melissa, knocked down by a car, and the breakdown of their marriage.

When Richard Holder fell ill in 1992, Nigel Coleman had already had his career, and a great deal more, taken away from him after a fall on the home turn at Worcester that April. With lacerations to the face and neck, the injuries he sustained were not thought to be serious by the hospital but the day after being released with stitches and paracetamol, he suffered a massive stroke from which he still carries profound disabilities. In the course of 12 seasons, he rode 114 winners.

~

Writing after the 2015 meeting, in the 85 Festival days since Ikdam's Triumph, heavy ground has been mentioned only once in the description of the official going. That was in 2007 when the cross-country course was soft, heavy in places. Apparently there would have been heavy ground had the 2001 Festival ever started but that was the year it was abandoned because of foot-and-mouth disease.

On the racecourse proper, it was described as soft for all three days in 1995; it was next soft for three races in 2007 and two in 2010; in 2013 it was soft on the Tuesday and for five races on the Friday, and in 2015 it was soft on the Friday. Ikdam would not have won the Triumph on soft.

One sure indication of just how testing the ground was when he set out in 1989 is the winning time of 4 minutes 18.8 seconds, comfortably the slowest for the race since 1982, the years of the old 'Cheltenham ground' and the slightly earlier renewals when the Triumph was nearly one furlong further. In the ten renewals from 2006 to 2015, the winning time was under four minutes on four occasions.

Contrary to popular belief, not all of Cheltenham Racecourse has had drainage installed. The major sections without it are the chute that contains the first three fences of the 2m4f and 2m5f courses and all points further away from the grandstand, apart from one area on the New Course on the bend between the fifth-last and sixth-last fences. Most of the downhill section on the New Course is drained, as is about a quarter of the downhill run on the Old Course.

I have a copy of the drainage map and the rest of it resembles an elaborate new tartan, a crazy kilt, but Simon Claisse, the Clerk of the Course, also stresses that 'management practices of the soil profile have changed – in terms of aeration and slitting, to try and maintain a profile through which water can travel to get to the drains. We do things differently. We've got different equipment.'

Arguably the most different thing about Cheltenham in March is the weather. With the benefit of a long-term view, it can be seen that the years 1975 to 1982 simply contained many in which rainfall in the region greatly exceeded the long-term average. In March 1981, for instance, the vast majority of England and Wales experienced more than 200 per cent of average rainfall.

It was so relentlessly wet in those days, it seemed as if it would always be that way. Consulting Met Office maps for UK rainfall every March compared to the area's

1961–1990 average, however, it appears that rainfall in the Cheltenham area has been clearly above that average only twice from 1990 onwards, whereas it has been clearly below it on 11 occasions.

Of most recent Festivals, Simon Claisse reported in late 2013 that: 'The watercourses have been low, the drains haven't been running and we've been watering in preparation for the Festival from up to three or four weeks out, just to prevent the ground going good to firm.' Water does not have to be pumped off the course these days, it has to be pumped on to it.

The odds of Ikdam alighting on a day at the Festival when the ground was heavy were long indeed, and when I think of a Festival race the result of which was directly attributable to the state of the ground, his Triumph Hurdle is the one I come up with first.

Reflecting on that race, Paul Holder says: 'Those were days when anything seemed possible. Father had had a small milking herd and a few sheep. He was constantly skint. And then there was this madness of the next ten years where anything seemed possible at any time.'

For those who lived and worked at Racecourse Farm, Ikdam's win was the highpoint of their racing careers. Compared to what followed for them, victory in a horserace is insignificant, but it meant a great deal at the time. It still counts for something now.

CHAPTER TEN

1989 TOTE CHELTENHAM GOLD CUP

Three Horses Striving to become Festival Greats

SUPERSTITIOUS CULTURES AND individuals have long believed that the sudden onset of extreme weather can be a sign or portent. Portentous of something more than that they are about to get wet. Thunder and lightning are probably the forms most often taken as compelling signals, and an intimation along those lines did pass through my mind while I waited in the grandstand at Newmarket in May 1993 as a mighty thunderclap reverberated around the heath just before the start of the 2,000 Guineas. The wonder-inducing event that followed was called Zafonic. It seemed as if winning a Classic could never have been easier.

At Cheltenham in the final minutes before the Champion Hurdle and Gold Cup, the feeling that something momentous is about to take place is an ever-present whatever the meteorological conditions. In anticipating these big races, the experience moves from the analytical to the emotional and the physical. The runners are paraded before the grandstand, canter to the start and, like the jockey with his toes in the stirrup irons, the world seems in abeyance. With jump racing, alongside the excitement and tension, there is also anxiety.

~

On Gold Cup day in 1989 the anticipation of what was about to unfold was heightened dramatically by the elements. As described in the preceding chapter, their sizeable contribution – to summarise, the weather was atrocious – was to turn the going heavy, very nearly unraceable. In the Gold Cup, with such conditions, but also with the cast assembled, there was an inescapable feeling that something remarkable was indeed about to happen. It could not be otherwise.

Top of the bill, without question, was Desert Orchid, the showman extraordinaire of my lifetime in jumps racing. Properly instituted perhaps on Boxing Day 1986, by March 1989 the cult of Desert Orchid had an awful lot of followers. 'If I was another trainer I'd have been fed up of hearing about him,' states Desert Orchid's trainer David Elsworth, but the racing public it seemed could not get enough. Despite snow, sleet and rain, the official attendance at Cheltenham was a then-record 51,549.

That season Desert Orchid had been unstoppable in all five races before the Festival. Usually uncatchable, in that sequence he was caught but still could not be beaten. Among those triumphs was the Gainsborough Chase in February and when Desert Orchid won there were scenes of some of the most spirited public support during and after a race that I had ever witnessed – and that was despite the fact that the Gainsborough was at Sandown and the racegoers who became so animated around me were watching it on television at Wetherby.

Dessie – everyone else seemed to call him that – was already among the greats of our sport. However, in the

1989 Gold Cup field I firmly believed that there were two other horses who possessed greatness in them. Aged nine and seven, whereas Desert Orchid was a ten-year-old, Ten Plus and Carvill's Hill were cases of promise that had yet to reach full fruition, but that promise was of the variety that could not be missed. Seeing these two walk around the parade ring that day at Cheltenham, although the cheers were all for Desert Orchid, there was no great leap of faith required to believe that they too could be Gold Cup winners.

From school I hazily remember a maths lesson in which we were told about the 'golden ratio' and the 'golden rectangle'. Those phenomena had their basis in mathematics but when expressed in architecture the results were also apparently the most pleasing to the human eye. They were employed in the construction of the Parthenon. With a mix of functional requirement and aesthetic appeal, both making themselves apparent from the experience of years watching thousands of individuals, it is hard to pin down exactly what makes the golden ratio in the architecture of a racehorse, but Ten Plus was my idea of the perfect-looking steeplechaser.

I still have a picture in my mind's eye of him about to be mounted in the parade ring at Newbury, almost certainly before the Mandarin Chase on the final day of 1988, when he was standing side-on to me, his neck arched and head bowed towards the ground, with his front feet pawing the turf ready for action. I have been a devotee of paddock watching, but in the preliminaries to a jumps race I do not know that I have ever seen anything more inspiring, or more suggestive of latent energy, than Ten Plus that afternoon.

'He was a fantastic specimen of a horse,' recalls Kevin Mooney, who rode him in every one of his races in Britain. 'He never was filling that frame when we first got him, but then he started to fill his frame and he was wonderful, a very good-looking horse. He stood over a lot of ground and was a very imposing horse, a good walker; he had everything.'

Expressing it even more strongly, Mark Bradstock, former assistant to his trainer Fulke Walwyn and the trainer himself of the 2015 Gold Cup winner Coneygree, says that Ten Plus 'was the most staggeringly beautiful individual you have ever seen in your life. His head, his physique, you name it. He was beautifully looked after by Peter Payne.

'He was just an exceptional individual. You could go into his stable and he just shone. His head was amazing, he was a fabulous colour. He was just everything you could possibly imagine wanting as a racehorse. He epitomised it. And he just had presence, didn't he?'

Payne had been on Walwyn's staff for more than 30 years and looked after Ten Plus from the day he drove him back from the Doncaster Sales in May 1984. 'The first time I saw him I thought he looked very much like Arkle,' Payne recollects, and the Walwyn team remembered Arkle all too well, having been stunned by him in the 1964 Gold Cup when he beat their stable star Mill House.

The big hope of Ireland in the 1989 Gold Cup came from the same yard as Arkle, from Greenogue, County Dublin, where Tom Dreaper had trained not only Arkle to three Gold Cup wins but also Fort Leney to another. Because of Dreaper's ill health, his son Jim took over in 1972 at the age of 20. Carvill's Hill was in a different mould from Ten Plus but also a striking individual in all that he did. Jim Dreaper describes his charge as 'a big, rangy horse. He was 16.3, bay. I think he'd be what they would now describe as an old-fashioned chaser. He was the type of horse who, if he was no good, people would say he's an ugly brute.' But from his first race, there had never been a time when Irish racegoers could think that Carvill's Hill was anything but very good indeed. Timeform would later observe that Carvill's Hill was 'in appearance very much most people's idea of the top-class, weight-carrying chaser.' On Gold Cup day, he stalked the parade ring with a heavyweight presence.

~

Divorcing the individual from the name is not always easy when taking in a horse's physical appearance but, in the midst of all the applause every time he walked around the paddock, Timeform certainly stuck resolutely to their objective approach when assessing Desert Orchid in ante-post betting, still describing him as 'the sturdy, useful-looking Desert Orchid' in their *Chasers & Hurdlers 1988/89*, useful-looking being the understatement of all time had it been applied – which, of course, it was not – to the sight of him actually racing.

Desert Orchid was the supreme athlete and anxious to show it. He would often sweat up before his races, as he did on Gold Cup day in 1989, but all of the evidence in its wake was that this was a sign of his relish at the impending action, not of any nervousness about it.

He would float over the ground in his faster paces and, having gone into training in November 1982 as a three-year-old, it was not long before Desert Orchid's faster paces proved somewhat faster than his trainer intended. At the end of a small canter – with a small stone wall in close proximity – his rider could not stop him. 'He was only green. He was very willing,' says Elsworth. 'He was doing his apprenticeship. We were feeding him a bit more. He was this big, leggy, backward, green horse who'd never been cantered probably before he got to us. On a daily basis he was improving and getting stronger.

'His schooling was in the same attitude – he wanted to do too much, he was always very willing. You just showed him the hurdles, and he'd jump them like a gazelle. He had confidence and he never hesitated.'

Had Desert Orchid opted to take on that stone wall, it would surely not have caused him any problems. In his first race at Kempton on January 21, 1983, however, there was one obstacle, the final one, which the promising newcomer did not negotiate safely. Tiring out of contention, he still attacked the hurdle and the result was a somersaulting fall. It was only after ten minutes had passed that Desert Orchid was able to get to his feet.

'I thought that will frighten him and steady him down a bit,' says his trainer, 'but the next time he schooled he was just the same – he didn't compromise.' That discretion might on occasions be the better part of valour was probably the last lesson Desert Orchid took on board, and even then it was never completely. In almost every race there came a point at which those watching his jumping could have asked themselves, 'Was that possible?' and, as the sport's attachment to him grew ever more devoted, 'Could it possibly be safe?' Just as Desert Orchid committed himself in every race, so watching him was no shallow commitment from his supporters.

In that first season, comprising four races and no wins, he was basically a tearaway. Elsworth's old friend Rodney Boult then joined the team and was soon asked to have a go on the then steel-coloured grey. On being informed that he had proved a bit too much for his initial riders, Boult's reaction apparently was 'I'm not bloody surprised – he tanks on.'

The work required to settle Desert Orchid was the work of years, and Elsworth states: 'Rodney, who rode him practically all the time, would have been more instrumental in making the horse what he was than anybody else. Rodney had a rapport with him and he had wonderful hands. He kept the lid on him.'

Reflecting on their grounding in the sport, Elsworth says, 'We were kids together and riding was like a competition – we always wanted to outride each other. If he could settle one I'd try and settle one. Horses bounce off the people, they're like dogs, and if you can have a rapport with a horse, and some people do, it's no coincidence that some people in racing yards seem to look after all the good horses.'

Born in December 1939 in Salisbury, there is nothing in Elsworth's background to say that he would become a racehorse trainer, or that he could have any career in racing, but it turned out that working with horses, and understanding them, was in his nature. A proud Wiltshire man, most of his training career in jumps racing was spent just over the county boundary. Sir Gordon Richards and Bill Marshall had overseen their strings at Whitsbury in Hampshire, but in truth the most illustrious pages of its history were now being written by the man who used to walk across the gallops there as a child while being taken to the pub by his grandfather.

Returning to Whitsbury as a racehorse trainer had not been easy, if only because becoming a trainer had not been easy. As a jumps jockey, there were two years between his first and second winners, and that stage of his career never threatened to set the racing world alight. One summer, when his trade as a jockey slackened and his income needed supplementing, Elsworth had the opportunity to survey the most famous landmark in Wiltshire history close up:

'They had only one applicant so I said I'd do it every night – every night for about six weeks I was night watchman at Stonehenge.'

Having attended parties at the summer solstice in his youth – 'you'd all be sitting there waiting for the sun to come up to throw the Heel Stone on the altar; it never happened' – he was already familiar with the prehistoric monument and in his new job he was now able to lap up the atmosphere there on his own. Or almost on his own:

'I enjoyed it. I used to be up there in solitude. I was doing haymaking during the day – I was earning more than I was in racing – and obviously I fell asleep. To be at Stonehenge in the summer months with the moon shining, it was quite eerie, you know, and one night I wake up and I hear music. I go over towards the music, I can see this dim light in the middle of the stones and there was this American fella, one of these old hillbillies, and he was there singing to the moon with his girlfriend, sat on the ground with their legs crossed. I said, "Do you know you're not supposed to be in here?" and they said, "Well, there's no one around boss." They had a bottle of wine, which made things easier. I told them all about Stonehenge and drank some of their wine, so some night watchman I was.'

His employers were so impressed with his work that they considered him a strong candidate for a new role, that of keeping the toilets clean. But that particular job offer was a good deal less well received and failed to seduce Elsworth away from his career plans in racing. He was a better racehorse trainer than a night watchman, which rapidly became apparent when he supervised the horses officially trained by Colonel Ricky Vallance in the early seventies, including the Mackeson and Hennessy Gold Cup winner Red Candle. When a fully fledged training career was denied him in the aftermath of Vallance being warned off in 1974, Elsworth's most publicised work was as a market trader selling cloth, but in 1978 the Jockey Club granted him a training licence and his impact was almost instantaneous.

After a first jumps winner in March 1979, his debut victory at the Festival was less than a year later. In between those jumps successes he had ten winners on the Flat and the most illustrious dual Flat and jumps training career of our time was underway. Heighlin at 40-1 in 1980 helped to give the Triumph Hurdle a major reputation for fluke results, as did Baron Blakeney at 66-1 a year later, but these start to look rather less serendipitous when you spot that those winners were the first at the Festival for David Elsworth and Martin Pipe, respectively.

Heighlin was the first of the many famous names to win top races for Elsworth, and Desert Orchid would become the most famous. There was a powerful clue in Desert Orchid's second season hurdling. It commenced with him still a novice and ended with six wins from eight races; and although he met with a heavy defeat on his final start, that was in the Champion Hurdle for which he was sent off second favourite. He ended the campaign as that season's highest rated novice hurdler with Timeform. The winning favourite that day at Cheltenham in 1984 was Dawn Run and it turned out to be the only occasion when those near-contemporaries matched strides up front. In the light of subsequent events, had the same happened over fences it would have been the ticket of the century.

To become a Gold Cup contender, every horse must go through phases of development and Desert Orchid reinvented himself as radically as any, sweeping aside a series of preconceptions that, if true, would have ruled him out of serious Gold Cup contention. He was such a striking individual that those preconceptions soon became equally decided. To break them, most of all he had to become more than a headstrong front-runner but for most of his first four campaigns, the norm was for him to blast off in front. While his jumping may have looked largely in the groove, in other respects it often seemed as if he was verging on out of control.

In the face of that, even in Desert Orchid's hurdling days, Elsworth had stated in a Timeform interview that he had 'always regarded him as a potential chaser; a three-mile chaser at that' but to most eyes there was still very little in Desert Orchid's way of going about things that suggested he had a chance of seeing out three miles, let alone the Gold Cup distance of three and a quarter. However, twice in his first season chasing he moved closer to that objective by showing he stayed two and a half.

Three Horses

At the 1986 Festival, at which Dawn Run joined the immortals, Desert Orchid took another step towards his own Gold Cup challenge but it may have been indiscernible to most observers. It came as no surprise that season that he could jump a fence with alacrity, but also for the first time at that Festival he showed when third in the Arkle that he could run creditably at Cheltenham. More than that, at the sixth attempt, it was his first performance of any consequence when racing left-handed.

Chasers & Hurdlers summed him up in that campaign as 'In his first season over fences Desert Orchid the chaser proved very similar to Desert Orchid the hurdler: a bold-jumping front runner inclined to make the odd costly mistake, one of the best of his generation though clearly not the best.'

~

Twenty-four hours after that 1986 Arkle, the Festival saw a horse whose future suitability for the Gold Cup distance looked a cast-iron certainty. Following one third place in a bumper at Down Royal for David MacNeilly, Ten Plus had been bought for 25,000 guineas at auction in May 1984, a not inconsiderable sum at the time, particularly when considering the buyer was told that Ten Plus had been detected with a heart murmur. Fulke Walwyn would later say that he was bought to win the Gold Cup. He was not alone in that but in this case it was not long before those at Saxon House Stables began to believe that that goal would, in time, prove entirely realistic.

Like Desert Orchid, Ten Plus did not win in his first season over hurdles but he had only three runs in that 1984/85 campaign and the third of those was the Sun Alliance at the Festival in which he made substantial late gains to finish sixth. He had shown plenty of ability at home from the word go and, as Kevin Mooney states, 'they were asking big questions of him'.

Of Ten Plus's response, Mooney says: 'He was a very forward-going horse, always loved to be out – he loved doing his work. And you could spot him a mile away. He always did the best he could.'

In 1985/86, while Desert Orchid was novice chasing, Ten Plus was still novice hurdling and when those big questions were asked of him once again, this time his answer was hugely in the affirmative. Unlike Desert Orchid, he was not the highest rated novice in his season but he could not have done much more to affirm his class in four starts than to win them all. His smallest winning margin was ten lengths, and the largest verdict was reserved for seemingly his stiffest task, against 27 opponents at Cheltenham in that 1986 Sun Alliance which he won by 15 lengths, an astronomical margin for a novice hurdle at the Festival.

Three out there were only two runners left anywhere near Ten Plus and they too had disappeared by the time he turned for home. He spoiled the photographs at the final flight but immediately resumed his relentless gallop. If ever a horse could stamp himself a Gold Cup prospect while competing in just a novice hurdle, this was it.

'A lot of people probably thought down the back I was doing a little bit too much on him,' comments Mooney, 'but it was only to keep him in the rhythm, to keep him jumping. If he could see one in his stride he would cover the length of this room.' We were not speaking on the front porch.

On the other hand, the jockey elaborates, 'If you were trying to ride a race on him he could never shorten his stride or anything. He was clumsy but it was just because he was being asked big questions.'

~

In May 1986, two months after Ten Plus had won at the Festival and Desert Orchid had come third, the four-year-old Carvill's Hill lined up for his first race of any description, a Leopardstown bumper. He came second of 22, the significance lying not just in the finishing position, but also that he was there in the first place. Outlining part of the owner's decision to send the horse to him at Greenogue, Jim Dreaper says: 'Especially with a big horse, he just liked someone who would let the horse decide when he was ready to run, rather than make a day for him.'

The Dreaper string would start off with slow, distance work on the bit and even then Carvill's Hill must have made quite an impression because one of his most striking features was his stride. 'I don't think that fills them full of joy,' observes Dreaper, when discussing what effect the sight of a long-striding young horse can have on his Flat-based training colleagues, because such horses are generally not associated with an ability to quicken. But Dreaper was a trainer of steeplechasers, and it was not long before Carvill's Hill indicated that he had not just a phenomenal stride but also an engine to go with it. Dreaper describes what transpired:

'It was in a stubble field and there might be six to eight horses going round in the mud, perhaps October time, and this was when Carvill's Hill was only a three-year-old. They'd all be told we're going to go a couple of rounds here, and the rule, as it still is with ours if they're doing long work, was as soon as they're tired stop, pull up, fine, and hope for better next day. We had some reasonable horses but after a week or two this fellow was still there – when the lads in front would pull up on the so-called fit horses, the better horses who were expected to be in front, he'd nearly always pull up beside them. He would have been big, fat and green, but he was able to do it naturally and that would have been in heavy ground.'

Summarising what Carvill's Hill was showing him at home compared to his normal charges, Dreaper says, 'This guy was doing it a whole year ahead.' Following that highly promising debut at Leopardstown, Carvill's Hill ran in two further bumpers, in February and March 1987, and won them both. Already he was one of Ireland's top prospects.

~

When that 1986/87 season opened, Ten Plus was a shorter price than Desert Orchid for the Gold Cup despite never having jumped a fence in public, but that was before Desert Orchid won the King George at Kempton by 15 lengths. That proved he stayed 3m, albeit on a sharp, flat track, and in April of the next season he won over 3m at Aintree, going left-handed, and followed up in the Whitbread at Sandown over three miles and five furlongs.

As well as a landmark performance in terms of proving his stamina, that first King George win was also the first in which he was ridden by Simon Sherwood. Desert Orchid was sent off at 16-1 and stable jockey Colin Brown abandoned him for the second favourite Combs Ditch.

Elsworth enthuses: 'Simon Sherwood was made for him. Colin Brown rode him beautifully and Richard Dunwoody rode him beautifully but with Simon, they were made for each other.'

Comparing Dessie with one of his Festival-winning stable mates, Givus A Buck, who needed plenty of galvanising and organising, Elsworth says: 'Desert Orchid didn't need any of that. Desert Orchid could have run loose, and with Simon he was running loose. Simon was a confidence jockey and he rode plenty of winners but he had a lot of falls – he totally trusted them [his mounts]. When he got on Desert Orchid that first day he was apprehensive. He thought he was riding the outsider of two because Colin was riding Combs Ditch but somebody knew he wasn't – I wanted him on this horse. By the time he jumped six fences I'm sure Simon said this is alright and, of course, in the end he had total confidence in the horse. He sat still as a mouse and the horse jumped from fence to fence with him.'

One week later, apprehension was also the feeling experienced by Kevin Mooney as he set out on Ten Plus's chasing debut at Newbury. The reason, states the jockey, was that 'he'd never jumped a ditch. He'd refused at every ditch we put him into. He refused point blank.' Mooney may have been on the 8-11 favourite but, in so many words, he advised his fellow jockeys in the race that, when approaching the ditch, it might prove best if they were to keep their distance.

Mercifully, when that juncture arrived Ten Plus did not react as if this part of the test was the emergency stop. Of his mount's overall performance that day, Mooney reports, 'He jumped adequate, gave them lots of daylight. He landed on all fours a couple of times. He didn't have to beat anything.' His veteran trainer was nonetheless immediately lobbied to aim Ten Plus at the Gold Cup. He felt vastly more inclined towards the Sun Alliance Chase against other novices, but in the event no decision had to be made. One morning, the Walwyn string were on a nearby road, with Peter Payne on Ten Plus.

'This lorry came by us a bit fast and he stumbled. I didn't realise he'd gone down to be quite honest, he was down and up, and it was the lad in front of me who said, "Peter! He's done his knees in."'

These were not merely grazes. 'They were bloody bad. It was straight down to the bone,' says Mooney. The season had ended for Ten Plus. After that one race, he was denied any further opportunity for race practice against fellow novices. Payne confides: 'We very, very seldom put knee boots on the horses, but we did after that.'

Having recovered from that injury and returned to training the next season, any chance for Ten Plus to gain early practice was then scuppered by an overreach. His first two starts were promising, most notably when a storming finish on the run-in saw him short-head Pegwell Bay over 2m5f at Wincanton, far more of a speed test than was ideal for Ten Plus, but at the end of January he crashed out of Gold Cup contention. At Cheltenham on the New Course, he was in a three-runner race, they went slowly, but he was going nowhere when taking what looked a mother-and-father of a fall at the second last. After that, he was switched back to hurdling and ran twice, including in the Stayers' Hurdle, but did poorly.

Mooney remembers: 'I kept wondering how a horse could give you so much and then give you nothing.' It turned out that Ten Plus had a bad chest infection. He was sent to his owner's estate for the summer.

~

Similarities in their brief chasing records – one novice chase; failing to complete at Cheltenham in January – at one stage prompted comparisons between Ten Plus and Dawn Run, but it was not long in the same campaign before the 1984 Champion Hurdle and 1986 Gold Cup winner was evoked far more often in the context of Carvill's Hill. Widespread speculation that he was the best Irish horse since Dawn Run might not sound quite so earth-shattering when it is remembered that his feted predecessor had died only in 1986 but subsequent events would indicate that Carvill's Hill also merited inclusion among top-class performers in a much longer-term context.

His bumpers had been highly promising but when sent over hurdles in 1987/88 Carvill's Hill won four of five starts, and by thumping margins on the last two occasions. He was rated by Timeform as that season's champion novice hurdler in Britain or Ireland. He was without question a stayer in the making but had not raced that season over even two miles and a half. Dreaper knew where Carvill's Hill's future lay from his home work and there were unmistakable clues to the horse's staying capabilities from the sight of him in full flow on the racecourse.

'He had a great stride but we wouldn't have considered him a very fast horse,' Dreaper reflects. 'Sometimes the heavy ground affects those long-striding horses but although he had a long, long stride, this guy was well able, in fact at his best, when the ground was really hard work for everything else. He would never have figured in a two-mile Champion Chase, he just did not have great speed, but he had a wonderful cruising speed.'

Notwithstanding those observations it was later reported that, in the build-up to the 1988 Festival, Dreaper's neighbour Al O'Connell had galloped his Cheltenham hope Classical Charm against the novice Carvill's Hill and that the Dreaper horse had given him weight, and beaten him out of sight. Classical Charm finished second in the Champion Hurdle.

Carvill's Hill himself, however, did not appear at Cheltenham or any of the other big spring meetings that year. It was said at the time that Cheltenham was given a miss in the interests of his long-term future as a chaser, which was true, but Dreaper also had another reason.

'Well, I wondered when you were going to introduce the problem bit,' responds the trainer at my first mention of Carvill's Hill's hurdling career. 'Jumping – that was the problem all his life. If you even had a telephone pole on the ground, a foot high, if he had the option he would rather run round the side of it. He did not like jumping.'

Of the bearing this had on whether to run Carvill's Hill at Cheltenham as a novice hurdler, Dreaper continues, 'We didn't go because we didn't trust him. Many of the build-up races in Ireland, he was winning them so easily that he wasn't actually learning a great deal, but you go to Cheltenham and they go flat out over the first three, in a crowd, and unless you really know how to do things, all of a sudden you could make one mistake and go from being fifth to fifteenth, and then you're under pressure. Now he may have been good enough to overcome that but because we couldn't trust his jumping we just didn't do it.'

The root of his jumping travails seems to have been that Carvill's Hill had a problem in his near-hind sacroiliac, in the pelvis area, and Dreaper reflects: 'My gut feeling is that it was something that happened to him as a yearling. You know, they'd be farting about in the field and he's skidded into a corner or he's lost his legs, and something went out, his pelvis was out of line, and because it wasn't noticed – he might not have even been lame – my feeling was that something in the physical shape of his backside changed to adapt to the new position.'

The trainer continues: 'We had a great man here looking after him, a man called Nicholas O'Connor who had been in racing all his life, the kind of man I don't think you'd see in racing now. He worked until he was about 65 here with us, having been in a number of other yards.'

O'Connor was one of those who would always think of his horses first and himself second, and the mental effort required on behalf of Carvill's Hill was often considerable. Dreaper elaborates: 'We could always tell if Nick thought Carvill's Hill wasn't right because you would hear him walking down the yard as if his boots were full of lead. Then you'd know by the look on the man's face, and then you'd just need to look at the horse's face – Carvill's Hill was in bad, bad humour, grumpy and so forth, when he was wrong. He was just an ordinary horse, a happy-go-lucky horse, on the relatively few days when he was right.'

~

Meanwhile Ten Plus was recuperating from his chest infection at the Warwickshire estate of owner Basil Thwaites. In the summer the paddocks contained Thwaites's retired racehorses as well as his horses in training. Possessed of a great love of the countryside, wildlife and conservation, he used to check on his horses and the rest of the estate early every morning and in the evening. Having made a success of Thwaites Engineering, the makers of a celebrated dumper truck, Thwaites discovered his love of racehorses late in life and in an unconventional manner.

Fulke Walwyn's wife Cath describes the first meeting with him: 'We were selling rather a bad horse at Ascot Sales. Fulke didn't go to the sales but said to the lad, "Whatever you do, don't bring him back." So that evening the box arrived back and out comes this horse. Fulke asked what the hell has happened, and he said, "Oh, a man bought it, he wants to send it to you and he is coming to see you tomorrow morning." So this huge Rolls-Royce or Bentley arrived in the yard the next day and Mr Thwaites wouldn't get out.'

All describe Thwaites as a very shy man: some would say eccentric. Mrs Walwyn continues: 'So Fulke went and sat in the car and he said, "You must get rid of this horse as soon as possible." Basil agreed and said, "Well, can I buy one and send it to you?" and Fulke said, "Please do."'

'He didn't like the limelight whatsoever,' says Mark Bradstock of the owner, which must have proved awkward when that next horse they bought was Dramatist, who developed into a top-class hurdler. He was third in a supreme line-up for the 1977 Champion. Thwaites used to stand away from everybody else when watching a race and the only occasion that Bradstock can remember him being in the winner's enclosure was when Dramatist won the Cathcart at the Festival.

All my interviewees from the Walwyn stable speak of Thwaites with great respect and affection. Simon Christian, one of Bradstock's predecessors as assistant at Saxon House and, like Bradstock, a Festival-winning trainer in his own right, says that 'He cut a rather extraordinary figure because he was very tall and he dressed in a rather old-fashioned way, usually in a mackintosh if the weather half required it, and with a big, long stick like a shepherd's crook. On the racecourse he was this extraordinary, slightly aloof, reclusive person who when you got to know him was utterly charming and modest, interested in the welfare of his horses and the people around him.'

When Ten Plus was turned out to grass at Thwaites's home for the summer months after his stricken 1987/88 season, he thrived on it. 'He was just totally a different horse,' says Mooney of the Ten Plus who returned to Lambourn to be readied for his third attempt at a proper campaign over fences. 'He looked a better horse, better in himself. He jumped ditches. Brilliant. We never schooled him again after that. You didn't have to – he was just a totally different horse.'

$\sim$

Five months before the 1989 Festival, two of the three eventual market leaders were now almost ready to commence their Gold Cup campaigns. The exception was Carvill's Hill, whose back was not in good order, and by the time he made it to Navan in the week before Christmas, Ten Plus had run three of his five races building to the Festival, Desert Orchid had had two of his five and Ten Plus's ring-rusty reappearance was the only time in those ten races that either of those British-trained horses met with defeat.

For Desert Orchid there were brash assertions of overwhelming superiority at first Wincanton and then in the Tingle Creek at Sandown over two miles, and the King George at Kempton over three. These were followed by him looking defeat in the face, and staring it down, under 12 stone in handicaps against Panto Prince, back over two miles at Ascot, and Pegwell Bay over three at Sandown, two of his triumphs that still cannot fail to stir when reviewed 25 years later.

While his form was taken to new heights and his versatility in alternating between contrasting race distances was astonishing, extravagance was still the most striking feature of Desert Orchid's jumping, but by now he was clever with it, and in almost every form he was above all extremely rapid. Where the process with most horses involved going up and over, with Desert Orchid it was over and on. The closing stages are the most exciting phase in the vast majority of races, but the soaring spectacle of Desert Orchid had the capacity to make any fence the highlight.

At Cheltenham, however, the fact remained that he had come nowhere in two Champion Hurdles, third in the Arkle, third and second in two Champion Chases. The outstanding horse of the era had not won a race at Prestbury Park.

The previous season's Chivas Regal Cup at Aintree had provided a ground-breaking first win going left-handed but he still looked fallible. 'I don't know why,' analyses his trainer, 'because he was a very well-balanced horse, he didn't hang, and he went round that gallop left-handed no problem.' In racecourse action, however, it was another matter, and as Elsworth accepts: 'The fact was he didn't get the wind in his sails for some reason. He was a much better horse going right-handed.'

For Ten Plus, the barriers to Gold Cup success were receding and although it had taken two years longer than many in the Press had predicted, he now looked very much the part. It was said at the time that the previous season's fall at Cheltenham had taught him a great deal but Mooney prefers to stress now that Ten Plus was simply a healthy horse again. He was not at all hard pressed in his four small-field chases – at Wincanton, Chepstow and Newbury (twice) – and his jumping in public, which for so long might best be described as deliberate, got better and better. 'He was measuring his fences,' says Mooney. 'He was just doing everything right.'

As Carvill's Hill had not jumped a fence in public before December 17 yet started second favourite in the same season's Gold Cup, it might be concluded at first glance that he too was doing everything right in the jumping department. But that conclusion would be wrong.

Jim Dreaper describes the critical moment that arrives when any horse first tries its hand over fences: 'If a horse meets a fence correctly, which you hope every horse will, they will jump it correctly but when they meet one wrong and they need to shorten up, which then involves more bending of the back to get them elevation, that's when you find out, that's really when you find out what kind of a jumper you've got. The fence they meet wrong is the one which tells you how you're fixed.'

He also describes what happened with Carvill's Hill: 'Ken Morgan rode him and made a great job of it, because he was a nightmare to ride. Going down to each fence, with the best will in the world, you hadn't a clue what was going to happen.'

Carvill's Hill won his chasing debut at Navan and on his second start looked very much the best horse at Leopardstown, but he did not win: approaching the second last in the Dennys Gold Medal Novice Chase, he stuttered and shuffled to his left, and when confronted with the final fence Carvill's Hill's forward and upward motion proved no match for that which he produced sideways. In careering to his left he fell, sending Morgan somersaulting into the rails.

When discussing how much schooling may be required for different horses, Dreaper recalls a saying from his father's time as a trainer – that you don't need to teach a university student how to read and write. Carvill's Hill was still doing his O level retakes. Included in the many and varied measures employed to improve his jumping, Dreaper says: 'A lot of it would be small fences, five strides apart and the next one seven strides after that and the next one six strides after that, to try and make him think about them – "what do I need to do here?" – and to try to get him to bend. I think it's what the eventing people would call grid work. Just to make him realise that not every fence is going to come in the same place and you've got to do something about it.'

In the course of his extra schooling sessions, did Carvill's Hill aggravate his injury? 'Almost certainly yes,' states the trainer. 'Because, to put it in common parlance, it was something ready to pop out of shape at any given time.'

When something did pop out, a call would most often be made to a man from Carrick-on-Suir who would then make the two hours plus drive to Greenogue to treat the horse. He got to know Carvill's Hill and his back very well but, as Dreaper puts it, 'We could fix him but we couldn't get it fixed permanently.'

Although the wider racing world was well aware of Carvill's Hill's recurrent problems, if not their extent, it was easy to be largely blinded to them given the show he put on that February. The result of the Red Mills Trial Chase at Gowran Park on his third chasing start may not have proved a great deal seeing as Carvill's Hill was the 7-2 on favourite, but he did win it by a distance. Then came the Vincent O'Brien Irish Gold Cup at Leopardstown, Ireland's top race for fully fledged chasers, for which the novice Carvill's Hill had had the benefit of just three previous runs over fences.

Held up at the rear, he pecked badly on landing over the first, but despite his rider's obvious preference for more patient tactics, which resulted in Carvill's Hill being repeatedly taken back through runners, some generally prodigious jumping took him almost into the lead at the third, fourth, fifth, sixth, seventh and eighth. When he emerged from the ninth in a two-length lead there was no choice this time but to go on, and thereafter for his supporters – despite the huge step up in class he was the 9-4 favourite – there was not the slightest moment of alarm, not even when Carvill's Hill met one of the fences on the wrong stride and jumped to his left on a couple of other occasions. It was a let-down that the next three in the betting all fell, including the 1988 Gold Cup winner Charter Party and soon-to-be Irish Grand National winner Maid Of Money – both five out – but no anti-climax when Carvill's Hill strode on to a 15-length victory, leaving an overwhelmingly positive impression.

At home at Greenogue, Dreaper's grass gallop was roughly a mile and a half long. Occasionally they would go two laps. 'Plenty of them could beat him over a mile and three,' says the trainer, 'but when you had to come up the hill a second time, he'd be the one still galloping.' On the racecourse it now looked as if he could do much the same against any horse in Ireland. The decision was taken that, if he was right and the ground was right, he would spurn the novice route at Cheltenham and go for the Gold Cup.

Dreaper explains: 'We reckoned that if he was in good nick and had a clear round he would have a chance if the ground was soft, regardless of the others. I still believe it to this day, because he had a wonderful, wonderful engine and it was just purely and simply dependent on how he jumped. Okay the opposition might have been less powerful in the novice race but the fences would have been the same.'

~

1989 GOLD CUP

In the newspapers on Gold Cup morning, Dreaper was quoted as considering whether to withdraw Carvill's Hill if the ground continued to dry. As it was, anybody attempting to read those newspapers needed to do so indoors. Instead of drying out, the ground became so saturated that conditions threatened something similar to those that prevailed in 1975 when Ten Up won, trained by the then 24-year-old Jim Dreaper.

As conditions cemented the participation of Carvill's Hill, so they cast that of Desert Orchid into doubt, in some quarters at least. Connections never seemed to duck any other challenge with him, which greatly boosted him in the public's estimation, but whether Desert Orchid and the Gold Cup would finally get together had already become the sort of 'Will they? Won't they?' saga that habitually propels two leading characters giddily through many a situation comedy. This was just the latest instalment. Connections could be excused some qualms about the prospective union, given the unexpected plot twist that ground conditions were turning towards the extreme, but one person would not shy away. 'I was dead keen to run him,' asserts his trainer. 'I was never in any doubt that we should run.'

Asked whether he was worried about the rain, Elsworth replies, 'No. I was worried about the prospect of racing, but he was better equipped to deal with it than anybody. He was such a good jumper. When the press said, "Is he running?" I said, "Of course he is running."'

Did he walk the course? 'No, I gave that up years ago.'

'I wanted to win the Gold Cup. I wanted to win everything,' states Elsworth, and talking to him even in 2013 there is absolutely no mistaking the exalted place the Gold Cup had in his ambitions, or his esteem. After our interview over a lunchtime pint at The Boot at Dullingham, the trainer gives me a lift back to his stables and, while we discuss the relative merits of recent Gold Cup winners Denman and Kauto Star, so animated is he that the car temporarily mounts the grass verge. Elsworth is a big fan of Denman.

'The Gold Cup was a big deal,' he tells me a little earlier. 'When I was a kid the first time I ever went to Cheltenham

Limber Hill won it. By Bassam out of Mindon. '55 was Gay Donald, '56 was Limber Hill. Tony Grantham rode Gay Donald, 33-1 trained by Jim Ford. He made all.'

By the time that Elsworth witnessed his first Gold Cup, Fulke Walwyn was already four years on from his first winner of the race as a trainer. As a jockey Walwyn had Festival wins in the County Hurdle in 1936 and the Gloucestershire Hurdle in 1939, as well as a Grand National in 1936 on Reynoldstown. The first of his Festival wins as a trainer was in 1946, a season in which he reportedly won 36 races with 18 horses. From the relatively humble start to his training career restoring broken-down horses to win selling hurdles, usually well backed in the process, Walwyn had by 1989 won more Festival races than any other trainer. Ten Plus's Sun Alliance was his 40th.

In one report on Gold Cup day in 1989 it was said that Ten Plus lived in the box formerly occupied by Mill House and The Dikler. Speaking in 2014, Peter Payne is not so sure and thinks he might have been in the one next door which used to house Mont Tremblant. Either way, Ten Plus was following in the footsteps of a former Gold Cup winner because Mont Tremblant won it in 1952, Mill House did so in 1963 and The Dikler triumphed in 1973, as did fellow Saxon House star Mandarin in 1962.

Talking about his time with Walwyn, Mark Bradstock reflects: 'I was there for 12 years and it was a phenomenal pleasure. He was an absolute, total, total genius. He likewise had the most incredible staff, who'd been there most of them 25, 30, 35 years. It was indescribable what it was like.'

Walwyn liked to have his most talented charges in a batch of the ten best boxes, 'The Top Ten', in which he could view a series of good horses all in a row. Ten Plus did not start in The Top Ten, but he was moved there in probably his second season. Cath Walwyn says her husband 'always thought that this horse was going to be a Gold Cup horse, that he was going to win a Gold Cup. He always had terrific faith in him.'

Mrs Walwyn and others assure me that her husband's motivation and ambition were undented, despite the fact that when the 1989 Gold Cup came round he was 78. As Simon Christian explains, that ambition was shared by Basil Thwaites:

'The Holy Grail for them both was to win the Cheltenham Gold Cup and the horse in their opinion had an outstanding chance of winning the Gold Cup, and at their age they weren't going to have another. I think it was something they wanted to do together because almost one supported the other. I don't think Mr Thwaites had a huge circle of friends outside his business and Fulke seemed to have a respect for him that was quite extraordinary. He seemed to have the most amazing, not just affection, but admiration for him.'

Crucial to the arguments for Ten Plus was that this was where his full strength in stamina would be demonstrated for the first time. He had run over 3m 2½ at Newbury in the Mandarin, but that four-runner race against that calibre of horse left reserves still to be tapped. This was a horse who would keep on galloping.

Of their belief going into the race, Mrs Walwyn states: 'In the Gold Cup you never can be very confident but we were as confident as you can be.'

Kevin Mooney's wife Sharon confides: 'When he was riding, Kevin was never any different, whether it was Cheltenham or Wincanton on a Wednesday, but the night before that Gold Cup he said to me, "If I'm in front at the top of the hill I think I'll win."'

~

What followed was, in 2005, voted the greatest race of all time by *Racing Post* readers. Under umbrellas in the ring, the bookmakers had Desert Orchid chalked up as 5-2 favourite at the off, with Carvill's Hill 5-1 and Ten Plus 11-2. The ten other runners included the previous two Gold Cup winners in The Thinker and Charter Party, plus the 1988 runner-up Cavvies Clown (Desert Orchid's stablemate) and the wide-margin Welsh Grand National winner Bonanza Boy. Desert Orchid was cheered to the start.

Jim Dreaper and Ken Morgan had walked the course, with Dreaper concluding that the ground was not quite as bad as in 1975, Ten Up's year, and Morgan reporting on television that in Ireland the ground would be called soft. But after the unrelenting precipitation, the protracted soul-searching of Desert Orchid's owners and the sight of staggering runners at the finish of the Triumph Hurdle, the first circuit in the Gold Cup was always going to be a matter of safety first. Desert Orchid was swiftly in his favoured position at the head of the field but by normal standards the pace he set was understandably very conservative. The Desert Orchid of old would have abhorred such behaviour. For nearly all of that first circuit, Charter Party raced close up on Desert Orchid's flanks, with Ten Plus adopting the same position on the outside of Charter Party.

For Carvill's Hill, held up in the rear, the signs were good when he flew the first and he continued to take most of the other early fences with plenty of air to spare. At the sixth, there was a scare for his supporters when Golden Freeze, carrying very similar colours, fell and hampered Cavvies Clown, who had only just worked his way forward after a slow start. At the seventh, though, Carvill's Hill's race was over.

It was the second open ditch and he met the fence on a good stride but tried to go through it rather than over it. 'He just disappeared under me,' reported Morgan, who was left with a dislocated shoulder.

Of his subsequent debriefing from the jockey, Dreaper recalls that 'it would have been along the lines of "Everything was fine until it wasn't." We're not much into post-mortems. I tried to do it myself, I know a little bit about raceriding, and when things go wrong they go wrong. It wasn't a huge surprise in all honesty.'

The scale of Carvill's Hill's error, though, just might have been. 'You know,' says the trainer, 'rather than trying to jump it a little bit in the approved manner, Jesus, what he did was kamikaze stuff.'

When the commentator announced the departure of Carvill's Hill, there were both groans and cheers from the crowd. Three fences later, as the field proceeded halfway down the hill, The Thinker also fell, slithering to the ground.

Up front, Desert Orchid was shifting to his right at his fences but travelling well within himself. For Ten Plus, too, everything was going well. 'It was wet, sloppy ground,' says Mooney, 'but they were getting through it, he'd jumped well out of the ground, so I made a decision after we'd gone a circuit. They were starting to slow the race up a little bit passing the stands, and that's not what I want, so I've gone past Desert Orchid.'

As they turned away for the final time, Ten Plus had the lead and Mooney was asking him to press on; Cavvies Clown also now attempted to serve it up to the favourite and the race had begun in earnest.

Charter Party was still on the heels of the leaders. Bonanza Boy, Slalom and Yahoo moved up ahead of Pegwell Bay. Over the plain fence, water jump and open ditch Ten Plus either had the lead from Desert Orchid or was disputing it with him, the pair taking it in turns to jump the better. All the while Mooney was nudging along on Ten Plus and Sherwood sat still on Desert Orchid, but that was entirely in keeping with the customary styles of horses and jockeys. Initially over that sequence of fences, there were only a couple of lengths or so between the first seven runners, but as he took the next fence the better and turned towards the ditch at the top of the hill, Ten Plus was taken to the inside rail and went three lengths clear. He did not take that final ditch as cleanly as Desert Orchid but when they emerged from it, Charter Party, Yahoo and arguably Ballyhane were the only other runners still in contention with them. Slalom had just unseated and others blundered badly. There were five fences remaining.

Ten Plus took the next with a higher trajectory than the neat jump of Desert Orchid but still had a two-length lead. Mooney pulled his goggles down. At the fourth last, where the ground on the landing side begins to drop away, Desert Orchid hit the fence hard. 'So I've kicked him down the hill and said, "Right, go on then," remembers Ten Plus's jockey. '"Go down to the bottom of the hill and then I'll give you a little bit of a breather."'

Three fences to go. Desert Orchid quickly made up two lengths approaching that downhill fence so that they took it almost head to head, but Mooney recalls that he was full of confidence in Ten Plus, believing that 'When he gets down the bottom and turns, all he's going to do is gallop up that hill. When he sets sail up that hill he'll win.'

It was not to be. 'I felt he still had loads left,' says Mooney, but Ten Plus struck the fence and fell. As the jockey hit the turf and tucked himself into a ball to avoid injury from the other runners, Ten Plus was up in an instant and set off after the others.

Suddenly, it was the 25-1 shot Yahoo, ridden by Ken Morgan's brother Tom, who emerged on Desert Orchid's inner and rapidly looked to be going much the better, as Sherwood's calm on the favourite was now definitely at an end. Yahoo entered the final straight ahead by a length and a half and he clung to the inner, while Desert Orchid characteristically drifted to his right, with another four or five lengths back to the Richard Dunwoody-ridden Charter Party who was only theoretically in contention. Yahoo looked the winner but, in Sherwood's words, 'once we were in a straight line Dessie knew what had to be done.'

The two horses were racing wide apart, but when they came to the second last everyone could now see that there was only half a length in it. At the final fence, both jockeys allowed their mounts all the time they needed to steady themselves and find their own stride. Yahoo took it just in the lead and seemed to get away the quicker, but for those beseeching Desert Orchid to battle his way to the front yet again, the answer came after a dozen strides.

Once the tide started to turn, could anyone with prior knowledge of Desert Orchid have doubted the outcome? Well, they shouted him on just to make sure. Tom Morgan has since said, 'I'd ridden in most big races, but I'd not heard anything like that. When we jumped the last it was almost as if the volume was turned up from a power of zero to ten in half a stride. I wonder still how many were cheering for Yahoo.'

Television viewers heard Peter O'Sullevan exclaim, 'He's beginning to get up! Desert Orchid is beginning to get up!' To hear what the course commentator was saying was impossible. Under a right-hand drive the grey hero veered to his left, so that, many have thought, he could really go head to head with his rival, and for the first time since the race began he was clearly on top. Desert Orchid beat Yahoo by one and a half lengths. Charter Party was eight lengths further away, with Bonanza Boy and West Tip tailed off as the only other finishers.

Umbrellas could be seen dancing in the infield. Peter Thomas, of the *Racing Post*, has written that 'brown trilbies, hurled skyward in jubilation, fell like righteous rain'. Richard Dunwoody on Charter Party clasped Sherwood's hand in congratulation; Tom Morgan did likewise and also gave Desert Orchid a pat on the neck. I wondered if the crowd would ever stop cheering. Perhaps they never did.

~

I cannot remember exactly when things changed for me. Ken Morgan reported: 'When I was coming back in the ambulance I heard them calling for a screen to be put up in front of the stands. I feared the worst.' Jim Dreaper was on the course looking for Carvill's Hill. A riderless horse came down towards him: 'He just came cantering as best he could. I thought, "Which horse is that?" and then when he got to me he was a lighter bay horse than ours. He more or less came to a halt where I was standing, so I grabbed on to him and then one of Mr Walwyn's men came and took him.'

When Ten Plus had risen from that fall at the third last, he had rapidly galloped off after the other horses but did so without putting his near-hind to the ground. The reason was a broken fetlock. 'It was heartbreaking,' says Peter Payne. 'I'd waited all them years to do a real good horse and win a top race and it had gone in a second.' Payne had looked after him for nearly five years. The green screens were raised and Ten Plus was put down.

~

With Richard Burridge at their quarters and Janice Coyle, the most famous stable lass or lad in Britain, at her horse's head, Desert Orchid and Simon Sherwood made their way back to the parade ring, through applauding crowds packed almost as deep as they could be. Making their way the length of the parade ring, the jockey had his hand shaken countless times and the horse received countless slaps and pats. On entering the winner's enclosure to a huge roar, the horse was greeted almost straightaway by his part-owner, Richard Burridge's father Jimmy. He it was who had bred Desert Orchid and his dam, the modest dual novice chase winner Flower Child, having purchased the grandam Grey Orchid for £175 as a ten-year-old in 1962. The assembled crowd gave three cheers for the winner. The paddock-side big screen announced that the winner was 'Desert Orchard'. When the 'Horses away' announcement was made the boos rang out, and when Desert Orchid was finally led away it was to a renewed bout of rapturous applause. His mesmeric appeal was such that nearly one hundred people hurried after him to the dope-testing area.

Standing at the other end of the parade ring were Fulke Walwyn and Basil Thwaites. Returning to them in an ambulance was Kevin Mooney. Concerning when he had unrolled himself and risen from his fall at the third last, the jockey relates, 'There were some people stood by that fence and I just said, "Did that horse get up and get away?" And they said, "Yes. He's got up and he was okay."' Mooney's thoughts turned to the cheering prospect of the Gold Cup in 1990.

Walwyn and Thwaites were also unaware of the fate that had befallen Ten Plus. The trainer remarked that they had not won the Gold Cup at the first attempt with The Dikler either. 'They hadn't got a clue until I walked up with the bridle,' says Peter Payne. 'That was the first time they knew that he'd been put down.'

Mooney sunk to his knees and broke down weeping, distraught, and had to be helped into the weighing room. Talking to me in 2013, his voice lowered: 'I'm not a soft person, but that was heartbreaking that was.' When I asked him whether he had ridden many other horses who were killed, his reply was 'Plenty'. Later on Gold Cup day, colleagues had to prevent him from coming out of the weighing room and declaring that he had finished as a jockey.

Mooney gives generous praise to Desert Orchid and says 'it's neither here nor there' whether Ten Plus would have won were it not for his fall, but he is adamant that his mount never got the chance to demonstrate of what he was truly capable. 'He'd had a mixed career, nothing was easy for him. People didn't know how good he was and he was just cut off in his prime. … Potentially he was a Gold Cup winner – for me he was a Gold Cup winner. I'll always say he was a Gold Cup winner. He didn't win a Gold Cup but I thought he could have gone on to win two or three. He was that sort of horse.'

I get the impression that Mooney has been asked about this race many times, and thought about it many more. His theory is that Ten Plus sustained an injury when dropping his hind leg on the bar of the take-off board at the last open ditch. After that his jumping did not feel the same over the next two fences and then, at the third last, 'he's gone to take off and then he's just done his leg – no propulsion from behind. He's probably had a hairline fracture and three fences later – gone.'

Peter Payne has also tried to work out what exactly befell Ten Plus, and he says, 'I've looked at the film that many times, but what happened there we don't know, not really.'

The day after the Gold Cup, Basil Thwaites came over to the Walwyn yard. He gave Payne the Silver Buck Trophy which Ten Plus had won at Wincanton four months earlier.

For all concerned with the horse, his loss was very hard to deal with. 'The yard was in shock,' recalls Mooney. 'It was empty, it was empty of any spirit. We'd just lost the best horse and we didn't have many good ones at that time. Fulke was winding down. That wasn't because he couldn't do the job, it was just because the people around him were dying. We didn't have the ammunition we had before.'

Of Walwyn himself, a trainer for 50 years, his wife recalls: 'He was just so upset by it. We went away, down by the sea, for a fortnight afterwards just to get him away from here. I just thought, get him away from seeing the horses.'

But nothing could fill the void that Ten Plus had left.

Three months later, Basil Thwaites died of a heart attack while out walking one morning on his estate. He was 77. In his will he left all his horses, geldings, mares and foals to Fulke Walwyn.

A victim of poor health for several years, the trainer had not been present when Ten Plus won the Sun Alliance Hurdle in 1986. Gold Cup day in 1989 was his final visit to Cheltenham Racecourse. Twelve months later, Walwyn did have a Gold Cup runner. Ten Of Spades had missed all of the previous season with injury, but Walwyn was sent him and brought him back in such good form that he was given his chance at Cheltenham. In the Lifestyles column in *The Sporting Life* that day, Walwyn revealed, among other things, that the Worst Day of his racing life was when Ten Plus was killed; his Funniest Racing Moment came one day at Folkestone when, having won the first five races with horses owned by Dorothy Paget, her sixth runner got beaten a length – and when asked by the Press how she felt she replied, 'Very disappointed'; his Music was Flanagan and Allen; his Racing Ambition was 'to win another Cheltenham Gold Cup.'

Comparing Ten Of Spades to Ten Plus, however, Mooney says that Ten Of Spades 'wouldn't be in the same furlong' and after duelling once more with Desert Orchid up front and holding the lead turning for home, Mooney's mount was weakening in fourth when he fell two out.

Ten Plus's Sun Alliance Hurdle was therefore the fortieth and last of Fulke Walwyn's Festival winners. Overall, his many decades in racing yielded more than 300 winners as an amateur jockey, about 2,300 as a trainer and he was champion trainer five times. He retired in May 1990 and died in February 1991. The following month, the Kim Muir Chase had its first running under the new title of the Fulke Walwyn Kim Muir.

Kevin Mooney retired from the saddle on a winner, By Line, trained by Cath Walwyn, in May 1991. Ten Plus was the best horse he rode, but Mooney is best known for his winning role in one of the most remarkable and celebrated finishes ever to a top steeplechase, when he was on board the Queen Mother's Special Cargo in the 1984 Whitbread Gold Cup. Having started his racing career as an apprentice with Barry Hills, his retirement as a jockey saw him return to Hills as assistant trainer, a position he still held with Hills's son Charlie more than 20 years later. The Hills yard is focussed on Flat racing but Mooney's switch of codes had nothing to do with what had happened to Ten Plus. 'My heart,' he says, 'was in jumping.'

∼

Judged on the rating given him for his win in the 1989 Vincent O'Brien Irish Gold Cup – with Timeform, the same that was accorded Yahoo at Cheltenham – Carvill's Hill would have been in the thick of the action in the Gold Cup had be jumped round safely. Carvill's Hill had one run 12 days after the 1989 Gold Cup and another the following month and he won both. In the Timeform *Chasers & Hurdlers* annuals, Carvill's Hill is easily the highest rated novice chaser from 1975/76 (when the annuals started) until Strong Promise in 1996/97. However, he was confined to four runs (winning two) the next winter and just two (winning one) the winter after that. The training of Carvill's Hill in those years seemed much more something to be endured than enjoyed.

The problem with him was the same that it had always been and, of his entire time with Dreaper, the trainer says: 'I would say that he was what we would call 100 per cent right on about three days, three race days.'

He continues, 'God knows we tried anything and everything. We bought a magnetic blanket for him and had various people poking at him, so called "back men", and to the best of my memory every one of them came in and said it was something different. However, the end result was that we never cured it. To put it in mechanical terms –

wonderful engine, serious chassis problem. That's the way he was.'

Of the horse's consequent issues with jumping fences, Dreaper says: 'In most of his races, he'd just make a desperate, desperate mistake. He'd do something that would have been painful for him to do, really plough and land on all fours, in fact land hind legs first, which must have had an awfully jarring effect on the whole horse's system. He just wasn't a natural jumper and I'd be the first to say it, we failed to cure it.'

Carvill's Hill was able to have another crack at the Cheltenham Gold Cup, in 1992, but by that stage Jim Dreaper was no longer his trainer. On what turned out to be his final run for the yard, in January 1991, Carvill's Hill became unsighted at the first fence and fell, fracturing his pelvis. Another injury had been added to injury and insult. Dreaper summarises his whole experience with Carvill's Hill as 'a hugely frustrating learning curve. Learning how to put up with negative comment – "If his father had him he'd be this, he'd be that, he'd be the other," that kind of crack. Ah but I've lived with that all my life, for understandable reasons. I'm well used to that. I used to take things very seriously in the first eight or ten years when I trained, but after that all you can do is your best and if it doesn't work it doesn't work.'

Paul Green had purchased a controlling share in Carvill's Hill for his curtailed final Irish season and transferred the horse to Martin Pipe, with absolutely no ill will on behalf of the Dreaper team. After Pipe and back specialist Mary Bromiley had worked on him, Carvill's Hill returned to racecourse action and won his next three starts by an aggregate of 45 lengths; the Welsh National he won by 20 in awesome style, conceding 19lb to the runner-up Party Politics, that season's Grand National winner. In the 1992 Gold Cup, therefore, despite some adverse rumours about his wellbeing, Carvill's Hill was sent off even-money favourite.

However, as Dreaper had described Carvill's Hill in his Irish days, 'he might go off down to the start in a race, jump one fence awkwardly and the whole thing would have gone pear shaped,' and that seems to be exactly what happened in this race and the fence in question was the first, which he hit halfway up, if that. Still in contention turning for home but ending up at a walk as the last of five finishers, Carvill's Hill was later found to have pulled muscles in his chest and to have a tendon injury.

'Pitman turns Delilah in cutting down Carvill's Hill' was one headline the next day in reference to the controversial, to say the least, confrontation up front between the favourite and the Jenny Pitman-trained 150-1 shot Golden Freeze, but if Carvill's Hill could not cope with it even over the first fence, then it was no surprise he did not emerge as that year's Gold Cup winner. He did not race again.

Jim Dreaper watched the 1992 Gold Cup on television at home, shuddered with his former charge at that first-fence blunder and watched the rest with sadness. 'Worse horses have won a Gold Cup,' he observes, and this is a considerable understatement. For evidence, take the Timeform rating for Carvill's Hill's win in the Welsh National (the middle leg of his last-season hat-trick) of 182. At that stage, since the days of Arkle only Desert Orchid and Burrough Hill Lad had achieved higher.

~

It is easily his most famous win but Desert Orchid's peak rating (187 with Timeform, 189 with the *Racing Post*) was of course not registered in the 1989 Gold Cup. The form he showed that day was not within a stone of his best. It is not high enough to rate in his top ten career performances. No matter. Speaking from a much longer-term perspective, both of the result and his horse's career, David Elsworth states, 'He did win a soft Gold Cup, make no bones about it, but I think it was a tremendous achievement of the old boy. I didn't think that Desert Orchid would ever win a Gold Cup.'

Elsworth watched him do it on television, almost alone, having been diverted just before the race to the Royal Box. He was with one other person, while everyone else was on the balcony. He assures me he maintained his composure: 'I did. I didn't even shout. I'm sure I didn't. Because I was never sure.' The enormity of becoming a Gold Cup-winning trainer may also have had its stunning effect.

After the race, Elsworth did not immediately go to the winner's enclosure. 'I thought the winner will look after himself,' says the trainer, who opted instead to commiserate with Mrs Ollivant, the owner-breeder of his other runner Cavvies Clown, who had not delivered one of his better performances. When he did move towards the winner's enclosure a gateman would not let him through, which surprised Elsworth – 'Most gatemen knew me, because I'd had a row with them all' – but there were thousands of other people there to put the gateman right.

In the aftermath Simon Sherwood asserted that 'I've never known a horse so brave,' which most who witnessed the race, and other races before it, could easily believe. It is striking that Elsworth has been the trainer not only of Desert Orchid but also of the monumental Flat stayer Persian Punch, another legend of courage, and indeed of the hurdlers Floyd and Muse, two more front-runners celebrated for their extreme tenacity. Can it possibly be a coincidence? When I invited Elsworth to discuss the concept of courage and gameness in the racehorse, his reply was: 'Fitness is a great thing. Despite the popular belief that Martin Pipe invented fitness, I did the rounds before I became a trainer. I used to ride at a very moderate level and I used to be frustrated by riding horses that got very tired. They were probably moderate horses anyway but trainers probably weren't aware of the fitness level required. I think the trainers are good now, they can all get them fit, but in those days I had wonderful facilities at Whitsbury and I fully exploited them and my horses were very fit. Every bit as fit as Martin Pipe's.'

Specifically of Desert Orchid, Elsworth says he could gallop him over a mile and a half on a Wednesday – 'you didn't have to "gallop" him, you just had to sit on him' – and run him on the Saturday. He was so durable that he could stand a 'proper preparation' and his fitness was always matched by his willingness.

'When a horse is good you tend to wrap him in cotton wool,' observes the trainer, 'but I said, "No, no, no. If you start getting him too fresh, he'll be too free." That was probably our biggest problem, deciding that although he was a superstar he still had as rigorous and as tough a preparation as anything did. He still did his work.

'He used to go through some incredible peaks of fitness. The day he won the Racing Post Chase [in 1990] under 12st 3lb, he was in the form of his life and I said, "I don't care what runs – they won't beat this horse today." He inspired me with such confidence. He flattened them that day and that was probably the best he's ever been.'

Comparing Desert Orchid to Persian Punch, Elsworth says: 'Both used to make the running but Punchie would pull up or ease off, he'd take his foot off the accelerator, whereas Dessie wouldn't. Dessie would die for you in front and he would battle back. I schooled Persian Punch but he had more chance of being a showjumper than a hurdler.'

Persian Punch was left to his Flat career, still showing his form at the age of ten, and Elsworth has almost entirely switched to his. He always trained Flat horses but within ten years of Desert Orchid's Gold Cup his Flat team had come to dominate. He even moved to Newmarket. From the summer of 2009 until the 2013/14 season he had no runners over hurdles and there have been hardly any since. There have been no Elsworth runners over fences since Black De

Bessy was tenth at 33-1 in the William Hill Handicap at the Festival in 2006.

He was already slowing down markedly with his jumps horses but in January 1997 there was a contributory factor when he lost another grey horse, called Fionans Flutter, one who was only just setting out on a chasing career. Elsworth must have explained what happened that day a fair few times before I ever spoke to him about it, but his emotions still could not be kept from the surface:

'He was a mad bastard – Desert Orchid, only worse – and he wanted to do everything in a hurry, he really did. He was wild but a nice horse. I schooled him over fences and he was just like Desert Orchid, he couldn't wait to get off the ground and land on the other side, and we went to Lingfield the first time he ran over fences and he took some unprecedented bloody chances over the first two. He wasn't as good a jumper as Desert Orchid but he thought he was. Anyway he went round the corner and he broke his leg. He hit the fence hard and turned arse over tip. I got there before they could shoot him and the horse knew me, because you had a job to catch him in his box. It's probably my concept of it not his, but I couldn't do anything and he thought I could, and they shot him. Not good. Put me off a bit, but I still love jumping.'

When I interviewed him early in 2013, Elsworth was relishing the prospect of the forthcoming Flat turf season. He lists the practical advantages of Flat racing over jumps – longer days, summer coats, better ground, lighter weights, etc. – and he does not even mention the greater financial rewards on the Flat, but then he states that his preference on a Saturday would be to watch jump racing at the likes of Sandown, Kempton or Cheltenham.

He continues: 'I would still go to Wincanton or Huntingdon to watch jumping horses. I wouldn't go to Yarmouth. Good Flat racing is good but the mediocre, it's boring. If you want to have a few quid on it's exciting but that's about it.' When summing up all-weather racing as an entertainment, Elsworth uses terminology that may well be similar to that employed when he was sounded out all those years ago about taking on the toilet duties at Stonehenge.

Desert Orchid lived until November 2006, having raced on until the 1991 King George. Other horses had the legs of him that season and connections were increasingly worried that, although his powers were waning, his approach to jumping fences remained the same – 'Never Compromise'. Whereas once if he met a fence on a long stride it was not a problem and he could produce one of those leaps that almost became his hallmark, now he was taking a chance. After he crashed out at the third-last fence in that 1991 King George Chase, attempting to win the race for a fifth time, retiring him was an easy decision to make.

In subsequent years Dessie would still appear at the King George to lead the parade and, usually ridden by Colin Brown, would comprehensively steal the show by basically bolting to post as he galloped past the stands. Most winters were spent with Elsworth, who has a photograph of him there in retirement, ridden still by Rodney Boult: 'Two old codgers together I put it. Rodney was 60 and Dessie was 20 something, but they were leading the yearlings.'

~

Dessie's most famous race, the 1989 Gold Cup, has been voted the greatest race of all time but it is not something I can go along with. Desert Orchid was incredible and I can see why so many voted for it, but it is simply not what I felt at the time and I do not feel it now. Jump racing is one of the few sports in which what is lost can be far more than just a race, and what happened to Ten Plus still wrings out the pleasure. The emotions associated with the winner and this loser that day in 1989 felt too contrasting and ran so deep. It may be hypocritical, because there are other races described in this book in which horses have died, but not every horse can mean the same to every individual. The crucial thing is that all will be mourned by somebody.

Deaths with horses are inevitable and there are horses in this book who met their ends in the most risk-free environments. When I interviewed Kevin Mooney, one of the prospective stars in the Hills Flat team the previous season had died in the stalls while awaiting the start of the 1,000 Guineas. 'I've always been told where there's livestock there's always dead stock,' one of the interviewees for this book told me, not at all matter of factly, and as David Elsworth says, 'I don't think they're pets – they're racehorses', but on the other hand the history of thousands of years shows that there is an affinity between man and horse and so does the experience of succeeding generations in racing. That horses can die in the sport must not be ignored nor in any way brushed under the carpet, but do not underestimate the care they receive in training or the depth of feeling that can be held for these horses by those who look after them. The BHA (British Horseracing Authority) website states that the equine fatality rate in British racing in recent years has been just over 0.2 per cent of runners.

There have been years when looking at the credentials of certain runners in the Grand National has begged the question of just how much their owners and trainers really cared for them, and every time there is a huge-priced National winner I partly shudder, because some owner will claim that the race is a lottery and any horse could have a go at it. On the whole, however, I do not believe that the sport treats issues of animal welfare at all lightly or casually. Training a jumps horse should be about development and the nurturing of talent over years.

Even for someone such as David Nicholson who spent his whole life in racing, the death of a horse was very hard to deal with. 'It would prey on his mind for a long time,' says his wife Dinah. 'He couldn't just snap out of it and forget it,' and of the bond that develops between stable staff and their charges, Nicholson's son John recalls, 'He would never ask a stable lad to hold the horse that was going to be put down. He would take it out to the field at the back of the stables and he would be the one holding it. He might give tears then but he'd always be the one to say that's not fair on the stable lads for that to happen – they're so close to their animals.'

Every regular racegoer at jumps meetings must have asked their conscience whether the cost of racing is acceptable and whether the challenges faced by participants are fair. That hurdlers and, in particular, chasers face stern challenges if a race is to be won is one reason the sport is so stirring, but this is categorically not an example of the bad times making the good times seem better.

The best sound on a racecourse is the applause that greets an apparently stricken horse when it rises to its feet, the green screens are taken down and it can walk away unharmed. This did not happen after the 1989 Gold Cup and I will not forget the fate of Ten Plus, but neither will I forget Desert Orchid. When I see a top racehorse racing I do not think this is an animal that has been subjugated. With racing I have above all been inspired by what the horse can do. And by what man and horse can do together.

CHAPTER ELEVEN

1990 TOTE CHELTENHAM GOLD CUP

The Festival's most unlikely Winner

IN THE CRUSH and din of a Cheltenham Gold Cup finish, it is not uncommon for racegoers to have their view of the action obscured, or for the commentator's shouts to be drowned out. Getting from one part of the racecourse to another on Gold Cup day is after all the nearest thing rural England has to rush hour, plus signal failure, on the London Underground. However, in 1990 even many of those who did succeed in getting an unimpeded view of the finish were immediately asking each other 'Who was that?' in reference to the winner. When the answer materialised that it was Norton's Coin, the biggest shock in the history of the Gold Cup, and surely of any race at the Festival, had made itself apparent.

In a startling series of improbable revelations, the first the crowd had to come to terms with – and some were struggling – was that this horse was not Desert Orchid. That much we could make out, his visage being better known than that of most Prime Ministers and a great deal more popular. I did not witness such distressing scenes myself, but the following day it was reported that 'grown men cried openly as the famous grey failed to quicken up the hill'.

The long-established *beau idéal* of jumps racing, Dessie was at the height of his powers that season. In terms of form, his highest *Racing Post* Rating in previous campaigns was 185 but he took that to 189 in February 1990 when winning the Racing Post Chase by eight lengths under 12st 3lb, two stone more than was carried by the next in the handicap, the runner-up Delius. On Timeform ratings that season his figure improved from 182 to 187, making him their highest rated chaser since the days of Arkle, Flyingbolt and Mill House in the 1960s.

The Racing Post Chase was Desert Orchid's last race before the Gold Cup. After it, he was a twelve-length winner of the Irish Grand National under 12st, giving between 26lb and 28lb to all his rivals. Norton's Coin, meanwhile, warmed up for the Gold Cup with placed efforts off 10st 7lb and 10st 6lb in relatively unassuming handicaps at Cheltenham and Newbury, in the former registering his best pre-Gold Cup Racing Post Rating, one of 152. At Kempton on Boxing Day, Norton's Coin had had his first crack at Desert Orchid and come off the worse by 39 lengths, the tailed-off last of six runners.

Unforgettably, among a host of triumphs, Desert Orchid had also staged his against-the-odds fightback in the previous year's Gold Cup. This time round, according to the betting anyway, it was the opposition, all eleven of them collectively, who would be struggling against the odds as Desert Orchid was sent off at 11-10 on.

The reported crowd of 56,884 was thought to be a record and not many were drawn there by the prospect of seeing Norton's Coin. Review the BBC pictures of the closing stages and it serves as a reminder of just what a grip Desert Orchid had on the public and broadcasting consciousness. Approaching the last fence the coverage went to a close-up of him when he was two lengths down and struggling. A dozen strides after the last they went to him again and this time it was when he was four lengths down and beaten.

Ahead of the vanquished hero, Norton's Coin still had to get past third-favourite Toby Tobias and none had managed to do it in that horse's previous four completed starts. Norton's Coin, however, had looked to be travelling clearly the best as soon as the four leaders straightened for home and proved on the run-in that this appearance was by no means deceptive by drawing level under a very powerful Graham McCourt drive and going on to win by three-quarters of a length. His RPR for this performance was 169.

As well as having to cope with the defeat of Desert Orchid, the crowd were now confronted by a 100-1 winner, the longest priced ever at the Cheltenham Festival, in its biggest race and in record time. The ground was very firm for a Gold Cup and the first six home all beat Dawn Run's course record, Norton's Coin doing so by more than four seconds. In the morning he was available not just at 100-1 but at 200-1. I knew of one friend who landed a tidy win on him (as you would) but he often had quite a few bases covered. The previous April I stood next to him at Aintree as 28-1 shot Little Polveir romped home in the Grand National and it was only that evening, or the following day, that he remembered backing him.

If there were clues to a Norton's Coin Gold Cup triumph in his previous form, they were in performances at the same course. A graduate from points and hunter chases, Norton's Coin had flourished the previous season and the most notable of those runs were at Cheltenham, when finishing strongly into second in the Cathcart (behind another outlandishly priced Festival winner, 66-1 shot Observer Corps) and winning a good conditions event at the April meeting. That was in addition to the aforementioned second place in a handicap six weeks before the Gold Cup, over 2m4f again and again staying on strongly.

The Welsh rugby union player and broadcaster Cliff Morgan, I have read, picked up on the clues that virtually everyone else dismissed and tipped Norton's Coin for the Gold Cup in his newspaper column. I am much more familiar with Morgan's legendary rugby commentaries – 'This is Gareth Edwards!' – than his tipping tactics but selecting Norton's Coin was quite a feat. In summing up the 1973 Barbarians try against the All Blacks, Morgan intoned, 'If the greatest writer of the written word would have written that story, no one would have believed it. That really was something,' and many pawing over the following day's newspapers must have had a very similar feeling about the 1990 Gold Cup.

Perhaps it helped to bring Norton's Coin to Morgan's attention that the horse was a fellow son of the valleys, from Nantgaredig near Carmarthen. It's on the A40.

The trainer was permit holder Sirrell Griffiths and I doubt whether many could have put a face to him prior to the Gold Cup celebrations. In the course of those celebrations, however, his checked cap was removed and he was revealed as very jovial-looking and without the full head of hair. Griffiths had not done that much hitherto to put Nantgaredig on the map for the bulk of racegoers, but that was understandable seeing as he trained only three horses. He was a farmer and had milked his cows on the morning of the Gold Cup, which rapidly became the single most celebrated act involving a member of the dairy industry since the mass delivery and unwrapping of milkmaids on the eighth day of Christmas.

Ten years earlier, in addition to his cows, Griffiths owned the stallion Mount Cassino and the mare Grove Chance. Together they had cost him little more than £1,000. Mount Cassino covered mostly ponies and cob horses before his death in 1983 and Grove Chance had only the one foal. Yet they were the sire and dam of Norton's Coin. The story of the 1990 Gold Cup was straining credibility to the limits.

The juxtaposition of Norton's Coin and Desert Orchid had been dramatic enough but consider also that of Sirrell Griffiths and Sheikh Mohammed. It may sound frivolous now, when the context of that Gold Cup is not in such sharp focus, but comparisons and contrasts were widely made at the time and not just because of their respective breeding empires. More pertinently, the Champion Hurdle had just been won by Kribensis and Kribensis was owned by Sheikh Mohammed.

Those who feared Maktoum hegemony on the Flat had been denied their refuge, and they could not have been greatly soothed by the fact that the trainer of Kribensis was the Flat champion Michael Stoute. If some romance had seemingly gone out of the sport with that Champion Hurdle result, Gold Cup day was like a multitude of Valentine's Days and candlelit dinners rolled into one. The defeat of Desert Orchid may have disappointed many, perhaps most, in the immediate aftermath but it was not long before that feeling was overtaken. Sirrell Griffiths has long since sold his cows but the victory of Norton's Coin will remain as one of the most cherished tales of the turf.

~

When setting off for Nantgaredig in January 2013 I thought I knew the Norton's Coin story, but it turned out that I did not know the half of it. For a start, Sirrell Griffiths is not Welsh. His wife Joyce is, originally from Builth Wells, but he was born just over the border. 'Hereford was my home until about 40 years ago,' he reports.

When the couple moved to Wales, drawn by cheaper land prices, it was not first to Nantgaredig and not everything went swimmingly, as Griffiths relates: 'I bought a farm about 25 mile away from here and we had a dry summer in 1976. There was no mains water and we couldn't find no water on the farm. The wells had dried up and all I was doing was ferrying water – two mile down the road and two mile back, five or six times a day. We tried to find water there and failed. The next person who came there went and found it. Now we've got too much water.'

Nantgaredig is a near-neighbour to the National Botanic Garden of Wales but the region's overwhelming passion is rugby not botany, and certainly not horseracing. One of the Griffiths' nephews, Mark Jones, is a Welsh international (rugby player, not botanist). Ninety per cent of the village of Nantgaredig is stretched out, it appears, alongside Station Road and at one end of that road there is a triple-arched stone bridge, built in 1786, over the River Towy. On the day of my visit, the centuries-old landmark seemed in danger of being swept away. Further up the valley, the river was firmly in flood. At the other end of the road there is a junction with the A40 and, as Station Road suggests, the village in between is not that ancient in origin. When the train arrived in 1865, so did the village. The pub is called the Railway Hotel but the line itself closed in 1963.

When the Griffiths family moved there, horses were always going to be with them. Elder son Linley says of his father, 'Horses mean everything to him, more than cows,' and Linley got his name because his father was a huge fan of jockey Jimmy Lindley. Sirrell Griffiths' own father had had a permit to train and he used to take young Sirrell to Cheltenham races as a schoolboy.

Before Norton's Coin, the stable star was Village Slave. 'Who is the best horse you've trained?' is probably not a question that Griffiths has been asked that often since 1990, but when he says that Village Slave was the best horse he has had, he means the best with Norton's Coin included. Village Slave was too good to be kept. Purchased from a Northern Irishman at Hereford market, he gained his first success by beating the Welsh pointing star Mandryka in the Clettwr Open with his owner-trainer in the saddle, Griffiths' only winner as a jockey. The following year, in

1974, Village Slave won all three of his completed starts, after which the Sale and Mackenzie annual described him as 'A sensational Pointer, whose scintillating performance at Belmont left experienced observers comparing him to The Dikler'. He was sold to join Fred Rimell but his career under rules was undermined by injuries.

At the same time that Village Slave was running for Griffiths in points, a bay colt called Mount Cassino was showing fairly useful form on the Flat in the care of Doug Smith. The son of an unexceptional Derby Italiano winner, he had won twice over 1m as a three-year-old in 1973 but went off the boil as his four-year-old career progressed and was well below his best on his only two starts at five before being sold for 700 guineas at the 1975 Newmarket Autumn Sales. In their 1973 annual, Timeform described him as a 'lightly made colt' and in 1975 they reported that he 'has been hobdayed', 'best form at up to 1m2f' and 'has worn bandages'.

The man who brought Mount Cassino to South Wales was Eryl Phillips, who had a small farm near Whitland, and among the many unlikely links in the chain of events that took Norton's Coin to the Cheltenham Gold Cup, this is one of the most tenuous. When in 2013 I asked Phillips why he had decided to purchase Mount Cassino, the surprising answer was that he hadn't. 'I went to Newmarket Sales with my friend looking for a stallion,' reveals Phillips. 'I fancied a horse and I'm a bit shy so I asked my friend to bid on it. So he did – on a horse which I didn't think I'd told him. He was in the collecting ring at the same time as the other one. My friend said, "Oh, that's a nice horse, isn't it?" So I didn't buy the one I meant. He bought this Mount Cassino and it was hobdayed. It was a mistake but I never said nothing to him afterwards.'

Phillips knew nothing at all about Mount Cassino, yet had become his owner. Had he realised he was hobdayed he would certainly not have bought him, but it was Mount

Cassino who made the journey back to South Wales to join Phillips' other stallion Welham. In 2013, as he describes Mount Cassino, it is hard not to feel that Phillips had a higher regard for his other charge: 'Mount Cassino was more of a racehorse than Welham. Welham was more bodied but not so big. Welham was one hell of a nice horse,' he says more than once, 'but Mount Cassino was alright.'

Mount Cassino covered about 20 to 30 mares a year, half-breds mostly, and Phillips charged '£20 for a half-bred, and a possible 30 for thoroughbreds.' There was competition locally from HIS (Hunters' Improvement Society) Premium horses whose owners were apparently quick to disparage the new arrival: 'They said when I bought Mount Cassino that he was hobdayed. They were telling everybody, "Oh, his stock couldn't be sound and they won't be any good."' Phillips would watch the career of Norton's Coin with great pleasure, but after Mount Cassino had spent about four years with him, he approached Sirrell Griffiths and sold the stallion on for £700.

'He was serving a few mares 20 mile down the road,' says Griffiths, 'so I thought I could do the same thing. I didn't have no thoroughbred mares. All I had were ponies and cobs. But it didn't matter to me – it was extra income, apart from milking cows. We had two boys leaving school and they wanted to stop at home, so I thought I had to do something else to get a little bit of income to keep them.'

While half a dozen or so horses of various types were always 'kicking about' on his farm, Griffiths had never previously had a stallion. He describes Mount Cassino as 'a good size – 16.2. He was quite a good stamp of a horse' and also as very straightforward to deal with. Linley Griffiths thought him 'a lovely-looking horse'. His brother Martyn points out that because of his wind operation Mount Cassino was unable to neigh.

For a charge of '£50 for a big horse and £25 for ponies,' Mount Cassino served about 30 or 40 mares a year in his time at Nantgaredig but only one that Griffiths can remember was a thoroughbred. In his entire stallion career from 1976 until he had to be put down in 1983 because of laminitis, Mount Cassino produced only six thoroughbreds and one non-thoroughbred who were registered with the racing and bloodstock industry's secretariat Weatherbys.

On 13 November 1982 at Klampenborg in Denmark, Dove O'Piece (or Dove O'Peace as it is called in the Danish form book) won the Leatherneck Handicap over 1m1f on the Flat, and that was Mount Cassino's only other winner under rules apart from Norton's Coin.

~

The covering that produced Norton's Coin may, on the face of it, have an air of inevitability about it, seeing as Griffiths owned both the sire and dam. Untypical of the vast majority of other coverings, theirs was no fleeting acquaintance; as lodgers on the same premises, the mare Grove Chance was more than the girl next door. However, the circumstances of how Grove Chance came to join Mount Cassino at Rwyth Farm in the first place were even more unconventional than those of the stallion. 'That's a long story,' says Griffiths. 'It's funny how the wheel turns and comes back to you.'

It is a long story, one that involved Griffiths being confronted by failures of a mechanical and legal as well as equine nature, and the starting point was a broken-down horsebox. Booked in to transport someone else's mare to the Newmarket hospital, his horsebox broke down five days beforehand. With not enough time to get it repaired, he happened to notice another one advertised for sale in the newspaper and bought that one to do the job. Safely returned and with his original vehicle mended, Griffiths had two horseboxes and not enough work to justify it. One would therefore be sold. A customer rang him up, came over and chose one of the boxes subject to it passing its test the following day, which it did. Seven months later, the same man was in touch again. As Griffiths relates, 'On a wet afternoon – I'll always remember it – I was out on the farm and he said, "I don't know what you're going to do, but there's a crack in the engine block and it's dripping water." I said, "Where have you been until now?"'

'In the end it went to court and I bloody lost, I lost,' says the dumbfounded and aggrieved vendor. His solicitor had assured him that the other side did not have a leg to stand on. Griffiths was also unconvinced about the impartiality of the judge: 'It lasted from 10 o'clock till 6 o'clock and after half an hour if I'd had my cheque-book I would have gone up to the judge and said, "Here, have it now." He didn't want to know my case at all. I had to purchase a new engine for them and pay their expenses.'

To Griffiths, the sale of this horsebox must have seemed cursed. It had resulted in him being hauled in front of an unfriendly judge in Carmarthen Crown Court and when the transaction took place he had not even been given the full purchase price. The buyer had suggested an alternative arrangement. He had a mare to sell who was only three years old but could not be raced because she threw her leg right out. Griffiths describes her as 'a nice big young mare. It was only when she trotted and cantered that this leg came out. When she walked you couldn't see it.'

For the cost of £400 off the price of his horsebox, Griffiths had become the owner of Grove Chance. 'This is why I say the wheel turns round, doesn't it?' he reflects. 'That man there went and done that on me but in a couple of years' time this mare bred a Gold Cup winner.'

It is fair to say that Griffiths did not immediately realise his good luck. His new mare was duly covered by Mount Cassino but by the time Grove Chance came to foal she was no longer in his ownership. 'I didn't intend doing that,' he says, but a friend from about four miles away, who used to go with them every time they went point-to-pointing, had turned up one day with the sad news that his own mare had been found dead in the field. He was looking for a replacement. Grove Chance must have been standing nearby. 'I said, "Give me the stud fee and she's yours,"' discloses Griffiths. 'So what I charged him actually was 50 quid. I felt a bit sorry for him.'

It is therefore Percy Thomas from Llanddarog who became the owner of Grove Chance a couple of months before she foaled and he is the one listed as the breeder of Norton's Coin. He raised the Gold Cup winner but Grove Chance died from complications resulting from the birth. On the morning of the birth, Thomas called Sirrell Griffiths and the Griffiths family went up to see the foal that same day. They also saw the horse often over the next few years. Linley Griffiths recalls, 'Me and my brother used to go and help Percy Thomas and his wife when they were on the hay or shearing or something like that, and I always can remember seeing him out in the paddock there by the house, as a yearling and two-year-old. I didn't think nothing special about him but Percy was proud of him.'

A far more regular visitor was Sirrell Griffiths, who remembers, 'We were always in touch. I was seeing it and having a look at it every month, and it grew up and as it got older it got bloody uglier.'

∼

Grove Chance's sire and maternal grandsire were stamina influences, and her dam and grandam were sprinters. In 1953, her third dam Bebe Grande had the unusual distinction of coming third in the 1,000 Guineas and second in the 2,000. Whether the latest representative of the family would contest a race of any description was considered unlikely, judged by the look of him in his youth, but at least one person who saw him was left with a more favourable impression. He was a former miner who worked for Thomas, as Griffiths relates:

'An old boy used to do a few jobs for them and he was down the field one day and he came up for his dinner at the farm and he said to Percy, "That horse down there, he's going round the field faster than a bloody Norton motorbike, he is."' What to name the horse had partly been resolved. A piece of local racing history inspired the second half, as the mare Nickel Coin had been sold at Llanybydder market and went on to win the 1951 Grand National. Thomas's youngster became Norton's Coin.

If there were any hopes that the Nickel Coin association might provide some sort of precedent, they were not held by Mr and Mrs Griffiths. 'When he was a three-year-old he was a horrible-looking animal,' he asserts. 'It was a terrible-looking thing, wasn't it?' adds his wife. Thomas's only previous winner was a pointer called Red Wasp who was trained by Griffiths, but when Thomas raised the subject of his latest prospect being broken in, his friend's response was 'I don't know whether it'll be worth breaking it in or not. Who's going to buy it?'

With the decision eventually taken that yes, he would be broken in, Griffiths thought it prudent not to volunteer his services: 'He was one hell of a naughty horse. We had terrible trouble.' Someone was found who did manage the job but when Thomas then asked his friend, 'Would you buy him now?', Griffiths' response was 'I don't want it.' He continues, 'So Percy said, "Well what am I to do with it?" I said, "I honestly don't know, to tell you the truth."'

Thomas took an innovative decision. In March 1990 the Welsh press would be acclaiming Norton's Coin the Gold Cup hero but little more than five years earlier the same horse featured in the classified ads. This was not with a view to him being sold, because Thomas did not think he was worth anything, but for someone to look after him for a year and to start riding him. After a surprisingly large response, Thomas favoured a coal merchant called Parry from Taff's Well, with Norton's Coin to be kept at livery stables in Wenvoe, between Cardiff and Barry.

When Griffiths found himself accompanying his friend to vet the place, one of the points he found in its favour was that there were chickens and bantams running about. In an interview in the Gold Cup build-up, Griffiths described how 'Norton's Coin used to be terribly bad tempered and would bite or kick you if you went anywhere near him. But then a lot of little bantam chicks started perching in his stable, playing on his back and scratching the floor under his feet – and I'm sure it was having the company and confidence that no one was going to hurt him that has made him so placid.'

Exactly how Norton's Coin passed the rest of his time at Wenvoe and who else sat on his back there are unrecorded – 'it was a bit of a riding school' is Griffiths' recollection – but hunting with the Pentyrch was part of his itinerary. In South Wales it is a lot less noteworthy and the scenery a lot more green than it sounds to someone who does not know the area, but Norton's Coin was indeed ridden over the old coal tips.

When the year was up, Thomas decided to try to get him prepared for a point-to-point. Approached to carry out the task were Nick and Julie Tamplin, who ran a long-established livery yard at Abertridwr, near Caerphilly. They had been responsible for plenty of good point-to-pointers but, in what was becoming a common reaction, Nick Tamplin was not impressed with his first sight of Norton's Coin.

'He was a bit on the lean mean side,' is one way in which Nick Tamplin describes him, with emphasis on the lean. The horse was sound and healthy but Sirrell Griffiths' description of him at that stage as gangly, to put it mildly, is one that Tamplin fully concurs with. 'He was never a horse who carried a lot of flesh. He weren't a great big bull but he was a good grubber,' says Tamplin of his longer-term experience with Norton's Coin. When he agreed to take him on it was only after insisting that the owner visit the stables as soon as possible so that there could be no misunderstanding about the unpromising material with which Tamplin was starting off: 'The words I said to Mr Thomas were "I'll try and get him to the course this year for you but there's no guarantee."'

At these stables, there were no bantams but it was a working hill farm, in a valley of its own, and with no shortage of livestock. Revisiting his years with Norton's Coin, Tamplin says, 'We've got a big mountain, and he'd be up the mountain and I used to ride him quite regularly and gather sheep on him and do all sorts of work on him. I think it keeps them sane, rather than just going out and up a gallop or on a horse walker – the bulk of them, that's how they're trained today, isn't it?'

About a decade earlier, following his transfer from a top Flat stable to Greystoke, a suspicious Sea Pigeon (see Chapter One) was described as having had to go through an at first tentative introductory process with the local wildlife and livestock. He stood transfixed at his first sight of a cow. Norton's Coin, having lived a rather less sheltered life, would never be so flummoxed. Other animals were old hat to him but there was one, in particular, with which he had to get acquainted at his new stables.

'We had pigs running about here,' says Tamplin, 'and we had an old sow that was like a guard dog. If anybody came here she used to play hell with them. She'd wander up around the yard every day.'

For all his initial doubts about getting him to the course, Tamplin had Norton's Coin ready to start his racing career on April 5 at the Llangibby point-to-point at Howick and Tim Jones was to ride him. 'During the cold weather, during the freeze-up, they used to take him down to Barry Island, on the sand there and he used to work with two

Open horses,' says Jones. They used to work in roughly a circle on the beach, going round three or four times, with Jones and Tamplin on board the established Open horses, but as Jones relates 'This horse, just before we pulled up, he came past us every time, and as soon as he came past us Tom [his rider] used to pull him up.'

If showing he could run took Norton's Coin not long at all, showing he could jump did not come quite so naturally. For his first proper schooling session over actual fences, it was decided to hack across the mountain to the old disused point-to-point course at Gelligaer, where the fences were still usable, and Tamplin recalls: 'It was the most hilarious morning we've ever had. We couldn't get him off the bloody floor, let alone jump a fence. He did eventually, like, but he had his own way of going.' Tim Jones remembers: 'We were there hours but in the end he did lift a leg and as soon as he lifted a leg he started to jump.'

When Norton's Coin set off towards the first fence on his pointing debut, Tamplin watched on with uncertainty. For Jones in the saddle it was trepidation, but that and the other fences passed without incident before Norton's Coin was eventually pulled up, which connections regarded as no great disaster.

One week later, in a maiden at St Hilary, Norton's Coin was out again and Sirrell Griffiths was a most interested spectator as the field approached the third last: 'It happened to run in the same race as I had one. It was one hell of a coincidence. I forgot to tell my jockey you must not use the stick – I bloody forgot to tell him – and as he come towards the jump he was up with the stick and this mare of mine went across instead of jumping. It turned across, stopped this horse here on the left and whose horse was that? It was Norton's Coin! He was as close as that, so of course he had to run out as well.'

According to Mackenzie and Selby's *Point-to-Pointers and Hunter Chasers* annual, the two horses were in second and third at the time of this melee. Was it a surprise to Griffiths that Norton's Coin had run so well? 'Oh, not half.' ['He was such an awkward, gangly looking horse,' says Mrs Griffiths.] 'We never expected anything like that. We thought that if he got round it would be a miracle.'

Putting the Griffiths' expectations for Norton's Coin in further context, their representative in that race was a 13-year-old mare called Pride Of Towy, whom Mackenzie and Selby described at the end of the season as 'Not amused at having her retirement interrupted after living a leisurely existence for eight years.' However, after further misadventure on the way to third place at Llantwit Major – 'I messed up,' declares Tim Jones. 'I tried to go up somebody's inside and got him murdered' – Norton's Coin returned to that course for the Ystrad meeting in May and ended his first season by registering a maiden win. Mackenzie and Selby noted that he 'won a humble contest readily, and may be able to make the transition to Restricteds.' Norton's Coin was on his way.

~

As a six-year-old in 1987, Norton's Coin opened up by winning a Restricted at Scoveston Fort in March and finishing second in an Adjacent at Talybont-on-Usk, but that was the sum of his appearances. 'I wouldn't run him,' states Tamplin. 'The ground was too firm. If you want to knacker a horse you run him on firm ground and I said no, he's too good a horse to run.' The terminology used to describe Norton's Coin had undergone an alteration.

Mackenzie and Selby concluded after that campaign that Norton's Coin 'seems sure to win again' and they were immediately proved correct when he reappeared as a seven-year-old in an Adjacent at the Llandeilo Farmers meeting at Erw Lon in February. From three further points that season, he won under Tim Jones's sister Pip when returned to Erw Lon for an Adjacent at the Vale Of Clettwr meeting in March.

'He was improving hand over fist,' affirms Tim Jones, and that campaign also featured his first two runs under rules, in hunter chases at Leicester and Chepstow. At Leicester, Norton's Coin had a disagreement with one of the fences on the first circuit and the rider was left with very limited use of the reins, but at Chepstow in April the partnership got up on the run-in to win from the Venetia Williams-ridden Sanber.

Tim Jones's summary of Norton's Coin's career in points is that 'He was a horse who had enormous talent really from Day 1. It was just harnessing it and getting everything into place. And he did strengthen enormously from a weak little five-year-old. As a seven-year-old he was a big, strong horse. The Tamplins were very, very good with him. They didn't abuse him when he was six, when he was still weak.'

Tamplin's assessment is that 'I was lucky I was involved with him. It was brilliant. He was no problems. He was a real nice horse. We had a lot of fun and it was a pleasure to have him.'

In their 1988 annual, the last time that he came under their remit, Mackenzie and Selby observed that Norton's Coin 'Has fulfilled earlier promise by developing into quite a useful performer and may have further scope ... Game and his determined finishing burst should ensure plenty more successes.'

By the end of that third season in points, Norton's Coin and that he possessed potential were now public knowledge and, as Griffiths says, the only way to make money pointing is by selling the good horses on. Percy Thomas had received bids. A bloodstock agent had phoned Griffiths as well, asking him to put in a good word on his behalf. Early in the summer of 1988, Thomas went to Griffiths and told him that he was thinking of selling.

'I said, "If you intend to sell it, give me first chance,"' Griffiths relates.

'Oh, you want him now!' was his friend's response.

A couple of months passed before the conversation was renewed. It is outlined here by Sirrell Griffiths:

'I think I'll sell that horse. How much do you think he's worth?' asked Thomas.

'It's your horse. I'm not going to say.'

'Alright, I'm going to give you first chance if you want it. Is he worth 5,000?'

'He's worth more.'

'Would you give 5,000?'

'Yes.'

'If you'll give me 5,000, I'll give you £200 "luck". I've had no end of people after me, but if you'll buy him off me, I'm very local, I come with you to point-to-points, I can still come with you and be part of it.'

'Of course you can.'

'So anyway,' reflects Griffiths in 2013, 'that's what happened.'

It is possible (but far from certain) that Norton's Coin would have won the Gold Cup had he joined a major yard, one with a high profile and dozens, if not scores, of other inmates. What is absolutely for certain is that had he done so, there is no way he would have reached the same celebrity as that achieved in his feats for Griffiths. The horse's name would have been subsumed. His roots would have been a footnote to the story, not an integral part of it, and the Welsh winner would not have been sent up from Wales. It is probably going much too far to say that a sense of history played a part in Thomas's decision over the sale of Norton's Coin, but a unique place in racing history was the result.

~

Before the ensuing 1988/89 season, the total number of winners trained by Sirrell Griffiths under rules (as opposed to point-to-points) stood at two: one in 1982/83 and one in

1986/87. He was a permit holder (training his own horses or those of his family) rather than a fully licensed trainer and in his first campaign with Norton's Coin only one other horse represented him under rules, the mare Fair Agnes who made the frame in two of her three bumpers. In his Gold Cup-winning season there was Norton's Coin, Fair Agnes (third in one of her novice hurdles), Official Lady (tailed off in one bumper) and that was it. They were the only horses he had in training. When it was reported that Griffiths trained 'a handful' of horses, that was overstating it.

'I didn't train him no different,' says Griffiths of the new arrival. 'People don't go out on the roads for an hour and a half now, do they? There are so many horses in these stables, they haven't got time to do what I used to do, which was to take them for at least an hour and a half up the road and round the lanes, five days a week. In the other two mornings I'd canter. Today it's all out on the gallops and back in, isn't it?'

For the vast majority of these excursions, the person riding Norton's Coin was Griffiths himself, weighing 15st 7lb according to reports at the time but he confesses now that it was probably more. The cantering was done on their farmland. A converted cowshed, also home to the farm cat, was Norton's Coin's stable and Griffiths also did the vast majority of the non-riding work with him. He used to do all the grooming, he would wash him, rub him down and muck him out. Of what followed, his younger son Martyn says, 'I was proud, very proud – I was proud about Dad. It was Dad who done it, simple as that.'

For fast work Griffiths senior would hand over the reins to Martyn, but of that fast work there was very little. To do it, the horse would have to be transported to someone else's gallops. Norton's Coin would sometimes be taken for exercise on the beach, as he had in his days with the Tamplins, but more often he would be seen on the common land of Llanllwni Mountain.

'It's about 12 mile up the road,' explains Griffiths. 'There's a road over the middle of it and there are several thousand acres of open hill. It's like riding across Dartmoor, only not so large. I definitely go once a week, maybe twice a week, for a change, somewhere different. Going to the same place day in day out, that's when a horse gets sick of being in training. You keep them happy by going different rides.'

'It's so steep you can't go fast – it's like that,' Griffiths continues, while indicating a precipitous angle. 'You can't do any damage because you can't go fast. The damage is done to a horse when you're going fast. So up there he couldn't go fast, but he was working hard at the same time.'

A rarity in fast work, Norton's Coin was also a stranger to schooling. How often was he schooled? 'Never,' asserts Griffiths. 'When a horse can jump and jump tidy, I can't see the point in jumping, jumping and jumping, because the more you jump the more chance you've got of doing damage, haven't you?'

There was another reason that Norton's Coin was not schooled, though, and that is because it was not just his trainer who was set against it. Griffiths discloses: 'It was no good having any jockey here because Norton's Coin wouldn't jump a fence on his own. He'd stop, you couldn't get him over. You had to have a lead.' In which the stable was seriously lacking. 'He couldn't jump two foot,' observes Mrs Griffiths. 'Even over something tiny he'd stop, wouldn't he?'

Norton's Coin's first race for them was on December 1 1988, at Warwick in a 2m4f handicap chase, in which he started 16-1 under Tim Jones in a 17-runner race and finished third. In the same month he was runner-up twice at right-handed Hereford and both Jones and Griffiths point out that he never won under rules going that way round. According to Tim Jones, 'He hated going right-handed. All his tricks were a lot worse going right-handed. It made him think a lot more.'

The Festival's most unlikely Winner

As already described, jumping a fence on his own was one issue but chief among the tricks was a general and strong preference for downing tools once he had hit the front. 'I'm sure we put that in his head,' confesses Jones, remembering the way the then new schoolboy Norton's Coin used to pass his seniors and then be pulled up at the end of his work on the beach at Barry.

Norton's Coin was ridden by professional jockeys for all his starts after Hereford and the first was Richard Dunwoody, who took over for a five-runner handicap at Chepstow. 'I said to him, "Whatever you do don't go to the front,"' states Jones. As described in Chaseform, Norton's Coin 'led 7th to 9th: led 12th: soon clear'.

Griffiths reports what happened next: 'He was a fence in front at the last, he slowed up into it as if he was going to bloody stop, and he went right up in the air and come down so steep he couldn't get his feet out of the mud. He fell.' Having remounted for fourth, Dunwoody apparently told Jones, 'Yes, sorry, you were spot on.'

Dunwoody won all his three other races that season on Norton's Coin. These too were not without their nervous moments, though, first of all at Bangor in March when Norton's Coin went on two out. 'That was the first time he gave me a feeling that this horse isn't too genuine,' recollects Griffiths. 'He went quite clear of them and started turning his head, looking for them, but he managed to stay in front.' At Newbury on April Fool's Day, Norton's Coin was left in front three out when the leader fell; Timeform observed that 'he had to be ridden out after tending to idle in front.'

In between those two races, eight days after Bangor, was a first appearance for Norton's Coin at the Cheltenham Festival, in the 2m4f Cathcart Challenge Cup Chase, for which Dunwoody was unavailable and the 25-1 shot was ridden by Hywel Davies, finishing eight lengths second to the total outsider of the field, Observer Corps. 'He should have won, should have won hands down,' laments Griffiths.

To précis, the trainer does not have a high opinion of the ride Norton's Coin was given that day, asserting that 'He didn't listen to what I asked him to do, he did the complete opposite.' At least Davies did not hit the front too soon. 'All I wanted to do,' says Griffiths, 'was run down there and move the winning post – up the hill, because he was absolutely flying. Some fella came up to me as he was coming back in and said, "We all make mistakes Griffiths, but the biggest mistake you made today was not having that horse in the Gold Cup."'

That unsolicited opinion from a stranger was not the only occasion on which the 1990 Gold Cup was mentioned that spring. The Cathcart gave Griffiths his first intimation of just how good Norton's Coin might turn out to be and on his final outing of the season, back at Cheltenham in a conditions event over 2m4f, he confounded odds of 20-1 to beat a field which included rivals who five weeks earlier had finished second, third and fourth in the Champion Chase. The form experts concluded that all the market leaders had underperformed – the runner-up was a 14-1 shot – but, in Griffiths' words, 'Dunwoody got off him and put his arm round my neck and said, "Promise me one thing." "What?" "Can I ride this horse in the Gold Cup next year?" I said, "Of course you can."'

~

In the summer of 1989 Richard Dunwoody had a choice to make, but it is possible that he did not view it in quite those terms. With Simon Sherwood having retired, Dunwoody was offered the ride on Desert Orchid.

'He rang me up and said, "I can't turn it down,"' recalls Griffiths. 'He said, "I'll ride your horse whenever I'm available" and I said, "That's no good, is it? I want somebody who is going to ride him in the Gold Cup, don't I?"' Dunwoody recommended that he be replaced by Graham McCourt.

'I was delighted because I never really had many Gold Cup riding opportunities,' says McCourt. 'As a freelance you just don't get that opportunity. So I was delighted and always going to try to make the most of it and I was lucky enough to speak to Woody and Woody said, "Gray, he's a proper horse this, you know. I don't think he's as good as what Sirrell would like him to be, but he will win a decent race and you want to ride him."'

The Gold Cup campaign began like any other, with Norton's Coin apparently not persuaded that his holidays were over, as Joyce Griffiths describes: 'When he'd been out for the summer and you went to put a saddle or a rug on him, you'd say no way has this horse ever been broken in.'

Martyn Griffiths explains: 'In the stable, you'd put the bridle on him then put the saddle on and once you'd start tightening the girth a little bit he would just go berserk. You had to do that for a week before you could think of getting on him. And he was like that in his later days, not just as a youngster. Once he got that out of his system, though, anybody could ride him. He had these little quirks you know, little things like that. But on the whole he was a very straightforward horse.'

One other unusual feature about Norton's Coin was that two bony growths started to appear on his head, one each side above the eye. Griffiths calls them horns. When visiting a horsedealer in Ireland, the man told him that if ever you find a horse with two horns like this, that horse will win you a Gold Cup.

For most of Norton's Coin's second season with Griffiths, however, horns or no horns, it looked as if Dunwoody was missing out on very little and that McCourt had taken on a dubious privilege. 'That didn't go very well, did it? That went very bad,' remembers Sirrell Griffiths of his programme leading up to the Festival. First was the King George on Boxing Day, his first clash with Desert Orchid, in which Desert Orchid was the nailed-on first and Norton's

Coin the tailed-off last. McCourt, though, was encouraged – 'he blew up and I thought ran a fantastic race.' In the aftermath, Griffiths also received positive feedback from an unexpected quarter. 'I thought it was somebody joking but it was him,' says Griffiths about taking a phone call from John Francome, who said he thought Norton's Coin had run extremely well and told Griffiths not to be disappointed.

There was no getting away from the disappointment of three other races before the Festival. First came what some will have considered an ambitious tilt at Ascot. Griffiths explains: 'He wasn't only a stayer, he had a lot of speed as well and I thought, well, with the handicap mark he's got, this horse could win over two miles so I entered him in the Victor Chandler.'

In his form book entry for January 13, 1990, of all that speed there is no mention. Their comment in running is a succinct one: 'always behind'. There is no doubt in the mind of Griffiths that there were occasions when his jockey failed to take him, or more importantly his horse, seriously enough and this, he believes, was one. 'If it was a well-known trainer like David Nicholson,' he asserts, 'these boys would probably do as I asked them to do, you know, but being as it's me they look after themselves don't they?'

McCourt and Hywel Davies were both unable to take the ride. McCourt is keen to defend his fellow jockeys, in this case Mark Perrett, but concedes that 'You probably, in your heart somewhere, don't take it quite as seriously as Sirrell would be taking it, because of the relatively obscure background. And, yeah, you can do that, but every jockey would ride him and come back and say, "Hang on, this could be a serious horse." And you might make the mistake once, you don't make it twice.'

Not all received the opportunity twice. McCourt was back on at Cheltenham at the end of the month and remembers, 'I could not believe something came by me going up the hill.' Two weeks later Norton's Coin was at Newbury for another 2m4f handicap, with McCourt assuring the trainer, 'He's the biggest certainty I've ever ridden,' but they were beaten again and by a good deal further. This defeat had a ready explanation but it was one that had far more serious repercussions for their hopes for Cheltenham 27 days later – Norton's Coin coughed 17 times between the unsaddling enclosure and the stable yard.

A scope revealed that he had blisters and pimples all the way down his throat and he was put on heavy antibiotics. The owner-trainer, however, still took him out on the roads around Nantgaredig, and says, 'I thought he had no chance really of going to Cheltenham but anyway I persevered, I persevered and we got him there.'

Griffiths himself was also affected after the Newbury race, by a dose of realism. The Gold Cup went off the agenda. Then, when investigating his other options at the Festival, he discovered that his charge was ineligible for a second crack at the Cathcart – the 1990 renewal was for horses which had not won a steeplechase before August 1, 1988, whereas Norton's Coin had previously won a hunter chase – and entries had already closed without him for the Festival handicaps. The Gold Cup was back on the agenda. Graham McCourt still jokes with Griffiths about his alternative theory: 'Sirrell always maintains he missed the entry for the Mildmay of Flete, and I don't think in his heart of hearts he wanted to run him in that. He wanted to run him in the Gold Cup. He always says it was a mistake but I don't know! He wanted to have a bash at it.'

With Norton's Coin showing signs of having recovered, on the Tuesday one week before the Festival, Mr and Mrs Griffiths sought confirmation by taking him to work on Peter Cundell's famous gallop at Compton, 1m4f and on the climb all the way. To accompany Norton's Coin on this workout, Cundell provided Ryde Again and he was the favourite for the Stayers' Hurdle. McCourt, a regular riding out at Compton, gamely fielded a series of small bets from the stable lads who all believed that Ryde Again would put Norton's Coin in his place. Cundell drove Mr and Mrs Griffiths up to their vantage point and Sirrell Griffiths describes the scene:

'When we got to the gallops we were stood on a bank and they started way down there, then came up to us on the most beautiful gallop you could ever see. It has never been ploughed, it was like a carpet. Peter Cundell said, "If your horse can work with this fellow, you'll run well."'

How did Norton's Coin's fare against Ryde Again? 'He ran all over him,' says Cundell. Griffiths remembers their host being rather quiet as he drove them back to the stables. 'I was a little bit surprised,' confesses Cundell. 'But Graham said, "This is a good horse." Graham was a good judge and the gallop is a very good judge as well.'

The Gold Cup was unquestionably reinstated as the target now, but with not much notice taken of it in the wider racing world. One newspaper which had lingered on Norton's Coin among the entries was *The Independent*, for whom Richard Smith was dispatched to Nantgaredig just before the Compton gallop. In that feature article, Griffiths expressed his chance in the Gold Cup as 'Each day I think about it and still can't believe it could be possible. Yet accidents happen don't they, and you never know where your luck may lie.'

In 2013 Martyn Griffiths remembers that 'Dad always said if he finishes sixth he'll cover his entry money. "We'll just go for a day out," he said. "We'll never do it again so we'll all go, and if they do finish in the first six we'll come home proud people."'

In more private moments, when Griffiths senior thought of his horse lining up in the race, the prospect stirred stronger emotions: 'I was riding him one particular morning, walking along and I was going through the race thinking about what I would tell the jockey, and as this was going through my mind these tears started coming down. The tears started running from my eyes. I remember saying to myself, "What the hell is happening to me?"'

~

When Gold Cup Day arrived but was some way off dawning, Griffiths and his two sons commenced milking their 70 Friesians. 'It was very quiet, concentrating on getting the work done and getting everything finished,' describes Martyn. Once the cows had been seen to, Norton's Coin was prepared. Their lorry had been readied the night before. With all three men going to Cheltenham instead of one staying behind, as usually happened on a raceday, it was 'all a mad rush'.

Mr and Mrs Griffiths went in the lorry with Norton's Coin and their friends Timmy Thomas and Ivor Davies. Martyn and Linley went with their wives Helen and Marion. On arrival, they had breakfast in the stable lads' canteen. Graham McCourt set off for the racecourse relishing the prospect of his Gold Cup ride but not thinking any more about it than his other four mounts, three of whom were among the market leaders: 'Any one of those horses, if they had won I would have been thrilled to bits.'

Having left Norton's Coin in his stable, the Griffiths family headed for the racecourse but the gates were closed. Sirrell Griffiths says: 'Charles Parkin [the racecourse announcer], he saw me stood outside waiting and took me to this wooden building and I sat in there until the gates were officially open. There was only one other person sat there and he was a big large fella sat looking out through the window. I'll speak to anybody, you know, so I happened to say to him, "You've got a runner, have you sir?" "Yes." He didn't want to speak.'

On volunteering the name of his horse, another Gold Cup contender, the other owner asked who the Griffiths representative was. He was told it was Norton's Coin, made an unimpressed sound, shrugged his shoulders and turned away. Griffiths continues, 'Our daughter-in-law Helen, she joined us and she had big faith in Norton's Coin and she said, "He'll be sorry he done that. He'll be sorry before the end of the day."' That owner would indeed leave Cheltenham with cause to remember Sirrell Griffiths, in more ways than one.

On finally gaining entrance to the course, Griffiths surveyed the official racecard. It described Norton's Coin as a candidate to finish nearer last than first. For the younger members of the Griffiths family, Linley remembers that they walked about the premises and came across some television personalities. The wives got their autographs.

In the days before, Helen Griffiths had been adamant that the stables should be painted because of the people who would come back there after they won the Gold Cup. She was also a source of helpful advice at the racecourse when they adjourned to the Owners and Trainers Bar and her father-in-law started tucking into a snack: 'For goodness sake stop eating those pickled onions. When you get the Gold Cup off the Queen Mother you'll be stinking."

One individual whose behaviour made no concession to the occasion was Norton's Coin. He had no difficulty coping with the big-race atmosphere. 'He was cool beyond,' states Martyn Griffiths. 'You were nearly ashamed to lead him round the paddock. That day I virtually had to drag him. He'd drop his old ears and he looked so miserable. Don't ask me why. Somebody came and asked Dad, "Is he all right? Is he always like that?" Well, that's how he was. He was just so laid back.'

Sirrell Griffiths continues, 'He looked terrible in the paddock, his coat was stuck up on end and my son was leading him round and Norton's Coin was dragging behind. Horses look round the paddock, don't they? His head was down here. As I was waiting to go into the paddock, a friend of mine was in front of me. David

Nicholson was stood by him with Princess Anne and my friend heard Nicholson say, "Look at this then, he ought to be in a bloody tin."'

Once in the parade ring, the Griffiths family met up with McCourt, whose first ride of the day had been co-third favourite Sayyure in the Triumph Hurdle. 'Sayyure was so unfortunate,' recalls the jockey. 'He burst two blood vessels at the bottom of the hill. He was running away at the time.' In a 12-runner race for the Gold Cup, McCourt was not on the complete outsider of the field. That was The Bakewell Boy who went off at 200-1. Norton's Coin, however, was freely available at triple-figure prices, and at the same time, the instructions of Sirrell Griffiths to his jockey as usual concentrated on not hitting the front too soon.

Ten minutes later the field paraded in front of the grandstand. Martyn Griffiths recalls, 'I led the horse out and Dad followed me down and as I let the horse go Dad looked back at the crowd and I'll never forget those words Dad said to me – he said, "What the bloody hell are we doing here?" I thought, "It's too late to think of that now."'

~

'Stay with the grey!' shouted the front page of *The Sporting Life* and most punters did, but Norton's Coin was not totally unbacked. Having chartered a small bus there for the day, a group of villagers from Nantgaredig stood to win £17,000. Another of Griffiths' friends mocked the rails bookmaker who offered him 100-1, exclaiming, 'A man like you, 100-1? You can have 200-1 down there!'

The bookmaker jabbed the punter in the chest:

'Will 200-1 do you?!'

'That's better, I'll have £60 each-way.'

Arrangements were later made for a representative of that bookmaker to be met at a bank the following Tuesday.

Elsewhere, Graham McCourt's friend Colin Tinkler senior had planned to have his 'wellington boot bet' on Desert Orchid but McCourt had advised him to have £100 each-way on Norton's Coin instead. Tim Jones was at Cheltenham and aiming for something similar. He had ridden in the previous race, the Foxhunter, returning tailed off: 'I'd taken money with me in my overcoat. I got changed quickly, I ran out and got to a Tote window, queued and because it was so warm I didn't put my coat on when I came out of the changing room. Instead of having £50 each-way, I only had a tenner in my trouser pocket, so I had a fiver each-way.'

At Compton, having suffered the disappointment of Ryde Again's fall two out in the Stayers' Hurdle, they now considered their options with Norton's Coin and, in the words of Peter Cundell, 'We all helped ourselves.'

'We're not betting people,' says Nick Tamplin, but at their farm that day various £2 each-ways and £5 each-ways were gathered and taken to the nearest bookmakers. Potential winnings were £4,500 or £5,000. A girl who was working with them and wanted to go on a skiing holiday had £2.50 each-way. Tamplin describes the day as 'very memorable.'

In Nantgaredig, the cowman hired to milk the herd in the Griffiths' absence had placed his first ever bet. Apparently he has never had a bet since. In Carmarthen, Eryl Phillips and his wife went up to a betting shop and contemplated having something each-way on Norton's Coin, but they decided against it.

Back in the packed grandstand at Cheltenham, the Griffiths family had never backed Norton's Coin in any of his races for them and were not about to make an exception. However, Helen, a nurse in Carmarthen Hospital, remembered that she had agreed to have £5 on for one of her patients. With her husband Martyn down by the track in the small stand reserved for stable staff, Linley went to the bookmakers for her. In Carmarthen Hospital, heart monitors were about to register some strange readings.

The Festival's most unlikely Winner

~

When the tapes went up and the field set off for the 1990 Gold Cup, the race appeared to be over as soon as it began for Desert Orchid's stablemate Cavvies Clown, who declined to start at the same time as his opponents, and Graham McCourt was led to believe that his hopes had not lasted much longer. Norton's Coin made a hash of the third fence. 'He absolutely bombed it,' reports the jockey. 'He didn't look like falling but he what we call bellied it and I sat up and thought, "Well that's it. It's all over now," because you don't win races like that making mistakes, and so I sat still for a circuit and when I came past the stands next time he was travelling really quite well.'

After that one incident, everything unfolded as smoothly as McCourt could wish for, as well as he had wished for: 'You always go through the race the night before in your mind and you dream how you might be going and what you might be doing. It went to plan. Everything he did. It went exactly to plan. It very rarely does in this world, does it? He was an easy ride because if he finished third everybody would be thrilled, so I was able to sit as long as I liked and when I got to the top of the hill I looked around and I'd got Desert Orchid beat.'

Whenever Desert Orchid had poked his head in front, Ten Of Spades had tried to wrest the lead back. Kevin Mooney was the jockey on Ten Of Spades, having also been on Ten Plus when that horse lost his life going head to head with Desert Orchid one year earlier. On this return, Mooney admits that the occasion got to him: 'I rode the wrong race completely. I was trying to beat Desert Orchid to be honest, and I beat myself, beat him and set it up for Norton's Coin and Jenny Pitman's. We just went too quick. I was taking him on all the time.'

Ten Of Spades was in front at the last open ditch at the top of the hill but Desert Orchid came back – he nearly always did – and they were side by side at the downhill fence three from home. All the while, Toby Tobias and Norton's Coin moved on to the heels of the leaders.

Martyn Griffiths says, 'I can never forget the commentary: "Norton's Coin travels well and goes into fourth place." I thought, "Oh my God, stop there." That's all I wanted, you know – if I could lead one in who'd finished fourth. "Stop there! Don't fall, don't fall." Then it was "Norton's Coin travels well and goes third," and I started shouting.'

From the grandstand, Linley Griffiths reports 'Dad was kicking me or punching me, saying, "We're in with a chance here, we're in with a chance here!"'

Straightening up for home, Ten Of Spades hung right and weakened. Desert Orchid was still there on the outside but, after an almost perfect run round, on or near the rails, Toby Tobias and Mark Pitman went into the lead. In between them, Norton's Coin was almost upsides Desert Orchid at the second last where Ten Of Spades was a faller, leaving Cavvies Clown in fourth. As Desert Orchid began to flag, the duel commenced up front.

'Riding at the last in those big races you just ride at them like your life depends on it,' says Pitman, who had noticed how well Norton's Coin was travelling a long way from home. They had raced almost upsides each other for more than a circuit. 'Toby Tobias was very brave and came up for me and I could sense that Norton's Coin was just on my right. He wasn't quite upsides but he was very close and I knew who it was, not that it would have made any difference – you're just trying to keep your focus and trying to get it right at the last and then trying to get away cleanly.'

Alongside him, McCourt was full of confidence. 'I honestly thought I would win from the top of the hill. Mark gave his horse such a fantastic ride and I was surprised how well he kept going, how good his horse was. With normal proceedings, I'd have gone by him with a flap of the elbows, but that horse he stuck to it, he really stuck to it.'

McCourt and Pitman were not the only ones who were riding the finish in deadly earnest. 'Coming to the last I could see that if Norton's Coin jumps this he's going to win, so of course I got excited,' explains Sirrell Griffiths. 'I was up on the step, I got hold of the chap in front of me by the shoulders and I was riding like this and shaking this man.'

Seeing the energy which the owner-trainer puts into it when telling the story 23 years later, it is not hard to imagine him riding a vigorous finish at the time, over the entire length of Cheltenham's daunting run-in, although thankfully his ride was not so strong as that of McCourt, who was given a three-day ban for his use of the whip. It took a while, but Norton's Coin gradually inched ahead.

When he passed the post three-quarters of a length to the good and his owner-trainer could finally drop his hands, the recipient of his animated attentions turned his head and was revealed as none other than the same owner who had been so unimpressed at the mention of Norton's Coin at the racecourse gate that morning.

'It was the same fella,' exclaims Griffiths, 'and he said, "Do you realise that was my fucking neck!" To think, of all those thousands that was there, what a coincidence that I had to put my hands round that bloke who shrugged me.'

In addition to all those who rode the finish at Cheltenham that day, one person ran it. Once the leaders had passed him at his position near the final fence, Martyn Griffiths sprinted all the way up the hill, shouting, to greet his winner near the finishing line. In a moving scene, when he got to Norton's Coin he grasped him round the neck. Martyn elaborates, 'It looked as if I was being loyal to him, patting him, but I was holding myself up because of the stitch.'

On recovering, he noticed that the winning jockey was very quiet: '"I don't know what to say," Graham said. He didn't know whether he was coming or going. He never.' The jockey's rather surreal experiences that day would later include having a shower with half a dozen reporters stood just outside it trying to get a quote.

Well before that, though, horse and jockey were led back into the parade ring and winner's enclosure, an experience that made an indelible impression on a stunned Martyn Griffiths who was leading them. Tim Jones was one of those at the horse's side.

Arriving from another direction was Sirrell Griffiths, who says, 'I remember trying to get back to the winner's enclosure thinking to myself, "Is it true? Is it?" It was a work of art to try and get back there through the crowd.' When he was reunited with his winner, his flat cap was grabbed by McCourt and launched into the air. One absentee, unfortunately, was Percy Thomas, apparently attending a planning meeting as the owner of land about to be developed for the M4, but in the bedlam that accompanies the winner in the aftermath of a Gold Cup, the Griffiths family saw that there were many more friends and neighbours present than they had realised. Linley remembers one particular moment: 'One of Dad's old bank managers was there and he was in the paddock as well and I went up and I kissed him.'

Also near at hand, David Elsworth escaped similar treatment and Linley did not attempt to plant a kiss on Mrs Pitman. 'I thought we would probably win but we were beaten fair and square,' says Desert Orchid's trainer. 'Sirrell was absolutely elated. I congratulated him and it was great.' Laughing, Elsworth adds, 'Listen, if I hadn't won a Gold Cup I might not have been so gracious.'

When Mark Pitman reflects in 2013 on the ride which Toby Tobias gave him that day, he says, 'I do remember thinking that there wasn't actually anything else I could have done. He'd run well, jumped well, given everything and just got chinned.'

He reasons, 'Those championship races, they always gave you a great thrill. They were always generally run at a really good clip and those horses are very, very special, because they have the ability to travel – their cruising speed is the speed that most horses can go flat out. You get a great thrill out of riding those very special horses.'

So coming second would have been a great thrill for him in that race? 'It was, looking back on it, but at the time it was quite crushing in a lot of ways. You don't know whether you are ever going to get another opportunity.'

In the midst of the human dramas on that racecourse, Norton's Coin was as unmoved after the race as he had been before it. His trainer relates, 'The man who examined him at the dope test tested his heart, as they always do, and he said, "This horse is either the fittest horse I've tested this week or he's a freak. He's one or the other because his heart rate is now like if he hadn't raced. It's back to normal."'

~

When the Gold Cup had been presented and Sirrell and Joyce Griffiths had enjoyed their chat with the Queen Mother, they did not celebrate in time-honoured fashion. Bottles were not uncorked. 'I was driving so I couldn't celebrate like that,' says Griffiths, 'so we went and sat and had a cup of tea in the stable lads' restaurant. Then we left round about 7.30. I said we'll sit here so a lot of the crowd will go.'

Trying to avoid a crowd would not be one of the day's successes. Martyn describes the arrival back at Nantgaredig: 'We just come home thinking, "Thank God we'll soon be to bed now. It's been a long day." But on the way home from the motorway you come down a bit of a hill and we looked down on the village. There's a rugby pitch just across one field from us, and it was gone 10 o'clock – a funny time to be playing rugby now we thought, but the lights were still on there. And Helen my wife said, "It's further over." The television people had found the plug points and they lit up the yard here as if it was a little town. And as you come down our drive and open the gates there were people parked there like it was a farm sale. There were people parked everywhere. There were banners up through the village and they're not racing people at all here you know. They're rugby boys.'

A field had been opened up for the parking, hundreds of people were present and there were banners across the road from one telegraph pole to another declaring 'Welcome home Norton's'. Most of the village had congregated, along with others from much further away. There were many non-racing people there and others the family had not seen for years. Someone was sent by Griffiths to the Railway Hotel to buy as many bottles of whisky as they could lay their hands on.

In the early hours of the morning, when scores of guests were still present, the trainer asked his son Martyn to go upstairs and fetch an envelope from his bedside table. In the envelope there was a note outlining something that had happened to Sirrell Griffiths one night shortly before the Gold Cup:

'I dreamt that Norton's Coin had won and I could see it plain as plain could be, and Toby Tobias was the horse he was with. So I got a bit of paper and I put it in an envelope, sealed it and put it in a drawer in my dressing table by the side of my bed. I never thought no more of it. That night there were crowds of people and after a lot of them went there were a few stragglers, 40 or 50. They were there until God knows what time and it wasn't until the early hours of the morning that I remembered about this envelope.'

'We read it out,' says Martyn, 'and that was his dream. It made us cry, you know. It made us cry.'

Of the nights that followed the Gold Cup, Griffiths senior says: 'I used to wake up in the morning thinking is this bloody true or is this a dream?' On Gold Cup night itself, however, there was very little time for sleeping: 'It was around about 4 o'clock that we got to bed and before it was 6 o'clock two cars pulled into the yard and they were both from London. They were paper reporters wanting to get a photograph of me milking a cow.' Did they get it? 'Yes they did.'

~

With success there comes responsibility as well as celebration, and after winning something that could only be dreamed of there can also be the fear of losing it. Griffiths experienced these in a large measure, and his responsibilities did not extend merely to purchasing everyone drinks at the post-race party. After he had posed for those photographs while milking, a deluge of telephone calls followed, from well-wishers and from the media. Another large crowd soon gathered, including a group of Irishmen on their way back from Cheltenham. With some of them Griffiths would later become the best of friends.

Over succeeding weeks, it seems that the maelstrom barely let up. Television and other interviews became a commonplace. 'After a couple of months I got fed up with it,' confesses the object of all this attention. 'The phone was bloody ringing all the time and I couldn't do nothing.'

For three weeks after the race, however, this was nowhere near the chief of his worries. That lay in something that happened in the immediate aftermath of the race, at Cheltenham. Running down from the grandstand, Linley Griffiths maintains that his father was able to think only about whether Norton's Coin had returned carrying the correct weight. When they eventually got to the parade ring, this concern was overtaken by another, as Sirrell Griffiths describes:

'When I got there, there was a chap holding the reins with Martyn which I never seen before, and another fellow walking across the paddock with his hand over the horse's backend, a chap I never seen before, but these two turned out to be mates. In the paddock they were making a fuss of him, stroking him and tapping him and all this.'

Edward Gillespie, the racecourse chief executive, asked the Griffiths whether these men were with them and was told that they were not. The gatecrashers were removed but the incident played terribly on the mind of Griffiths: 'I spoke to Gillespie later on and said I'm worried stiff now, because that chap walked across the paddock with his hand on the horse's backend and he could easily have put a needle in there and he'll fail a dope test. It'll be no good saying I haven't done it because they're not going to accept that, are they?'

Gillespie promised to investigate whether the men had tried anything similar elsewhere and phoned back the next morning to say that they had also been seen in the winner's enclosure at the Arc de Triomphe. He urged Griffiths not too worry too much: 'He said if you are worried it'll be 21 days before we know the verdict. We'll just hope and pray that that's all they were there for, as a gimmick.'

It comes as a shock to hear just how badly this affected Griffiths, when his wife adds, 'Sirrell said if they had have done something I think I'd have drowned myself.'

Griffiths explains further: 'I couldn't let myself down, you know. I kept saying to her, "If this has gone wrong after all the letters we've had – we'd had hundreds of letters, from complete strangers, everywhere, from Australia, God knows where – and say if this fails, I don't think I can face up to it. I honestly don't think I can."'

The 21 days passed without him being notified of anything untoward and he could begin to feel totally comfortable with his success. At Cheltenham's April meeting he was back there to judge a best-turned-out horse award and was invited to lunch, at which he found himself sitting next to David Nicholson. Griffiths' mind wandered back to The Duke's comment on Gold Cup day. The one regarding Norton's Coin and his suitability for a tin. 'I thought I'd mention it to him,' says Griffiths. 'I thought he was going to say "I never" but he said, "Yes, I did say it." He said "Now you know, I'll stand up and tell the rest of the table what I said," and that's what he did. I admired him for that.' After that, the two trainers always had a chat when they met.

Back home, celebration of Norton's Coin and his owner-trainer continued apace. Rugby did not provide the only sporting feat recognised in their part of Wales, for a short while anyway. Norton's Coin was given the freedom of Carmarthen. He opened betting shops, among other celebrity appearances, and loved the attention from young and old.

He also continued at the day job for another three seasons. In terms of historical ratings, he does not rank highly among Gold Cup winners but demonstrated clearly that the level he achieved that day in March 1990 was not a fluke. Graham McCourt affirms, 'On that day, that horse was an absolute flying machine. He recovered from that mistake and you can see from the way he jumped the last – it was long and he came up with a big weight on his back, after three and a quarter miles. He was a good horse.'

There was only one further win, but to register that, at the end of a very slowly run race over 2m4f at Cheltenham in April 1991, he had to outsprint one of the top 2m chasers in Waterloo Boy. In that year's Gold Cup, defending his trophy, Norton's Coin was still in contention about three lengths off the lead when falling six out, although not travelling with the same fluency as the year before. When he fell, Mark Pitman was again just off the lead, this time on Garrison Savannah, and approaching the final fence Pitman was in front once again. He discloses: 'I had flashbacks to the year before. Driving at the last, I just had that vision, of almost déjà vu.' In Jenny Pitman's autobiography she says that she thought 'The nightmares are about to return'. On this occasion, though, fighting it out against The Fellow with Desert Orchid 15 lengths back, Pitman's mount held on by a short head.

Norton's Coin ended that season with a Timeform squiggle. At Leopardstown in February he refused three out, but that was after he had been badly affected by the journey over and struck into during the race. In between the Gold Cup and his 2m4f win, he ran at Aintree, of which appearance McCourt says: 'I rode him and it was probably the worst riding performance of my career. Disgraceful. I just couldn't believe he could get beaten and hadn't realised what he could do when he was in front too long.'

Richard Dunwoody did know it and he was on Aquilifer, the only other horse who ran his race. Sirrell Griffiths describes how McCourt and Norton's Coin were at odds with each other in the closing stages: 'He found himself in front two out and tried to put the bloody brakes on. It had been raining and he slithered into the fence and couldn't stop. He broke the fence. He got him going again and by the time he got to the last he was back in front, and he tried to do the same again. If he'd only just sat still he would have won so comfortable.'

Over the subsequent two seasons, the problem was physical. Griffiths had his own opinion that it was a sinus issue, with early evidence as far back as the 1990 Gold Cup Day. In the stables after his greatest triumph, Norton's Coin had a drink – rare for him – and in the bottom of the bucket, in front of a disbelieving audience, he left a discharge which from Griffiths' description seems to have been substantial and colourful. However, when much later the owner-trainer was searching for an explanation for Norton's Coin's disappointing performances, he bowed to an expert veterinary opinion that his horse had a breathing problem and needed a tie-back operation. 'It was an unnecessary operation and he's done a bad job of it as well,' is how Griffiths sums up that intervention. The racing career of Norton's Coin was effectively over.

Once retired, he was never ridden. Plenty of his time was, as formerly, spent in the field with the Griffiths dairy herd. 'If you turned him out with the cows and the cow had a calf, he'd send the cow off and he'd look after the calf,' remembers Griffiths. 'He'd stand by it all day long. He had a few odd things.'

As with huge numbers of other dairy farmers, however, the time was not far away when Griffiths decided that keeping his dairy herd was no longer economically viable. Within five years of the Gold Cup, they were gone. His flock of black-faced ewes would eventually follow them and when I visited in 2013 the farm housed only horses, many more of them than in 1990. 'About 30 horses, all kinds,' says Griffiths.

Describing their years on the farm, son Martyn says: 'We've always got a few horses about here. There's only us here. It's the same now really, we don't employ nobody. All we like to do is buy a little cheapie, you know, and hope it turns out well.'

Norton's Coin died at the age of 20. Sirrell Griffiths turned him out in the field one morning, returned with some hay and found him dead, from a heart attack. 'We would have buried him on the lawn,' says Griffiths, 'but it was wet at the time so we buried him in the field and put a stone on the lawn with a brass plaque on it. When he was first buried, the grandchildren used to take flowers over there and put them on his grave.'

~

One of the letters Griffiths received following the death of Norton's Coin was from Lester Piggott, who had ridden him on his only Flat race, when eighth in the 1991 Queen Alexandra at Royal Ascot. Graham McCourt's father

Matt was listed as the trainer that day, because Griffiths' licence was not sufficient. Upgrading his involvement in the sport was something which Griffiths had to consider.

'I had no end of letters and phone calls to ask would I be interested in training their horse, and the answer I gave them was that I'd have to move away from here because I'm too far away. Too far away to travel to the races. I would have loved to have done it if I'd lived in Gloucester or Cheltenham or somewhere like that.'

As it was, Griffiths continued as a permit holder. He has trained a couple of dozen winners under rules since the Gold Cup, recording three in a season twice in the mid 1990s. His best horses since Norton's Coin were the fairly useful Forestal, Noble Colours and U B Carefull, the first two of whom won at Cheltenham meetings other than the Festival. He stood one other stallion after Mount Cassino but with no great success.

His life may not have changed that much in terms of his career in racing but it has in many other ways. Sirrell and Joyce Griffiths have made many friends and seem to get a particularly warm reception whenever they are in Ireland. They had been there on their honeymoon but hardly ever again until after the Gold Cup and now they are regular visitors.

'In Ireland I can be walking down the street and it doesn't matter where it is, someone will come up to me,' vouches Griffiths.

In the course of these trips they have visited the world bloodstock powerhouse of Coolmore and the Ballydoyle stables run by Aidan O'Brien. They have also been to Sheikh Mohammed's Kildangan Stud and speak in awe of what they saw there, from the entry gates, to the paddocks, to the stables and the brass on the stable door. 'Oh, that was an experience wasn't it?' recalls the Gold Cup-winning trainer.

Given the current state of the sport, with so much strength concentrated in so few hands, it has been said that there is no way that an underdog of the Norton's Coin variety could ever win the Gold Cup again. Considering how unlikely that story was in the first place, it is probably a reasonable percentage call. There were shades of his story in 2015 when the magnificent novice Coneygree won the Gold Cup for Mark Bradstock's small team, but overall a very small number of stables have come to dominate.

Among owners, Sheikh Mohammed added to his 1990 Champion Hurdle win with another in 1992, thanks to the Graham McCourt-ridden Royal Gait, but he decided against launching any task force to try to conquer British jumps racing like the one he has commanded on the Flat. Jump racing was apparently not for him. I do remember, however, a 1996 television interview in which Sheikh Mohammed tipped Rough Quest to win the Grand National.

It is tempting to speculate idly that Sheikh Mohammed may also have been paying close attention to the jumps game two days after his first Champion Hurdle triumph, when Norton's Coin struck his blow for the underdog in the 1990 Gold Cup, and that he may have derived something important from it – an insight into the satisfaction that might be gained from a more hands-on approach to having horses in training and the wealth of publicity that could be generated for the place those horses came from. In 1992 Sheikh Mohammed founded Godolphin and, in his own way, set about trying to do for Dubai what Sirrell Griffiths and Norton's Coin had done for Nantgaredig.

CHAPTER TWELVE

1991 COUNTY HANDICAP HURDLE

The Miraculous Powers of Winnie The Witch

STAMINA – IT'S NOT just the horses who need it. While many a Cheltenham horse is said to 'stay all day', the committed Festival racegoer and punter is now required to stay all Tuesday, Wednesday, Thursday and Friday. Officially it may have gone from three days to four in 2005 but for me the Festival has often felt as if it were of indeterminate length. In the very rare instances when I could not attend for one of the days, it felt as if the meeting were one day shorter. Being there was not everything but it was incomparably more than the snatched opportunity to watch some of the races on TV.

More happily in a glorious and sustained period when circumstances were at their most conducive, the Festival was three days officially but I could make that state of mind stretch to seven or eight, commencing in the week before Cheltenham with three days in London. Included in that preliminary search for cultural diversions, readying myself for the main event, I examined a large tank of sump oil at the Saatchi Gallery and Flemish locks at the Victoria and Albert Museum, and gazed for the first time at Manet's *A Bar at The Folies-Bergère*. On one London visit, my friend Martin and I found ourselves sat on opposite sides of the Whispering Gallery in St Paul's Cathedral and, lo and behold, the words that emerged from the ether comprised the name of a horse that was running in about half an hour's time. We swapped St Paul's for a betting shop on the other side of the street, placed our bets and, as I hazily remember it, the horse in question either fell or blundered badly at the second last.

Rather more time was spent in London pubs. When warming up, in racing terms, at Sandown for the Imperial Cup on the Saturday, further drinks and heavy losses had to be avoided at all costs but if we were lucky or inspired, such as when Collier Bay won in 1995, it could pay for all of Cheltenham too. I say 'we' because London was predominantly a social thing, and for many years in very happy succession some of the same determined cast members would reunite at the Festival the following week.

One stimulus to excess for the racegoer is that the Festival is fundamentally a celebration. It is not just individual horses and humans who are feted; the whole sport is because this event is the best that the sport has to offer, and the tens of thousands who turn up tend to toast it in the traditional manner. In 1985 it was reported that this involved the consumption of 6,000 bottles of champagne and 70,000 bottles of beer. In 2012, the booze inflation rate had taken those figures to 18,000 bottles of champagne and 214,000 pints of Guinness, while in 2014 the stocktakers reported back that 120,000 bottles of wine were drunk at the Festival and the number of Guinness pints was up to 236,472. Not all of these are consumed by lonely, disillusioned punters propping up the bar after the latest loser.

Personally, when it comes to drinking during racing hours, surveying the runners for the next race is usually far more important. An exception to this abstinence was before the Gold Cup in 1987, when because the immediate build-up was stretched by an additional one hour and 20 minutes thanks to a snowstorm refuge was taken at a whisky stall and to dilute the glass involved simply reaching outside to catch the falling snow.

However, outside those racing hours the week is not generally a dry affair. The Festival is a major life event, one to be shared with best friends and usually it is the same addicted friends back year after year, witnessing some of the great days in sport and sharing in the experience of trying to negotiate all the highs and lows. Difficult as it is to comprehend, not everyone of my acquaintance feels nearly as crazy for Cheltenham as I do, but there have always been enough who got close. Rejoicing one evening, drowning our pecuniary sorrows the next, regaling the world with tales of what might have been and trying to shout home the winners at regular junctures in between, the camaraderie of Festival week is one of the very best parts of it.

From 2005, with the onset of the four-day meeting, not every member of our Festival fraternity could be there every day. Even the hard core of our original group was fractured. Some have had to join the real world and one became an absentee when he broke a cardinal rule – never to risk conceiving a child nine months before the Festival. The cast list has changed. The show has most definitely gone on but I will always reflect on the adventures and misadventures of that original, youthful group with particular affection, and of all the moments shared by that band of brothers the best has to be the closing stages of the 1991 County Hurdle.

~

At the head of the betting, Imperial Brush was trained by Desert Orchid's handler David Elsworth and second-favourite One For The Pot by the bookmakers' nemesis Lynda Ramsden, while leading trainers David Nicholson, Dermot Weld, Josh Gifford, Jenny Pitman, Gordon Richards, Philip Hobbs and Martin Pipe all had runners. Pipe had three. For some of those big names, a first Cheltenham Festival winner had not come at all easily. But for Ken Bridgwater, the trainer of Winnie The Witch, success in any race had hitherto been a triumph. Bridgwater first took out a trainer's licence in 1969 and his seasonal win totals over jumps were 0, 1, 0, 1, 0, 2, 0, 2, 2, 0, 0, 1, 0, 2, 0, 2, 3, 1, 2, 3 until in 1989/90 there were eight wins and it must have seemed like Eldorado. With four wins, 1978 was easily his best season on the Flat.

Outlining the decision in the late 1950s that eventually led to Ken Bridgwater becoming a trainer, his wife Mary reveals: 'He was a very good footballer. He had a trial for Birmingham City and passed his trial. We were going to get married, I was only 18, and it was a toss-up whether he had £25 a week [with the football] – which was a lot of money in those days – or whether he went with horses. He went with horses and we were on £4 a week.'

Bridgwater spent about ten years looking after other people's horses, first while also humping meat at the Bull Ring in Birmingham for butcher Arthur Rymond, who used to have some hunters, and then for the Lord Mayor of Birmingham Dr Glass and Les Fletcher of Capel Transport. It was Fletcher who gave them the £100 required by Weatherbys for Bridgwater to start as a trainer and when they settled down properly to the task it was at Bear House Farm in Lapworth, near Solihull.

Training did not make the Bridgwaters money. Other sources of income had to be found and one was for Ken to take his horsebox to the horse sales at Doncaster and Ascot, where horses who had passed through the sales ring now needed someone to take them away again. Rather like Peter Jones or Deborah Meaden on *Dragon's Den*, his wife was sometimes unimpressed with his entrepreneurial expertise and commitment in extracting money from his customers. 'If Ken knew him, he'd just say, "Oh, give us 20 quid,"' she says. Late in the year, Bridgwater would make their Christmas money by going clipping – he had a round of customers he would visit to clip their horses' winter coats.

On the racecourse, the golden period for the stable during their first 20 years was in 1977 from April 30 to September 3, embracing the end of one jumps season and the start of another, when under the 7lb-claiming rider Jerry Walsh the six-year-old novice Old Chad won four races over fences. The fourth and easily highest profile was at Stratford in the Virginia Gold Cup Handicap, in which the famed front-running 2m chaser Tingle Creek carrying 12st 7lb was caught in the final strides by Old Chad carrying 9st 8lb. Nearly two months later, the 11-year-old Tingle Creek broke his own course record at Sandown when putting up what Timeform ratings reckoned was the best performance in a 2m chase all season. For the Bridgwaters, however, those victories for Old Chad were as good as it got in either 1976/77 or 1977/78 – there were no other wins in either of those jumps seasons.

Mary Bridgwater describes those years, far and away the majority of her husband's training career, as being 'hard, very difficult', but says it was a wonderful life: 'Ken was very sound, genuine, honest as the day is long, very hard-working. He was just a solid, sound chap. He loved his family, he loved his job and he was very, very happy with his life. Whatever stage we went through he was happy, he was content. He loved his kids. He loved his family life and he always used to say, "It's great I'm doing a job that I love." It was hard work but he loved it.'

By the 1988/89 season, youngest son David was a conditional rider with David Nicholson, having first been apprenticed with Lester Piggott, but eldest sons Kenny and Gary were working alongside their parents. At Lapworth, they had a small circular gallop in the paddock, although it sounds as if gallop may be putting it too strongly. They had to use someone else's when the horses needed to do some fast work. 'It was like a cinder track really,' is how Mary Bridgwater describes their own circuit. The chief ingredient in that surface was supplied by one of their owners from the waste of a foundry in Birmingham, larger items of industrial flotsam being painstakingly removed from the foundry dust.

Gary Bridgwater describes the usual type of horse they had and their usual routine at home: 'We used to train our horses on steady work. We used to canter for 20 minutes solid one way and 20 minutes solid the other way. And the lads would come in and be absolutely knackered, the horses would have white foam pouring off them. Unfortunately our horses were useless; the only other thing they were was fit.'

More than 20 years on there is a danger of these descriptions sounding a note of romantic poverty, but when Mary Bridgwater recalls their position in the training ranks in those days, she sums it up, bluntly, as 'We were just bottom of the pile, weren't we?'

~

The horse who was to transform the Bridgwaters' racing lives joined them on December 6, 1988. Winnie The Witch was a Christmas present they bought themselves at almost the racing equivalent of the charity shop, Ken and Mary Bridgwater having gone to Leicester races and claimed her for £4,100 out of a selling hurdle. She finished third of five finishers in that six-runner race, seven lengths off the winner. In four previous novice hurdles there had been a hint of ability on one occasion but she had been beaten at least 20 lengths in all four. Between them, the other runners in that seller went on to win one race, worth £1,548.

Four days later, the following appeared in the classified advertisements of *The Sporting Life*:

PADDOCKS THOROUGHBRED RACING LTD
YOU LUCKY PEOPLE!
Here's your first early Christmas present
A RACEHORSE
WINNIE THE WITCH
This delightful filly will run for you on Boxing Day
We are looking now for our next horse
Come on, have fun, there's still time
£200 for two years racing, stable visits, stud visits

The Bridgwaters were looking to launch an owners' syndicate and had been searching for a suitable horse. What had persuaded them that Winnie The Witch might be the one? On the face of it there was not much to recommend her from her racing record, but the trainer had noticed her on the racecourse before she ran in that seller and they were also drawn to her by her sire, Leading Man, and found some attraction in what Mary Bridgwater describes as the mare's 'tough, old-fashioned jumping stock'. Winnie The Witch's dam, Star Ruler, was a point-to-point winner, as was her dam, and Ken Jr was later quoted as saying: 'Claiming Winnie The Witch is about the only thing Dad and I have ever agreed on – we just liked her breeding.'

With the benefit of hindsight, after 20 years in which Winnie The Witch turned out to be the only winner from her dam and Winnie herself failed to produce anything with ability, Mary Bridgwater sums her up now simply as 'a freak of nature'.

That was not, however, the first description applied to Winnie The Witch at Bear House Farm, once she had first been put through her paces. 'Slow, very slow, extremely slow,' is how Gary Bridgwater assessed her.

The Miraculous Powers of Winnie The Witch

Applications to join the nascent syndicate did not exactly flood in and she did not make that mooted Boxing Day engagement. When the time did come for the mare to make her debut for her new yard in early January, divisions appeared within the family about which race would be most appropriate for her level of ability. Ken Bridgwater had one view and his two eldest sons had another, as Gary describes: 'Dad entered her up at Warwick first time up in a novice handicap (on the Saturday) and I think she was number 23 of 23, and we'd entered her in a selling hurdle at Chepstow (on the following Monday) and me and Kenny were absolutely adamant that we've got to run her in the seller because she's bloody useless. We worked her at home and she's the slowest thing that you've ever sat on in your life. I used to ride her nearly all the time because she was so slow. And anyhow, she got in at Warwick and Dad goes there and he tells all the owners to back her! All the old boys on the gate backed it too. Dave didn't want to ride her – he thought she was useless – so Steve Bridle rode her claiming 7lb and, if you've ever seen a video of it, it was like watching Arazi. She's come from the back, jumped the last on the far side and gone from third to 25–30 lengths clear round the bend – all over!'

At 50-1, Winnie The Witch won by 20 lengths. At the initial entry stage, she had in fact been 55th out of 61 in the list of entries and the maximum field for the race was 25. There was no such scrum for a berth in the selling race at Chepstow and had that winning performance taken place in a seller, it would have been extremely hard, probably impossible, for the Bridgwaters to retain her at the subsequent auction.

As it was, the newly feted heroine was safely back at Lapworth and the following Saturday, one week after the Warwick revelation, the following message appeared at the foot of page 26 of the *Racing Post*, in their classified section:

PADDOCKS THOROUGHBRED RACING LIMITED
Join the 'WINNIE' team
WINNIE THE WITCH wins first time out by 20
lengths at 50-1
CONGRATULATIONS to our founder members
WHAT A START!
New members welcome to join now
COME ON AND HAVE FUN & WIN
Telephone Ken Bridgewater [*sic*] for application
details on ...

The registration of the club had not been completed in time for her debut win, and at that stage there were not nearly enough members anyway, so Winnie had recorded that surprise triumph carrying the orange, white sleeves and black cap colours of the trainer's wife. However, some who had got in touch after the first advert were also present at the track. Jim Kelly had flown in from Derry; Barbara Neale had not come across the Bridgwaters before – she had not even heard of them – but she also arranged to meet them at Warwick. She was impressed, and not just by the win:

'I went to Warwick and they'd got a couple of runners and what made me look at them was how lovely the horses were turned out and the way the lad leading them was talking to the horses all the way round. So that was it. I thought it wasn't an expensive journey into racehorse ownership so we'll give it a go.'

For those absent from the track, her startling success ensured the effectiveness of the second advert. The Bridgwaters were inundated with new applications and when the line was drawn, the syndicate was 60 strong. Mrs Neale reports that the star of the show was less than communicative when off the main stage – 'she used to go and hide in the back of her box when we tried to talk to her' – but that seems to have been the only anti-social thing about her. For a start, the Bridgwaters had determined to enjoy the increased interest but not to milk it. 'We just wanted our money back,' says the trainer's wife. After the succession of years in which winners often came along less frequently than birthdays, they also knew how to go about it when there was something to celebrate. Every other Sunday was syndicate day, when all the members could bring their families to the farm. Later, for an annual owners' open day, a marquee was put up, bands were hired and other entertainments and refreshments were laid on.

'We had what we called a "dirty dancer" – I mean it wasn't; now it wouldn't be anything,' backtracks Mary Bridgwater, 'but Big Jim from Ireland he got a bit merry, we took pictures of him, and his missus went mad. We had some Indians who said, "No, we no drink." I said, "Have a bit of that punch. It's only fruit." Well, Jim had brought me some poteen and of course I put it into the punch. I tell you what, they had a whale of a time. It was phenomenal.'

Crucially it was not just some of the owners who perked up with the Bear House Farm experience. Winnie The Witch, it seemed, relished her new regime and the taste of winning. 'She completely altered,' says Mrs Bridgwater. 'She was so snooty when she won. She was a complete show-off.'

David Bridgwater cannot put his finger on one particular explanation for what was about to unfold but he says, 'The way my dad trained suited her because mares are quite funny really. Sometimes you get horses off other people and they improve, and sometimes you lose horses and they improve. It's just, you know, different water, different food, any number of reasons really, but it certainly clicked there.'

In her work at home there was never much sign of it – 'David would come and ride her work and say she's bloody useless,' comments his mother – and Winnie The Witch did not win again in her first season at Bear House. But after nearly a year off she came back an improved horse on the track. First time out a market move from 16-1 into 8-1 came unstuck when she fell at the second last while moving strongly. David Bridgwater rode another horse in that race but at Leicester two weeks later both he and Winnie The Witch made all the right decisions as he took the ride and she gave the 19-year-old his first winner as a jockey.

The ground-breaking wins, new friendships and all the tickertape may be what springs to mind when remembering Winnie The Witch but none of it came as a matter of course; it was not the inevitable result of her being in their stable. Chiefly this was because training her was not easy, as she was not the soundest behind and kept going lame. 'She was a lovely mare but she wasn't straightforward,' says Gary Bridgwater. 'She had a lot of problems. It was a fantastic training performance.'

Also vivid in his memory, though, is one frightening episode in the build-up towards her County Hurdle season, when all the time and care that had been spent on her nearly came to nothing. 'About six months before the race, one day she got loose,' says Gary. 'She'd been turned out in the field. We were all in the yard and heard this horse galloping up the road, looked out and it's bloody Winnie, isn't it? She went straight up towards the main road and I thought she was going to die.' Among all the skills of animal management, he had never had to deploy those he'd seen before only on television, used by men trying to herd rhinoceros. 'We got in the van, I got upsides her and managed to bang her and bang her and then got her down a lane. She went down this lane and we got her, not a mark on her.'

When Winnie The Witch returned to more conventional action towards the end of 1990 she improved again and this time it was a major step forward. Second time out, at the end of December, she breezed home in front under David Bridgwater in a 2m handicap at Warwick. Two subsequent races at around 2m4f did not go so well but the first of those, when unseating her rider on the far side at Warwick in a Coral Golden Hurdle qualifier, had a positive side nevertheless as the final of that series was scrapped from her possible Cheltenham itinerary. The trainer's wife had also entered her in the County Hurdle.

When that engagement was almost upon her, Winnie The Witch was as usual showing no signs in her work that she had any hope of a big-race success. 'Before she ran at Cheltenham,' Gary Bridgwater reveals, 'we took her to Twiston's [Nigel Twiston-Davies's] and Dave came down to ride her; he rode her up the gallops, jumped off and said, "You can't run this, you can't run her." We said that was how she works. She was the worst horse you ever sat on in your life and you'd take her to the track and she'd just come alive.'

One last detail had to be finalised before she could be taken to Cheltenham for the County Hurdle and that was for her to get into the race. With her still lowly handicap mark of 118, the family had serious fears that she might not make it, but when the five-day entries came out she was 31st on the list and only one horse had to be withdrawn for her to make the field. In the final declarations, she was number 23 of 26 and the withdrawals included two horses scheduled to head the weights, so Winnie The Witch was not only in the race, she was also in the handicap proper, scheduled to carry 10st 1lb, minus David Bridgwater's 7lb allowance.

∼

The closing race holds an importance at the Festival that far exceeds its place in terms of status or prize money. For racegoers whose year revolves around this week in March, it is the last race before the sunset, and for punters not prepared to lie down quietly it can be the 'getting-out stakes'. One essential maxim for the serious, regular punter

447

is that 'there is always another race,' meaning that there is absolutely no need to chase one's losses on a certain day, or meeting. Being able to fight another day is the imperative. But it's hard to deny that a winning Festival has a nice ring to it.

When I went to the Festival for the first time, in 1981, the final race of the meeting was 'the Cathcart'. The Cathcart Challenge Cup Chase was a conditions event with idiosyncratic conditions, one that habitually attracted a small field and gave punters the chance to lump on a short-priced favourite. In those double-or-quits days, Half Free, for instance, won it at 11-8 in 1986 and 5-4 in 1987.

In 1988, however, the Cathcart was switched in the running order with the County Hurdle, and bar 1992's flirtation with the Champion Bumper, for which there was hardly any solid form to go on, it was the County Hurdle which closed proceedings until 2009. The form is not in short supply for this race. Where once, in the Cathcart era, the punters would alight on a small line-up in which a very small number of horses usually stood out on form, now their last throw of the dice would be in a near maximum field of 20-something runners in a handicap for which, in theory, all the participants were weighted so that their chance was exactly the same. Not many have claimed that successful punting at the Festival is easy.

In my group of Festival-going friends, as independent thinkers, there have been countless occasions when one of us has been shouting his head off for one horse, while standing a couple of feet away someone else in the group has been doing exactly the same about another. When the head-to-head has been resolved, the winner is usually ecstatic and often unable to conceal it; the loser offers his congratulations. When in the latter category, those congratulations may not always be my first instinct, but if I cannot win I want my friends to do so and can usually share in their rejoicing. There is always the comforting knowledge that at least one of us should be able to buy the first round of evening drinks. In all these currents of sometimes conflicting emotions and behaviour, I have not the slightest qualm in completely rejecting the slogan of one gaming website, the one that reads 'Beating the bookies feels good … but beating your mates feels better!' Cheering home a winner I have backed feels great but the pleasure increases exponentially when all of us are on it.

When the first two days of the 1991 Festival were over and it was the morning of the County Hurdle and I was scanning through the names in the race, my memory contained an image of Winnie The Witch that was positive and persuasive, the image of that latest easy win at Warwick. The phone lines hummed among my friends that morning as Dave sought corroborative evidence in the form books and it turned out that Martin too had an image of Winnie The Witch in his mind. His was from a dream.

Let me state now that, while I do not believe that revelatory dreams are necessarily the preserve only of biblical characters, Roman emperors or sickly songs by Abba, I am no believer in the efficacy of dreams as a predictor of who will win horse races. If you think about as many racehorses as I have during my waking hours you will also dream about plenty of them at night. I would prefer to dream about almost anything else. Strangely, one dream I did have on the eve of the 1987 Grand National was that Steve Smith Eccles found himself hanging on underneath his mount Classified at the Canal Turn and something very similar did actually happen, but I have also dreamt that I was the jockey on board a Grand National winner and that never came to pass. David Nicholson had his red socks and Jack Berry his red shirt, and we have often remarked on the form of lucky ties, lucky underpants and even the lucky Milletts bag, but I have always thought that this was more for theatrical than practical purposes. Martin pores over the racing pages as diligently as anyone on raceday, but perhaps on this day he was swayed by something extra.

With different methods of analysis, ways of looking at betting and concepts of value, it has not happened that often that all of our group have backed the same horse but, for whatever reasons, Winnie The Witch was one runner for whom everyone fell into line. Legends are woven into the fabric of every society and Winnie The Witch is one of ours. She was a serious fancy and a big price. We set out for the racecourse full of hope and we were not the only ones to do so.

After the race, it was reported that all of the owners had also leapt at the available odds when the phone lines opened in the morning. Ken Bridgwater was a very quiet man but if he were ever going to wax lyrical this was the day to do it. 'We've laid her out for this and they [the syndicate] were all on at 40-1 with Ladbrokes in the morning,' said the trainer in one report. 'We really fancied her.'

Making their way to Cheltenham, one of those in the car with Ken and Mary Bridgwater was Big Jim and by the time they arrived at the course confidence levels seem to have risen appreciably thanks to some sightings I had not previously appreciated the significance of.

'We went under a bridge with a train going over the top and Dad said, "Jim, we're going to have a good day,"'explains Mary Bridgwater. 'A bit further on we saw a wedding and he said, "God Jim, we're going to have a good day today you know – all I need to see now is a Dalmatian." So we're going along and Big Jim shouts, "Jairsus Ken! There's a Dalmatian, look!"'

That day's racing at the Festival was every bit as engaging as ever – Oh So Risky won the Triumph by 12 lengths; Dun Gay Lass lost the Foxhunter when her rider's stirrup broke close home; Garrison Savannah short-headed The Fellow, from Desert Orchid, in the Gold Cup; Seagram became a strong Grand National fancy when winning the handicap chase; Chatam came home 12 lengths clear in the Cathcart – but for those who had a gamble underway in the County it felt as if all that action was something of a warm-up act for Winnie The Witch. When the preliminaries to that final race of the 1991 Festival at last arrived, I went to check on how she looked in the parade ring, liked what I saw and set off to have another bet on the Tote. Perhaps, though, I should also have given some attention to the appearance of her jockey, David Bridgwater.

When he was first briefed of the riding plans for Winnie The Witch, his boss David Nicholson had apparently questioned the 7lb claimer's readiness for the task. It was after all his first ride at the Festival, but Ken Bridgwater asserted: 'My horse, my lad.' In the parade ring, the jockey did not share quite the same confidence as his father:

'I was a 20-year-old 7lb claimer, still a virgin, I hasten to add, in every respect, so I was a bit bewildered by the whole occasion. It was massive, to me anyway it seemed massive, and I was just in a different world, I was just zoned out. The thing I can remember is that my dad, when I got into the paddock, he said, "down the inner, blah blah blah, hit the front going to the last, and don't win too far."'

David Bridgwater stresses that he would never have sworn at his father. But some very colourful language, accompanied by plenty of exclamation marks, was racing through his mind as he prepared to be legged up for his first Festival ride and his dad told him not to win too far. With all the expletives edited out, he was thinking 'What? Are you for real?'

Not for the first time during Winnie The Witch's years with Ken Bridgwater, the trainer's optimism when others may have lacked it was proved correct. And how. I'm really not too fussy how a horse I've backed wins, but one who moves steadily through from the rear in a big field must rank highly. In a 26-runner race, Winnie The Witch was 22nd of 25 turning away from the stands, one rival having

451

fallen at the first. The early pace was strong. After the third flight Bridgwater took her forward into the pack. Through binoculars there were only fleeting and indistinct sights of her yellow cap thereafter and racecourse commentator Raleigh Gilbert had not mentioned her since the turn into the back straight, but as the field started to get strung out not long after the sixth, the flight at the top of the hill, there she was! In a close seventh as the field turned down the hill, there were only two flights to be jumped. By the time the first of those was negotiated Winnie The Witch was two or three lengths off the lead, on the outside of the four leaders.

So far I have mentioned no other runner by name in this race description and that is because my attention was exclusively on the one horse. Perhaps the binoculars started shaking at this point. Only the second favourite One For The Pot looked to be travelling as well as they went into the final bend and I suppose we should have been worried given the fearsome reputation for handicap success that attended his trainer Lynda Ramsden; but any doubt now lasted for only a few seconds. One For The Pot's rider took a glance to his right and he was in for a nasty shock as Winnie The Witch moved alongside and wasted no time in going past. On the run to the last hurdle, Gilbert proclaimed, with a surprised tone, that it was 'Winnie The Witch quickly going on' but I doubt very much whether we heard him. Our group's shouts – somewhat isolated, I seem to remember – had reached a new volume. Exhortation had already turned to exultation. Reviewing the race in 2012, David Bridgwater says that the finer details of his father's instructions had not really registered, 'but going to the last I was about four clear and I was like "****** hell!", winged the last and whoosh, away she's gone, and it was fantastic.'

Winnie The Witch won by seven lengths.

Gary Bridgwater led Winnie The Witch back into the winner's enclosure. He asked his brother what he was thinking as they came down the hill and 'Dave said, "I'm sat there like this [indicating a double handful] and I thought if only she could pick up, but there's no chance she could pick up because they've gone a suicidal pace – and she picked up."'

Gary continues, 'It's the only time I've known this, even all the Gold Cups – we came into the winner's enclosure and all the valets, all the jockeys, came out of the weighing room, stood there and cheered.'

They were not alone. The feeling for me and the others in my group was one of delirious joy. We booked a table at the second-best Chinese restaurant in Cheltenham.

~

Norton's Coin one year earlier tends to put all other tales of Cheltenham victory for the underdog slightly in the shade. In 1982, striking a resonant note in a politically and economically divided Britain, the Coral Golden Hurdle Final was won by Tall Order, one of a handful of horses, if that, trained in Cumbria by Louis Foster, a steelworker who had been made redundant the previous August and claimed unemployment benefit. Winnie The Witch's County Hurdle was firmly in the same camp, though, as Mary Bridgwater was well aware, judged by her comments in the following day's *The Sporting Life*: 'The big trainers have so much success and you get tired of reading about it. This time we have stuffed them all and I love it!'

Eventually, the victorious connections returned to the car park, with the mood somewhat different from when they had arrived. 'We had an old white Orion, it was an old rusty thing and when we pulled into the owners' car park we parked between two Rolls-Royces. At the one Rolls-Royce they were drinking champagne out of the boot and they went oooh like this,' says Mrs Bridgwater, imitating a snooty air, 'and Ken turned round and he says about the rust, "I wouldn't get too close because this is catching, you know, this is contagious."'

After racing, the same Rolls-Royce was still there, along with its champagne-quaffing occupants, and this time the trainer was accompanied by an object that did not have a trace of rust on it. As Gary Bridgwater remembers it, his father 'put his trophy on the top of the car and said, "You could have done with that, couldn't you?" He got in his car and he was the happiest man alive.'

Others in the party may have come close to that and Big Jim had just got a bit bigger: 'I don't know how much money he shovelled on, but he couldn't get it in his pockets,' observes Mrs Bridgwater. A call was made home with instructions to go in search of champagne and for all of the syndicate members who had not been at Cheltenham to gather at the house. The place was decked with balloons. The dirty dancer might have been the only one not invited.

Barbara Neale describes her part in the convergence on Bear House Farm, the merriment that broke loose and how Ladbrokes were not the only ones who paid for it: 'We were working so we couldn't go but we went up to the local bookies, a William Hill in Coventry, to watch the race and absolutely everybody in the bookies was cheering for Winnie. We went over to Lapworth with a load of bunting and flags and we put them all round the stable, and more of the owners turned up and we made sandwiches. We got all the champagne from the local off-licences and we had a real good evening. And all the while we were there, dressing the place up, every car that went past tooted their horn. It was wonderful.'

The hangovers had barely subsided and the bunting been put away before there was cause to do it all again. Ken Bridgwater's instructions 'not to win too far' may have seemed pretty ridiculous to his bewildered jockey son at the time but they took on some relevance when Winnie The Witch's next race was the even more valuable Swinton

Insurance Trophy Handicap – first prize £27,400 as opposed to the County's £23,995 – at Haydock at the start of May and she had been raised a stone in the weights. The pace was not so strong and the other jockeys were on the look-out for her this time, so the 8-1 co-third favourite got boxed in, but David Bridgwater managed to switch her wide between the last two flights and Winnie The Witch did the rest, winning by one and a half lengths.

Haydock's chief executive at the time was Charles Barnett (subsequently chief executive at Aintree and Ascot) and he had the pleasure of watching the track's most valuable hurdle race won by a horse he had bred himself. Ten years earlier he had been the one in the saddle when Winnie The Witch's dam Star Ruler gained narrow hard-fought wins in point-to-points at Mollington and Kimble. Seemingly lacking the overdrive her daughter displayed at Warwick, Cheltenham and Haydock, Star Ruler was described in the *Horse And Hound Annual* as 'consistent, stays extra well, and tries hard, but one-paced.'

'It was an emotional day,' Barnett says of Winnie The Witch's Swinton triumph, and while, to public eyes, Winnie The Witch's pre-Bridgwater years appeared to predict a career of little consequence on the racecourse, in other words one fairly typical of the majority of horses, Barnett had cause to remember her as something out of the ordinary from the word go, given the circumstances of her birth, as he relates: 'When I came back from work the foal was outside having just been born and the mare was inside the stable. Somehow or other she'd foaled it through the door and the door had then shut, so we had a rather splendid time picking the foal up and putting her back in with her mother. It must have happened immediately. She must have kicked the door, opened the stable, foaled the foal out on to the cobbled yard and then the door shut with the wind or something.'

~

The successes of the 1990/91 season were not matched in her subsequent campaigns – how could they be? – but Winnie The Witch made two further visits to the Cheltenham Festival. She was about 15 lengths tenth of 16 to Royal Gait in the 1992 Champion Hurdle and fifth, hampered and well behind the first two, to Travado in the 1993 Arkle. She won three novice chases (two at Warwick) in the latter season and a handicap chase at Worcester in April 1994. On retirement she had recorded nine wins and six seconds from 42 starts, for total prize money of £82,474.

As a fully fledged jockey, David Bridgwater went on to further Festival success in the 1994 Grand Annual (Snitton Lane), the 1996 Stayers' Hurdle (Cyborgo) and Cathcart (Challenger Du Luc), and the 1997 National Hunt Handicap (Flyer's Nap). He won the 1994 Scottish Grand National on Earth Summit and in 1996 was second in the Grand National itself, on Encore Un Peu. In the latter season he rode 132 winners in all, second only to Tony McCoy. The enabling factor in that haul was that he had succeeded Richard Dunwoody as first jockey at the winners' factory presided over by Martin Pipe, but the connection lasted for only one season. The trainer and jockey did not share the same priorities and Bridgwater walked away. In Chris Pitt's superb book *Go Down To The Beaten*, Bridgwater compared his first Festival winner with the two he had in 1996: 'To ride a winner at the Festival should be the pinnacle. I remember how it felt with Winnie The Witch. But to ride two winners for Mr Pipe wasn't like "That was fantastic"; it was "Thank God for that." It was expected and there was no enjoyment about it. When I'd come back from riding a winner at the Festival, it felt like I'd just won a selling hurdle at Hereford.'

At the Grand National meeting in 1997, Bridgwater's elbow was shattered in a fall over the Mildmay fences and, after further falls, he never regained full fitness. He was forced into retirement from the saddle in February 1998, having ridden 435 winners under National Hunt rules in Britain, plus one on the Flat and two in Australia. In his early days as a trainer, that same year, a double-barrel kick from a horse as he rode back from the gallops resulted in him sustaining a badly broken leg. His first three runners as a trainer all won but most of what followed were lean years, reminiscent at least statistically of his father's early career, until 2010/11 when seven wins were put on the board and the leader of the team was The Giant Bolster, the horse who in 2012 went so close to securing David Bridgwater's name on the list of Festival-winning trainers in the biggest race of all. The Giant Bolster got the better of his battle with the favourite Long Run in that Gold Cup but Synchronised stormed past them both on the run-in. The Giant Bolster then finished fourth in the 2013 Gold Cup and a somewhat unlucky, hampered third in the 2014 version.

Reflecting in 2012, the upwardly mobile trainer admitted that the full significance of that County Hurdle was almost lost on him at the time. But it isn't now:

'Winnie The Witch was a family thing and it was my first one – my first Festival ride, first win – just unbelievable. Looking back, that was so special and it almost passed me by. That was pretty awesome, especially for Dad. What you've got to remember is that I've had a leg up in life because my dad was a trainer, and because blood is thicker than water I naturally got rides for him. Dad had it hard because he started from absolutely diddly squat. For Dad to do that, to train a Festival winner – it's bloody hard. The only thing is that Dad never really capitalised on it because he was very old-fashioned. On the back of that he should have trained 50 horses but he never did. I've learned from that.'

Apart from youth, one good reason why the full import of his County Hurdle win might almost have passed him by at the time is that he was not at Lapworth for the celebrations afterwards. In his position as a conditional jockey employed by another trainer, he was back at David Nicholson's for evening stables.

Of his other Festival wins as a rider and how they compare, Bridgwater says: 'I wanted to be a professional jockey and that is what professional jockeys do, win at the Festival. Great, it was wonderful – being a jock and being a trainer is always more than just a job – but it's not as important as Winnie was. She was a very special horse for a small yard. With a big yard it's just another number and she only won the County Hurdle. It's all relative. When you've struggled as a trainer all your life, or whatever Dad did, and struggled to clothe us as kids, to then win that – it means so much more than Nicky Henderson winning the Gold Cup with Long Run, or any other Gold Cup winner trained by a big yard. It's just so much more.'

At David Bridgwater's stables near Stow-on-the-Wold, his wife Lucy is a vital member of the team, as is brother Gary, and Mary Bridgwater only recently handed over the reins after running his office. His daughter Poppy is now a winning amateur jockey on the Flat who hopefully will turn apprentice. They are still a close-knit family. For the 2014/15 jumps season he had 49 horses run for him and 33 wins.

It was at his stable that Winnie The Witch died in 2005, aged 21. 'For more than 15 years the lives of my whole family have revolved around her,' said the trainer at the time, to the *Racing Post*. 'She got me on the map and she got Dad on the map too. These things happen but it has hit me hard. She was a darling and more than a racehorse. She's the first horse I've ever cried over.'

Her progeny may have been 'useless' as racehorses (the Bridgwaters never bred from her daughters) but nevertheless two of them were still there with the family in 2012. The old stables at Bear House Farm in Lapworth have long since been transformed into Bear House Farm Mews and one of those houses was called Winnie.

Speaking on the evening of the 2012 Champion Stakes, Barbara Neale says: 'Winnie was our Frankel.' Although Paddocks Thoroughbred Racing's ownership of Winnie The Witch gave her and her husband their best moments in racing and was a hard act to follow, she extended her involvement in the sport and has been the breeder of four winners out of her mare Sweets, three of them trained by David Bridgwater.

Of Ken Bridgwater, Mrs Neale affirms: 'He was a lovely man. Everybody says so and won't hear a word against him. He was a true gentleman.'

Seventy-five per cent of his stable's £72,333 in win prize money in the 1990/91 season was provided by Winnie The Witch, but he had 19 horses run for him in that campaign and a total of eight won 11 races between them. In 1993/94 he had ten wins and £33,211 but after Winnie The Witch's retirement the stable disappeared from the headlines. Having suffered longstanding heart problems, the trainer died in November 1999 at the age of 66. He had just fed the fillies and mares, including Winnie The Witch, when he had a heart attack.

In trying to sum up their involvement with Winnie The Witch and the story of their County Hurdle triumph, Gary Bridgwater says, 'All you've got to do is just put down that it was all down to Dad. And that was it. She wouldn't have been there but for him.'

His thoughts go back to the first race Winnie The Witch ran for them and the moment they knew for the first time that they had a good horse, when Ken Bridgwater's instructions to jockey Steve Bridle had been to sit at the back, improve down the far side and lead at the last: 'On the bend she has gone 25 lengths clear! Everybody just couldn't believe what they saw. We were absolutely dumbfounded. Dad always stood at the second last – his ashes are spread there – and I can always remember him jumping up and down. We all were. It was unbelievable that she was so far clear.'

When Winnie The Witch did something similar at the Festival two years later, Ken Bridgwater had beaten the odds to win on one of sport's greatest stages.

Bibliography

Bradley, Graham, with Steve Taylor, *The Wayward Lad*, Greenwater
    Publishing, 2000
Budden, John, *The Boss*, Mainstream, 2000
Burridge, Richard, *The Grey Horse*, Signet, 1993
Chaseform, *The Jumps Annual*, Raceform
Chaseform, *The Form Book: Jumping Season*, Raceform
Chaseform, *Jumping Form Book*, Raceform
Clayton, Michael, *Prince Charles: Horseman*, Stanley Paul, 1987
Clower, Michael, *The Legend Of Istabraq*, Cassell
Cope, Alfred, *Cope's Royal Cavalcade Of The Turf*, David Cope, 1953
Curling, Bill, *The Sea Pigeon Story*, Michael Joseph, 1982
Fitzgeorge-Parker, Tim, *Great Racehorse Trainers*, Pelham Books,
    1975
Fitzgeorge-Parker, Tim, *The Ditch On The Hill*, Simon & Schuster,
    1991
Francome, John, *Born Lucky*, Pelham Books, 1985
Godfrey, Nicholas edited by, *Racing Post 100 Greatest Races*,
    Highdown, 2005
Herbert, Ivor, *Six At The Top*, William Heinemann, 1977
Hislop, John, *Steeplechasing*, J A Allen, 1982
Holland, Anne, *Dawn Run*, Arthur Barker, 1986
Holland, Anne, *Steeplechasing*, Little, Brown, 2001
Irish National Hunt Steeplechase Committee, *Irish Point-To-Point
    Results*, Michael Keogh
Jackson, Florence E, *A Portrait Of Prestbury*, Peter I. Drinkwater, 1987
Lee, Alan, *Cheltenham Racecourse*, Pelham Books, 1985
Lee, Alan, *Fred*, Pelham Books, 1991
Mackenzie, Ian, and Selby, Terry, *Point-to-Pointers And Hunter
    Chasers*, Mann Publications and later Racing Post
Mottershead, Lee, *Persian Punch*, Highdown, 2004
Newton, David, edited by, Timeform *Chasers & Hurdlers* annuals,
    Portway Press
Newton, David, edited by, Timeform *Racehorses* annuals, Portway
    Press
Nicholson, David, with Jonathan Powell, *The Duke*, Hodder and
    Stoughton, 1995
Oakley, Robin, *The Cheltenham Festival*, Aurum , 2011
Oaksey, John, *Oaksey On Racing*, Kingswood, 1991

O'Neill, Jonjo, with Tim Richards, *Jonjo: An Autobiography*, Stanley Paul , 1985

O'Neil, Peter and Boyne, Sean, *Paddy Mullins: The Master Of Doninga*, Mainstream, 1995

Pickering, Martin, editor, *Directory of the Turf*, Pacemaker Publications

Pitman, Jenny, *Jenny Pitman: The Autobiography*, Partridge Press, 1998

Pitt, Chris, *A Long Time Gone*, Portway Press, 1996

Pitt, Chris, *Go Down To The Beaten*, Racing Post Books, 2011

Powell, Jonathan, *Golden Days*, Stanley Paul, 1991

Powell, Jonathan, *Monksfield*, World's Work, 1980

Raceform, *Raceform Flat Annual*, Sporting Chronicle Publications and Raceform

Raceform, *Raceform Up-To-Date Form Book: Flat Racing Season*, Sporting Chronicle Publications and Raceform

Raceform, *Raceform Up-To-Date Form Book: National Hunt Annual*, Sporting Chronicle Publications and Raceform

Randall, John, and Morris, Tony, *Guinness Horse Racing: The Records*, Guinness, 1985

Rimell, Mercy, *Reflections On Racing*, Pelham Books/Stephen Greene Press, 1990

Sale, Geoffrey and Mackenzie, Ian, *Hunter Chasers and Point-To-Pointers*, IPC

Scally, John, *Them and Us*, Mainstream Sport, 2000

Scott, Brough, *Front Runners*, Victor Gollancz, 1991

Scott, Brough, *Of Horses And Heroes*, Racing Post, 2008

Scudamore, Peter, *Scu: The Autobiography Of A Champion*, Headline, 1993

Sherwood, Simon, *Nine Out Of Ten*, The Lambourn Press, 1989

Smith, Raymond, *Better One Day As A Lion*, Sporting Books, 1996

Smith, Raymond, *The High Rollers Of The Turf*, Sporting Books, 1992

Smith, Raymond, *Tigers Of The Turf*, Sporting Books, 1994

Stevens, Peter, *History Of The National Hunt Chase*, Peter Stevens, 2010

Tanner, Michael, *The Champion Hurdle*, Pelham Books/Stephen Greene Press, 1989

Timeform, *Timeform Black Book*, Portway Press

Timeform, *Favourite Racehorses*, Portway Press, 1997

Welcome, John, *The Cheltenham Gold Cup*, Pelham Books, 1984

West, Julian, editor, *Racing Post The Turf Directory*, Kilijaro Ltd